THE AMERICAN LANGUAGE IN THE 1970S

THE AMERICAN LANGUAGE

Boyd & Fraser Publishing Company
3627 Sacramento Street, San Francisco, California 94118

IN THE 1970s

HERMAN A. ESTRIN
Newark College of Engineering

DONALD V. MEHUS
Fairleigh Dickinson University

THE AMERICAN LANGUAGE IN THE 1970s

Herman A. Estrin and Donald V. Mehus

Composition by Dharma Press, Emeryville, California

Library of Congress Catalog Card Number: 73-90425

ISBN: 0-87835-044-6

1   2   3   ●   6   5   4

ACKNOWLEDGEMENTS

Grateful acknowledgement is made to the following publishers and individuals for permission to reprint material which is in copyright, or of which they are the authorized publishers:

THE AMERICAN SCHOLAR: For "Polluting Our Language" by Douglas Bush. Reprinted from THE AMERICAN SCHOLAR, Volume 41, Number 2, Spring, 1972. Copyright © 1972 by The United Chapters of Phi Beta Kappa. By permission of the publishers.

AVON BOOKS: For "Contemporary Literature" by Richard Kostelanetz. Reprinted from ON CONTEMPORARY LITERATURE by Richard Kostelanetz, by arrangement with Avon Books. Copyright c 1964, 1969 by Richard Kostelanetz.

COMMONWEAL: For "Black English" by Dorothy Z. Seymour. Reprinted by permission of Commonweal Publishing Co., Inc.

THOMAS Y. CROWELL COMPANY, INC.: For "American Slang" by Stuart Berg Flexner. From DICTIONARY OF AMERICAN SLANG by Harold Wentworth and Stuart Berg Flexner. Copyright © 1967, 1970 by Thomas Y. Crowell Co., Inc. With publisher's permission.

CUE MAGAZINE: For "Stasio on Theatre" by Marilyn Stasio. Reprinted from CUE, October 17, 1970 by permission of the publisher.

FAMILY CIRCLE MAGAZINE: For "Can You Influence People Through 'Body Language'?" by Julius Fast. Reprinted from FAMILY CIRCLE MAGAZINE, November, 1970, by permission of the publisher.

WEBB GARRISON: For "You'd Be *Tongue Tied* Without Poker." Reprinted from AMERICAN LEGION MAGAZINE, January, 1968, by permission of the author.

HAMMOND ALMANAC, INC.: For "Current Words and Phrases" by Laurence Urdang Inc. Reprinted from THE OFFICIAL ASSOCIATED PRESS ALMANAC 1973, page 426–428. © *The Official Associated Press Almanac* 1973. By permission of the publisher.

HOLT, RINEHART AND WINSTON, INC. For "The Magic and Mystery of Words" by J. Donald Adams. Adapted from THE MAGIC AND MYSTERY OF WORDS by J. Donald Adams, as it appeared in SATURDAY REVIEW. Copyright © 1963 by J. Donald Adams. Reprinted by permission of Holt, Rinehart and Winston, Inc.

INTERNATIONAL FAMOUS AGENCY: For "Rock Lyrics are Poetry (Maybe)" by Robert Christgau. Reprinted by permission of International Famous Agency. Copyright © 1967 by Robert Christgau; first appeared in *Cheetah Magazine*.

J. B. LIPPINCOTT COMPANY: For "Nonlinguistic Systems of Communication" by Mario Pei. From THE STORY OF LANGUAGE by Mario Pei. Copyright 1949, © 1965 by Mario Pei. Reprinted by permission of J. B. Lippincott Company.

LOS ANGELES TIMES: For "Space Language is Out of Sight" by Nicholas Chriss. Copyright, 1971, Los Angeles Times. Reprinted by permission.

THE MACMILLAN COMPANY: For "The American Language" by Henry Louis Mencken. Reprinted from LITERARY HISTORY OF THE UNITED STATES, 3rd Edition, by Robert E. Spiller *et. al.* with permission of The Macmillan Company. Copyright © 1946, 1947, 1948, 1953, 1963 by The Macmillan Company. Also, for "Censorship" by Henry J. Abraham. Reprinted with permission of the publisher from the ENCYCLOPEDIA OF THE SOCIAL SCIENCES, David L. Sills, editor-in-chief. Volume II, pages 356–360. Copyright © 1968 by Macmillan Publishing Co., Inc.

MODERN AGE: For "The Language of the Election and Watergate Years" by Mario Pei. Reprinted from MODERN AGE, Volume 17, Number 4, Fall, 1973, pages 387–398 by permission of the publisher and the author.

NATIONAL COUNCIL OF TEACHERS OF ENGLISH: For "The Language of White Racism" by Haig A. Bosmajian. Reprinted from COLLEGE ENGLISH, December, 1969. Copyright © 1969 by the National Council of Teachers of English. Reprinted by permission of the publisher and Haig A. Bosmajian. Also, for "Some Effects of Science and Technology Upon our Language" by W. Earl Britton. Reprinted from COLLEGE

COMPOSITION AND COMMUNICATION, December, 1970. Copyright © 1970 by the National Council of Teachers of English. Reprinted by permission of the publisher and W. Earl Britton. Also, for "The Making of a Dictionary–1969" by William Morris. Reprinted from COLLEGE COMPOSITION AND COMMUNICATION, October, 1969. Copyright © 1969 by the National Council of Teachers of English. Reprinted by permission of the publisher and the author.

NEWARK NEWS: For "Woodbridge Seeks to Better Image of School System" by Campbell Allen. Reprinted from NEWARK NEWS, April 3, 1966 by permission of the publisher.

NEWSWEEK, INC.: For "New Peak for Newspeak." Reprinted from NEWSWEEK, May 6, 1968. Copyright Newsweek, Inc., May 6, 1968.

THE NEW YORK TIMES: For "The Fork–Tongued Phrase Book" by Russell Baker. Reprinted from THE NEW YORK TIMES, September 24, 1970. © 1970 by The New York Times Company. Reprinted by permission. Also, for "Is It Possible for a Woman to Manhandle the King's English?" by Israel Shenker. Reprinted from THE NEW YORK TIMES, August 29, 1973. © 1973 by The New York Times Company. Reprinted by permission. Also, for "Walking–and Talking–on the Moon." Reprinted from THE NEW YORK TIMES, November, 1969. © 1969 by The New York Times Company. Reprinted by permission.

MARIO PEI: For "The American Language in the Early '70s" by Mario Pei. Reprinted from MODERN AGE, Fall, 1971, pages 409–414. Copyright 1971 by Modern Age. Reprinted by permission. Also, for "English in 2061: A Forecast" by Mario Pei. Reprinted from SATURDAY REVIEW, January 14, 1961. By permission. Also, for "The Revolt Against English" by Mario Pei. Reprinted from SATURDAY REVIEW, April 6, 1968. By permission.

PHI DELTA KAPPAN: For "Jargon . . . Sacred and Profane" by Andrew W. Halpin. Reprinted from PHI DELTA KAPPAN, March, 1962, pages 237–239. By permission of the publisher.

RANDOM HOUSE, INC. For "Usage, Dialects, and Functional Varieties" by Raven I. McDavid, Jr. From THE RANDOM HOUSE DICTIONARY OF THE ENGLISH LANGUAGE, copyright 1970, 1969, 1967, 1966 by Random House, Inc. Reprinted by permission.

SCHOLASTIC EDITOR GRAPHICS / COMMUNICATIONS: For "The Collegiate Press: Irresistible, Irreverent, but Relevant" by Herman Estrin. Reprinted from SCHOLASTIC EDITOR GRAPHICS / COMMUNICATIONS, May, 1973, pages 8–11. By permission.

DONALD A. SEARS: For "A Linguistic Look at Aerospace English" by Donald A. Sears and Henry A. Smith. Reprinted from WORD STUDY, April, 1969, pages 1-8 by permission of the authors and G. & C. Merriam Co. Copyright © 1969 by G. & C. Merriam Co.

SR PUBLISHING ASSETS INDUSTRIES, INC.: For "Body Language." Reprinted from SATURDAY REVIEW OF EDUCATION, May, 1973. Copyright 1973 by Saturday Review Co. First appeared in SATURDAY REVIEW, May 1973. Used with permission.

TIME INC.: For "The Euphemism: Telling It Like It Isn't." Reprinted from TIME, September 19, 1969. Reprinted by permission from TIME, The Weekly News-magazine; Copyright Time Inc. 1969. Also, for "Words from Watergate" by Stefan Kanfer. Reprinted from TIME, August 13, 1973. Reprinted by permission from TIME, The Weekly Newsmagazine; Copyright Time Inc. 1973. Also, for "Sispeak: A Msguided Attempt to Change Herstory" by Stefan Kanfer. Reprinted from TIME, October 23, 1972. Reprinted by permission from TIME, The Weekly Newsmagazine; Copyright Time Inc. 1972. Also, for "A Women's Lib Exposé of Male Villainy" by Ann Bayer. Reprinted from LIFE, August 7, 1970, page 62A-62B. Ann Bayer, LIFE Magazine © 1970 Time Inc. Reprinted with permission. Also, for "Right You Are If You Say You Are–Obscurely." Reprinted from TIME, December 30, 1966, pages 14-15. Reprinted by permission from TIME, The Weekly Newsmagazine; Copyright Time Inc. 1966. Also, for ". . . And Now a Word About Commercials." Reprinted from TIME, July 12, 1968. Reprinted by permission from TIME, The Weekly Newsmagazine; Copyright Time Inc. 1968. Also, for "The New Pornography." Reprinted from TIME, April 16, 1967. Reprinted by permission from TIME, The Weekly Newsmagazine; Copyright Time Inc. 1967. Also, for "Pornography Revisit-ed: Where to Draw the Line" by Ruth Brine. Reprinted from TIME, April 5, 1971. Reprinted by permission from TIME, The Weekly Newsmagazine; Copyright Time Inc. 1971. Also, for "Violent Protest: A Debased Language." Reprinted from TIME, May 18, 1970. Reprinted by permission from TIME, The Weekly Newsmagazine; Copyright Time Inc. 1970. Also, for "The Limitations of Language" by Melvin Maddocks. Reprinted from TIME, March 8, 1971. Reprinted by permission from TIME, The Weekly Newsmagazine; Copyright Time Inc. 1971.

THE WORLD PUBLISHING COMPANY: For "The Development of The English Dictionary" by Harold Whitehall. Reprinted from the WEBSTER'S NEW WORLD DICTIONARY OF THE AMERICAN LANGUAGE, COLLEGE EDITION by permission of the World Publishing Company. All rights reserved.

CONTENTS

PREFACE

During the past decade the United States has experienced an era of unprecedented national ferment. Rapid social change, broad new developments in many fields, and widespread debate on countless vital issues have marked the decade. Explosive social, political, economic, and military problems have clamored unceasingly for attention and for solution. At the same time the country has seen an expansion in education, many innovations in the arts and the mass media, and startling alterations in customs and modes of living.

Paralleling and reflecting these many changes have been corresponding developments in the American language. As new concerns and problems have arisen, new vocabularies—often vivid and imaginative, sometimes irreverent —have come into being. Countless new words and novel expressions as well as new meanings and uses for established words have been created.

Slang and jargon have assumed greater prominence, not only among various originating groups but also in the mass media and with the public at large. Hitherto esoteric expressions in the arts, sciences, military, sociology, and minority groups have increasingly filtered into the mainstream of American English. Scatalogical words once taboo are more often appearing in standard books and periodicals as well as on television and on the stage.

While this never-ending flood of innovations pours into the American language, the upholders of tradition—teachers, linguists, and lexicographers—find themselves hard-pressed in their attempts to determine acceptable standards of usage. Language inevitably changes as people, customs, and countries change. But certain questions never seem to be resolved satisfactorily. How much of this change can be readily accepted as "good usage" or "standard usage"—and by what and by whose standards? How can we determine which slang, jargon, neologisms, foreign terms, even obscenities we may confidently regard as "standard English?"

If too much of the new in language is rejected, so the argument goes, language tends to become somewhat rigid, even archaic; it does not truly reflect the particular times. If on the other hand too much of the new–such as recent slang of certain groups–is quickly accepted as standard, this element of the language may be incomprehensible to large numbers of contemporaries. Further, if much of the new usage turns out to be ephemeral, it would not be readily understandable to most readers in the future. Even dictionaries seem unable to settle this complex issue satisfactorily, and lexicographers, teachers, writers, and others continue in the 1970s, as they have long before, to debate this perplexing question.

In order to present a sense of the innovations, developments, and state of the American language in the 1970s, this book is published. It consists of a wide range of articles, many by well-known writers and established authorities, written for the most part within the past decade. (A few earlier articles, still timely, help to place the present state of the American language in a broader historical context.) Many of the articles originally appeared in leading publications such as *The New York Times*, in scholarly journals, in widely-read magazines, and in various books. Together the articles represent a broad spectrum in subject matter and in point of view. Among the subjects discussed are dictionaries and usage, slang and graffiti, the language of the blacks and of women's liberation, the arts and the mass media, and modern living and behavior. Additional perspective on the contemporary American language is provided by articles on the development of American English and on the future of English.

While this book ranges widely over the vast and many-faceted field of the American language in the 1970s, it makes no claim to comprehensiveness. Some readers might prefer additional material on certain areas. The editors can only reply that space limitations have forced them to omit a number of excellent articles that they would like to have included. Still, it is their hope that the book conveys a lively sense of the many new developments, of the freshness and vitality of much of the current language, and of the controversies over the American language during the past decade.

The American Language in the 1970s has been planned primarily as a textbook for the college freshman English course. The book's main purpose is to help the individual student–through his becoming more aware of many aspects of the current American language–to improve his own ability to write good, clear, expository compositions on a variety of topics. Major criteria used in selecting the articles for inclusion in the text, in addition to their concern with language, are their overall excellence, their timely quality, and their potential interest to the college freshman. The editors have, in fact, already used many of the articles in this text in their college English courses success-fully. Other important considerations in choosing the articles are their clarity in presenting the relevant material, a good fluent style, and appropriate organization of the respective material.

As the selections in *The American Language in the 1970s* range from scholarly topics to timely, controversial subjects (women's liberation, black English, political ethics), each class will have considerable individual choice of materials and approaches. While many of the articles will inevitably aid the student to gain a greater understanding of contemporary American life, they will also help him to learn about his own language.

Through study of this text the student can learn about the history of, and recent developments in, the American language; about subtleties and ambiguities in language; and about the potentialities and the power of words. The articles should help the student to improve his own written and spoken language by serving as a stimulus to classroom discussion and to compositions on current topics of vital concern to many students.

While this book is designed primarily for the college freshman, it could also be studied profitably in upper-level courses in language and linguistics, in contemporary history and social problems, in psychology and sociology, as well as in other subjects. The book should also prove of considerable interest to the general reader as a panorama of both the changing language and the infinitely variegated scene in the United States in the 1970s.

Herman A. Estrin
Department of Humanities
Newark College of Engineering

Donald V. Mehus
Department of English
Fairleigh Dickinson University

1
INTRODUCTION

"Has it ever occurred to you how much words have in common with money? They are, first of all, counters of exchange; they are sometimes inflated and frequently devalued, put in circulation and withdrawn. They, too, accumulate interest, they are coined; they are borrowed, they grow blurred with use, they are hoarded, and they are spent lavishly." With this analogy J. Donald Adams, former New York Times *book editor, begins the following essay, adapted from his book* The Magic and Mystery of Words. *In his essay Mr. Adams continues to examine various aspects of words: their origins, their subtleties and possibilities, their future, and their power for good and for evil.*

This article serves to introduce both the subject and the scope of The American Language in the 1970s.

The Magic and
Mystery of Words

J. Donald Adams

Has it ever occurred to you how much words have in common with money? They are, first of all, counters of exchange; they are sometimes inflated and frequently devalued, put in circulation and withdrawn. They, too, accumulate interest, they are coined; they are borrowed, they grow blurred with use, they are hoarded, and they are spent lavishly. They can be counterfeit. They convince and they seduce. They are accepted (too often) at face value, and they lend themselves easily to speculation, or I would not be writing these particular words.

As a subject for comment, words are almost on a par with the weather in their universality of appeal. We all use them, poorly or well, and for good or ill; we all have some interest in them, if only in solving crossword puzzles. Books about them multiply; newspapers run prize contests based on their use; magazines prod us into enlarging our vocabularies. Is it paradoxical that so much attention should be paid them at a time when they are more carelessly used and more rapidly debased than ever before, or is this increased attention the result of their abuse?

In either case, the situation is strange. Surely there was never a time in which so many different groups of people—including hipsters, horseplayers, sportswriters, sociologists, gossip columnists, psychoanalysts, educators, mobsters, fashion experts, hucksters, physicists, and technologists, bureaucrats and teenagers—have insisted on divorcing themselves from the common tongue and developing a distinctive lingo. At the present rate of acceleration, the time cannot be distant when, in the interest of easier communication, we shall have to devise a new *lingua franca*. Perhaps it would be simpler to take over the old sign language that served the Plains Indians so well.

Whatever the present situation, words remain one of the most living things of man's creation; indeed, one might argue that they have more vitality than anything else we have fashioned. What else is there that seems to lead an independent life? Words do; they acquire strength and lose it; they may, like people, become transformed in character; like certain persons, they may gather evil about them, or, like others, prod our wits or lift our hearts. Like ourselves, some of them suffer from hardening of the arteries. They seem to pursue their own ends with a dogged intention, and when, utterly spent and cast out from the common tongue, they fall into obsolescence, not all the lexicographers and etymologists together can revive them.

During wars and immediately after them, words—particularly those that stand for big and ideal concepts—are likely to have a hollow sound and to grow frayed at the edges, if not somewhat rotten at the heart. Except in their most simple and direct uses, they are not much good in time of war, though we are then pelted with them even more than we are in the intervals of peace. However much we may talk about them as weapons—which they can be—when armies are on the march and the earth shakes, words assume a triviality that belies their true nature. They have a lot to do with making wars, but save for those we speak of as cold, not much with winning them.

Our greatly increased interest in semantics, the science of meanings, is not, I think, a merely chance matter. Words are more important today than ever before, because men have become less united in their attitudes, and have increasing difficulty in understanding one another. Words were less important in the Middle Ages, when people were sustained by a deeply felt religious faith that permeated their lives and when all values were more clearly defined and more universally shared. Even as recently as the nineteenth century Western man, at least, firmly believed in continual progress and the perfectibility of man. Our divisions today are found in more intangible barriers than those of the Berlin wall and the Iron Curtain. As Albert Camus observed, it would seem now as if "man's long dialogue" had come to an end. I said earlier that words have much in common with money, but there is a great difference too, in that they are living tissue, sensitive organisms that require the most careful handling. When they are casually shoved in the slot like tokens on a bus, or when they are used, as they so often are in an age of universal and insistent propaganda, to act as the inky effluvia of the squid, they become obscuring and destructive forces of great potency.

Man's other creations all require a material embodiment of some kind. Words stand alone. Although they appear in type or on the phonograph disc, they are not dependent on them as architecture is dependent upon steel and stone, or painting upon colors and canvas. Words alone are as disembodied as when man first drew them from his stream of thought. Though they are transmitted by his vocal cords, by the gestures of his hands, or by the medium of print, they are capable of free existence in his brain, like a wish, an ambition, a love. They had to exist there before he could utter them, or by sign communicate their meaning.

Nothing in man's development from the so-called lower orders seems to me as fascinating, as teasing to the mind, as the process by which he developed the capacity for speech. All of us who use words, whether as tools in our work or merely as the means of day-to-day communication with our fellows, must sometimes pause to ponder over their beginnings and to wonder at the frequently brilliant suggestiveness of the symbols chosen by those remote ancestors who looked with fresh eyes upon the phenomena of nature and sought to find, in speech, sounds that would convey what they saw. For all the theories that have been spun about the origins of language, we know with certainty very little about them. All is conjecture, all is shrouded in the mists of an age of which our only records lie in the rocks, or in the forms of animal and vegetable life—and these records, however much else they may tell us, have nothing to say of speech. The question of its origin is the more teasing because the likelihood of our ever learning any more than we now know about it is small indeed.

How we would like to know! Did the old man of the tribe say we will call this thing that, and give it a name? Was there a council, and were other suggestions offered? There are too many obviously echoic words, words that attempt to approximate in sound the things for which they stand, for us not to believe that there sometimes was a conscious effort toward duplication in speech of what had been observed or heard in experience. To use what is for me an enticing example, consider the ancient Greek word for the sea, which was *thalassa*. To my ear, it conveys the sound of water slapping against a rock or the side of a boat. It is easy to carry these things too far, and I know that the scientific students of language distrust many so-called echoic words. Yet, knowing as little as we do, can't we guess?

Let's consider for a moment words that do not achieve their effect by imitating certain sounds, but nevertheless seem admirably suited to call up the image of what they are meant to stand for. There are two old English words that have come down unsullied through the centuries, unchanged in pronunciation and meaning, and singularly figurative: *dawn* and *dusk*. I have always taken pleasure in both the sight and sound of these words. To me, there is slowly spreading light in the word *dawn,* both to the eye as we see it in print, and to the ear as we hear it spoken. So far as the eye is concerned, this effect is partly due, I think, to the fact that "a" is a bright letter; it lets in light. For that reason, I prefer the spelling "grey" to "gray," because the first seems to me more shadowed. And when we hear the sound that *dawn* makes, surely the lengthiness and opening out of that single syllable suggest the gradual filling of the sky with light. Similarly, when we hear the word *dusk*, there is about the sound of it a suggestion of stealthiness, of the creeping up of night. Old as they are, unspoiled as they are, these two words are used more commonly in writing than in speech. No words could be simpler or more expressive, but in ordinary speech we are more likely to use *sunrise* and *twilight*, or, in certain localities of the United States, *sunup* and *sundown*. Is it because of the beauty of *dawn* and *dusk* that they have acquired a somewhat literary character, so that we are a trifle self-conscious about their casual use? Certainly they are still fresh and unstained; yet *dawn* comes down to us from the Anglo-Saxon verb *dagian*, which in Middle English became *dawnen*, and *dusk* from the Anglo-Saxon *dosc* and the Middle English *dosk* or *dusk*. Fifteen centuries have failed to stale them.

Words have a magic and mystery. It is interesting to note how much the effect of certain words upon us can be altered by a slight change in them, and how a certain phrase can be undermined by the substitution of one word for another of almost but not quite equivalent meaning. In *The Summing Up,* although Somerset Maugham contends that the language of the King James version has had a deleterious effect upon subsequent English prose, he refers to its *majestical* quality. Normally I prefer a short word to a longer one, but in this instance *majestical* adds a measure of weight where it is needed that *majestic* does not have.

In the matter of phrases in which slight alteration has disproportionate effect, suppose we consider the Biblical phrase "beside the still waters." *Quiet* is a synonym for *still*, but if it is substituted for the word chosen by the King James translators, the magic of the phrase is impaired. *Still* seems to me a quieter word than *quiet*, which is actually rather noisy. *Still* is like dropping a pebble in an unruffled pool, and watching the circles silently widening out. With *quiet* you have just the plop of the pebble.

"Words," Elihu Root once said, "are like those insects that take their color from their surroundings. Half the misunderstanding in this world comes from the fact that the words that are spoken or written are conditioned in the mind that gives them forth by one set of thoughts and ideas, and they are conditioned in the mind of the hearer or reader by another set of thoughts and ideas, and even the simplest forms of expression are frequently quite open to mistake, unless the hearer or reader can get some idea of what were the conditions in the brain from which the words come."

I suspect that one of the first steps necessary to getting ourselves and the world out of the mess we are in, is to become clear in our minds as to just what we mean by certain words, and also what other people mean, who use them in what may seem to us a quite different sense. I am thinking, of course, of words like *democracy, liberal,* and *conservative.* George Orwell may have hit on a profound truth when he assumed that the present political chaos is connected with the decay of language, and that some improvement might be brought about by starting at the verbal level.

There is much more to this situation, however, than the loose or inappropriate use of words arising out of carelessness or ignorance. Orwell called attention to the fact that in our time a good part of political speech and writing is devoted, through a carefully disingenuous use of words, to "the defense of the indefensible." He had particular reference to the dishonest nice Nellieness with which some of the characteristic deviltries of our era are described. The bombardment of defenseless villages has too often gone by the deceptively innocent term, *pacification.* When men are sent to prison without trial, or bundled off to concentration camps, phrases like *elimination of unreliable elements* are called into use. In this fashion it is possible to name horrible things without creating mental pictures of them. Such is the power of words.

Orwell hazarded the guess that the German, Italian, and Russian languages all deteriorated as a result of the word-jockeying that ensued as soon as dictatorship in one form or another fastened itself upon these peoples. Indeed, even in Great Britain and the United States the growth of bureaucracy has encouraged an increase of muddiness, clumsiness, and circumlocution, and the changes have been definitely on the side of deception and concealment. We like to think of ours as a time when plain speaking and writing are better appreciated than they were in some periods of the past; we are proud of the fact that Fourth of July oratory now sounds hollow in our ears, and we boast of our readiness to call a spade a spade, but we are guilty of some strange contradictions of that attitude.

Language being the responsive medium it is, one deeply affected by the temper and attitudes of the period to which it belongs, it is only natural that the way in which words are used in our times should reflect our confusion and our awareness of shifting values. But language is not only acted *upon*—it is an active force itself, capable of affecting our attitudes and ideas; and that is why we must give increasing thought to words and to the power within them.

Emerson said, "Every word was once a poem." A few of them, I think, still are. This is true even of some place-names, whose beauty is solely that of sound, like *Susquehanna* and *Shenandoah*. Words, then, are like money, counters of exchange; they are living entities; they were, and sometimes still are, poems, they are persuaders and fortifiers, tranquilizers and irritants; and they are forces for good or evil—builders and destroyers.

Words are not static. All civilized tongues—and possibly those of primitive peoples—are in continual flux, and this is more true, perhaps, of our own than of any other. I daresay that English has suffered more sea changes since the fourteenth century, when it began to assume a character recognizable to us now, than French, Spanish, Italian, German, or Russian. Nowhere have these changes been as constant or as pronounced as in the United States. English on its home grounds has altered much, of course, but not as markedly as here, where it separated itself sufficiently from parental usage for H. L. Mencken to be emboldened to issue a declaration of verbal independence in *The American Language*.

What Mencken did not foresee was that British and American English, both written and spoken, would draw closer together. This *rapprochement* has been in progress since World War I, following several decades in which American writers were forging a native style, more closely approximating the differences that distinguished our speech from that of the mother country. The source of this development has been too commonly attributed to Mark Twain, who, though he did more to advance it than Thoreau, was by no means the pioneer that Hemingway called him in stating flatly that "American writing begins with Mark Twain." Not only did Thoreau precede Twain in arriving at a native style; so, too, at times did his mentor Emerson. Earlier still, there are definite traces in Franklin's *Autobiography* of an emerging native idiom. If, prior to Mark Twain, we were prevailingly influenced by English models—and continued to be even past the turn of the century—the balance of power began perceptibly to shift with the coming of World War I. The influence of our own speech and writing on the British began then, too, and has proceeded since at an increasingly accelerated pace. This type of coexistence, though a matter of indifference to us, has not been universally welcomed by our British brethren. Occasional angry voices are lifted in the *Times* of London and other publications, protesting that this linguistic miscegenation must be halted at once.

The march of language, forward or backward, however, cannot be halted. Although that march is speedier and more insistent in matters of speech, it is no less perceptible on the printed page. Though Hollywood may have set the pace for British borrowings from us, the periodical press, though not books, has not been too far behind. The *Times* of London may remain adamant, but some other English papers have not been above a flattering interest in American newspaper style. And if Sydney Smith could once–and not wholly without justification–inquire, "Who reads an American book?" no literate Englishman today would raise such a question. Even *Punch* would laugh at him.

The gulf between us and the British in manner of speech, choice of words, and even of cadence, grows steadily narrower. The once famous, and to our ears unintelligible, Oxford drawl has almost passed from hearing, and the speech of the cultivated Britisher and the cultivated American approximate each other more and more. Where we still differ widely–and this much to our discredit–is in the rhythms of speech. Ours holds to an almost deadly monotone; the British manner of running up and down the scale, when not exaggerated, is far more pleasing and far less boring to the ear. We are still baffled, though, by the speech of the cockney; more so, perhaps, than an Englishman is by the Brooklyn accent.

My concern with the words of tomorrow is by no means limited, however, to such further verbal fellowship as may come about between the British and ourselves. I am thinking also of such current menaces as the speedreading craze. The proponents of this fiendish effort to convert the human reader into some kind of IBM computer put a very low value on quality in words and the manner in which they are assembled. They will dispute this charge, of course, but I do not think they can disprove it. Words as they wish us to see them become like so many nickels, dimes, quarters, or cartwheels that you might drop in the maw of a one-arm bandit in the expectation of hitting the jackpot. One quarter or cartwheel serves this purpose just as well as another.

It is not my intention or my wish to throw their entire effort into the ashcan. Their methods, which they guarantee will make it possible for you to consume several pages of print in the time it now takes you to consume but one, may serve very well for certain menial purposes; they will enable you to swallow whole a mass-produced article that you now nibble at piecemeal; they will assist you to get through your favorite newspaper (provided it is not the *New York Times*) before you have finished your morning grapefruit; they will make it possible for you to cut in half the time you now spend on the latest whodunit—but I will bet dollars to doughnuts that they will not increase your appreciation of any first-rate writer, whether he be poet, novelist, or essayist. You will, in fact, lose the greater part of what you were able to get before, even if your eyes formerly had the speed of a moving tortoise. It isn't humanly possible to take in a fat paragraph at a glance, and, beyond absorbing the general sense of it, receive any adequate notion of its structure, its music, its shadings of meaning, or its subtleties of thought. Reading is not a one-way street; you get from it in proportion to what you give, and if all you give is a rapid-fire runover, what can you expect for your money? Try reading the Twenty-third Psalm at a glance. That is not perhaps a satisfactory example, for the words are too well-known, even today, although I would wager there are fifteen million teen-agers who couldn't distinguish it from a TV commercial. I know there are thousands of bright, even brilliant, and reasonably well-read teen-agers, for I have listened to some of them; I am talking, however, in terms of national averages.

Speedreading is not the only menace that threatens the words of tomorrow. We pride ourselves on our bluntness of speech, on our distaste for old-fashioned oratory—or any oratory, for that matter—and yet we coin as many or more nice Nellieisms as the Victorians, with their *limbs* for *legs*. They were, as a matter of fact, more honest in some respects, for they simply declined to use the words they thought offensive, instead of devising pale substitutes for them, as we so often do. I say "we"; what I really mean is that these Uriah Heepish words are foisted on us by the sociologists, the bureaucrats, and other dangerous elements in our society.

One phrase now much in the news, which I would like to see cast into outer darkness, is *senior citizens*. This euphemism for the elderly or downright old is almost as offensive as *funeral home*. Whoever concocted it—and the originators of these minor monstrosities somehow always remain anonymous—should be baked in oil and then served as a soufflé in the hell he will sometime inhabit. There will, of course, be a special corner of the infernal regions reserved for the Madison Avenue luminary who thought up "Get that greasy kid stuff out of your hair"; he will be afflicted forever with an itching scalp. As for those smirking dolls who caress their own skins while promoting the last thing in lotions, they will suffer the tortures of perpetual acne.

The words of tomorrow, as foreshadowed in the recent controversial new edition of the Merriam-Webster, will, of course, include a host of technological terms as yet unborn. They will, I predict, be increasingly abstruse and increasingly polysyllabic. Everybody, if Mr. Kennedy has his way about shooting for the moon, will feel obliged to learn them. The question remains: What will we do with them after they have been acquired? Just as we may ask ourselves: What will we do with the moon after we have set foot on it?

The Scientists (now so important in our lives that I feel compelled to capitalize the word for them as we capitalize the Deity) have announced that Venus, once just a lovely apparition in the early evening and morning skies, has a prevailing temperature of 800° Fahrenheit, and that its inhabitants, if any, look upward into a smog thicker than any that ever hung over Pittsburgh or Los Angeles. Then came word of their conclusions as to what Mars is like. The sensitive recording instruments dispatched to that planet have revealed that Mars is almost completely a desert, and that if any life exists there, it must be of a very low order. When will man get it through his head that his choice of a celestial speck to inhabit was a very shrewd one, and that in spite of the mayhem he has committed upon his native Earth, it remains the one hospitable world he is likely to encounter. Let him, then, redouble his efforts to improve it, instead of horsing around beyond its stratosphere.

Space? You can have it. In my estimation, it's for the birds. It was theirs in the first place; let them keep it. Man, God bless him, is a primate, who came down out of the trees only to end up riding bumper to bumper on endless ribbons of concrete, strangling himself in city traffic, cooping himself up in oversized boxes built out of steel, concrete, and glass. He seems at the moment to emulate, above all other forms of animal life, the goldfish. Bankers, once the most secretive of men, now build themselves enormous glass-walled bowls in which their questionable activities are laid open to every passer-by. When at home, *Homo sapiens*, as he has conceitedly christened himself, delights in burrowing into a huge steel-framed anthill in which, by current building standards, he is privy to whatever noises are most pleasing to his immediate neighbor. This curious compulsion is in full spate from New York to New Delhi. Men once went traveling to remind themselves that not everybody lives alike; now they venture forth to remind themselves that they have never left home.

What can we do about it? Not much, probably, but we might make a try by using words as weapons. Properly employed, they have within them more force than a hundred-megaton bomb.

2
THE DEVELOPMENT OF AMERICAN ENGLISH

In the opening article of this chapter Henry Louis Mencken traces the development of the American language from the settlement of the first colonies in the early 17th century through the growth of the country to the United States of the mid–twentieth century. Editor, critic, and author, Mencken was the compiler of the monumental volume The American Language.

The chapter continues with an examination of more recent developments in the American language during the early 1970s. The writer of this article is the distinguished linguist Mario Pei, author of the book The Story of Language *and many other books and articles on language.*

The chapter concludes with a list of 133 words and phrases (with definitions) that have only recently made an appearance in English or that have had some restricted usage over a period of time but are now acquiring widespread usage. The compiler of this list is Laurence Urdang, editor of The Random House College Dictionary.

The American
Language

HENRY L. MENCKEN

I⊤ WAS THE great movement to the West that finally fixed the character of the American language, preserving as it did the Elizabethan boldness which characterized the speech of the first settlers. "Our ancestors," said James Russell Lowell in his "On a Certain Condescension in Foreigners," "unhappily could bring over no English better than Shakespeare's." This, of course, was mere rhetoric, and its aim was only to confute the English chauvinists who for more than half a century had been howling against American speechways. As a matter of record, not many of the colonists who stumbled ashore during the seventeenth century were steeped in the poetical glories of the Elizabethan age, and four-fifths of them, in all probability, had never so much as heard of Shakespeare. But if we dismiss the exact meaning of Lowell's words—often a safe plan in dealing with a literary critic—and consider rather their underlying drift, it turns out that a good deal of truth was in them. The newcomers to the wilderness, if they lacked both information and taste, were at least Englishmen, and they shared with all other Englishmen the enormous revolution in the national language, as in almost every other cultural trait, that had gone on during the forty-five years of Elizabeth's reign.

Those years saw the disappearance of the last trace of medieval resistance to change. The English, once predominantly insular and introspective, became an eager and expansive race, full of strange curiosities and iconoclastic enterprises. They began to investigate the world beyond the sky rim; they made contact with outlandish and inexplicable peoples; they looked with sharp and disillusioned eyes upon many of the ideas and ways of life that had sufficed them for centuries. All this ferment of fresh concepts and unprecedented experiences had its inevitable effect upon the language in which they expressed their thoughts, and it began to burgeon in a manner truly amazing. The last of the bonds that fastened it to the other tongues of the Indo-European family were loosed, and it settled into a grammatical structure so slipshod that, in more than one detail, it suggested less the related German, French, Latin, and Greek than Chinese. Simultaneously, there was a sudden increase in its vocabulary, with new words and idioms coming in on all levels, from that of the street boys of London to that of the court poets and university illuminati. The contribution of Shakespeare himself, whether as inventor or as introducer, was heavy, and in part at least it was lasting. Not infrequently, to be sure, he failed to find a market for his novelties, as when he launched *to happy, to child,* and *to verse,* but his successes were quite as numerous as his failures, and it would be hard to imagine English today without some of the terms he introduced, e.g., *to fool, disgraceful, barefaced, bump, countless, critic, gloomy,* and *laughable;* or without the swarming coinages of his contemporary poets and dramatists, e.g., *dimension, conscious, jovial, rascality, scientific, audacious,* and *obscure.*

All these locutions are now universally accepted, and no one apparently has ever challenged them. But as Tudor license began to succumb to Puritan dogmatism, there was a tightening of the whole English *Kultur,* and the language did not escape its effects. Grammarians arose, and efforts were made to break English to the patterns of Latin. All novelties in speech were received hostilely, and the doctrine was launched that there were enough words already, and no more were needed. The Restoration had but little corrective effect upon this foolishness, and it went roaring into the eighteenth century when Samuel Johnson became its chief fugleman. No man who ever undertook to write a dictionary knew less about speechways. He was all theory—and nine-tenths of his theory was nonsense. It may seem incredible today, but it is nevertheless a fact, that he tried to put down *touchy* and *to coax;* what is more, *stingy* and *to derange;* what is yet more, *chaperon* and *fun.* Nor did he battle alone; for example, Jonathan Swift had frowned upon *banter* and *sham, bubble* and *mob, bully* and *to bamboozle.* Under such attacks English became again a highly policed language, and lost almost altogether its Elizabethan hospitality to novelty. The writer who thought of a new word kept it to himself, for the penalty of using it was infamy. The tony English style became an imitation of Johnson's quasi-Latin, and no term was countenanced by the elegant that was not in his dictionary. Thus the old libido for word making went underground, and there it has remained in England, to this day. Ardent neologists, of course, have arisen since Johnson's time–notably Thomas Carlyle–but they have had but little influence upon the language, and a good three-fourths of the novelties it has adopted in our own time have come from the United States, and have been on the level of the vulgar speech.

Why the people of America, despite their general subservience to Puritan ideas, have preserved the Elizabethan boldness of speech remains a bit mysterious; perhaps it is mainly because the life they have led has continued to be predominantly Elizabethan. They had, during their first two centuries, an immediate and menacing wilderness to subdue, and the exigencies of their daily lives did not favor niceness, whether in language or otherwise. It was not until the early years of the nineteenth century that the influence of English purism began to be felt here, save only upon the higher levels, and by that time the great movement into the West had begun–a movement that seems to have fixed finally the character of American speech. Moreover, it is not to be forgotten that, to the immigrants who swarmed in during the century following, life in the United States continued to be a sort of frontier life, even in the East, and that niceness was beyond their powers, even if they were aware of it. Whatever the chain of causes, American English refused to be policed, and it continues in a kind of grammatical, syntactical, and semantic outlawry to this day. The schoolma'am has tried valiantly to bring it to heel, and only too obviously in vain. Most of the native grammarians of any sense have long since deserted her, and the rules they now propagate tend to be more and more inductive. If she continues to war upon *ain't, it's me,* and the confusion of *will* and *shall*, it is only because most of the supergogues who train her are apparently unaware of this collapse of the old-time grammar. New words and idioms swarm around her in such numbers that she is overwhelmed, and her function as an arbiter of speech withers away. In this great free Republic the verdict of life and death upon a neologism is not brought in by schoolma'ams, whether in shorts or step-ins, but by a jury resembling a *posse comitatus*, on which even schoolboys sit. In brief, the American language is being molded by a purely democratic process, and, as on the political level, that process is grounded upon the doctrine that any American is as good as any other.

II

The first Americanisms, naturally enough, were nouns borrowed from the Indian languages, designating objects unknown in England. Some of them reached the present bounds of the United States by way of the older colonies to southward or northward, e.g., *tobacco, canoe,* and *potato,* but the great majority entered the colonial speech directly, and nearly all the earlier ones came from the Algonquin dialects, e.g., *hickory* (1634[1]), *hominy* (1629), *moccasin* (1612), *opossum* (1610), and *pone* (1612). The colonial chronicles are full of such loans, and though many of them survive mainly in place names or have become obsolete altogether, e.g., *cockarouse* (1624), *sagamore* (1613), and *tuckahoe* (1612), others remain alive in the general American speech, e.g., *moose* (1613), *persimmon* (1612), and *raccoon* (1608). Not a few, indeed, have been absorbed by standard English, e.g., *tomahawk* (1612), and *squaw* (1634), and even by other languages, e.g., *totem* (1609). "The Indian element" in American English, said Alexander F. Chamberlain in 1902, "is much larger than is commonly believed to be the case. . . . In the local speech of New England, especially among fishermen . . . many words of Algonkian origin, not familiar to the general public, are still preserved, and many more were once current, but have died out within the last one hundred years."[2]

At later stages American English was destined to receive many loans from the languages of non-English immigrants, especially the Dutch, French, Spanish, and Germans, but before 1700 they seem to have been relatively small in number. *Portage,* from the French of Canada, has been traced to 1698 and is probably somewhat older, but *bureau, chowder,* and *rapids* are not recorded until the time of the French and Indian War, and many other familiar French loans, e.g., *prairie* and *gopher,* did not come into general use until the Revolutionary era. The same time lag is observed when Spanish loans are investigated, and there was no appreciable infiltration from the German until the middle of the eighteenth century. Even the borrowings from Dutch, save in New York, were very few before 1700. *Scow* is traced to 1669, and *hook* (as a geographical term) to 1670; but most of the loans now familiar are later, e.g., *sleigh* (1703), *stoop* (1755), *span* (of horses, 1769), *cooky* (1786) and *coleslaw* (1794). It was not, indeed, until after Yorktown that there was any considerable infiltration of Dutch into the common speech, and some of the loans now known to every American are surprisingly recent, e.g., *spook* (1801), *cruller* (1805), *waffle* (1817), *boss* (1818), and *Santa Claus* (1823). John

Pickering omitted all these save *scow, sleigh,* and *span* from his pioneer *Vocabulary* of 1816, but by 1859 John Russell Bartlett was listing *boss, cooky, hook, stoop,* and *cruller* in the second edition of his *Dictionary of Americanisms. Yankee,* perhaps the most conspicuous contribution of Dutch to American English, was at first applied to the Dutch themselves, and it was not until the years immediately preceding the Revolution that it came to signify a Northern American.

Of far more importance than these loans were the new words that the colonists made of English materials, mainly by compounding but also by giving old words new meanings. *Snowshoe* is traced by the *Dictionary of American English* to 1666, *backlog* to 1684, *leaf tobacco* to 1637, *statehouse* to 1662, *frame house* to 1639, and *selectman* to 1635. By the middle of the eighteenth century the number of such neologisms was very large, and by its end they were almost innumerable. Many were invented to designate natural objects not known in England, e.g., *bluegrass* (1751), *catbird* (1709), *tree frog* (1738), *slippery elm* (1748), *backwoods* (1784), *salt lick* (1751), and *garter snake* (1775), and others were names for new artifacts, e.g., *smokehouse* (1759), *ball ground* (1772), *breechclout* (1757), *buckshot* (1775), *shingle roof* (1749), *sheathing paper* (1790), *springhouse* (1775) and *hoecake* (1755). But not infrequently, as if delighting in the exercise, the colonists devised novel appellations for objects that were quite well known in England, e.g., *broomstraw* (1785), *sheet iron* (1776), *smoking tobacco* (1796), *lightning bug* (1778), and *bake oven* (1777), and almost as often they gave old English names to new objects, e.g., *corn, shoe, rock, lumber, store, cracker, partridge,* and *team.* Some of the latter were extended in meaning, e.g., *rock,* which meant only a large mass of stone in England, and *barn,* which meant only a building for storing crops, with no accommodations for cattle; others were narrowed, e.g., *corn,* which indicated any kind of edible grain to the English, and *boot,* which indicated any leather footgear; and yet others underwent a complete change in significance, e.g., *freshet,* which the English applied to a small stream of fresh water, and to which the Americans gave the meaning of an inundation, and *partridge,* which the English applied to *Perdix perdix* and the Americans to *Bonasa umbellus, Colinus virginianus,* and various other birds.

By 1621 Alexander Gill was noting that some of the new words bred in America were coming into recognition in England, by 1735 Francis Moore was denouncing one of the most vivid of them, to wit, *bluff,* in the sense of a precipice or escarpment, as "barbarous," and by 1754 Richard Owen Cambridge was suggesting that a glossary of them would soon be in order. But so far as the studies of such philological historians as Allen Walker Read, M. M. Mathews, and W. B. Cairns have revealed, there was no attempt at an orderly treatise upon them until 1781, when John Witherspoon printed a series of papers on the subject in the *Pennsylvania Journal and Weekly Advertiser* of Philadelphia.[3] This Witherspoon was a Scots divine who came out in 1768 to be president of the College of New Jersey (Princeton). When the Revolution shut down his college he took to politics, was elected a member of the New Jersey Constitutional Convention, got promotion to the Continental Congress, and signed both the Declaration of Independence and the Articles of Confederation. But though he was thus ardently for independence as a political idea, he was outraged by its appearance in speech, and denounced not only the common people for daring to exercise it, but also the bigwigs who showed signs of it "in the senate, at the bar, and from the pulpit." His animadversions, in the main, were only echoes of the pedants then flourishing in England, and they had but small effect. Thus when he protested against the peculiar American use of *to notify*, as in "The police were notified"–"In English," he said, "we do not notify the person of the thing, but the thing to the person"–he roared in vain. The politicians, lawyers, clergy, and journalists of the time paid little heed to him, and the generality of Americans never heard of his attempt to improve their speech.

Of much more potency were the English reviewers who began, after the Revolution, to notice American books. They were, with few exceptions, bitterly hostile to the new republic, and their hostility often took the form of reviling Americanisms. Thomas Jefferson was one of the first victims of this crusade, which went on violently for almost a century and is not infrequently revived in our time. When he used the verb to *belittle*–apparently his private invention–in his *Notes on the State of Virginia*, the European Magazine and London Review* showed as much dudgeon as if he had desecrated Westminster Abbey, and during the years following nearly all the other contemporary American writers were attacked almost as savagely, notably John Quincy Adams, John Marshall, Noah Webster, and Joel Barlow. It would be too much to say that all this fury had any substantial effect upon the national language, but it undoubtedly shook some of the national literati. Even Noah Webster was influenced more or less, and in his earlier writings he was extremely polite to English opinion. As for Benjamin Franklin, he yielded to it with only the faintest resistance.

III

This complaisance was broken down at last by the War of 1812, but there were still signs of it in the first formal study of American speech–the before-mentioned *Vocabulary* of John Pickering. Pickering was no dilettante like Witherspoon, but a diligent and learned student of language, and Franklin Edgerton has described him as "one of the two greatest general linguists of the first half of the Nineteenth Century in America."[4] His observations on Americanisms first appeared in a paper he read to the American Academy of Sciences of Boston in 1815. This paper attracted so much attention that in 1816 he expanded it into a book that is still well worth study, for it is admirably documented and contains a great deal of valuable matter. Unhappily, it is mainly devoted to the objurgations of the English reviewers, and even more unhappily, it shows a lamentable tendency to yield to them. Though he might produce some English authority, says Pickering, for many of the Americanisms he lists, "yet the very circumstance of their being noticed by well-educated Englishmen is a proof that they are not in use at this day in England, and of course ought not to be used elsewhere by those who would speak correct English." This position was fatal to any really rational discussion of them, and in consequence Pickering's book probably did more harm than good. Its influence hung over the discussion of the national speech for a long while, and is not altogether thrown off today. A number of American writers, during the thirty years following its publication, dissented sharply from its thesis, notably James K. Paulding; but many more acquiesced, and it was not until 1848, when Bartlett brought out the first edition of his *Dictionary of Americanisms*, that American English found an anatomist willing to take it for what it was, without any regard for what Englishmen or Anglomaniacs thought it ought to be.

Pickering was thoroughly the scholar, and showed some of the deficiencies that occasionally go with that character. His outlook was rather narrow, and he was more than a little cautious. He omitted all mention of Indian loans from his *Vocabulary*, probably because they were predominantly uncouth, and he dealt only gingerly with the common speech. The great movement into the West was already under way as he wrote, and was already coining the gaudy neologisms that were to give color to the national language, but he seems to have been either too pained to deal with them or unaware of them altogether. By Bartlett's day they were everywhere visible; indeed, they were so numerous after 1840 that all novelties in speech came to be called Westernisms. Bartlett not only listed hundreds of them; he obviously relished them, and he found the same relish in a large number of readers, for his *Dictionary of Americanisms* had to be brought out in a revised and expanded form in 1859, again in 1860, and yet again in 1877, during which time its bulk doubled. It is still on the shelves of most public libraries, and copies often turn up in the secondhand bookstores. Bartlett, unlike Pickering, was not a schooled philologian; but he had a fine feeling for language, and in his preface to his fourth edition he discussed the sources of Americanisms with great perspicacity. Most of them originated, he noted, in the argots of the more raffish trades and professions, and entered the common speech as slang. There they entered upon a struggle *à outrance* for general acceptance, with no assurance that the fittest would survive. Some of the best succumbed, and some of the worst gradually took on respectability, were passed by lexicographers, and became integral parts of the language. Such was the history, for example, of *to lynch, squatter, to hold on,* and *loafer.*

There were various other writers on American speech in the period between the Revolution and the Civil War—for example, Jonathan Boucher, David Humphreys, Charles Astor Bristed, James Fenimore Cooper, Robley Dunglison, and Adiel Sherwood—but their studies were fragmentary and not of any importance.[5] Noah Webster, though he was an ardent reformer of spelling and believed in the future autonomy of American English, gave relatively little attention to Americanisms, and did not list them in any number until his *American Dictionary* of 1828. The first discussion of them on a large scale by a man trained in language studies was in Maximilian Schele de Vere's *Americanisms: The English of the New World* (1871). Schele was a Swede educated in France and Germany, and was brought out to the University of Virginia to profess modern languages. He arrived in 1844, and save for four years in the Confederate Army, held his chair until 1895. In his book he attempted a classification of Americanisms, and was the first to give adequate attention to the loan words among them. After him there was a hiatus until 1889, when an Englishman, John S. Farmer, published *Americanisms, Old and New,* a useful compilation but not altogether free from English prejudice. A year later the American Dialect Society was formed, and the publication of *Dialect Notes* was begun. The ostensible field of the society was narrow, but it soon branched out into wider studies of the national speech, and there is a vast richness of material in the files of its journal. Its projectors included many philologians of sound distinction—for example, Charles H. Grandgent, E. S. Sheldon, E. H. Babbitt, J. M. Manly, and F. J. Child; and in the course of time it attracted the interest and collaboration of many younger scholars of ability, including especially Louise Pound, who became the first editor of another valuable journal, *American Speech*, in 1925. But the Dialect Society, though it had a profound influence, flourished only feebly, and the publication of *Dialect Notes* was often delayed by lack of money.

Next to the appearance of *Dialect Notes* the event that had most to do with putting the study of American English on a scientific basis was the publication of Richard H. Thornton's *American Glossary* in 1912. Thornton was an Englishman who migrated to the United States in 1874. He was a lawyer by training, and died in 1925 as dean of the Oregon Law School, but a good part of his leisure of half a century was given over to an attempt to produce a really comprehensive dictionary of Americanisms. Pickering, Bartlett, and Farmer before him had introduced the practice of illuminating the subject by dated quotations, but he went much further than any of them. Among other things, he seems to have read the whole file of the *Congressional Globe*, along with a multitude of early newspapers. The result was a work of wide range and very high merit. There were a few slips in it, but not many. Unhappily, no American publisher would venture to publish it, and Thornton had to turn to a small firm in London.⁶ He continued his researches afterward, and between 1931 and 1939 the printing of his posthumous materials went on in *Dialect Notes*. His work was not only valuable in itself; it also paved the way for the much more comprehensive *Dictionary of American English*, edited by Sir William Craigie and published between 1938 and 1944 by the University of Chicago Press. Meanwhile, a *Linguistic Atlas of the United States and Canada* was begun in 1939 under the supervision of Hans Kurath.

IV

"For some two centuries, roughly down to 1820," said Craigie in 1927,⁷ "the passage of new words or senses across the Atlantic was regularly westward; practically the only exceptions were terms which denoted articles or products peculiar to the new country. With the nineteenth century, however, the contrary current begins to set in, and gradually becomes stronger and stronger, bearing with it many a piece of drift-wood to the shores of Britain, there to be picked up and incorporated in the structure of the language." This eastward current, at the start, was resisted with the utmost violence, partly because of the lingering English suspicion of all neologisms, but mainly because of an increase in the political hostility that had begun with the

Revolution. From the turn of the century until after the Civil War, the Americans, to all right-thinking Englishmen, were the shining symbols of everything infamous. "They have," wrote Southey to Landor so early as 1812, "acquired a distinct national character for low and lying knavery; and so well do they deserve it that no man ever had any dealings with them without having proofs of its truth." To which the Very Reverend Henry Alford, Dean of Canterbury, added in 1863:

> Look at those phrases which so amuse us in their speech and books. . . ; and the compare the character and history of the nation–its blunted sense of moral obligation and duty to man; its open disregard of conventional right when aggrandisement is to be obtained; and I may now say, its reckless and fruitless maintenance of the most cruel and unprincipled war in the history of the world.

The literati–for example, Dickens–were in the forefront of this fray, for they had a special grievance: to wit, the refusal of the United States to make a copyright treaty with Great Britain, and the consequent wholesale piracy of their works by American publishers. But there were also deeper and more general considerations. The population of the United States had gradually overtaken that of the United Kingdom during the first half of the century, and in the fifties it went bounding ahead. American commerce and manufactures began to increase at a rate which offered an alarming menace to English world trade, American agriculture and mining developed in almost geometrical progression, and the discovery of gold in 1848 and of oil in 1859 gave promise of new and almost illimitable floods of wealth. Thus the English, once only contemptuous, began to view the republic with a mixture of envy and dread, and it is no wonder that most of their chosen augurs hoped (and predicted) that the Civil War would wreck it.

The insular hostility to American ways of speech hardly needed any fresh fillip; it had been active and violent, as we have seen, since the palmy days of the English reviewers. But now it was augmented by a gathering sense of futility. What could be done to stay the uncouth novelties that so copiously barged in? Apparently not much. Every returning English traveler brought them in his baggage, and every American book bristled with them. In 1820, at the precise moment fixed by Sir William Craigie for the turn of the tide, Sydney Smith could still launch his historic sneer at American literature; but only a few years later Cooper and the early American humorists were beginning to break down the English barrier, and they were soon followed by authors of greater heft and beam. The English purists, of course, did not surrender without a bitter fight. Moreover, they had some successes, especially against such shocking Westernisms as *gone coon, semioccasional, to scoot, to skedaddle, to stay put,* and *to shell out.* But when they encountered the more decorous and plausible American novelties, e.g., *outdoors, telegram, anesthetic, presidential, to belittle, to progress, reliable, mileage, and caucus,* they objected in vain. These words were sorely needed, and England itself had nothing to offer in place of them—nothing so logical, so apt, so good. The Elizabethan gift for bold and vivid neologisms had been transferred to this side of the water, and here it has remained. The dons of Oxford, perhaps, still make some show of clinging to the waspish precepts of Johnson, but the English plain people, ever since the Civil War era, have exhibited an increasing and, in late years, overwhelming preference for the novelties marked "Made in America."

It was the American movie, of course, that gave the final impulse to this revolution. When the first American-made films reached England, in 1907, they were too few and too crude to attract the attention of the guardians of the national speech; but this age of innocuousness did not last long. By 1910 the English newspapers began to print an increasing spate of letters from Old Subscribers protesting against the new words and phrases that the silent legends were bringing in, and during the fifteen years following, the protest gradually mounted to a roar. In 1927 legislation was adopted limiting the influx of American films, and it was hoped that the onslaught might be stayed. That hope was renewed on the advent of the talkie, for most authorities declared that the patriotic English people would never tolerate the abomination of American spoken speech. Even the American movie magnates seem to have been of that mind, for they showed a considerable perturbation in the talkie's early days, and even got out English versions of their masterpieces, manned by proper English actors. But within a short while they had trained their native performers to give a tolerable imitation of English speech, and soon afterward they began to discover that English audiences really did not object to what remained of the Yankee twang. By the middle thirties a wholesale imitation was in progress, and on December 14, 1930, a woman contributor to the London *Evening News* was writing:

> An American, coming over to England for the first time, was struck by the fact that English children in the streets of London and elsewhere talked exactly the same as children in the United States. An American impresario came to this country to make films. He was anxious to secure a crowd of English-speaking

children, but he utterly failed to find English children who could talk English, and he had to abandon that part of his programme.

To which D. W. Brogan, of Cambridge University, added in 1943:

> There is nothing surprising in the constant reinforcement, or, if you like, corruption of English by American. And there is every reason to believe that it has increased, is increasing, and will not be diminished. If American could influence English a century ago, when the predominance of the Mother Country in wealth, population and prestige was secure, and when most educated Americans were reverentially colonial in their attitude to English culture, how can it be prevented from influencing English today, when every change has been a change of weight to the American side?[8]

V

There was a time when most Americanisms originated in the Western wilds, but by 1940 their source was mainly among city sophisticates, many of whom were devoted professionally to inventing them. They appeared in the compositions of gossip columnists, comic-strip artists, sporting reporters, press agents, advertisement writers, and other such subsaline literati, were quickly gathered into the movies, and were then on their way. They were first adopted in England, as at home, on the lower levels of speech, but if they had the requisite pungency they gradually moved upward. It is curious to note that the very few Briticisms that enter American take a different route: they appear first on pretentious levels, and then sink down. But not many of them ever really survive. English speech seems affected and effeminate to the 100 per cent American, and he would no more use *civil servant, liftman, luggage van,* or *boot shop* than he would stuff his handkerchief into his wristband.

American spelling and pronunciation, like the American vocabulary, have departed considerably from English standards. Efforts to simplify and rationalize the spelling of the language were begun in English so early as the sixteenth century, but it remained for Noah Webster, the American, to work the first effective reforms. It was he who induced Americans to drop the *u* in the *-our* words, the redundant consonants in *traveller, jeweller,* and *waggon,* and the final *k* in *frolick* and *physick*; and to change *gaol* to *jail, plough* to *plow, draught* to *draft, barque* to *bark,* and *cheque* to *check.* In the first flush of his enthusiasm Webster advocated a large number of other reformed spellings, including such bizarre forms as *bred, giv, brest, bilt, relm, frend, speek, zeel, laf,* *dawter, tuf, proov, karacter, toor, thum, wimmen* and *blud,* but by the time he came to his first dictionary of 1806, he had abandoned them. To the end of his days, however, he had a weakness for *cag* (keg), *hainous, porpess,* and *tung,* and it remained for other lexicographers to dispose of them. Two pets of his later years were *chimist* and *neger,* but they never got a lodgment. Perhaps his partiality for them arose from a desire to change the common American pronunciation. *Neger,* which seems to have been borrowed by the early colonists from some Northern dialect of English, survived until the nineteenth century, though *negro* had been challenging it from the start, and *nigger* has been traced to 1700.

The Simplified Spelling movement, which was launched by Francis A. March, W. D. Whitney, F. J. Child, and other eminent philologians in 1876, languished until 1906, when Theodore Roosevelt, then in the White House, gave it his imprimatur and Andrew Carnegie financed it. In its heyday, during the fifteen years following, it brought out long lists of proposed new spellings, including *corus, giv, stomac, brekfast, harth, bluf, activ, hostil, giraf, ar,* and *wer;* but the country would not have them, and after 1919, when both Roosevelt and Carnegie died, it ceased to trouble. Its efforts, however, succeeded in reducing words of the *programme, catalogue,* and *quartette* classes to their *program, catalog,* and *quartet* forms, and in giving *tho, thoro,* and *thru* a certain amount of countenance. It also promoted the exchange of the last two letters in words of the *theatre* class. In England the reform of spelling at the turn of the century was chiefly furthered by the brothers Fowler. Their *Concise Oxford Dictionary,* which first appeared in 1911, retained the *-our* ending; but it abandoned the English *-ise* for the American *-ize,* and the *y* in *cyder* and its analogues for *i,* and made various other concessions to American practice.

The first Englishmen to observe American speechways all reported that there were no dialects in this country. This was an exaggeration; but it remains a fact, as John Witherspoon wrote in 1781, that "there is a greater difference in dialect between one county and another in Britain, than there is between one state and another in America." More painstaking investigation has revealed three major speech areas. The first includes the New England states, the second the South, and the third all the rest of the country. These areas are divided into subareas more or less narrow, and the speech of Boston differs from that of New England in general just as the speech of the Southern tidewater differs from that of inland regions. But these differences, which mainly have to do with the pronunciation of *a* and the treatment of terminal *r,* are not important, and even on the most ignorant levels an American of one speech area readily understands an American of another. Noah Webster based his recommended pronunciations upon the cultivated usage of New England, and for many years this practice was inculcated by the schoolma'am; but it has been losing ground since the Civil War, and most authorities seem to believe that what is commonly called General American or Western American will eventually prevail everywhere. It is, on all counts, an admirable form of English, and its great superiority to the Oxford form fashionable in England is manifest. A great many educated Englishmen, indeed, denounce the Oxford form as affected and absurd, and it shows no sign of spreading hereafter. General American is much clearer and more logical than any of the other dialects, either English or American. It shows a clear if somewhat metallic pronunciation, gives all necessary consonants their true values, keeps to simple and narrow speech tunes, and is vigorous and masculine.

---

[1] The dates here and hereafter are of the earliest examples found by the searchers for the *Dictionary of American English*.

[2] *Journal of American Folk-Lore*, XV (1902), 240. The best account of such loans is to be found in the etymologies by Joseph Coy Green in *Webster's New International Dictionary*, 1934.

[3] They appeared under the heading "The Druid." They are reprinted in full in M. M. Mathews, *The Beginnings of American English*, Chicago, 1931.

[4] "Notes on Early American Work in Linguistics," *Proceedings of the American Philosophical Society*, July, 1943, p.27. The other was Peter Stephen Du Ponceau.

[5] Humphreys, Cooper, Dunglison, and Sherwood are reprinted by Mathews in *The Beginnings of American English*.

[6] The J. B. Lippincott Company of Philadelphia brought out 250 sets of the London sheets in 1912; but they sold slowly, and there was never a genuinely American edition.

[7] *The Study of American English* (S.P.E. Tract No. XXVII), Oxford, 1927, p. 208.

[8] "The Conquering Tongue," London *Spectator*, Feb. 5, 1943.

The American Language in the Early '70s

Mario Pei

THINGS ARE HAPPENING to the English language, as they always have. They may be viewed benignly, as picturesque innovations or useful additions, or they may be regarded with alarm and deplored. Either way, it won't change the changing picture of the language. They can, however, be recorded, discussed, and, above all, classified. The first major classification that occurs to us is into those innovations which are purely accidental, or due to ignorance, and those that are deliberate and foisted upon us for a purpose. The year 1970 has brought to us more of the same things that we discussed in earlier articles, but at a quickened pace. Does this mean that the English language is degenerating faster than it used to? Perhaps, if "degenerating" is the right word.

I

More and more the press media bring to us misspellings like *permissable* and *advisible,* or *supercede* for *supersede,* which are due to the fact that the ear tends to deceive both the eye and the memory of what was once, we hope, learned. There are cases of alternate spellings, like *busing* and *bussing,* the first of which lends itself to being pronounced like *using,* the second to confusion in meaning with *kissing.* Hoary rules of grammar are openly disregarded on TV (not merely "like a cigarette should," but also, at the opening of every Star

26

Trek program, "to boldly go where no man has gone before," with the infinitive split right down the middle). Open defiance is flaunted at puristic viewers: "What do you want, good grammar or good taste?" Actually, some of us might settle for a little of both. Then there are all the words and expressions taken from the "young" language ("Wow!"; "Together!"). *Wow*, incidentally, is described as originating in Scottish English in 1513, then spreading to America, where in the 1920's it even underwent an extensive process of functional change ("She's a wow!"; "We wowed them last night!"). There are other words taken from the tongue of journalism (*birthquake* for *population explosion; thighscraper* for *miniskirt; to be in Splitsville* for *to be on the point of divorce*). Perhaps the greatest outrages inflicted on the language are those perpetrated by the younger generation. David Susskind, whom no one can accuse of being over-conservative, came out at the end of 1970 with a protest about the monosyllabic language of his daughters and their associates, which he described as consisting mainly of such things as "Ya know, man," "It's like aaaaa . . . ," "It's like heavy, ya know." "Shouldn't we be teaching them to speak better, to think straighter . . . how to make their points with appropriate English?" he plaintively concluded.

But the younger generation is also creative. To them we owe such recent additions to a growing family of words as *mill-in, rock-in* (for a music festival), *sick-out*, along with *groupies* (the modern equivalent, in hippie circles, of the medieval camp followers); *Flunkenstein*, applicable to a student who consistently fails to make the grade; perhaps also, on the sexier side, *beddable* and *lewdity* (the analogy of *nudity* is obvious); and the ingenious written or gestured symbol L + 7, which adds up to a "square" whom you don't want to call that to his face. The "kids" (often graduate students well over 21) seem responsible for the current use of the verb *to trash*, which means to wreck, burn, or otherwise devastate a university building or other property. This word, whose origin is "obscure," appears as a verb 1618, but is described by all our dictionaries as in the meaning of "to hold back or restrain a dog," or, at the most, "to trim dead leaves and branches from a tree." The British Oxford Dictionary further informs us that it appears in 1859 in Western U.S. usage with the meaning of "to efface"; this is confirmed by none of our American dictionaries, but might supply a plausible genealogy for its use by rebellious students.

The black element of our population supplies, as usual, an abundant contribution to vocabulary growth. A very recent work by Mrs. Hermese Roberts entitled *The Third Ear: a Black Glossary* ("third ear," by the way, is an expression taken from African story-tellers, who ask their audiences to lend a "third ear" when they want more attention), offers such choice bits as "Man, he's putting down his Ralph Bunche to his old lady!" (talking his way out of a tight situation by the use of diplomatic language), and "the day the eagle flies," meaning payday. Other coinages reported are *landprop* (a telescoping of *landlord* and *proprietor*), *rap* for talk and *hang-up* for preoccupation (but these have been around a while, and have penetrated the general teenage language), *rip off* for steal, *squeeze* for girl or boyfriend, *sweatbox* for a crowded party, *happy shop* for liquor store. There is also a curious inversion of *bad* to mean "good." When the *Black Glossary* first appeared, columnist Russell Baker of *The New York Times* thought it was time to issue a counterpart *White Glossary* that would interpret the language of the suburbs to the blacks. He, too, offers *Ralph Bunche*, but in the sense of one of the few persons of any race who could move in next door without lowering real estate values. *Pig*, which to many blacks is the standard term for policeman, is presented to them by Baker as having the secondary meaning of "a four-footed animal, often used for comparison with young sons in such expressions as 'This room is not fit for a pig.' " (Interestingly, in German slang usage, *pigs* is used for students, not for the police, with *Schweinebums* for snobs, and even a book entitled *Versuch über Schweine*, "Research about Pigs" in the sense of students.) Baker even translates suburban "Er-uh-er" into "Like man, I mean," "Like man, y'know"; a general signal that the brain is temporarily idling.

In more serious vein, we have the coinage of *blackthink* on the analogy of *poorthink*, to indicate anyone whose thinking is black-oriented; the use of *reparations* to indicate money demanded, under duress, of churches and universities to make up for indignities suffered over a century ago; and the use of two thoroughly legitimate expressions, not only by blacks, but by their left-wing, often unwanted white allies in a sense that gives us pause: *community*, where older usage would have preferred *neighborhood*, and the slogan "Power to the people!," which makes one wonder who are the people that are meant to have the power. One journalistic usage for which the blacks cannot be held responsible is the omission of any qualifying adjective in a news item if the youthful offender is black, coupled with a definite "white youth" if he is not. This might be labeled "description by omission."

Before passing on into the area of true weasel words, where the desire to create a given effect is evident, a few more coinages bear mention. *Folknik* and *smutnik* have been added to the ever-growing family of *-niks; zodiatronics* has been formed to indicate casting of a horoscope by computer; *satisficer* has been built out of *satisfy* and *suffice*.

All ingenious creations are by no means American. Professor Edward Misken, of the London School of Economics, is given credit for the following: *growthmen, illfare, uglifying, Newfanglia,* and even *bads,* the opposite of *goods.*

Among expressions that seem to display weasely intentions are the scientific *demute* (to turn up the sound volume); the medical *pregnancy interruption* for abortion; the labor *job action* to betoken a work slowdown, like the one carried on by the New York City police (wouldn't *job inaction* be more appropriate?); the educational *no-time syndrome* (where the professor can't take time to explain); *interpersonal relationships* (redefined as "kid fights"); *ancillary civic agencies for the support of discipline* (which really means to call in the cops to restore order); and columnist John Roche's *ivory foxholes,* to describe what the professors retreat into when the storm breaks over the university.

II

The four prime areas for weasel words are, as usual, the military, government, politics, and commercial advertising.

In the lower army ranks, innovations in usage are few and down-to-earth. The picturesque, unprintable vocabulary of the enlisted men was developed, for the most part, during the Second World War, and only a few terms are of recent origin. It is altogether uncertain whether an expression like *to freak out,* which appears in none of our major dictionaries, even of slang, originated in Vietnam or in the big city slums. The noun *freak,* in the sense of whim or prank, first appears in 1563; the sense "monstrosity," as in "a freak show," is added in 1847; that of "homosexual" in the early twentieth century; the only dictionary use of *freak* as a verb is in the sense of to speckle or streak something with color.

There is a use of *to waste* in the sense of to kill, again not offered in even our most recent dictionaries, but heard repeatedly in connection with the My Lai testimony and elsewhere. *To lay waste* goes back to Middle English, and there is an antiquated legal use of *to waste* in the sense of to destroy property (but not human life). From 1689 on we find *to waste* (to do away with) used in connection with such impersonal things as sin and sorrow. Shakespeare comes a shade closer to the modern usage in "Would he were wasted, marrow, bones and all." Wentworth and Flexner's *Dictionary of American Slang* informs us that the verbal use of *waste* originated with teenage gangs, becoming current in the 1950's in the sense of to defeat decisively, to destroy. This is still not the precise counterpart of "We were ordered to waste all the villagers," and it is possible that this ultimate semantic shift originated in Vietnam.

The *doughboy* of World War One and the *G.I. Joe* of World War Two have turned into a *grunt*, so far as the Vietnam war is concerned. While *grunt*, both as a noun and as a verb, goes back to the sixteenth century, only Webster III among our comprehensive dictionaries gives the acceptance of the noun as a ground lineman employed by public utilities as a helper to the man who is up on a ladder doing the actual repairs, and volunteers the suggestion that he was called a *grunt* because of the noises he made as he lifted and passed on weighty objects. Wentworth and Flexner offer a further connection with the suggestion that the Army *grunt* was in origin a member of the Army Signal Corps. If all this is true, the question is: how did the Signal Corps usage become extended to cover all Armed Forces members?

The real military contribution to language comes from the higher echelons. Here we find not only those reprehensible and often deplored terms, *kill ratio* and *body count* (they have been in use for some years, yet none of our dictionaries records them), but also *greenbacking*, used to describe the hiring of mercenary troops or the financing of such responsive governments as those of South Vietnam and Cambodia, likewise unreported by any dictionary (*greenback* itself, for U.S. currency, goes back to 1778). *Protective reaction* is Pentagonese for such operations as Cambodia and Laos, and displays the usual euphemistic quality of the language of the generals. Other gems of military gobbledegook are seemingly non-deliberate: *accidental delivery of ordnance equipment* to indicate shelling of our own or allied troops by mistake; *combat emplacement evacuator* for a shovel; *aerodynamic personnel accelerator* for a parachute. The finest sample is perhaps the one coined by the Air Force to replace the word *demonstration*, previously used for an accounting review of a contract, to which General Teubner had objected on the ground that *demonstration* had become a dirty word in other connections. He suggested *audit review* as a replacement, which would have been reasonable enough; but the staff writers gave him more than he had bargained for: *Data Accounting Flow Assessment*, with a suitable abbreviation, DAFA.

The word *acceptable*, which in military parlance is applied to casualties or damage inflicted by the enemy, began to supply a good line with the language of government in general when it was applied to unemployment: *acceptable unemployment* was, in the concept of the administration, what the country could take without too much damage to its economy. The trouble with this use of the term is that it is far too subjective; what is *acceptable unemployment* to a bureaucrat who is still working and drawing his salary may not be at all acceptable to the man who is thrown out of his job despite the fact that he has a family to support.

Relatively old administrative parlance, such as *grandstanding* and *jawboning* (the latter sometimes ironically redefined by columnists as the *open-mouth policy*), has been joined by the brand-new terms, *incomes policy* (this means a highly modified version of price-wage-profits control), *inflation alert*, a sarcastic *Nixonomics*, the use of *high* and *low profile* to apply to the attitude taken by a country or administration (we are said to assume a fairly high profile in our dealings with the Soviet Union and North Vietnam, but a low profile when it comes to facing inflation coupled with recession). Two expressions for which either President Nixon himself or his immediate entourage seem responsible are *workfare* (the President's substitute for public welfare, designed to bring to a victorious conclusion the war on poverty, hunger and crime); and *governess government* (the overshadowing of the States by an all-powerful Federal establishment, which doles out its bounty to the deserving in the form of grants with strings attached, and for which the replacement would be stringless *revenue sharing*).

One additional formation which may bear fruit is the *Finlandization* which indicates a peaceful economic take-over of a small nation by a big one, as of Finland by the USSR. This readily lends itself to such extensions as *Czechoslovakization* (take-over by a display of overwhelming force), or even *Hungarization* (take-over by the actual use of such force).

Needless to say, the majority of these words, expressions and usages go unrecorded in our most recent dictionaries, although *jawboning* has a definite ancestry in the verbal use of *jawbone*, which even Webster III calls slang, in the sense of to talk convincingly for the purpose of obtaining credit or trust. Its first application to presidential exhortations to labor and business to exercise some voluntary restraint in the matter of price and wage hikes seems to stem from the Johnson era.

The language of politics, in addition to an ironical telescoped form *lawnorder*, favored by leftist writers and designed to betoken the semi-literacy of those among us who actually believe in law and order, shows the *lib-lash* coined by Lenore Romney in the course of her Michigan Senatorial campaign (she stated that a *lib-lash* exerted by the Women's Liberation Front had hurt her chances). Moynihan's *benign neglect* in connection with black problems and aspirations also deserves mention.

One term that has gained a new acceptance is *Middle America*. This is defined in all dictionaries as a geographical unit embracing Central America, Mexico, and often the islands of the Caribbean. The term, not too often used in English, which prefers separate listing of the component parts, is much favored in German ("*Nord-Amerika, Süd-Amerika und Mittel-Amerika*"). There is another geographical use of *Middle* in connection with States (the *Middle States* are defined in some dictionaries, mostly British, as being those intermediate between New England and the South: New York, New Jersey, Pennsylvania, Delaware, possibly Maryland). Casual questioning brings out the fact that most of the uninitiated, when they hear "Middle America," think of the Central or Midwestern States. The new political acceptance, however, is economic rather than geographic, pointing to the middle classes or middle income groups, which constitute at least 60% of our population, as against the 30% poor and the 10% rich. The implications are that Middle America tends to vote as a unit in defense of its class interests, which does not seem too well borne out by the facts.

Silent majority has been with us for a while, but comes up perennially every time there is an election or a demonstration, in spite of which it is ignored by the dictionaries. Again, the implication is that there exists a group, constituting a majority of the voters, which normally does not demonstrate or even raise its voice, but reveals its true feelings at the polls. To the extent that this may be true (the indications are mixed), the question may arise: "Why is this majority silent?" Can it be because it is far too busy working to provide sustenance not only for itself, but also for those who are engaged in noisy demonstrations?

During 1970, Vice-President Agnew was by far the best purveyor of political catchwords, slogans, and usable clichés. Starting out with forms like *troglodytic* and *effete snobs*, he went on to alliterative gems worthy of the poetic tongue of the Anglo-Saxons: *pusillanimous pussyfooting, politicians of panic, troubadours of trouble, vicars of vacillation;* then, warming up to the literary device, *nattering nabobs of negativism, covey of confused congressmen, hopeless, hysterical hypocondriacs of history.* His political opponents tried to reply in kind by dubbing him a *functional alliterate* and denouncing his *lurid lexicon of 'literation,* but they were hopelessly outgunned. La Guardia's denunciation of *punks, tinhorns and gamblers,* back in the 1930's was only a faint foretaste of the Agnevian language.

III

Last, but anything but least on our topical index is the ineffable (or shall we switch to the Anglo Saxon etymological equivalent and call it "unspeakable"?) language of commercial advertising. Advertising has been defined as "boloney disguised as food for thought," but it has the merit of being frank. When you see or hear a commercial, you know, or should know what its purpose is, even without benefit of Ralph Nader or Bess Myerson Grant. You are told how much you can *save* by buying a certain product at a certain time; of course you can save much more by not buying it at all. *Fewer cavities* are said to be the result of using a certain toothpaste; why not *no cavities?* Why only one? Sometimes the slogan in the jingle is a covert, or perhaps not so covert, criticism of a competing product ("It's the real thing!"; are all the others "unreal"? "Greasy kid stuff!"; do only kids use the others?; "When you're out of Blitz, you're out of cheer!"; no "cheer" whatsoever in the other brands?). There are the jingles and slogans so oft repeated that a built-in antagonism arises ("It's worth a trip!"; "What's worth a trip?"; "Decisions, decisions!" I, for one, will never take that trip, and I hope I may always have something more important to decide than a cigarette brand).

At times, the jingle takes on the aspect of a religious rite, like the Invocation to the Great God Nab ("Oh, Nab! We're glad they put boloney in you!"). At others, there are sexual overtones, some obscure and leering, like the story of Little Red Riding Hood that winds up with "We'll have to put our heads together!"; others frank in their appeal to the boisterous younger generations, like "pucker power" and "mouthwash for lovers"; a few with rather extreme connotations, like "My kind of guy, my kind of male," or the Simpering Swede who urges you to "Take it all off!"

Some commercials are a challenge to your creative, or at least your imitative ability. I sometimes dream of a competing detergent-cleanser that will be a *Blue Hurricane*, or a mouthwash that will have *sox appeal*. An airline ad makes me long to "get out of this world!" Butter (or margarine; I'm not quite sure which) evokes visions of "the continuing soap-opera of Engelbert's Mother." The Federal Communications Commission has freed us of cigarette ads on radio and TV, so we no longer have to put up with "What a bad time for a Scent!" "You can take Sell 'em out of the country but–," and "You've

come a short way, Baby, if all you've learned to do is smoke like a chimney."
But it is too much to expect relief from "the smelliest mouth in town,"
"Rooster makes beer, and I don't care—especially for you!," or "Hot dogs are
doggi-er, yummies are yummi-er, crummies are crummi-er, tummies are
tummi-er, because coffee is coffee-er."

But why complain? Life, the language, and its speakers will go on,
irregardless!

Current Words
And Phrases

LAURENCE URDANG INC.

THE FOLLOWING LIST of words and phrases consists of terms and meanings that have only recently made an appearance in English or of terms that have had some restricted usage over a period of time but are now acquiring widespread usage. Many of these words have passed the test of time and have already entered the dictionaries. Some will prove to be fleeting, however, and will remain only as a curious reminder of some passing vogue.

acupuncture, the medical practice, originating in China but now gaining currency in the West, of inserting needles under the skin to relieve pain or cure illness

Afro, a full, bouffant hair style, as worn by some Negroes

audible, a football play decided upon and called by the quarterback at the line of scrimmage

au pair, of or designating young girls accepting hospitality from foreign families in return for domestic service or as part of an international exchange scheme

biomathematics, the application of mathematical methods to the structure and functions of living organisms

black nationalism, a movement advocating the establishment of a separate Negro nation within the borders of the United States *black power,* political and economic power as sought by black Americans in the struggle for civil rights

bleep, to censor (something said), as in a telecast by substituting a beep

brown fat, a heat-producing tissue stored in certain areas of the body by a hibernating animal: it prevents freezing and helps to warm the awakening animal

busing, the transporting of school children to schools outside their regular district

CATV, acronym for *Community Antenna Television,* a cable system by which signals from distant stations are relayed from a large antenna to subscribers' television receivers

chart, [Slang] an arrangement of a musical composition, as for a jazz band

Chicano, a U.S. citizen or inhabitant of Mexican descent: also chicano

chill factor, the effect of low temperatures and high winds on exposed skin, expressed as a loss of body heat

cinémathèque, a library of motion pictures, as in a museum, shown for study and critical analysis

cityscape, the physical aspect or view of a city or town, often the result of deliberate aesthetic planning

coffee table book, a large, expensive, commercially popular book, extravagantly illustrated but with a poorly written or trivial text

cold duck, a drink made from equal parts of sparkling burgundy and champagne

commune, a small group of people living communally and sharing in work, earnings, etc.

comsat, any of various communications satellites for relaying microwave transmissions, as of telephone, television, etc.

consumerism, 1. the practice and policies of protecting the consumer by making him aware of defective and unsafe products, misleading business practices, etc. 2. the consumption of goods and services

containerization, a method of through-transportation in which goods are packed into containers at a factory or depot and delivered to their destination without being unpacked in transit

counterculture, the culture of many young people of the 1960's and 1970's manifested by a life style that is opposed to the prevailing culture

crash pad, [Slang] a place to live or sleep temporarily

credibility gap, a situation or state of affairs in which there is an apparent disparity between what is said, especially by a government spokesman, and the actual facts *cyborg,* a cybernetic organism, a hypothetical human being modified for life in a nonearth environment by the substitution of artificial organs and other body parts

cyclazocine, a pain-killing, nonaddictive, synthetic drug that blocks the effects of heroin or morphine

dashiki, a loose-fitting, usually brightly colored robe or tunic of a kind worn ceremonially by some African tribes

Day-Glo, a trademark for a coloring agent added to pigments, dyes, etc. to produce any of a variety of brilliant fluorescent colors

defoliant, a chemical used to destroy vegetation, especially in warfare

deschooling, the process of abandoning conventional or traditional methods of education

disadvantaged, deprived of a decent standard of living, education, etc. by poverty and lack of opportunity

downer, [Slang] 1. any depressant or sedative, as a tranquilizer, barbiturate, alcoholic drink, etc. 2. a depressing situation, letdown, etc. Also *down*

dystopia, a very bad or defective place, society, etc.: the opposite of utopia

earthrise, the appearance of the earth above the lunar horizon (opposed to *earthset*)

ecocide, the destruction of the environment by the use of defoliants and other pollutants

eidetic, designating mental images that are unusually vivid and almost photographically exact

encounter group, a small group of people that meets for a kind of therapy in personal interrelationship, involving a release of inhibitions, an open exchange of intimate feelings, etc.

EVA, acronym for *extravehicular activity,* any task performed by an astronaut outside his spacecraft, either in space or on the surface of the moon

EVR, Electronic Video Recorder, a device for playing back a prerecorded sound film through an ordinary television receiver

exobiology, 1. the study of extraterrestrial living organisms 2. the study of the effects of space on living organisms

first-strike, of the initial stage or attack in a nuclear war

flash forward, a shot of a future event interjected at an earlier point in a film, for any of various artistic or philosophical reasons

flat out, at maximum speed, pace effort, etc.

fragging, [Slang] the killing or wounding by a U.S. serviceman of his superior officer, etc., as by rolling a fragmentation grenade under the victim's bunk *freak,* [Slang] 1. a user of a specified narcotic, hallucinogen, etc.: as, an acid *freak* 2. a devotee or buff as, a rock *freak* 3. a hippie

free university, a loosely organized forum for the study of subject matter not offered in regular university courses

G, general audience: a movie rating meaning that the film is thought suitable for persons of all ages

game plan, a long-range plan of operations and strategy, like that in advance of a football game, designed to accomplish a specific goal

gay liberation, a movement organized to promote a more tolerant attitude toward homosexuals

gazump, to raise the price of a house beyond that already negotiated with the buyer

GP, general audience, parental guidance suggested: a movie rating meaning that persons of all ages will be admitted, but parents are cautioned as to the film's content

greenie, [Slang] an amphetamine pep pill used by some athletes for extra energy during the competition

greening, a becoming less naive and more mature, esp. in one's understanding of social and political forces

gricer, a railroad enthusiast

groove, [Slang] to react in a nonanalytical, empathetic way to persons, situations, sensations, etc., surrounding one

grotty, [Brit. Slang] dirty, grimy, shabby, etc.

groupie, a young woman who is a fan of rock musicians or other performers, and who follows them about, often in the hope of achieving sexual intimacy

hadron, any of a group of atomic particles, including the baryons and mesons, that are strongly interacting

hard drug, [Colloq.] any drug, such as heroin or cocaine, that is addictive and potentially very damaging to the body or mind

hard hat, 1. a protective helmet worn by construction workers, miners, etc. 2. such a worker, especially one regarded as holding strongly conservative views.

hard line, characterized by an aggressive, unyielding position in politics, foreign policy, etc.

headshop, a shop selling commodities associated with hippies, such as pipes and other items used in smoking, fashionable clothes and accessories, posters, etc.

heavy, [Slang] 1. very good or pleasing; a general term of approval 2. deep; serious; profound: as, a *heavy* book 3. sophisticated; aware; fashionable; stylish; hip

heliox, a breathing mixture consisting of 98 percent helium and 2 percent oxygen, used in deep dives to avoid the hazardous effects of compressed air at great depths

hot pants, very brief shorts worn by girls and women, often with long, soft boots

-in, a use of the preposition *in* with verbs to form nouns expressing the mass occupation of a place for the purpose of performing the action described by the verb, often as a protest, as in sit-*in*, love-*in*, be-*in*, work-*in*, etc.

into, [Colloq.] involved in or concerned with: as, he is very much into astrology now

irtron, a hypothetical infrared body proposed as the fundamental body in certain galaxies and from which new matter is assumed to be formed

IUD, acronym for *intrauterine device,* a plastic or stainless steel loop worn as a contraceptive within the uterus

jawbone, to attempt to persuade by using one's high office or position to apply pressure, as the President might in proposing price and wage controls to business and labor

ketamine, a quick-acting anesthetic that affects the central nervous system so as to eliminate pain and other sensory perceptions without producing unconsciousness; it may cause delirium, hallucinations, etc.

KREEP, an acronym for a lunar soil material that has a rich concentration of potassium (K), Rare-Earth Elements, and phosphorus (P)

L-asparaginase, an enzyme that has produced a temporary remission of certain types of leukemia in some patients, seemingly by depriving cancerous cells of an essential nutrient

lib, a short form of *liberation,* as in women's *lib*

life, [Colloq.] another chance: often used in the phrase *get a life*

life style, the consistent, integrated way of life of an individual as typified by his manner, attitudes, possessions, interests, etc.

light show, a combination of projected slides, flashing colored lights, etc., used usually to accompany rock music

low profile, an unobtrusive, barely noticeable presence, or concealed, inconspicuous activity

lunar module, the detachable, separately powered section of an Apollo spacecraft which transports astronauts to and from the surface of the moon while the remainder of the craft is in orbit. Also called *LEM (lunar excursion module)*

mammography, an X-ray technique for the detection of breast tumors before they can be seen or felt

mascon, any of several regions on the moon where the gravitational force sharply increases, causing distortion in the orbits of spacecraft

maxi-, 1. maximum, very large, very long, as in *maxicoat* 2. of greater scope, extent, etc. than usual, as in *maxi*-power

microsphere, any of various minute globules, as an encapsulated isotope

microtonal, designating or of musical intervals that are less than a halftone, often employed in such a way as to produce a wailing effect

Middle America, the American middle class, characterized generally by moderate or conservative political attitudes and conventional social values; sometimes, specifically, the middle class of Midwestern America

midi-, of moderate size, length, etc., as a skirt of mid-calf length

mini-, 1. minimum, very small, very short, as in *mini*-skirt, *mini*-dress. 2. of lesser scope, extent, etc., than usual, as in *mini*-revolution

MIRV, acronym for *multiple independently targetable re-entry vehicle,* a tactical guided missle containing several warheads which may be separately aimed at selected targets with considerable accuracy

Mobot, a remote-control, mobile robot designed to work in hazardous environments, as on the ocean floor, or to handle hazardous materials, as rocket propellants

modem, a device that converts data to a form that can be transmitted, as by telephone, to data-processing equipment, where a similar device reconverts it

monetarism, an economic theory which holds that economic stability and growth are not determined by government spending and taxing policies but rather by the maintenance of a steady rate of growth in the supply of money

Moog synthesizer, a computerized, electronic musical instrument capable of creating a wide variety of sounds

moonquake, a trembling of the surface of the moon, thought to be caused by internal rock slippage or, possibly meteorite impact

narc, [Slang] an undercover police official who specializes in apprehending violators of the narcotics laws: also *narco, nark*

neutron star, a heavenly object hypothesized to be a collapsed star consisting of immense numbers of densely packed neutrons

new math, an ordered system for teaching fundamental concepts of mathematics by the use of set theory

OD, 1. (*noun*) an overdose of drugs 2. (*verb*) to take an overdose of drugs

outreach, designating or of a branch office of a social agency, governmental department, etc. set up to accommodate those who cannot or will not utilize the services of the main offices

outtake, a scene or segment shot for a motion picture or television show, but not included in the shown version

paraprofessional, a person not fully qualified in a profession, yet able to perform work in the profession to relieve a fully qualified person, especially in a crisis

participatory democracy, a political system, as in universities, local communities, etc., in which all individuals participate in administrative decisions directly affecting them

patrial, a person whose parent or grandparent was born in a specified country, especially Great Britain. Opposed to *non-patrial*

PBS, Public Broadcasting Service, a non-profit organization which distributes programs to independent, non-commerical television stations subscribing to its services

Peter Principle, a facetious proposition stating that in the hierarchy of a business organization, every employee tends to rise to the level at which he is no longer competent in discharging his duties

pick up on, [Slang] to become familiar with

Picturephone, a trademark for a device combining a telephone and television camera and receiver, which permits two-way visual contact as well as sound

polywater, a viscous laboratory substance formed in minute quantities in capillary tubes, variously identified as a colloidal disperson, a new form of water, contaminated water, etc.

porno, [Slang] pornography: also called *porn*

quadraphonic, designating or of sound reproduction, as in records, tapes or broadcasting, using four channels to carry and reproduce the sounds

R, restricted: a movie rating meaning that no one under the age of seventeen will be admitted unless accompanied by a parent or guardian

right on, [Slang] 1. (*interjection*) that's right! you said it!: an exclamation of approval 2. (*adjective*) sophisticated, informed, current, etc.

rip off, [Slang] 1. to steal 2. to exploit, cheat, or take advantage of

samizdat, (literally, "self-published") books and manuscripts circulated clandestinely in typescript or mimeograph form in the Soviet Union

sensitivity training, a popular adaptation of group therapy in which a group of people under a leader try through discussion and performance of behavioral experiments to achieve improved mutual understanding or to solve problems of the individuals

sexism, the economic exploitation and social domination of members of one sex by the other, specifically of women by men

shoot (up), [Slang] to inject a drug directly into the blood-stream

shuck, [Slang] 1. (noun) a deception or hoax 2. (verb) to deceive or hoax, or to talk exaggerated nonsense

sitcom, in television, a situation comedy, a weekly series of comic episodes involving the same characters

skinflick, [Slang] a pornographic motion picture

skinhead, [Slang] any of the gangs of antihippie British youths who wear their hair closely cropped and often engage in violence

skyjack, to seize control of (an airplane) and hold its passengers and crew to ransom for personal or political ends

smack, [Slang] heroin: also called *skag*

SST, a *supersonic transport* airliner, such as the Anglo-French *Concorde,* which can carry up to 100 passengers

Talwin, a trademark for pentazocine, a pain-killing synthetic drug used as a substitute for morphine, with about one-half its analgesic effect

toke, [Slang] 1. (*noun*) a puff on a cigarette especially a marijuana or hashish cigarette 2. (*verb*) to take a puff on (such a cigarette)

trendy, [Colloq.] of or in the latest style, or trend; ultrafashionable; faddish

Tuinal, a trademark for a combination of barbiturates used as a quick and relatively long-acting sedative

upper, [Slang] any drug containing a stimulant, especially an amphetamine: also called *up*

VAT, acronym for value-added tax, an indirect taxation assessed as a percentage of the value added at every stage of the production, distribution, etc., of a commodity

water bed, a vinyl bag filled with water, often with an electric heating element, used as a kind of mattress

with-it, [Slang] alert, fashionable, sophisticated, hip, etc.

X, a movie rating meaning that no one under the age of seventeen will be admitted to a film's showing under any circumstances

3
DICTIONARIES
AND USAGE

An article by Harold Whitehall on the history of the English dictionary opens this chapter.

The next article tells how the highly regarded American Heritage Dictionary *was planned, compiled, and edited.*

Raven McDavid then discusses regional and social dialects in the United States, standard and non-standard usage, vocabulary, and slang.

The Development
of the English Dictionary

Harold Whitehall

The evolution of the English dictionary is rooted in the general evolution of the English language. In this development the chief pressures were exerted by the steady increase in the word stock of English from the 50,000–60,000 words of Anglo-Saxon through the 100,000–125,000 words of the Middle-English vocabulary to the huge total of some 650,000 words which could theoretically be recorded in an exhaustive dictionary of contemporary English. Such an overall increase as this made the dictionary *necessary*. The pressure of vocabulary, however, has always been influenced and reinforced by the intellectual climate of each successive period of the language. A dictionary is not exactly a work of art, yet it bears as strongly as an artistic production the impress of the age that bore it. For that reason, the history of the dictionary is a fascinating chapter in the history of ideas.

The beginnings of dictionary history are neither national nor concerned with any of the national languages. They are concerned with the international language of medieval European civilization: Latin. Our first word books are lists of relatively difficult Latin terms usually those of a Scriptural nature, accompanied by glosses in easier or more familiar Latin. Very early in the Anglo-Saxon period, however, we find glosses containing native English (i.e., Anglo-Saxon) equivalents for the hard Latin terms, and it may be that two of these–the *Leiden* and *Erfurt Glosses*–represent the earliest written English we possess. Such glosses, whether Latin-Latin or Latin-English, continued to be compiled during the entire Anglo-Saxon and most of the Middle-English period.

The next stage of development, attained in England around 1400, was the collection of the isolated glosses into what is called a *glossarium*, a kind of very early Latin-English dictionary. As it chances, our first example of the glossarium, the so-called Medulla Grammatica written in East Anglia around 1400, has never been printed; but two later redactions were among our earliest printed books, and one of these, the *Promptorium Parvulorum sive clericorum*, issued by Wynkyn de Worde in 1499, was the first work of a dictionary nature ever to be printed on English soil. Significantly enough, this version of the *Medulla* places the English term first and its Latin equivalent second.

The first onset of the Renaissance worked against rather than in favor of the native English dictionary. The breakdown of Latin as an international language and the rapid development of international trade led to an immediate demand for foreign-language dictionaries. The first of such works, Palsgrave's *Lesclaircissement de la Langue Francoyse* (1523), was rapidly followed by Salesbury's Welsh-English dictionary (1547), Percival's English-Spanish dictionary (1591), and finally, by the best known of all such works, Florio's Italian-English dictionary (1599). Meanwhile, the first great classical dictionary, Cooper's *Thesaurus* (1565), had already appeared. The history of dictionaries is larded with strange occurrences: we are not surprised, therefore, that the publication of Cooper's work was delayed five years because his wife, fearing that too much lexicography would kill her husband, burned the first manuscript of his magnum opus. It should be noted, in passing, that none of these various word books of the 16th century actually used the title *dictionary* or *dictionarium*. They were called by various kinds of fanciful or half-fanciful names, of which *hortus* "garden," and *thesaurus* "hoard" were particularly popular.

During the late 16th century, the full tide of the Renaissance had been sweeping a curious flotsam and jetsam into English literary harbors. Constant reading of Greek and Latin bred a race of Holofernes pedants who preferred the Latin or Greek term to the English term. Their principle in writing was to use Latino-Greek polysyllabics in a Latino-English syntax. Their strange vocabulary—studded with what some critics call "inkhorn"terms—eventually affected English so powerfully that no non-Latinate Englishman could ever hope to read many works in his own language unless he was provided with explanations of elements unfamiliar to him. The "Dictionary of Hard Words," the real predecessor of the modern dictionary, was developed to provide precisely such explanations. It is significant that the first English word book to use the name *dictionary*, Cokeram's *The English Dictionary* (1623), is subtitled "An Interpreter of Hard Words." Among those explained on its first few pages are *Abequitate, Bulbulcitate,* and *Sullevation.* In point of time, the first "dictionary of hard words" was Robert Cawdrey's *Table Alphabeticall of Hard Words* (1604). Of the various works of the same class appearing after this date may be mentioned John Bullokar's *English Expositor* (1606) and Edward Phillip's *New World of Words* (1658), both of which reveal a strong interest in the reform of spelling, Blount's *Glossographia* (1656) containing the first etymologies ever to appear in a printed English dictionary, and Thomas Kersey's *Dictionarium Anglo-Brittanicum* (1708), which also includes legal terms, provincialisms, and archaisms. If the 16th was the century of the foreign-language dictionary, the 17th was the century of the dictionary of hard words.

Between 1708 and 1721, hard-word dictionaries began to be replaced by word books giving ever-increasing attention to literary usage. The Latino-Greek borrowings of the earlier century had been either absorbed into the language or sloughed away. The French influence, from 1660 onwards, had replaced Renaissance stylistic ideas with notions of a simple elegance in syntax and a quiet effectiveness in vocabulary. These stylistic virtues were actually achieved in the works of Swift, Addison, Steele, and lesser writers. The literary mind of the early 18th century, therefore, was convinced that English had finally attained a standard of purity such as it had never previously known; it was also convinced that the brash outgrowth of mercantile expansionism, later to be reinforced by the infant Industrial Revolution, might very well destroy this hard-won standard of literary refinement. What more natural than that the standard should be enshrined in a dictionary for the admiration and guidance of posterity?

The first word book to embody the ideals of the age was Nathaniel Bailey's *Universal Etymological Dictionary of the English Language*, originally published in 1721, and then, in a beautiful folio volume with illustrations by Flaxman, in 1731. This, one of the most revolutionary dictionaries ever to appear, was the first to pay proper attention to current usage, the first to feature etymology, the first to give aid in syllabification, the first to give illustrative quotations (chiefly from proverbs), the first to include illustrations, and the first to indicate pronunciation. An interleaved copy of the 1731 folio edition was the basis of Samuel Johnson's *Dictionary* of 1755; through Johnson, it influenced all subsequent lexicographical practice. The position of dictionary pioneer, commonly granted to Johnson or to Noah Webster, belongs in reality to one of the few geniuses lexicography ever produced: Nathaniel Bailey.

Johnson's *Dictionary* (1755) enormously extends the techniques developed by Bailey. Johnson was able to revise Bailey's crude etymologies on the basis of Francis Junius' *Etymologicon Anglicanum* (first published in 1743), to make a systematic use of illustrative quotations, to fix the spelling of many disputed words, to develop a really discriminating system of definition, and to exhibit the vocabulary of English much more fully than had ever been attempted before. In his two-volume work, the age and following ages found their ideal word book. Indeed, a good deal of the importance of the book lies in its later influence. It dominated English letters for a full century after its appearance and, after various revisions, continued in common use until 1900. As late as the '90's, most Englishmen used the word *dictionary* as a mere synonym for Johnson's *Dictionary*; in 1880 a Bill was actually thrown out of Parliament because a word in it was not in "the Dictionary."

One of the tasks taken upon himself by Johnson was to remove "improprieties and absurdities" from the language. In short, he became a linguistic legislator attempting to perform for English those offices performed for French by the French Academy. From this facet of his activities we get the notion, still held by many dictionary users, and fostered by many dictionary publishers, that the dictionary is the "supreme authority" by which to arbitrate questions of "correctness" and "incorrectness." The dictionaries of the second half of the 18th century extended this notion particularly to the field of pronunciation. By 1750, the increasing wealth of the middle classes was making itself felt in the social and political worlds. Those who possessed it, speakers, for the most part, of a middle-class dialect, earnestly desired a key to the pronunciations accepted in polite society. To provide for their needs, various pronunciation experts—usually of Scottish or Irish extraction—edited a series of pronunciation dictionaries. Of these, the most important are James Buchanan's *New English Dictionary* (1769), William Kenrick's *New Dictionary of the English Language* (1773), Thomas Sheridan's *General Dictionary of the English Language* (1780), and, above all, John Walker's *Critical Pronouncing Dictionary and Expositor of the English Language* (1791). In such works, pronunciation was indicated by small superscript numbers referring to the "powers" of the various vowel sounds. Despite the legislative function exercised by the authors of almost all of these works, we must admit that they did indicate contemporary pronunciation with great accuracy, and when

Walker's pronunciations were combined with Johnson's definitions the result was a dictionary which dominated the word-book field, both in England and the United States, until well after 1850.

If the chief contributions of the 18th century to dictionary making were (1) authoritative recording of literary vocabulary and (2) accurate recording of pronunciation, those of the 19th were unmistakably (1) the recording of word history through dated quotations and (2) the development of encyclopedic word books. Already in 1755, Samuel Johnson had hinted in his preface that the sense of a word "may easily be collected entire from the examples." During the first twenty-five years of the century, the researches of R. K. Rask, J. L. C. Grimm, and F. Bopp clearly defined the historical principle in linguistics. It was only a question of time, therefore, before someone combined Johnson's perception with the findings of the new science of historical linguistics. That person was Charles Richardson, who, in this *New Dictionary of the English Language* (1836), produced a dictionary completely lacking definitions but one in which both the senses and the historical evolution of the senses were accurately indicated by dated defining quotations. Richardson's work leads directly to the great *New English Dictionary on Historical Principles,* first organized in 1858, begun under Sir James Murray in 1888, and completed under Sir William Craigie in 1928. With its supplement (1933), the *New English Dictionary* or *Oxford English Dictionary* (N.E.D. or O.E.D.) covers the vocabulary of English with a completeness of historical evidence and a discrimination of senses unparalleled in linguistic history. No other language has ever been recorded on anything approaching this scale, and no dictionary of English since the *New English Dictionary* was completed has failed to reveal a profound debt to this monumental work. As compared with the effort represented by the N.E.D., the attempt to record the technological vocabularies of the language as first seen in John W. Ogilvie's *Universal Dictionary of the English Language* (1850) seems to be of minor importance, although it has had great practical effect on subsequent American dictionaries.

Since the publication of the O.E.D., the only important British dictionary has been Henry Cecil Wyld's *Universal Dictionary of the English Language* (1932), a work of somewhat restricted vocabulary coverage but one which may well point the way to the dictionary of the future. Wyld has discarded the older logical definitions for definitions of a more functional nature; his examples delve deeply into idiom; his etymologies are of a completeness and modernity unparalleled until this present dictionary in any medium-sized word book. The failure of Wyld's book to achieve much popularity on this side of the Atlantic underlines the fact that the typical American dictionary of the English language is a work *differing in kind* from any of those so far mentioned. It differs because the conditions of American life and culture differ from those of English life and culture.

The modern American dictionary is typically a single compact volume published at a relatively modest price containing: (1) definitive American spellings, (2) pronunciations indicated by diacritical markings, (3) strictly limited etymologies, (4) numbered senses, (5) some illustrations, (6) selective treatment of synonyms and antonyms, (7) encyclopedic inclusion of scientific, technological, geographical, and biographical items. It owes its development, within the general framework of the evolution sketched above, to the presence of a large immigrant population in this country, to the elaborate American system of popular education, and to the vast commercial opportunities implicit in both of these.

The first American dictionaries were unpretentious little schoolbooks based chiefly on Johnson's *Dictionary* of 1755 by way of various English abridgments of that work. The earliest of these were Samuel Johnson Junior's *School Dictionary* (1798), Johnson and Elliott's *Selected Pronouncing and Accented Dictionary* (1800), and Caleb Alexander's *Columbian Dictionary* (1800). The most famous work of this class, Noah Webster's *Compendious Dictionary of the English Language* (1806) was an enlargement of Entick's *Spelling Dictionary* (London, 1764), distinguished from its predecessors chiefly by a few encyclopedic supplements and emphasis upon its (supposed) Americanism. The book was never popular and contributed little either to Webster's own reputation or to the development of the American dictionary in general.

The first important date in American lexicography is 1828. The work that makes it important is Noah Webster's *An American Dictionary of the English Language* in two volumes. Webster's book has many deficiencies—etymologies quite untouched by the linguistic science of the time, a rudimentary pronunciation system actually inferior to that used by Walker in 1791, etc.—but in its insistence upon American spellings, in definitions keyed to the American scene, and in its illustrative quotations from the Founding Fathers of the Republic, it provided the country with the first *native* dictionary comparable in scope with that of Dr. Johnson. It was not, as is often claimed, the real parent of the modern American dictionary; it was merely the foster-parent. Because of its two-volume format and its relatively high price it never achieved any great degree of popular acceptance in Webster's own lifetime. Probably its greatest contribution to succeeding American dictionaries was the style of definition writing–writing of a clarity and pithiness never approached before its day.

The first American lexicographer to hit upon the particular pattern that distinguishes the American dictionary was Webster's lifelong rival, Joseph E. Worcester. His *Comprehensive, Pronouncing, and Explanatory Dictionary of the English Language* (1830), actually a thoroughly revised abridgment of Webster's two-volume work of 1828, was characterized by the addition of new words, a more conservative spelling, brief, well-phrased definitions, full indication of pronunciation by means of diacritics, use of stress marks to divide syllables, and lists of synonyms. Because it was compact and low priced, it immediately became popular–far more popular, in fact, than any of Webster's own dictionaries in his own lifetime. As George P. Krapp, in his *The English Language in America,* says: "If one balances the faults of the Webster of 1828 against the faults of the Worcester of 1830, the totals are greatly in the favor of Worcester." One might feel the same about its merits as compared with those of Webster's own revision of his *American Dictionary* (1841), which featured the inclusion of scientific terms compiled by Professor W. Tully. The first Webster dictionary to embody the typical American dictionary pattern was that of 1847, edited by Noah Webster's son-in-law, Chauncey A. Goodrich, and published by the Merriams.

Temperamentally the flamboyant Noah Webster and the cautious Joseph Worcester were natural rivals. Their rivalry, however, was as nothing compared with that which developed between the rival publishers of the Webster and Worcester dictionaries. By 1845, the great flood of immigration and the vast extension of the school system had suddenly lifted dictionary making into the realm of big business. In a "war of the dictionaries" that reflects the rudimentary business ethics of the period, the rival publishers used every device of advertisement and every stratagem of high-powered salesmanship to drive each other off the market. Unsavory as this war appears in retrospect, it certainly helped to force rapid improvement of the dictionaries that these publishers controlled. Worcester's initial advantages were surpassed in the Merriam-Webster of 1847; the innovations in Worcester's edition of 1860 were more than paralleled in the Merriam-Webster of 1864, one of the best dictionaries ever to appear, but one from which almost everything really characteristic of Noah Webster himself was deleted. The battle was finally decided in favor of the Webster dictionaries, chiefly because the popularity of Webster's "Little Blue Back Speller" had put their name in every household, partly because of the death of Joseph Worcester, and partly because of the merit of the Merriam product from 1864 onwards.

Since about 1870, the climate of American dictionary making has been much more peaceful. In the field of unabridged dictionaries, the most important accretion is the *Century Dictionary* (1889), edited by the great American linguist, William Dwight Whitney, and issued in six volumes. Unfortunately, this magnificent work, considered by many authorities to be basically the finest ever issued by a commercial publisher, has lost much of its popularity because of inadequate subsequent revision. The fact that it was not in a one-volume format undoubtedly also worked against its popular success. The only other new unabridged dictionaries that have appeared in the period are Webster's *Imperial Dictionary of the English Language* (1904), and Funk and Wagnalls *New Standard Dictionary* (1893). The first of these, the only unabridged dictionary ever published west of the Appalachians, was issued in Chicago by George W. Ogilvie, a publisher who carried on his own private guerrilla "war of the dictionaries" against the Merriam Company between 1904 and circa 1917. At the moment, the most important advances in lexicography are taking place in the field of the abridged collegiate-type dictionaries.

Meanwhile, the scholarly dictionary has not been neglected. Once the *New English Dictionary* was published, scholarly opinion realized the need to supplement it in the various periods of English and particularly in American English. The first of the proposed supplements, edited by Sir William Craigie and Professor J. R. Hulbert, is the *Dictionary of American English on Historical Principles,* completed in 1944. This was followed by a *Dictionary of Americanisms,* edited by Mitford M. Mathews and published in 1951. A *Middle English Dictionary,* a *Dictionary of the Older Scottish Tongue,* and a *Dictionary of Later Scottish* are in preparation, and work on the *American Dialect Dictionary* of the American Dialect Society is now finally under way.

The Making
of a Dictionary – 1969

WILLIAM MORRIS

First, PERHAPS, I should note that the title of this article is a misnomer. More accurate would be "The Making of a Dictionary, 1963 to 1969," with the added reservation that at least one of the major elements in the new *American Heritage Dictionary of the English Language* was being planned as early as 1955.

A question that I am sure must occur to every reader is simply "Why another new dictionary?" After all, Merriam-Webster, Funk & Wagnalls, and Random House have all made substantial contributions to lexicography during the past decade and the World Publishing Company promises a new edition of their admirable *Webster's New World Dictionary* in the near future.

The answer, then, is that there is neither need nor excuse for a dictionary that simply duplicates the coverage of the existing dictionaries and presents the essential lexical data in the same humdrum fashion.

When the executives of *American Heritage*, Houghton Mifflin, and I began our talks about dictionaries in 1963, they shared a feeling then widely voiced in such media as the New York *Times, The New Yorker, The Atlantic Monthly,* and *The American Scholar,* that Webster's Third New International Dictionary had failed both press and public by eliminating virtually all usage labels and other indications of standards of usage.

So an idea that I had been nurturing for nearly a decade was received with enthusiasm. I proposed that there would–of course–be no return to the prescriptive dictates of earlier lexicographers like Frank Vizetelly who, as recently as 1913, was able to decree that "*Raise* should never be used of bringing human beings to maturity; it is a misuse common in the southern and western United States. Cattle are *raised*; human beings are *brought up* or, in an older phrase, *reared*."[1] This pose of dogmatic prescription had, indeed, long been abandoned by responsible lexicographers. For example, *Webster's New International Dictionary*, second edition, published in 1934, under the editorship of William Allen Neilson, had recorded the language descriptively, not prescriptively, though its editors did employ a considerable number of usage labels (*slang, vulgar, colloquial,* and the like) to guide the user of the dictionary in selection of words appropriate to the various contexts in which they might appear.

But my feeling was that restoring such labels as "slang," "vulgar," "informal," "nonstandard," and the like–while helpful–was not enough. We felt that the dictionary user wants to be given sensible guidance in how to use the language. And where better to get that information than from the men and women who have demonstrated their ability to use the language with felicity, facility, grace, and power. So we organized a Panel on Usage, consisting of more than 100 writers, editors, public figures–poets like Marianne Moore, Langston Hughes, and John Ciardi; newspapermen like Walter Lippmann, Russell Baker, and Red Smith; critics like Dwight Macdonald, Winthrop Sergeant, and John Bainbridge; historians like Bruce Catton, Barbara Tuchman, and Eric Goldman; scientists like George Gamow, Harlow Shapley, and Isaac Asimov; public figures like Senators McCarthy, Neuberger, and Hatfield.

To these panel members over a four-year period we sent more than 600 questions about linguistic problems, debatable usages. For instance, Merriam had indicated that "imply" and "infer" could be used interchangeably, "that to discriminate between "semi-monthly" and "bi-monthly" was hairsplitting, and that "ain't" was–in the words of Merriam-Three–"used orally in most parts of the United States by many cultivated speakers."

Not surprisingly, there was nothing like unanimity in the replies of the panelists. Here are a few typical questions, with the percentages of response and comments from some of the respondents. Writers, being writers, like to write, so we were careful to provide a very wide margin for these comments–many of them highly amusing as well as to the point.

Myself, as in "He invited Mary and myself" and "Neither Mr. Jones nor myself is in favor of this."–*Panel Verdict: Yes 5%, No 95%*

No, no–a genteelism.

—Malcolm Cowley

Prissy evasions of *me* and *I*.

—Gilbert Highet

Unforgivable. *Myself* is the refuge of idiots taught early that *me* is a dirty word.

—Walter W. (Red) Smith

Mutual   in "mutual friend" and "mutual aid."—*Panel Verdict: Yes 86%, No 14%*

Anything else would be pedantic.

—Malcolm Cowley

Dickens settled this.

—Mark Van Doren

Media,   (as singular form) and *medias* (as plural).—*Panel Verdict: Media—Yes 12%, No 88%; Medias—Yes 5%, No 95%*

In Latin I prefer Cicero to BBD&O.

—Russell Baker

Used only by modern sociologists, etc., who never had first-year Latin.

—Herbert Brucker

I know a lot of people who would answer *yes* to these questions. They are all illiterate.

—David Ogilvy

Mighty, for *very,* as in "It's a mighty good book."—*Panel Verdict: Acceptable in writing: 11%; Acceptable in speech: 56%*

No, except as a humorous rusticism.

—Sheridan Baker

No, except for a deliberate homespun effect.

—Sydney J. Harris

A solid southern (Negro) improvement.

—Arna Bontemps

Nauseous for *nauseated* —*Panel Verdict: Yes 12%; No 88%*

People who say "nauseous" when they mean "nauseated" *are* nauseous.

—Isaac Asimov

An illiteracy of the genteel.

—Russell Baker

Absolutely no—excepting from the girl at Woolworth's.

—Hodding Carter

A vicious, ignorant misuse.

—Katherine Anne Porter

Negotiate,   in "Though the hill was steep, we negotiated it easily."—*Panel Verdict: Yes 46%; No 54%*

Yes, without enthusiasm.

—John Ciardi

Yes, but why so fancy? Why not climb?

—John K. Hutchens

A form of double negation,   as "He would not surrender, not even in the face of impossible odds."—*Panel Verdict: Yes 71%; No 29%*

Seems stuffy to object.

—Marianne Moore

This, in my opinion, lends strength.

—George Gamow

It is informal but adds to the character of his resistance.

—Katherine Anne Porter

Nouns as qualifiers of other nouns,   as in "health reasons," "disaster proportions," "sex-education courses," "platform employees."

I weed every one of these out of everything I can.

—Sheridan Baker

This represents an important change and simplification of English (or American) usage, resembling, in some points, the construction of Chinese—a language which also tends to confuse nouns and adjectives. Languages tend to become simpler the longer they are in use as living languages.

—Charles Berlitz

Some of these examples sound a bit clumsy, but the construction itself is part of the genius (and economy) of the language. Unimpeachable examples abound, and their number must grow and grow. When new or ill-matched, they sometimes seem clumsy; when long and heavy, they often sound German.

—Louis Kronenberger

Shakespeare gave his authority to this (in general).

—Lewis Mumford

The seriousness of the panel's approach to their assignment is reflected in this comment from Barbara Tuchman: "English is a language of marvelous qualities. I like to see it properly used just as one likes to see a shirt properly washed or a dinner table properly set."

So, on the basis of the replies of the panelists, we prepared some 600 Usage Notes. These appear immediately after the entry referred to, so that the user of the dictionary will have authoritative—not dogmatic or prescriptive—guidance right where he wants it. In a sense we have built a Usage Dictionary right into our main general dictionary.

However, the inclusion of these Usage Notes was not the only innovation, not the only departure from established dictionary practice. Perhaps even more radical was the decision to abandon the cryptic, even cabalistic, signs and symbols, that, acting as a kind of lexicographic shorthand, have long perplexed dictionary users. If we want to say "for example," we spell it out—"for example"—not "e.g." When we want to say "derived from Old High German" we don't use a backwards running arrow followed by OHG—we spell the phrase out. We have, indeed, made every possible effort to communicate our concepts and definitions as quickly and clearly as possible to the reader of the dictionary. What's more, we have added many hundreds of quotations—illustrative citations, to use lexicographer's jargon. These have not been chosen from the writings of travel writers and the like, but from works of writers, including many contemporaries, whose works appear on reading lists of undergraduate and graduate literature courses.

Now that we have, perhaps, answered the question: "Why a new dictionary?" let us direct our attention to the second inevitable query: "Where do you get your words?"

Linguists call the total word stock of a language its lexicon. The linguist would define a dictionary as an objective record of the lexicon of a language. But the lexicon of English is open-ended. It is not even theoretically possible to record it all as a closed system; so the task of the dictionary maker is to determine a selection of items from the lexicon that form a reasonable group for a purpose. Such a group is called a corpus. (This problem faces all dictionary makers.) There is a notion in America that a so-called unabridged dictionary records the unabridged lexicon, that is, all the words of the language. This is nonsense. Philip Gove, editor of the largest American dictionary now in print, wrote in his preface that it could have been many times larger, but it would have been impossible to bind. His predecessor, John P. Bethel, once told me that it would be possible to fill a dictionary the size of the largest "unabridged" with names of compounds of carbon alone. How then does the lexicographer select his words? In the past there were only one way that offered any objectivity—making a file of citations from reading. All respectable dictionaries have done and still do this, though no one will ever again compile such a file as the great *Oxford English Dictionary,* which has extensive lists of citations for each word to establish its history.

The reason such a job won't be done again is simply because nobody can afford it. All the reading for the Oxford was done without pay by scholars and enthusiasts all over the English-speaking world. R. W. Burchfield, the editor of the forthcoming Oxford supplement, assures me that he now has to pay. This is the first difficulty of such a method: the enormous expenditure of time and money.

But there is a flaw in such a collection, even if one could afford it. The citations are collected by readers who are interested in words as words and they tend inevitably to record the odder, more extended meanings rather than the basic obvious meanings. In the Merriam-Third file it was discovered at one point that there were 150 citations for *bump* as in burlesque stripping but not one for the bump in the road. Marganita Laski, who has been reading for the Oxford supplement, recently wrote a series of articles about the *OED* in the *Times Literary Supplement.* An amusing footnote to the half-century of reading for the main work was her account of a party given on completion of the fascicle in 1928. All the readers still alive were invited to Oxford and they came—from every part of the Empire. When all had checked in, it was discovered that, of all the living readers, only two had failed to appear. One, it developed, was in an insane asylum, the other in jail.

The ideal citation file would be made up of citations chosen at random, but nevertheless within a defined limit on the kinds of material used, so that the corpus would be balanced and purposeful. When we started work we explored the computer to see if it could help us with such a task. We were lucky beyond anything we could have expected. At that time just such a corpus was being completed by Brown University scholars using the latest IBM equipment; and the use of it was ours at the cost of programs and printouts to suit our purposes.

At Brown, under the direction of Professors Nelson Francis and Henry Kučera, a project had studied the total output of all kinds of publishing in

America during a calendar year and had divided it into fifteen categories. These categories were given weight in the number of words to be allotted to each according to the amount published within each. Then selections were made by scientifically random means. The result was a million words of running text fairly representing a year's publishing in America. This is called the Standard Corpus of Present-Day Edited English. The "edited" is significant. The corpus tells nothing about how we talk, just how we write–after copy-editors having had their innings.

Thus through no special virtue of our own, we had become the first dictionary to have access to such a random corpus. It has given us the assurance that we have as the core of our dictionary a meaningful vocabulary. It has also been entertaining. It is interesting to know that the first ten words in order of frequency are *the, of, and, to, a, in, that, is, was, he.* This contains no surprises, but some of the analyses of Professor Kučera may. One fact which he hasn't published is that newspapermen use a richer vocabulary than scholars.

However, we immediately found that a million words was not nearly enough for the corpus to do the whole job of selecting words. At the present time–now that this computer study as well as some larger ones in Europe have shown the way–there are linguists demanding that all lexicographical material be pooled into a giant word bank. The notion of having such a thing available naturally pleases any lexicographer–however well he knows that it won't happen. But even if such a project were feasible, it still would not eliminate judgment in selecting a dictionary vocabulary. We discovered that there are, especially in science, words that would appear very rarely in even a large corpus, but are central to the concepts of a whole science. We also found that there are groups of words that form systems such that the omission of the less frequent ones would make it difficult to define the others. Such a group would be the divisions of geologic time. These are words that appear only a few times, for example, in the Bible, but are of great literary significance. Another instance is "madding," as in Gray's "far from the madding crowd."

So we have concluded that frequency alone is not an adequate criterion to establish the most useful dictionary vocabulary. We supplemented the corpus in several ways. We continued the reading for citations, concentrating on new words. We directed many of our 150 or so consultants in specialized areas to produce vocabularies for their areas. We ransacked specialized dictionaries and glossaries and indexes, usually having an expert review what we drew out of them.

And that brings us to the third question asked by the more hostile critics:

"Don't you just copy other dictionaries?" After five years of work by more than 200 people spending four million dollars, I hope it's plain that we do very much more than that. But we very definitely have examined and re-examined every reputable general dictionary. One check we must make with other dictionaries is to make sure we haven't duplicated wording of a definition without meaning to.

So far we've talked mostly about what words to include in a dictionary. I should say something about what is and ought to be expected in the way of information about the words. The traditional elements have been for some time: spelling and syllabication, pronunciation, definition, and etymology. To these we have added the new dimension of large-scale information about usage.

Spelling is rather well established, thanks to generations of copy-editors, but we have been able to confirm preferred choices statistically with the Brown corpus.

In the definitions, aside from such literary qualities as economy, precision, completeness, and style, there is the question of arrangement which remains variable in dictionary practice. When a word has many senses, what should be the order of presenting them? The Oxford established a historical order since the explication of the history of words was its chief concern. Even the Oxford admits to violating historical order sometimes "for convenience." One may ask whose convenience? I think they mean theirs. The one difficulty is that the general user finds it confusing to wade through obsolete, archaic, or rare meanings first.

More recently some dictionaries have chosen to represent the order of their definitions as based on frequency. First, there is not enough evidence for this practice and second, if there were, it would often throw unrelated senses together.

We have attempted an approach that abandons both alleged historical fact and alleged statistical fact and that arranges the meanings of a word in a natural flow. This consists of finding a central sense and arranging the others from it. Such a method, designed for the convenience of the reader, represents the "shape" or pattern of the word in the mind of the native speaker, regardless of how the pattern came about.

When we described the plan at the first meeting of our linguistic panel, Morris Halle of MIT, one of the leading modern linguists, became quite excited and felt we were getting on to some of the most exciting new work in linguistics, dealing with semantic intuition.

The technique of organizing definition by what we sometimes call the "analytical method" was only one of several basic concepts that we discussed with the members of our linguistic panel, a group of scholars who attended a number of policy and planning meetings with our senior editors. Each of these linguists later contributed an article on his specialty to the front matter of the dictionary. As a matter of fact, an extraordinarily wide range of current linguistic thought is reflected in these articles by such diverse figures as Morris Bishop, Calvert Watkins, Morton Bloomfield, Henry Lee Smith, Jr., Richard Ohmann, Henry Kučera, and Wayne O'Neil. Taken together these articles, which range from O'Neil on phoneme-grapheme correspondence to Kučera on the use of computers in linguistic analysis and lexicography, should prove informative guides for layman and scholar alike.

The etymologies – the word histories – have long been treated as a kind of step-child among the elements of a dictionary. They are often given with many confusing abbreviations and symbols, and it is very rare that the full story of a word, even the main line of its ancestry, is carried as far back as present knowledge would permit.

At the inception of the project we enlisted the aid of Calvert Watkins of Harvard, who is one of the great Indo-European scholars. Working with him became so exciting that we decided to make every effort to exhibit the total ancestry of our language.

As we know, most European languages have been traced to a single parent language – Indo-European. The work of reconstructing this language has been going on for more than 100 years, but few people other than scholars realize how much is known or what a fascinating light it sheds on English.

In a special appendix to the main dictionary, we seek nothing less than to give every Indo-European root that contributes an English word recorded in our dictionary. All the words that derive from each root are traced by their separate paths. For example *door, forensic, forest, foreign,* and *thyroid* are from the same root *dwher.*

We cannot know until scholars and students have tested this Indo-European root appendix if such information is of any substantial value, but if one is to have etymologies, why not, we thought, give the whole story. To make the story as clear and readable as possible we also eliminated all abbreviations and symbols from etymologies in the body of the book, and, in large measure, from the appendix.

Now that the task of creating the new dictionary is completed, I can only echo the remark made by Dr. Johnson as he delivered the last folio of his great work to the printer: "Every other author may aspire to praise; the lexicographer can only hope to escape reproach."

---

[1] Funk & Wagnalls New Standard Dictionary, copyright 1952 (original copyright 1913), p. 2045.

Usage, Dialects, and Functional Varieties

RAVEN I. MCDAVID, JR.

SINCE LANGUAGE IS the most habitual form of human behavior, the details of usage often become class markers. Social anthropologists have noted that the more ostensibly "open" a society happens to be, the more tolerant it is of the rise of its members to higher class status and the more subtle are the values used for setting one group above another. In the United States, where it is accepted that the grandsons of immigrants and laborers may fill the highest offices in the land, concern with acquiring certain forms of usage as indications of social status is likely to replace the slow acculturation to upper-class mores that has characterized older and more traditionally oriented societies.

Although actually there are subtle distinctions in usage which will determine the appropriateness of a given form on a particular occasion, and which can be appreciated only by long observation and intuitive experience, the prevailing public attitude is that certain forms of usage are "correct" and others are "incorrect." Teachers, especially of English, are supposed to know the difference between "right" and "wrong" in language. And entrepreneurs who make fortunes out of public anxieties stand ready to provide what the schools haven't given, by warning against "common mistakes" in the language of even the best educated. Furthermore, "right" usage is supposed to be stable, as opposed to "wrong" usage which is changing, while in fact some widely spread forms, favored by authoritarians, are clearly innovations and are still regarded by many cultivated speakers as pretentious affectations of the half-educated.

The cold fact about usage in natural languages is that it is diverse and is subject to change. Essentially, in the usage of native speakers, whatever is, is right; but some usages may be more appropriate than others, at least socially. It is not merely the number of speakers and writers that determines the appropriateness, but their age, education, sophistication, and social position. Within any living language there will be varieties of usage associated with geographical origin (*regional dialects* or simply *dialects*), social status (*social dialects* or *social levels*), and relationships (*styles* or *functional varieties*), as well as such special varieties as *slang, argot,* and *technical language.* All of these arise out of the normal interactions of human beings in a complex society.

Regional dialects originate in a variety of ways. Most commonly they come about from settlement, whether old, as of the Germanic tribes between the Rhine and the Elbe, or recent, as of Southern Englishmen in eastern Virginia and Ulster Scots (more commonly called Scotch-Irish) west of the Blue Ridge. Dialects spread along routes of migration and communication. For example, words and pronunciations characteristic of western New England mark the progress of Yankees across New York State and the Great Lakes Basin. In this Northern dialect area we find such grammatical forms as *dove* for the past tense of *dive,* "sick *to* the stomach" for "nauseated," and *darning needle* as the popular name of the dragonfly. Settlements by speakers of other languages may leave their mark. In the Hudson Valley, which was settled by the Dutch, *stoop,* derived from *stoep,* is commonly used for "porch." In Pennsylvania and settlements elsewhere by Pennsylvania Germans, *smearcase,* modified from *Schmierkäse,* denotes "cottage cheese" or any soft cheese suitable for spreading. The Scandinavian loan translation, to *cook coffee,* is used in place of to *make, brew,* or *fix* it in the Upper Midwest. The Spanish *frijoles,* plural of *frijol,* is used to denote the kidney beans widely used in Texas and other parts of the Southwest.

A dialect area with an important cultural center, whose characteristic speech forms tend to spread, is a *focal area.* Older focal areas in the United States are southeastern New England (Boston), the Delaware Valley (Philadelphia), the Upper Ohio Valley (Pittsburgh), the Virginia Piedmont (Richmond and its neighboring cities), and the South Carolina Low-Country (Charleston). Among newer focal areas that have been identified are the Carolina-Georgia Piedmont (Atlanta-Charlotte), Metropolitan Chicago, New

Orleans, Salt Lake City, and the San Francisco Bay area. Others are in process of developing, even as older areas like Richmond and Charleston have lost their preeminence.

An area lacking an important center, whose characteristic speech forms are preserved mainly by the older and less educated, is a *relic area*. Among the more noticeable relic areas are northeastern New England (Maine and New Hampshire), Delmarva (the eastern shore of Chesapeake Bay), the North Carolina Coast, and the Southern Appalachians. Similar regional dialects are found in other parts of the English-speaking world. They are much more sharply defined in the British Isles, much less sharply in Australia. In Canada, as in the United States, regional and local differences are sharpest in the older coastal settlements (New Brunswick, Nova Scotia, Prince Edward Island, and especially in Newfoundland), least sharp in the prairie and Rocky Mountain areas where there was almost no permanent settlement before the building of the transcontinental railroads. But no geographic region is without its local subtypes, and in the United States there is nothing that qualifies as a mythically uniform General American Speech.

Cutting across regional distinctions are social ones. In every linguistic community there are certain people whose speech and writing is admired as a model of *cultivated usage*, because of their wealth, education, family connections, or social position. In sharp contrast is the usage of those with little formal education, experience acquired from travel, or other marks of sophistication, and this we would call *folk usage*. In between is *common usage*. How distant from each other the three types are depends, essentially, on the social structure of a particular community.

What is standard usage may sometimes be determined by an official body charged with setting the standard. In England in the 17th and 18th centuries there was a movement toward setting up an academy for the English language, a manifestation of the appeal of the idea of linguistic legislation to the neoclassical era. The movement drew its strength in part from the classical model of Plato's Academy, but more from the example of the extant academies on the Continent, the Italina Academia della Crusca (1592) and especially the Académie Française (1635), founded by Richelieu. Other academies developed in Europe, notably in Spain and Russia, but no English academy ever arose. Although Dryden, Defoe, Pope, Swift, and Addison and Steele, among others, viewed with alarm the "decay" of the English language and agreed that only an academy could set things right, they could not agree on who was to head it, and the Royal Society, the one learned body that might have assumed the role, confined its interest to the physical sciences. Samuel Johnson originally proposed to set himself up as the arbiter of the English language through his dictionary, but the result of his labors was to convince him that such a role was impracticable.

Nevertheless, the learned of Johnson's day vested in his dictionary the authority of the academy that Johnson had eschewed, and established the Anglo-American tradition of dictionary worship, which assumes that a dictionary must and does include within its covers more accurate information on any word than any layman could possibly have. The yearning for an academy is not a thing of the past; laymen are far less likely to criticize a dictionary or a grammar for unwarranted assumptions of authority than for abdicating its responsibility to make decisions the public are bound to obey.

Academies usually select one local variety of educated speech to impose as an official standard: Roman-Florentine in Italy, Parisian in France, Castilian in Spain, and Moscovian in Russia. Their legislative power induces a conservatism that prevents their decisions from accurately representing cultivated usage. If the Académie Française overlooks or rejects a word or meaning at its weekly meeting, no reconsideration is possible for several decades, until the rest of the dictionary has been revised and the same part of the alphabet comes up again. As a result, there is a growing split between academic usage, subservient to the Academy, and popular educated usage, defiant of it.

Inasmuch as the academy-sponsored prestige dialects of Italy, France, Spain and Russia had achieved their positions before the academies were set up, essentially the academies merely recognized accomplished facts. In Great Britain the grammar and pronunciation used by educated men from the south of England, called Received Standard, have informally achieved highest status without an academy. Fostered by the "public schools," Winchester, Eton, and the like, and by the two great universities, Oxford and Cambridge, Received Standard has long been a badge of office for those who handle the affairs of church and state. Used normally by upper-class families, Received Standard as taught in the public schools to children of the newly rich has been one of the ways for the established order to accommodate the new wealth. A merchant or manufacturer who has risen in society cannot acquire the accent or forms of usage of his new class, but his children can—and the status that goes with it. Yet even in its heyday Received Standard was never uniform or unchanging. Observers have commented on many changes over the past two generations.

Today, with the expansion of education under the welfare state, it is no longer possible to bestow Received Standard on every recruit to the intellectual elite, and it has consequently lost much of its glamour.

Until the 1920's, Received Standard was the usual model for teaching English to native speakers of other languages. It is the basis for the local varieties of English that have arisen in the new nations developing out of the Commonwealth in Asia and Africa. The educational systems of these countries have been modeled on British practice, and some of their institutions of higher education are still affiliated with British universities. In Europe there is still a notion in some quarters that Received Standard is "better" or "more elegant" than any variety of American English. However, as overseas students come to the United States in increasing numbers, and as American commercial and educational operations develop overseas, the prestige of Received Standard is no longer unquestioned.

The American criteria for separating standard from nonstandard usage are of yet another sort. On the one hand, a predominantly middle-class society, believing in the importance of formal education, is likely to accept authoritarian judgments; on the other, Americans have inherited traditions of democratic individualism, and are likely to resent the proscription of habitual pronunciations, words, and even grammatical forms. But contributing most to the American multivalued standard is the history of strong local cultural traditions. Before the American Revolution and for some time thereafter, communication between the colonies, or the new states, was difficult. In Boston, New York, Philadelphia, Richmond, and Charleston, indigenous cultivated English developed in different ways. In the new cities to the west similar developments took place. In some rural areas and in a few cities, notably New York, the rapid assimilation of large numbers of immigrants with languages other than English has almost swamped traditional local educated usage and pronunciation.

Throughout the English-speaking world and particularly in America, the grammar of the educated is much more uniform than their pronunciation. In fact, grammar is the surest linguistic index of a speaker's education and general culture. There are almost no structural differences from region to region. The familiar use of such verb phrases as *might could* and *used to could* by educated Southerners stands almost alone. Even in matters of incidence there are few regional differences in the grammar of educated people. One of these is the Northern use of *dove* (dōv) for the past tense of *dived*.

As we might expect, grammatical variations are greater in folk and common usage than among the cultivated. Alongside the standard past tense *saw* we find *see, seed,* and *seen.* The last is common everywhere but in New England, the two others are restricted regionally. Beside the standard *climbed,* we have *clam, clim, clom, clome, cloom,* and *clum,* with fairly clear regional patterns, though the last is the most common.

In vocabulary, the sharpest regional distinctions concern matters of humble and rustic life before the mechanization of agriculture. Many such words are only faintly remembered as supermarkets and mass advertising substitute national terms for local ones. But at the same time, new local and regional terms are developing. A dry cleaning establishment is a *cleanser* in Boston; a rubber band is a *rubber binder* in Minnesota. The grass strip between sidewalk and street is a *boulevard* in Minneapolis, a *devil strip* in Akron, a *tree lawn* in Cleveland, and a *tree belt* in Springfield, Massachusetts; a sandwich of many ingredients, in a small loaf of bread, is a *poor boy* in New Orleans, a *submarine* in Boston, a *hoagy* in Philadelphia, a *hero* in New York City, and a *grinder* in upstate New York.

Regional and social differences are not to be confused with style. Both educated and uneducated usage, wherever encountered, have formal and informal modes though the educated speaker has more gradations at his command. Informal usage is neither better nor worse than the formal usage of the same speaker. What really matters is that each usage should be appropriate for the situation. An educated speaker will transfer from informal *haven't* to formal *have not.* The uneducated speaker who informally uses *I seen* or *I done gone* may adjust to the formal mode with *I have saw* and *I have went.*

Slang is usually but not inevitably associated with the informal style. Characterized by novelty and impermanence, it is used to indicate that one is up to date, but it often merely indicates that one is dated. Within a few years *hot* as a general adjective of approbation gave way to *cool,* and *cool* in turn to *boss.* Recently, however, old slang terms have been temporarily revivified by the rerunning of old movies on television.

Slang was once a synonym for argot, the ingroup language used by those who participate in a particular activity, especially a criminal one. In fact, much slang still derives from small, specialized groups, some of it nursed along tenderly by press agents. Popular musicians have originated many slang expressions now in general use. The word *jazz* itself is a good example: a Southern term meaning to copulate, it was used by the musicians who entertained in New Orleans brothels to describe their kinds of musical improvisations and soon came into general use despite the horror of Southerners who had previously known the word as a taboo verb. Today much slang originates with narcotic addicts, spreads to popular musicians, and then gains vogue among the young, while falling into disuse among its inventors. Other argot, however, is restricted to the practitioners of a particular field: *boff*, meaning variously "a humorous line," "a belly laugh," or "a box office hit," seems restricted in its use to theatrical circles; *snow*, as it means "cocaine or heroin," is a common term only among drug addicts.

The fate of slang and argot terms is unpredictable. Most of them disappear rapidly, some win their way into standard use, and still others remain what they were to begin with. *Mob*, deplored by Swift and other purists of 1700, would never be questioned today, but *moll*, meaning "a prostitute" or "the mistress of a gangster," has been in use since the early 1600's, and is still slang.

Technical terms arise because it is necessary for those who share a scientific or technical interest to have a basis for discussion. The difference between scientific and popular usage may be seen most strikingly in the biological sciences. A Latin term like *Panthera Leo* (lion) has a specific reference, while *cougar* may refer to any large wild American feline predator, or *partridge* may designate the bob-white quail, a kind of grouse, or some other game bird, according to local usage. Common words may be used with specific reference in a given field: *fusion* denotes one thing in politics, another in nuclear physics. As a field of inquiry becomes a matter of general interest, its technical terms will be picked up and used with less precision. Because of popular interest in Freudian psychology, such terms as *complex, fixation,* and *transference* are bandied about in senses Freud would never have sanctioned.

Despite some yearnings for authorities who would prescribe how people should use their language, the tendency in the English-speaking world is toward teaching based on objective description of the language. This does not mean an abandonment of standards. Indeed, in some situations this approach may call for rigorous drill so as to make habitual the features which everywhere set off standard usage from other varieties. It may also lead to systematic and rigorous drill to impart a fuller command of the rhetorical possibilities of standard English. At the same time, it should provide a more flexible attitude, an acceptance of varieties of cultivated speech other than one's own, and an understanding of the ways in which varieties of a language arose.

4

SLANG, GRAFFITI, AND EUPHEMISMS

The vivid, irreverent, and imaginative language of slang and graffiti as well as the often opaque language of euphemisms are discussed in this chapter. Stuart Berg Flexner, *co-editor of* Dictionary of American Slang, *presents a detailed survey of many aspects of current American slang.*

Next is an article by Donald V. Mehus on contemporary American graffiti, with examples of this spontaneous form of unauthorized wall writing—which may show up anywhere in addition to walls these days.

In a Time *essay on the surge of euphemisms in the United States today, the writer declares, "The persistent growth of euphemism in a language represents a danger to thought and action, since its fundamental intent is to deceive."*

American Slang

Stuart Berg Flexner

AMERICAN SLANG, AS used in the title of this dictionary, is the body of words and expressions frequently used by or intelligible to a rather large portion of the general American public, but not accepted as good formal usage by the majority. No word can be called slang simply because of its etymological history; its source, its spelling, and its meaning in a larger sense do *not* make it slang. Slang is best defined by a dictionary that points out who uses slang and what "flavor" it conveys.

I have called all slang used in the United States "American," regardless of its country of origin or use in other countries.

In this preface I shall discuss the human element in the formation of slang (what American slang is, and how and why slang is created and used). Linguistic processes are described in the appendix matter under The Mechanical Formation of New Words.

The English language has several levels of vocabulary:

Standard usage comprises those words and expressions used, understood, and accepted by a majority of our citizens under any circumstances or degree of formality. Such words are well defined and their most accepted spellings and pronunciations are given in our standard dictionaries. In standard speech one might say: *Sir, you speak English well.*

Colloquialisms are familiar words and idioms used in informal speech and writing, but not considered explicit or formal enough for polite conversation or business correspondence. Unlike slang, however, colloquialisms are used and understood by nearly everyone in the United States. The use of slang conveys the suggestion that the speaker and the listener enjoy a special "fraternity," but the use of colloquialisms emphasizes only the informality and familiarity of a general social situation. Almost all idiomatic expressions, for example, could be labeled colloquial. Colloquially, one might say: *Friend, you talk plain and hit the nail right on the head.*

Dialects are the words, idioms, pronunciations, and speech habits peculiar to specific geographical locations. A dialecticism is a regionalism or localism. In popular use "dialect'" has come to mean the words, foreign accents, or speech patterns associated with any ethnic group. In Southern dialect one might say: *Cousin, y'all talk mighty fine.* In ethnic-immigrant "dialects" one might say: *Paisano, you speak good the English,* or *Landsman, your English is plenty all right already.*

Cant, jargon and *argot* are the words and expressions peculiar to special segments of the population. *Cant* is the conversational, familiar idiom used and generally understood only by members of a specific occupation, trade, profession, sect, class, age group, interest group, or other sub-group of our culture. *Jargon* is the technical or even secret vocabulary of such a sub-group; jargon is "shop talk." *Argot* is both the cant and the jargon of any professional criminal group. In such usages one might say, respectively: *CQ-CQ-CQ . . . the tone of your transmission is good; You are free of anxieties related to interpersonal communication;* or *Duchess, let's have a bowl of chalk.*

Slang[1] is generally defined above. In slang one might say: *Buster, your line is the cat's pajamas,* or *Doll, you come on with the straight jazz, real cool like.*

Each of these levels of language, save standard usage, is more common in speech than in writing, and slang as a whole is no exception. Thus, very few slang words and expressions (hence very few of the entries in this dictionary) appear in standard dictionaries.

American slang tries for a quick, easy personal mode of speech. It comes mostly from cant, jargon, and argot words and expressions whose popularity has increased until a large number of the general public uses or understands them. Much of this slang retains a basic characteristic of its origin: it is *fully* intelligible only to initiates.

Slang may be represented pictorially as the more popular portion of the cant, jargon, and argot from many sub-groups (only a few of the sub-groups are shown below). The shaded areas represent only general overlapping between groups:

Eventually, some slang passes into standard speech; other slang flourishes for a time with varying popularity and then is forgotten; finally, some slang is never accepted nor completely forgotten. *O.K., jazz* (music), and *A-bomb* were recently considered slang, but they are now standard usages. *Bluebelly, Lucifer,* and *the bee's knees* have faded from popular use. *Bones* (dice) and *beat it* seem destined to remain slang forever: Chaucer used the first and Shakespeare used the second.

It is impossible for any living vocabulary to be static. Most new slang words and usages evolve quite naturally: they result from specific situations. New objects, ideas, or happenings, for example, require new words to describe them. Each generation also seems to need new words to describe old things.

Railroaders (who were probably the first American sub-group to have a nationwide cant and jargon) thought *jerk water town* was ideally descriptive of a community that others called a *one-horse town.* The changes from *one-horse town* and *don't spare the horses* to a *wide place in the road* and *step on it* were natural and necessary when the automobile replaced the horse. The automobile also produced such new words and new meanings (some of them highly specialized) as *gas buggy, jalopy, bent eight, Chevvie, convertible,* and *lube.* Like most major innovations, the automobile affected our social history and introduced or encouraged *dusters, hitch hikers, road hogs, joint hopping, necking, chicken* (the game), *car coats,* and *suburbia.*

The automobile is only one obvious example. Language always responds to new concepts and developments with new words.

Consider the following:

wars: *redcoats, minutemen, bluebelly, over there, doughboy, gold brick, jeep.*

mass immigrations: *Bohunk, greenhorn, shillalagh, voodoo, pizzeria.*

science and technology: *'gin, side-wheeler, wash-and-wear, fringe area, fallout.*

turbulent-eras: *Redskin, maverick, speak, Chicago pineapple, free love,·fink, breadline.*

evolution in the styles of eating: *applesauce, clambake, luncheonette, hot dog, coffee and.*

dress: *Mother Hubbard, bustle, shimmy, sailor, Long Johns, zoot suit, Ivy League.*

housing: *lean-to, bundling board, chuck-house, W.C., railroad flat, split-level, sectional.*

music: *cakewalk, bandwagon, fish music, long hair, rock.*

personality: *Yankee, alligator, flapper, sheik, hepcat, B.M.O.C., beetle, beat.*

new modes of transportation: *stage, pinto, jitney, kayducer, hot shot, jet jockey.*

new modes of entertainment: *barnstormer, two-a-day, clown alley, talkies, d.j., Spectacular.*

changing attitudes toward sex: *painted woman, fast, broad, wolf, jailbait, sixty-nine.*

human motivations: *boy crazy, gold-digger, money-mad, Momism, Oedipus complex, do-gooder, sick.*

personal relationships: *bunky, kids, old lady, steady, ex, gruesome twosome, John.*

work and workers: *clod buster, scab, pencil pusher, white collar, graveyard shift, company man.*

politics: *Tory, do-nothing, mug-wump, third party, brain trust, fellow traveler, Veep.*

and even hair styles: *bun, rat, peroxide blonde, Italian cut, pony tail, D.A.*

Those social groups that first confront a new object, cope with a new situation, or work with a new concept devise and use new words long before the population at large does. The larger, more imaginative, and useful a group's vocabulary, the more likely it is to contribute slang. To generate slang, a group must either be very large and in constant contact with the dominant culture or be small, closely knit, and removed enough from the dominant culture to evolve an extensive, highly personal, and vivid vocabulary. Teenagers are an example of a large sub-group contributing many words. Criminals, carnival workers, and hoboes are examples of the smaller groups. The smaller groups, because their vocabulary is personal and vivid, contribute to our general slang out of proportion to their size.

Whether the United States has more slang words than any other country (in proportion to number of people, area, or the number of words in the standard vocabulary) I do not know[2]. Certainly the French and the Spanish enjoy extremely large slang vocabularies. Americans, however, do use their general slang more than any other people.

American slang reflects the kind of people who create and use it. Its diversity and popularity are in part due to the imagination, self-confidence, and optimism of our people. Its vitality is in further part due to our guarantee of free speech and to our lack of a national academy of language or of any "official" attempt to purify our speech. Americans are restless and frequently move from region to region and from job to job. This hopeful wanderlust, from the time of the pioneers through our westward expansion to modern mobility, has helped spread regional and group terms until they have become general slang. Such restlessness has created constantly new situations which provoke new words. Except for a few Eastern industrial areas and some rural regions in the South and West, America just doesn't look or sound "lived in." We often act and speak as if we were simply visiting and observing. What should be an ordinary experience seems new, unique, or colorful to us, worthy of words and forceful speech. People do not "settle down" in their jobs, towns, or vocabularies.

Nor do we "settle down" intellectually, spiritually, or emotionally. We have few religious, regional, family, class, psychological, or philosophical roots. We don't believe in roots, we believe in teamwork. Our strong loyalties, then, are directed to those social groups—or sub-groups as they are often called—with which we are momentarily identified. This ever-changing "membership" helps to promote and spread slang.

But even within each sub-group only a few new words are generally accepted. Most cant and jargon are local and temporary. What persists are the exceptionally apt and useful cant and jargon terms. These become part of the permanent, personal vocabulary of the group members, giving prestige to the users by proving their acceptance and status in the group. Group members then spread some of this more honored cant and jargon in the dominant culture. If the word is also useful to non-group members, it is on its way to becoming slang. Once new words are introduced into the dominant culture, via television, radio, movies, or newspapers, the rapid movement of individuals and rapid communication between individuals and groups spread the new word very quickly.

For example, consider the son of an Italian immigrant living in New York City. He speaks Italian at home. Among neighborhood youths of similar background he uses many Italian expressions because he finds them always on the tip of his tongue and because they give him a sense of solidarity with his group. He may join a street gang, and after school and during vacations work in a factory. After leaving high school, he joins the navy; then he works for a year seeing the country as a carnival worker. He returns to New York, becomes a longshoreman, marries a girl with a German background, and becomes a boxing fan. He uses Italian and German borrowings, some teen-age street-gang terms, a few factory terms, slang with a navy origin, and carnival, dockworker's, and boxing words. He spreads words from each group to all other groups he belongs to. His Italian parents will learn and use a few street-gang, factory, navy, carnival, dockworker's, and boxing terms; his German in-laws will learn some Italian words from his parents; his navy friends will begin to use some of his Italian expressions; his carnival friends a few navy words; his co-workers on the docks some carnival terms, in addition to all the rest; and his social friends, with whom he may usually talk boxing and dock work, will be interested in and learn some of his Italian and carnival terms. His speech may be considered very "slangy" and picturesque because he has belonged to unusual, colorful sub-groups.

On the other hand, a man born into a Midwestern, middle-class, Protestant family whose ancestors came to the United States in the eighteenth century might carry with him popular high-school terms. At high school he had an interest in hot rods and rock-and-roll. He may have served two years in the army, then gone to an Ivy League college where he became an adept bridge player and an enthusiast of cool music. He may then have become a sales executive and developed a liking for golf. This second man, no more usual or unusual than the first, will know cant and jargon terms of teen-age high-school use, hot-rods, rock-and-roll, Ivy League schools, cool jazz, army life, and some golf player's and bridge player's terms. He knows further a few slang expressions from his parents (members of the Jazz Age of the 1920's), from listening to television programs, seeing both American and British movies, reading popular literature, and from frequent meetings with people having completely different backgrounds. When he uses cool terms on the golf course, college expressions at home, business words at the bridge table, when he refers to whiskey or drunkenness by a few words he learned from his parents, curses his next-door neighbor in a few choice army terms–then he too is popularizing slang.

It is, then, clear that three cultural conditions especially contribute to the creation of a large slang vocabulary: (1) hospitality to or acceptance of new objects, situations, and concepts; (2) existence of a large number of diversified sub-groups; (3) democratic mingling between these sub-groups and the dominant culture. Primitive peoples have little if any slang because their life is restricted by ritual; they develop few new concepts; and there are no sub-groups that mingle with the dominant culture. (Primitive sub-groups, such as medicine men or magic men, have their own vocabularies; but such groups do not mix with the dominant culture and their jargon can never become slang because it is secret or sacred.)

But what, after all, are the advantages that slang possesses which make it useful? Though our choice of any specific word may usually be made from habit, we sometimes consciously select a slang word because we believe that it communicates more quickly and easily, and more personally, than does a standard word. Sometimes we resort to slang because there is no one standard word to use. In the 1940's, *WAC, cold war,* and *cool* (music) could not be expressed quickly by any standard synonyms. Such words often become standard quickly, as have the first two. We also use slang because it often is more forceful, vivid, and expressive than are standard usages. Slang usually avoids the sentimentality and formality that older words often assume. Taking a girl to a *dance* may seem sentimental, may convey a degree of formal, emotional interest in the girl, and has overtones of fancy balls, fox trots, best suits, and corsages. At times it is more fun to go to a *hop*. To be *busted* or without a *hog* in one's *jeans* is not only more vivid and forceful than being penniless or without funds, it is also a more optimistic state. A *mouthpiece* (or *legal beagle*), *pencil pusher, sawbones, boneyard, bottle washer* or a course in *biochem* is more vivid and forceful than a lawyer, clerk, doctor, cemetery, laboratory assistant, or a course in biochemistry–and is much more real and less formidable than a legal counsel, junior executive, surgeon, necropolis (or memorial park), laboratory technician, or a course in biological chemistry.

Although standard English is exceedingly hospitable to polysyllabicity and even sesquipedalianism, slang is not. Slang is sometimes used not only because it is concise but just because its brevity makes it forceful. As this dictionary demonstrates, slang seems to prefer short words, especially monosyllables, and, best of all, words beginning with an explosive or an aspirate[3].

We often use slang *fad* words as a bad habit because they are close to the tip of our tongue. Most of us apply several favorite but vague words to any of several somewhat similar situations; this saves us the time and effort of thinking and speaking precisely. At other times we purposely choose a word because it is vague, because it does not commit us too strongly to what we are saying. For example, if a friend has been praising a woman, we can reply *"she's the bee's knees"* or *"she's a real chick,"* which can mean that we consider her very modern, intelligent, pert, and understanding – or can mean that we think she is one of many nondescript, somewhat confused, followers of popular fads. We can also tell our friend that a book we both have recently read is *the cat's pajamas* or *the greatest.* These expressions imply that we liked the book for exactly the same reasons that our friend did, without having to state what these reasons were and thus taking the chance of ruining our rapport.

In our language we are constantly recreating our image in our own minds and in the minds of others. Part of this image, as mentioned above, is created by using sub-group cant and jargon in the dominant society; part of it is created by our choice of both standard and slang words. A sub-group vocabulary shows that we have a group to which we "belong" and in which we are "somebody" – outsiders had better respect us. Slang is used to show others (and to remind ourselves of) biographical, mental, and psychological background; to show our social, economic, geographical, national, racial, religious, educational, occupational, and group interests, memberships, and patriotisms. One of the easiest and quickest ways to do this is by using counter-words. These are automatic, often one-word responses of like or dislike, of acceptance or rejection. They are used to counter the remarks, or even the presence, of others. Many of our fad words and many student and quasi-intellectual slang words are counter-words. For liking: *beat, the cat's pajamas, drooly, gas, George, the greatest, keen, nice, reet, smooth, super, way out,* etc. For rejection of an outsider (implying incompetence to belong to our group): *boob, creep, dope, drip, droop, goof, jerk, kookie, sap, simp, square, weird,* etc. Such automatic counters are overused, almost meaningless, and are a substitute for thought. But they achieve one of the main purposes of speech: quickly and automatically they express our own sub-group and personal criteria. Counter-words are often fad words creating a common bond of self-defense. All the rejecting counters listed above could refer to a moron, an extreme introvert, a birdwatcher, or a genius. The counters merely say that the person is rejected—he does not belong to the group. In uttering the counter we don't care what the person is; we are pledging our own group loyalty, affirming our identity, and expressing our satisfaction at being accepted.

In like manner, at various periods in history, our slang has abounded in words reflecting the fear, distrust, and dislike of people unlike ourselves. This intolerance is shown by the many derogatory slang words for different immigrant, religious, and racial groups: *Chink, greaser, Heinie, hunkie, mick, mockie, nigger, spik*. Many counters and derogatory words try to identify our own group status, to dare others to question our group's, and therefore our own, superiority.

Sometimes slang is used to escape the dull familiarity of standard words, to suggest an escape from the established routine of everyday life. When slang is used, our life seems a little fresher and a little more personal. Also, as at all levels of speech, slang is sometimes used for the pure joy of making sounds, or even for a need to attract attention by making noise. The sheer newness and informality of certain slang words produces a pleasure.

But more important than this expression of a more or less hidden esthetic motive on the part of the speaker is slang's reflection of the personality, the outward, clearly visible characteristics of the speaker. By and large, the man who uses slang is a forceful, pleasing, acceptable personality. Morality and intellect (too frequently not considered virtues in the modern American man) are overlooked in slang, and this has led to a type of reverse morality: many words, once standing for morally good things, are now critical. No one, for example, though these words were once considered complimentary, wants to be called a *prude* or *Puritan*. Even in standard usage they are mildly derisive.

Moreover, few of the many slang synonyms for drunk are derogatory or critical. To call a person a standard drunk may imply a superior but unsophisticated attitude toward drinking. Thus we use slang and say someone is *boozed up, gassed, high, potted, stinking, has a glow on*, etc., in a verbal attempt to convey our understanding and awareness. These slang words show that we too are human and know the effects of excessive drinking.

In the same spirit we refer to people sexually as *big ass man, fast, John, sex pot, shack job, wolf*, etc., all of which accept unsanctioned sexual intercourse as a matter of fact. These words are often used in a complimentary way and in admiration or envy. They always show acceptance of the person as a "regular guy." They are never used to express a moral judgment. Slang has few complimentary or even purely descriptive words for "virgin," "good girl," or "gentleman." Slang has *bag, bat, ex, gold digger, jerk, money mad, n.g., old lady, square,* etc.; but how many words are there for a good wife and mother, an attractive and chaste woman, an honest, hard-working man who is kind to his family, or even a respected elderly person? Slang–and it is frequently true for all language levels–always tends toward degradation rather than elevation. As slang shows, we would rather share or accept vices than be excluded from a social group. For this reason, for self-defense, and to create an aura (but not the fact) of modernity and individuality, much of our slang purposely expresses amorality, cynicism, and "toughness."

Reverse morality also affects slang in other ways. Many use slang just because it is not standard or polite. Many use slang to show their rebellion against *boobs, fuddy-duddies, marks,* and *squares.* Intellectuals and politicians often use slang to create the "common touch" and others use slang to express either their anti-intellectualism or avant-garde leanings. Thus, for teen-agers, entertainers, college students, beatniks, jazz fans, intellectuals, and other large groups, slang is often used in preference to standard words and expressions. Slang is the "official" modern language of certain vociferous groups in our population.

In my work on this dictionary, I was constantly aware that most American slang is created and used by males. Many types of slang words –including the taboo and strongly derogatory ones, those referring to sex, women, work, money, whiskey[4], politics, transportation, sports, and the like–refer primarily to male endeavor and interest. The majority of entries in this dictionary could be labeled "primarily masculine use." Men belong to more sub-groups than do women; men create and use occupational cant and jargon; in business, men have acquaintances who belong to many different subgroups. Women, on the other hand, still tend to be restricted to family and neighborhood friends. Women have very little of their own slang.[5] The new words applied to women's clothing, hair styles, homes, kitchen utensils and gadgets are usually created by men. Except when she accompanies her boy friend or husband to *his* recreation (baseball, hunting, etc.) a woman seldom mingles with other groups. When women do mingle outside of their own neighborhood and family circles, they do not often talk of the outside world of business, politics, or other fields of general interest where new feminine names for objects, concepts, and viewpoints could evolve.

Men also tend to avoid words that sound feminine or weak. Thus there are sexual differences in even the standard vocabularies of men and women. A woman may ask her husband to set the table for dinner, asking him to put out the *silver, crystal,* and *china*—while the man will set the table with *knives, forks, spoons, glasses,* and *dishes.* His wife might think the *table linen* attractive, the husband might think the *tablecloth* and *napkins* pretty. A man will buy a *pocketbook* as a gift for his wife, who will receive a *bag.* The couple will live under the same roof, the wife in her *home,* the man in his *house.* Once outside of their domesticity the man will begin to use slang quicker than the woman. She'll get into the *car* while he'll get into the *jalopy* or *Chevvie.* And so they go: she will learn much of her general slang from him; for any word she associates with the home, her personal belongings, or any female concept, he will continue to use a less descriptive, less personal one.

Males also use slang to shock. The rapid tempo of life, combined with the sometimes low boiling point of males, can evoke emotions—admiration, joy, contempt, anger—stronger than our old standard vocabulary can convey. In the stress of the moment a man is not just in a standard "untenable position," he is *up the creek.* Under strong anger a man does not feel that another is a mere "incompetent"—he is a *jerk* or a *fuck-off.*

Men also seem to relish hyperbole in slang. Under many situations, men do not see or care to express fine shades of meaning: a girl is either a *knockout* or a *dog,* liquor either *good stuff* or *panther piss,* a person either has *guts* or is *chicken,* a book is either *great* or nothing but *crap.* Men also like slang and colloquial wording because they express action or even violence: we *draw pay, pull a boner, make a score, grab some sleep, feed our face, kill time*—in every instance we tend to use the transitive verb, making ourselves the active doer.

The relation between a sub-group's psychology and its cant and jargon is interesting, and the relation between an individual's vocabulary and psychological personality is even more so. Slang can be one of the most revealing things about a person, because our own personal slang vocabulary contains many words used by choice, words which we use to create our own image, words which we find personally appealing and evocative—as opposed to our frequent use of standard words merely from early teaching and habit. Whether a man calls his wife *baby, doll, honey, the little woman, the Mrs.,* or *my old lady* certainly reveals much about him. What words one uses to refer to a mother *(Mom, old lady),* friend *(buddy, bunkie, old man),* the bathroom *(can, John, little boy's room),* parts of the body and sex acts *(boobies, gigi, hard, laid, score),* being tired *(all in, beat),* being drunk *(clobbered, high, lit up like a Christmas tree, paralyzed),* and the like, reveal much about a person and his motivations.[6]

The basic metaphors, at any rate, for all levels of language depend on the five senses. Thus *rough, smooth, touch; prune, sour puss, sweet; fishy, p.u., rotten egg; blow, loud; blue, red, square.* In slang, many metaphors refer to touch (including the sense of heat and cold) and to taste.

Food is probably our most popular slang image. Food from the farm, kitchen, or table, and its shape, color, and taste suggest many slang metaphors. This is because food can appeal to taste, smell, sight, and touch, four of our five senses; because food is a major, universal image to all people, all sub-groups; because men work to provide it and women devote much time to buying and preparing it; because food is before our eyes three times every day.

Many standard food words mean money in nonstandard use: *cabbage, kale, lettuce.* Many apply to parts of the body: *cabbage head, cauliflower ear, meat hooks, nuts, plates of meat.* Many food words refer to people: *apple, cold fish, Frog, fruitcake, honey, sweetie pie.* Others refer to general situations and attitudes: to *brew* a plot, to receive a *chewing out,* to find oneself *in a pickle* or something *not kosher,* to be unable to *swallow* another's story, to ask *what's cooking?* Many drunk words also have food images: *boiled, fried, pickled;* and so do many words for nonsense: *applesauce, banana oil, spinach.* Many standard food words also have sexual meanings in slang. The many food words for money, parts of the body, people, and sex reveal that food means much more to us than mere nourishment. When a *good egg brings home the bacon* to his *honey,* or when a *string bean* of a *sugar daddy* takes his *piece of barbecue* out to get *fried* with his hard-earned *kale,* food images have gone a long way from the farm, kitchen, and table.

Sex has contributed comparatively few words to modern slang,[7] but these are among our most frequently used. The use of sex words to refer to sex in polite society and as metaphors in other fields is increasing. Sex metaphors are common for the same conscious reasons that food metaphors are. Sex appeals to, and can be used to apply to, most of the five senses. It is common to all persons in all sub-groups, and so we are aware of it continually.

Slang words for sexual attraction and for a variety of sexual acts, positions, and relationships are more common than standard words. Standard non-taboo words referring to sex are so scarce or remote and scientific that slang is often used in referring to the most romantic, the most obscene, and the most humorous sexual situations. Slang is so universally used in sexual communication that when "a man meets a maid" it is best for all concerned that they know slang.[8] Slang words for sex carry little emotional connotation; they express naked desire or mechanical acts, devises and positions. They are often blunt, cynical and "tough."

The subconscious relating of sex and food is also apparent from reading this dictionary. Many words with primary, standard meanings of food have sexual slang meanings. The body, parts of the body, and descriptions of each, often call food terms into use: *banana, bread, cheese cake, cherry, jelly roll, meat,* etc. Beloved, or simply sexually attractive, people are also often called by food names: *cookie, cup of tea, honey, peach, quail, tomato,* etc. This primary relation between sex and food depends on the fact that they are man's two major sensuous experiences. They are shared by all personalities and all sub-groups and they appeal to the same sense—thus there is bound to be some overlapping in words and imagery. However, there are too many standard food words having sexual meanings in slang for these conscious reasons to suffice. Sex and food seem to be related in our subconscious.

Also of special interest is the number of slang expressions relating sex and cheating. Used metaphorically, many sex words have secondary meanings of being cheated, deceived, swindled, or taken advantage of, and several words whose primary meaning is cheating or deceiving have further specific sexual meanings: *cheating, fucked, make, royal screwing, score, turn a trick,* etc. As expressed in slang, sex is a trick somehow, a deception, a way to cheat and deceive us. To curse someone we can say *fuck you* or *screw you,* which expresses a wish to deprive him of his good luck, his success, perhaps even his potency as a man.[9] Sex is also associated with confusion, exhausting tasks, and disaster: *ball buster, screwed up, snafu,* etc. It seems clear, therefore, that, in slang, success and sexual energy are related or, to put it more accurately, that thwarted sexual energy will somehow result in personal disaster.

Language is a social symbol. The rise of the middle class coincided with the period of great dictionary makers, theoretical grammarians, and the "correct usage" dogma. The new middle class gave authority to the dictionaries and grammarians in return for "correct usage" rules that helped solidify their social position. Today, newspaper ads still implore us to take mail-order courses in order to "learn to speak like a college graduate," and some misguided English instructors still give a good speaking ability as the primary reason for higher education.

The gap between "correct usage" and modern practice widens each day. Are there valid theoretical rules for speaking good English, or should "observed usage" be the main consideration? Standard words do not necessarily make for precise, forceful, or useful speech. On the other hand, "observed usage" can never promise logic and clarity. Today, we have come to depend on "observed usage," just as eighteenth- and nineteenth-century social climbers depended on "correct usage," for social acceptance.

Because it is not standard, formal, or acceptable under all conditions, slang is usually considered vulgar, impolite, or boorish. As this dictionary shows, however, the vast majority of slang words and expressions are neither taboo, vulgar, derogatory, nor offensive in meaning, sound, or image. There is no reason to avoid any useful, explicit word merely because it is labeled "slang." Our present language has not decayed from some past and perfect "King's English," Latin, Greek, or pre-Tower of Babel tongue. All languages and all words have been, are, and can only be but conventions mutually a-greed upon for the sake of communicating. Slang came to America on the Mayflower. In general, it is not vulgar, new, or even peculiarly American: an obvious illustration of this is the polite, old French word *tête*, which was originally slang from a Latin word *testa*—cooking pot.

Cant and jargon in no way refer only to the peculiar words of undesirable or underworld groups. Slang does not necessarily come from the underworld, dope addicts, degenerates, hoboes, and the like. Any cultural sub-group develops its own personal cant and jargon which can later become general slang. All of us belong to several of these specific subgroups using our own cant and jargon. Teenagers, steel workers, soldiers, Southerners, narcotic addicts, church-goers, truck drivers, advertising men, jazz musicians, pick-pockets, retail salesmen in every field, baseball fans—all belong to typical sub-groups from which slang originates. Some of these sub-groups are color-ful; most are composed of prosaic, average people.

Many people erroneously believe that a fundamental of slang is that it is intentionally picturesque, strained in metaphor, or jocular. Picturesque me-taphor (and metonymy, hyperbole, and irony) does or should occur frequently in all levels of speech. Picturesque metaphor is a frequent characteristic of slang, but it does not define slang or exist as an inherent part of it. The picturesque or metaphorical aspect of slang is often due to its direct honesty or to its newness. Many standard usages are just as picturesque, but we have forgotten their original metaphor through habitual use. Thus slang's *jerk* and *windbag* are no more picturesque than the standard *incompetent* and *fool*. *Incompetent* is from the Latin *competens* plus the negating prefix *in-* and equals "unable or unwilling to compete"; *fool* in Old French, from the Latin *follis* which actually equals "bellows or wind bag"; slang's *windbag* and the standard *fool* actually have the same metaphor.

As for picturesque sounds, I find very few in slang. Onomatopoeia, reduplications, harsh sounds and pleasing sounds, even rhyming terms, exist on all levels of speech. Readers of this dictionary will find no more picturesque or unusual sounds here than in a similar length dictionary of standard words. Many slang words are homonyms for standard words.

As has been frequently pointed out, many slang words have the same meaning. There seems to be an unnecessary abundance of counter-words, synonyms for "drunk," hundreds of fad words with almost the same meaning, etc. This is because slang introduces word after word year after year from many, many sub-groups. But slang is a scattergun process; many new words come at the general public; most are ignored; a few stick in the popular mind.

Remember that "slang" actually does not exist as an entity except in the minds of those of us who study the language. People express themselves and are seldom aware that they are using the artificial divisions of "slang" or "standard." First and forever, language is language, an attempt at communication and self-expression. The fact that some words or expressions are labeled "slang" while others are labeled "jargon" or said to be "from the Anglo-Saxon" is of little value except to scholars. Thus this dictionary is a legitimate addition to standard dictionaries, defining many words just as meaningful as and often more succinct, useful, and popular than many words in standard dictionaries.

---

[1] For the evolution of the word "slang," see F. Klaeber, "Concerning the Etymology of Slang," *American Speech*, April, 1926.

[2] The vocabulary of the average American, most of which he knows but never uses, is usually estimated at 10,000–20,000 words. Of this quantity I estimate conservatively that 2,000 words are slang. Slang, which thus forms about 10 per cent of the words known by the average American, belongs to the part of his vocabulary most frequently used.

The English language is now estimated to have at least 600,000 words; this is over four times the 140,000 recorded words of the Elizabethan period. Thus over 450,000 *new words or meanings* have been added since Shakespeare's day, without counting the replacement words or those that have been forgotten between then and now. There are now approximately 10,000 slang words in American English, and about 35,000 cant, jargon, and argot words.

Despite this quantity, 25 per cent of all communication is composed of just nine words. According to McKnight's study, another 25 per cent of all speech is composed of an additional 34 words (or: 43 words comprise 50 per cent of all speech). Scholars do differ, however, on just which nine words are the most popular. Three major studies are: G. H. McKnight, *English Words and Their Background*, Appleton-Century-Crofts, Inc., 1923 (for spoken words only); Godfrey Dewey, "Relative Frequency of English Speech Sounds," *Harvard Studies in Education*, vol. IV, 1923 (for written words only); and Norman R. French, Charles W. Carter, and Walter Koenig, Jr., "Words and Sounds of Telephone Conversations," *Bell System Technical Journal*, April, 1930 (telephone speech only). Their lists of the most common nine words are:

McKnight's speech	Dewey's written	Bell Telephone conversations
	a	a
and	and	
be		
have		
	in	
		I
	is	is
it	it	it
		on
of	of	
	that	that
the	the	the
to	to	to
will		
you		you

³ Many such formations are among our most frequently used slang words. As listed in this dictionary, *bug* has 30 noun meanings, *shot* 14 noun and 4 adjective meanings, *can* 11 noun and 6 verb, *bust* 9 verb and 6 noun, *hook* 8 noun and 5 verb, *fish* 14 noun, and *sack* 8 noun, 1 adjective, and 1 verb meaning. Monosyllabic words also had by far the most citations found in our source reading of popular literature. Of the 40 words for which we found the most quotations, 29 were monosyllabic. Before condensing, *fink* had citations from 70 different sources, *hot* 67, *bug* 62, *blow* and *dog* 60 each, *joint* 59, *stiff* 56, *punk* 53, *bum* and *egg* 50 each, *guy* 43, *make* 41, *bull* and *mug* 37 each, *bird* 34, *fish* and *hit* 30 each, *ham* 25, *yak* 23, *sharp* 14, and *cinch* 10. (Many of these words, of course, have several slang meanings; many of the words also appeared scores of times in the same book or article.)

⁴ It would appear that the word having the most slang synonyms is drunk.

⁵ Women who do work usually replace men at men's jobs, are less involved in business life than men, and have a shorter business career (often but an interim between school and marriage). The major female sub-groups contributing to American slang are: airline stewardesses, beauty-parlor operators, chorus girls, nurses, prostitutes, and waitresses.

⁶ For just the last example, *clobbered* may indicate that a drinker is punishing himself, *high* that he is escaping, *lit up like a Christmas tree* that he is seeking attention and a more dominant personality, and *paralyzed* that he seeks punishment, escape or death.

⁷ Many so-called bedroom words are not technically slang at all, but are sometimes associated with slang only because standard speech has rejected them as taboo. However, many of these taboo words do have further metaphorical meanings in slang: *fucked, jerk, screw you*, etc.

⁸ On the other hand, Madame de Staël is reported to have complimented one of her favorite lovers with "speech is not his language."

⁹ See F. P. Wood, "The Vocabulary of Failure," *Better English*, Nov., 1938, p. 34. The vocabulary of failure is itself very revealing. Failure in one's personality, school, job, business, or

an attempted love affair are all expressed by the same vocabulary. One gets the *brush off,* the *gate,* a *kiss off,* or *walking papers* in both business and personal relationships. As the previous discussion of counterwords demonstrates, slang allows no distinction or degree among individual failures. Incompetence does not apply to just one job or facet of life—either one belongs or is considered unworthy. This unworthiness applies to the entire personality, there are no alternate avenues for success or happiness. One is not merely of limited intelligence, not merely an introvert, not mere ugly, unknowing, or lacking in aggression—but one is a failure in all these things, a complete *drip, jerk,* or *square.* The basic failure is that of personality, the person is not a mere failure—he is an outcast, an untouchable; he is taboo.

Contemporary American Graffiti

DONALD V. MEHUS

New York City has long been waging a seemingly losing battle against air pollution and trash-littered streets. In an appeal for public cooperation to help alleviate these conditions, the municipal sanitation department recently put up posters around the city asking: "Did you make New York dirty today?" On one of the posters a long-suffering resident scribbled a plaintive retort: "New York makes *me* dirty *every* day!"

This heartfelt remark is a characteristic example of the American version of graffiti, the ancient art of anonymous, unauthorized wall writing. Graffiti dates back at least as far as the Egypt of the Pharaohs; scholars have long busied themselves collecting and deciphering specimens from the ancient walls of Egypt, Athens, and Pompeii.

During the past few years the United States has witnessed its own flowering of this special form of spontaneous, personal expression. The best examples of contemporary American graffiti, whether lightly humorous or bitterly vitriolic, are often witty and provocative comments on some of the most vital concerns of our time—war and peace, government and politics, the individual and society.

Until recently comparatively little serious attention has been given to American graffiti. Lately, however, this often vividly imaginative writing has been accorded a measure of respectful recognition. Such publications as the *New York Times* and *Newsweek* have devoted substantial articles to the subject. Several authors readily admit that they took titles for some of their works directly from graffiti. The playwright Edward Albee first saw the conundrum

"Who's Afraid of Virginia Woolf?" on a restroom wall in a bar of New York's Greenwich Village. Robert Saffron found the title for his book "Is the U. S. Ready for Self-Government?" scribbled beneath an assortment of protest slogans on a subway wall.

A number of short book collections, including *Graffiti* and *Great Wall Writing*, both compiled by Robert Reisner, have been published. During recent years, as Reisner points out, the best American graffiti has gradually become more sophisticated, more intellectual and witty. Partly this is because simple obscenities scrawled on walls—a large share of graffiti everywhere, both past and present—have in this permissive age lost much of their shock value. At the same time people have become more alert to the problems, complexities, and absurdities of the age. Reflecting the mood of the troublous times, graffiti has also become more cynical.

According to some observers, American graffiti came of age during the late 1960s, when the widespread protest movement against United States involvement in the Vietnam War and against a range of national ills reached its peak of intensity. Much of the best wall writing suddenly became more pointed and articulate, more socially conscious, much more vitriolic. One bitter comment reported first seen at Harvard University read: "War is good business—invest your sons." Another proclaimed: "Bombing can end the war—bomb the Pentagon." A third cynic caustically urged: "Ban the H-bomb; save the world for conventional warfare."

While much of the best graffiti opposes rather than favors something, a protest slogan may occasionally be amended so as to reverse its original intention. Thus someone once appended to the traditional anti-American sign long familiar throughout the world, "Yankee Go Home," this personal request: "–and take me with you!"

Where is the best graffiti found? Who creates it, and why? Reisner reports that the best graffiti is often seen in large urban areas, particularly at universities and in the restrooms of coffee-houses and smart bars. Graffiti seems to be written predominantly by men; lately, however, women have become increasingly productive. The liveliest writing is often by students, hippies, and young business people. Graffiti is produced for a variety of reasons: to express an opinion, to voice an insult, to share a joke, to assert one's own individuality, to protest social and political conditions.

Some of the wittiest and most learned graffiti, according to Reisner, is on religious subjects. One pithy exchange by several persons ranged through various abstruse areas: contemporary theological debate, the atheistical views of the 19th century German philosopher Nietzsche, the position of Odin as the supreme deity of Scandinavian mythology.

The exchange began with the now-famous two lines: "God is dead. Nietzsche." Immediately following, in another hand, appeared: "Nietzsche is dead. God." A third writer dismissed both assertions: "They are both dead. Odin." Elsewhere an anonymous philosopher-theologian made a brilliant if somewhat heretical attempt to resolve the dilemma: "God is not dead. He just doesn't want to get involved."

The public seems to take particular relish in striking back at the inflated claims of omnipresent advertising. Some businessmen, however, actually welcome anonymous additions to their posters; they hope that graffiti may suggest—as some has—ideas for future ads. Graffiti writers are quick to deflate rhetorical questions even on altruistic posters for worthy causes. When a placard asked: "If the President finds time to help the mentally retarded, what are you doing that's so important?" some disgruntled citizen wrote underneath: "Working to get them out of Washington."

Predictably, America's racial troubles and the Federal laws against discrimination in housing, employment, and education have prompted widespread comment by wall writers. Much of this writing is regrettably virulent and bitter, the targets fairly clear. But occasionally one is not quite sure how to interpret certain graffiti, such as this equivocally misanthropic remark seen in a bar: "We hate all people, regardless of race, creed, or color."

By far the most popular subject of graffiti has doubtless always been the relation between the sexes. Much of this kind of wall writing is of course merely meaningless obscenities. But some is marked by genuine wit. One such example enjoins the reader to "Love thy neighbor, but don't get caught." Another offers a suggestion for alleviating a water shortage: "Save water; bathe with friends." A third smacks of what has been termed "pseudo-graffiti"—a pithy statement that while wittily pregnant yet lacks the apparent spontaneity of true graffiti: "Before Freud, sex was a pleasure; now it is a necessity."

As amusing and perceptive as graffiti may sometimes be, it has by no means won universal approval. Often graffiti merely defaces, like much of the huge, psychedelic lettering covering the sides of many New York subway cars. We have no idea how many people simply look in dismay at such graffiti and refrain from comment. But not infrequently a dissenter registers his objection. Wrote one: "I think people who write on walls are immature and troubled and need psychological help."

Pleas by authorities do not seem to help much to stem the flood. When a sign appeared in a bar requesting: "Do not write on walls," a patron retorted: "You want we should type maybe?" But perhaps the ultimate futility of trying to halt the spread of graffiti was reflected in this injunction written on a freshly-painted wall: "Stop vandalism—don't scribble on walls."

The Euphemism:
Telling It Like It Isn't

TIME

MODERN AMERICAN SPEECH, while not always clear or correct or turned with much style, is supposed to be uncommonly frank. Witness the current explosion of four-letter words and the explicit discussion of sexual topics. In fact, gobbledygook and nice-Nellyism still extend as far as the ear can hear. Housewives on television may chat about their sex lives in terms that a decade ago would have made gynecologists blush; more often than not, these emancipated women still speak about their children's "going to the potty." Government spokesmen talk about "redeployment" of American troops; they mean withdrawal. When sociologists refer to blacks living in slums, they are likely to mumble about "nonwhites" in a "culturally deprived environment." The CIA may never have used the expression "to terminate with extreme prejudice" when it wanted a spy rubbed out. But in the context of a war in which "pacification of the enemy infrastructure" is the military mode of reference to blasting the Viet Cong out of a village, the phrase sounded so plausible that millions readily accepted it as accurate.

The image of a generation blessed with a swinging, liberated language is largely an illusion. Despite its swaggering sexual candor, much contemporary speech still hides behind that traditional enemy of plain talk, the euphemism.

NECESSARY EVIL

From a Greek word meaning "to use words of good omen," euphemism is the substitution of a pleasant term for a blunt one–telling it like it isn't. Euphemism has probably existed since the beginning of language. As long as there have been things of which men thought the less said the better, there have been better ways of saying less. In everyday conversation the euphemism is, at worst, a necessary evil; at its best, it is a handy verbal tool to avoid making enemies needlessly, or shocking friends. Language purists and the blunt-spoken may wince when a young woman at a party coyly asks for directions to "the powder room," but to most people this kind of familiar euphemism is probably no more harmful or annoying than, say, a split infinitive.

On a larger scale, though, the persistent growth of euphemism in a language represents a danger to thought and action, since its fundamental intent is to deceive. As Linguist Benjamin Lee Whorf has pointed out, the structure of a given language determines, in part, how the society that speaks it views reality. If "substandard housing" makes rotting slums appear more livable or inevitable to some people, then their view of American cities has been distorted and their ability to assess the significance of poverty has been reduced. Perhaps the most chilling example of euphemism's destructive power took place in Hitler's Germany. The wholesale corruption of the language under Nazism, notes Critic George Steiner, is symbolized by the phrase *endgültige Lösung* (final solution), which "came to signify the death of 6,000,000 human beings in gas ovens."

ROSES BY OTHER NAMES

No one could argue that American English is under siege from linguistic falsehood, but euphemisms today have the nagging persistence of a headache. Despite the increasing use of nudity and sexual innuendo in advertising, Madison Avenue is still the great exponent of talking to "the average person of good upbringing"–as one TV executive has euphemistically described the ordinary American–in ways that won't offend him. Although this is like fooling half the people none of the time, it has produced a handsome bouquet of roses by other names. Thus there is "facial-quality tissue" that is not intended for use on faces, and "rinses" or "tints" for women who might be unsettled to think they dye their hair. In the world of deodorants, people never sweat or smell; they simply "offend." False teeth sound truer when known as "dentures."

Admen and packagers, of course, are not the only euphemizers. Almost any way of earning a salary above the level of ditchdigging is known as a profession rather than a job. Janitors for several years have been elevated by image-conscious unions to the status of "custodians"; nowadays, a teen-age rock guitarist with three chords to his credit can class himself with Horowitz as a "recording artist." Cadillac dealers refer to autos as "pre-owned" rather than "secondhand." Government researchers concerned with old people call them "senior citizens." Ads for bank credit cards and department stores refer to "convenient terms"–meaning 18% annual interest rates payable at the convenience of the creditor.

Jargon, the sublanguage peculiar to any trade, contributes to euphemism when its terms seep into general use. The stock market, for example, rarely "falls" in the words of Wall Street analysts. Instead it is discovered to be "easing" or found to have made a "technical correction" or "adjustment." As one financial writer notes: "It never seems to 'technically adjust' upward." The student New Left, which shares a taste for six-syllable words with Government bureaucracy, has concocted a collection of substitute terms for use in politics. To "liberate," in the context of campus uproars, means to capture and occupy. Four people in agreement form a "coalition." In addition to "participatory democracy," which in practice is often a description of anarchy, the university radicals have half seriously given the world "anticipatory Communism," which means to steal. The New Left, though, still has a long way to go before it can equal the euphemism-creating ability of Government officials. Who else but a Washington economist would invent the phrase "negative saver" to describe someone who spends more money than he makes?

A persistent source of modern euphemisms is the feeling, inspired by the prestige of science, that certain words contain implicit subjective judgments, and thus ought to be replaced with more "objective" terms. To speak of "morals" sounds both superior and arbitrary, as though the speaker were indirectly questioning those of the listener. By substituting "values," the concept is miraculously turned into a condition, like humidity or mass, that can be safely measured from a distance. To call someone "poor," in the modern way of thinking, is to speak pejoratively of his condition, while the substitution of "disadvantaged" or "underprivileged," indicates that poverty wasn't his fault. Indeed, writes Linguist Mario Pei in a new book called *Words in Sheep's*

Clothing (Hawthorn; $6.95), by using "underprivileged," we are "made to feel that it is all our fault." The modern reluctance to judge makes it more offensive than ever before to call a man a liar; thus there is a "credibility gap" instead. No up-to-date teacher would dare refer to a child as "stupid" or a "bad student"; the D+ student is invariably an "underachiever" or a "slow learner."

FORBIDDEN WORDS

The liberalization of language in regard to sex involves the use of perhaps a dozen words. The fact of their currency in what was once known as polite conversation raises some unanswered linguistic questions. Which, really, is the rose, and which the other name? Is "lovemaking" a euphemism for the four-letter word that describes copulation? Or is this blunt Anglo-Saxonism a dysphemism for making love? Are the old forbidden obscenities really the crude bedrock on which softer and shyer expressions have been built? Or are they simply coarser ways of expressing physical actions and parts of the human anatomy that are more accurately described in less explicit terms? It remains to be seen whether the so-called forbidden words will contribute anything to the honesty and openness of sexual discussion. Perhaps their real value lies in the acidic, expletive power to shock, which is inevitably diminished by overexposure. Perhaps the Victorians, who preferred these words unspoken and unprinted, will prove to have had a point after all.

For all their prudery, the Victorians were considerably more willing than modern men to discuss ideas—such as social distinctions, morality and death—that have become almost unmentionable. Nineteenth century gentlewomen whose daughters had "limbs" instead of suggestive "legs" did not find it necessary to call their maids "housekeepers," nor did they bridle at referring to "upper" or "lower" classes within society. Rightly or wrongly, the Victorian could talk without embarrassment about "sin," a word that today few but clerics use with frequency or ease. It is even becoming difficult to find a doctor, clergyman or undertaker (known as a "mortician") who will admit that a man has died rather than "expired" or "passed away." Death has not lost its sting; the words for it have.

PSYCHOLOGICAL NECESSITY

There is little if any hope that euphemisms will ever be excised from mankind's endless struggle with words that, as T. S. Eliot lamented, bend, break and crack under pressure. For one thing, certain kinds of everyday euphemisms have proved their psychological necessity. The uncertain morale of an awkward teenager may be momentarily buoyed if he thinks of himself as being afflicted by facial "blemishes" rather than "pimples." The label "For motion discomfort" that airlines place on paper containers undoubtedly helps the squeamish passenger keep control of his stomach in bumpy weather better than if they were called "vomit bags." Other forms of self-deception may not be beneficial, but may still be emotionally necessary. A girl may tolerate herself more readily if she thinks of herself as a "swinger" rather than as promiscuous. Voyeurs can salve their guilt feelings when they buy tickets for certain "adult entertainments" on the ground that they are implicitly supporting "freedom of artistic expression."

Lexicographer Bergen Evans of Northwestern University believes that euphemisms persist because "lying is an indispensable part of making life tolerable." It is virtuous, but a bit beside the point, to contend that lies are deployable. So they are; but they cannot be moralized or legislated away, any more than euphemisms can be. Verbal miasma, when it deliberately obscures truth, is an offense to reason. But the inclination to speak of certain things in uncertain terms is a reminder that there will always be areas of life that humanity considers too private, or too close to feelings of guilt, to speak about directly. Like stammers or tears, euphemisms will be created whenever men doubt, or fear, or do not know. The instinct is not wholly unhealthy; there is a measure of wisdom in the familiar saying that a man who calls a spade a spade is fit only to use one.

5

THE LANGUAGE OF GOVERNMENT AND POLITICS

The recent Watergate investigations have focused renewed attention on the often ambiguous language of government and politics. Douglas Bush opens this section with an article showing how language can be polluted through distortion of various kinds.

Next, Mario Pei discusses the language of the past presidential election year and of Watergate.

Stefan Kanfer follows with a devastating critique of euphemisms frequently heard from those summoned to testify before the Senate Watergate Committee.

In another article, Newsweek *editors declare that "euphemisms, circumlocutions, jargon and other high-flown forms of linguistic obfuscation have now become as pervasive as pollution."*

Finally, the New York Times *columnist Russell Baker brilliantly satirizes the cliché-laden campaign speeches of American politicians.*

Polluting Our Language

Douglas Bush

ALONG WITH OUR overriding anxieties about the state of the world and our own country, we are resentfully aware of shoddiness in cars, foods, services, in almost everything except the language we use. While an aroused public applauds the exposure of civic corruption and environmental pollution, neither the public at large nor officialdom has any concern with the corruption and pollution of language except to contribute to it. And this kind of corruption is quite as disastrous as any other, if not more so, partly because common violation of traditional usage is an ugly debasement of our great heritage, partly because sloppy English is a symptom and agent of sloppy thinking and feeling and of sloppy communication and confusion. To the famous question, "How do I know what I think till I hear what I say?" the answer might be "Do you and I know then?"

The history of this relatively modern country has created problems that have not existed in the same way or degree in the older, smaller, and much more cohesive European nations. In England the South-East Midland dialect in which Chaucer wrote became standard English, although down to our time other regional dialects have maintained an active nonstandard existence among the lower classes. But in the United States obvious historical factors have worked against such an accepted standard; the legacy of a frontier civilization, with its individualistic indifference or hostility toward cultivated speech; the relative absence of class distinctions (apart from those caused by economic and hence educational disparities); the increasing intermixture of diverse races and nationalities; and so on. Thus, according to the irate linguist (or the lighthearted American librettist) of *My Fair Lady*, the French don't care what you do so long as you speak correctly, while in America English hasn't been spoken for years. At any rate we can see much recent evidence of the conspicuous spread of bad English; Gresham's law operates no less in the linguistic than in the monetary sphere. And it seems plain that among many writers, editors, publishers, and printers there is growing indifference to the lowly but not insignificant matters of misspelling and misprints.

Whatever may be the case in other countries, in ours efforts to establish or reestablish serious respect for the mother tongue, for the precise use of words, for clarity, simplicity, and discriminating taste, have encountered much apathy or resistance, tacit or vocal, from average unconscious practice and, in recent decades, from very conscious academic doctrine. The only "errors" familiar to the mass of people seem to be the split infinitive and the ending of a sentence with a preposition, and neither of these usages is an error. As for academic doctrine, the publication in 1961 of the third edition of Webster brought on an immediate battle in which much ink and some blood were spilled. On one side were the makers and the defenders of the dictionary's widely permissive policy and procedure; the "standard" set up was current American speech; aiming at description, not prescription, the dictionary recorded, and by implication endorsed, all words, meanings and usages actually in use; it normally avoided invidious distinctions between "right" and "wrong." On such principles the idea of "error" has no validity; any intelligible expression that any people utter becomes automatically right and acceptable, no matter how it may violate orthodox rules of diction, grammar or idiom. Such wholesale pragmatism was decidedly a challenge, at least to those who believe that tennis requires a net. Along with much silent revulsion, a considerable number of writers, while recognizing the historical process of continuous change, reacted vehemently against a Philistine view of language based on the habits of the man in the street and insisted on traditional standards of language as molded by time and taste, by old writers and speakers as well as those of the moment. To such champions of good English the linguists replied with charges of pedantic schoolmarmishness, elitism, and the like.

That pitched battle died down, but people who have a conscience about language, who see the far-reaching consequences of linguistic corruption, have continued to express concern, because corruption continues to spread not merely in everyday speech and writing but in public utterances on war and peace, indeed in all areas and on all levels. A generation ago George Orwell emphasized the close connection between disorder in language and disorder in society (as, for instance, Roger Ascham, the Tudor humanist, and Milton had done in earlier ages), In an interview in the *New York Times* of October 19, 1971, W. H. Auden said: "As a poet–not as a citizen–there is only one political duty, and that is to defend one's language from corruption. And that is particularly serious now. It's being so quickly corrupted. When it's corrupted, people lose faith in what they hear, and this leads to violence." But such protests do not much affect the multitude, who need to be jolted out of their complacent insensitivity, a multitude that includes not only a large proportion of the upper-middle class but persons of such exceptional intelligence and cultivation as writers and politicians.

To cite examples from these two elite groups, the front-page review in the *New York Times Book Review* of September 19, 1971, carried, as a boldface heading, a pronouncement of John Hawkes as "feasibly, our best writer"; a couple of months before that, Secretary of the Treasury John Connally, according to a highly reliable member of his audience, fervently proclaimed that "In the early sixties we were strong, we were virulent. . . . " These are only two recent reminders of the kind of English that has become increasingly common among the educated; such blunders, and countless others, would, we may believe, have been quite impossible a hundred years ago, when educated people were literate. During the past generation or two neither early teaching (often by doubtfully literate teachers) nor reading seems to have had much effect in holding back the tide of illiteracy. Very readable authorities on English and American usage, from the canonical Fowler to William Strunk and E. B. White, Theodore Bernstein and Wilson Follett, apparently are not read by the masses of people who need them; instead, these people, both upper- and lower-middle classes (if such terms may be used), create, absorb, and propagate an ever-increasing body of what are no longer merely vulgar errors but constituent elements of American English. And American English, whatever its violations of established diction and idiom, always has chauvinistic force and heat behind it; many people would rather be wrong than be tainted with English English (not that contemporary English English is of flawless purity). Correctness smacks of effete gentility, which is abhorrent to American virility (or, to echo Secretary Connally, virulence). And recent American literature has yielded a notable flowering of the native tradition of toughness.

To intermix the concrete with the general, we might observe some random examples of the illiteracy that we meet on all sides, in print and on the air. It is more or less commonly accepted that there is such a word as "pablum," an item, if my memory serves, in Mr. Agnew's copious vocabulary (I don't know how the Latin "pabulum" came to be both syncopated and domesticated); that "torturous" means "tortuous"; that "transpire" means "happen," "occur"; that "humanitarian" is the adjective corresponding to "the humanities"; that you "convince" someone to do something; that "otherwise" is an adjective (and that any noun may be converted into an adverb by the addition of "-wise"); that "reticent" means "reluctant" (for example, in a *New York Times* editorial of some years ago, "The commission's reticence to assess blame"); that "sensuous" means "sensual" and vice versa; that "fulsome" (that is, "grossly excessive") means something like "extremely good or favorable" ("The chairman gave a fulsome eulogy of the speaker"); that "connive" means "conspire"; that "hopefully" may be thrown into a sentence anywhere as a floating rib; that "media" and "data" are singular nouns; that the past tense of "fit" is "fit" (for example, *New Republic,* June 12, 1971, p. 36; August 7-14, p. 14). I might add a few examples perhaps less common than those cited, which I have heard on the air: "The delegation's arrival was upheld by the weather"; "Two trustees escaped from prison last night"; and—on public TV—"I demure to that" (to render the commentator's pronunciation).

Wilson Follett affirmed that "affectation in an advanced culture is the chief agent of linguistic corruption." In regard to origins (or jargon, which will come up later) that may well be true, but the wholesale spread of corruption may surely be ascribed to mere infection, to the careless, unthinking assimilation of the floating germs that envelop us. The abolition, years ago, of "shall" (except for some freakish misuses) in favor of "will" as maid-of-all-work has wiped out the important distinction between simple futurity and determination ("I will not cease from mental flight, / Nor shall my sword sleep in my hand"). There is the ugly and almost universal use of "like" for "as" (legislative anxiety about cigarette advertising did not extend to cancerous grammar), and, in a lesser degree, the use of "as" for "like"—a reversal of accepted usage that has no warrant in ease, informality, or anything except perversity and contagion. Some indispensable words have been so thoroughly corrupted that they can no longer be used correctly without the probability of being misunderstood. A well-known American poet speaks of an artist's "flaunting of polite society"; a distinguished critic says that Milton "flaunts" botanical fact; the press secretary at the White House cannot think that the governor of Texas would "deliberately flaunt the wage-price freeze"

(*New York Times*, August 20, 1971, p. 1). This misuse of "flaunt" for "flout" is of course sanctioned by Webster. Contrariwise, R. G. Martin's popular biography, *Jennie*, tells of "the flouting, fashionable beauties" of late Victorian times (vol. 1, New York, 1969, p. 45). The use of "wrack" (wreck) in the sense of "rack" (torture) seems to be obliterating the right word. Bergan Evans, coauthor of *A Dictionary of Contemporary American Usage*, avows himself "wracked with admiration" for Theodore Bernstein, in a pamphlet issued by the publishers of Webster. The *New Republic* misfires in both words of a compound "dissention-wracked" (December 11, 1971, p. 7). In the long catalogue of linguistic corruptions one of the most grievous—or in the common phrase, "nerve-wracking"—is the case of "disinterested," which is almost always used in place of the now abandoned "uninterested." It is not clear why, since the usurper is not at all easier to utter than the right word; the result is that, as I said, one can't use "disinterested" correctly without the probability of being misunderstood—and there is no real synonym to fall back on.

All this adds up, not to greater force, enrichment and refinement, or clearer communication, but to the steady coarsening and blunting of the expressive and discriminating power of the language. For one thing, it threatens to cut us off from the great heritage that is a large part of what we possess. We can hardly echo Wordsworth's proud boast that we "speak the tongue / That Shakespeare spake," since we may before long lose the ability to read him: indeed many young people have lost it already. Perhaps if the counterculture or subculture does not sweep away all literature but the immediately contemporary, a favorite comedy for schools will be abridged, rewritten in the language of the street, and rechristened *Like You Like It*. The sentiments I have been expressing are of course damned as old-fogeyish by progressive thinkers. Of the compilers of the third edition of Webster and their dropping of standard authors of often insignificant contemporaries, Dwight Macdonald said: "They seem imperfectly aware of the fact that the past of the language is part of its present, that tradition is as much a fact as the violation of tradition." They seem also imperfectly aware that the use of language is, on varying levels of sophistication, an art (an unawareness shared by some modern and scholarly translators of the Bible); and the practice and judgment of art are not egalitarian and quantitative—except in the world of "pop art."

It may be replied, even by those who do not believe that whatever is is right: "So what? Misused words are the only grit in the porridge, and such things have been assimilated for centuries. They don't spell doom." Well, grit in porridge is not agreeable to taste or digestion, and consumed in quantity may be fatal; since nowadays, as we have seen, there is no effective check on the spread of illiteracy, such particles – or should we say pockets of fog? – multiply very rapidly and nourish carelessness, crudity, and confusion not merely of expression but of thought. Easy tolerance of corruption recalls, in Thomas Peacock's *The Misfortunes of Elphin* (1829), a satirical flick at Tory opposition to electoral reform: refusing to repair a dike that was in a dangerous state of decay, the tipsy prince insisted: "But I say, the parts that are rotten give elasticity to those that are sound: they give elasticity, elasticity, elasticity. If it were all sound, it would break by its own obstinate stiffness."

We know that language is always changing and growing (and also in a much smaller degree, shrinking), but acceptance of the perpetual process does not or should not mean blind surrender to the momentum or inertia of slovenly and tasteless ignorance and insensitivity. Ideally, changes should be inaugurated from above, by the masters of language (as they often have been), not from below. Language is not a tough plant that always grows toward the sun, regardless of weeds and trampling feet. From the Greeks (notably Plato) and Romans onward, many men of good will have been concerned about the use and abuse of language, the relation between the rhetoric of persuasion and private and public ethics, and all the attendant questions; and they did what they could to curb barbarism and foster taste, discipline, and integrity. One great agent of discipline, though, has lost much or most of its traditional power. In our century and our country, and perhaps somewhat less conspicuously elsewhere, classical education, with the clear-eyed concreteness of mind it nourished (not that all its products were all angels of light), has greatly declined, and whatever the great virtues of modern writing, they are not an adequate substitute for some central and instinctive qualities of the ancients. One might call many witnesses on this point, Matthew Arnold, Santayana and others, but there is a special aptness in some remarks of Evelyn Waugh, a contemporary and, whatever the general merits of his novels, a stylist of repute. In *A Little Learning: An Autobiography* (Boston, 1964), he thus sums up his schooling:

> My knowledge of English literature derived chiefly from my home. Most of my hours in the form room for ten years had been spent on Latin and Greek, History and Mathematics. Today I remember no Greek. I have never read Latin for pleasure and should be hard put to it to compose a simple epitaph. But I do

not regret my superficial classical studies. I believe that the conventional defense of them is valid; that only by them can a boy fully understand that a sentence is a logical construction and that words have basic inalienable meanings, departure from which is either conscious metaphor or inexcusable vulgarity. Those who have not been so taught—most Americans and most women—unless they are guided by some rare genius, betray their deprivation. The old-fashioned test of an English sentence—will it translate?—still stands after we have lost the trick of translation. [P. 139]

A multitude of educated people (including teachers) do not seem to be deeply concerned about language *per se* or its manifold implications. If we need illustrations of the obvious, we have evidence both rough and ready—or cloudy or slick—in the speech of many of our public men compared with that of many of their predecessors back through the seventeenth century; the urbane elegance of Adlai Stevenson was, in point of popular appeal, a heavy handicap in contrast to the amiable bumbling of General Eisenhower. It may be noted that the official proprietors of language, while they support the uninhibited, uninstructed freedom in speech in opposition to what they regard as archaic rigidity, do not themselves—apart from occasional jargon —exploit the liberty they defend. That liberty, it appears, is both scientifically sound and in accord with the spirit of American democracy; it was not, however, the creed of the founding fathers and belongs rather to the obsolete principle of *laissez faire*.

In the past, new words, new meanings, and new idioms had of necessity to undergo a period of probation; if they proved useful, they survived to enrich and refine the language. But the modern probationary period has greatly shrunk or vanished. Thanks especially to the mass media of the air, bad English can be established overnight, and not merely for the uneducated; it becomes current usage. (The same agencies, it may be added, help to inaugurate or propagate mispronunciation. We may wonder why nearly all Americans give a semi-French pronunciation to age-old English names, Bernard and Maurice; or why the third edition of Webster, departing from the strictness of the second edition, accepts such common but quite unwarranted pronunciations as "skitsophrenia" and "par-li-a-ment.") And while on occasion opponents of "standard" English delve into the past for meanings not now approved by conservative orthodoxy, the same procedure must not be allowed to uphold the great mass of traditional words and idioms that remain standard if thought, feeling, and communication are to carry their immense responsibility. Was it Churchill who said "When it is not necessary to change, it is necessary not to change"?

To the heterogeneous atoms of illiteracy that have been sampled might be added a different but related kind of bad English, although only a word can be said about its manifold varieties: that is, jargon. There is the simple jargon of pretentious padding, sometimes pseudo-technical: no one ever teaches in college but always "at the college level"; a crow is not black but basically or essentially black; nothing happens before anything else but always "prior to." No one feels pleasure or anxiety or fear; he feels a sense of pleasure, a sense of anxiety, a sense of fear. A politician doesn't say "Yes" but—if he is relatively forthright—"My answer is in the affirmative." Official and political rhetoric is not, of course, peculiar to our time or country. We remember that words are to be understood "in a Pickwickian sense"; we remember too Dickens' opinion of the parliamentary debates he reported. But it would appear that in modern times the mildew has grown much thicker. The recent death of Sir Alan Herbert recalls an example he once provided: if, he said, Nelson had lived during the Second World War, he would not have signaled to the fleet "England expects that every man will do his duty," but would have proclaimed: "England anticipates that as regards the current emergency, personnel will face up to the issues and exercise appropriately the functions allocated to their respective occupation groups." And we cannot forget the exquisite *jeu d'esprit* of an American journalist, the Gettysburg address written in the style of General Eisenhower. On a less innocent level, political and official deception and downright lying may be accomplished directly (since the public is assumed to have a short memory) or through a smoke screen of evasive verbiage. Volumes could be filled with this kind of rhetoric, but the subject is too depressingly familiar to dwell upon.

A prime creator of "sophisticated" jargon has been advertising—who would not be allured by a baroque cocktail costume?—but that, like officialese, is too familiar to linger with. There are the kinds of jargon purveyed by the various tribes of scientists, social scientists, and literary critics. While there are technical ideas and data that require a special language, it may be used to conceal a lack of ideas or to give thin ones impressive authority. I once had a visit from a bright and buoyant sophomore who having received a C, wished to explain, first, that he was a Thomist in his thinking, and, secondly, that his writing, which I had termed clotted jargon, was "the English of the future"—a prophetic oracle that left me vanquished and dumb. Among parodies of psychological jargon a favorite of mine—because it exposes more than linguistic flatulence—is one that readers may not have met, the opening of the Twenty-third Psalm, rendered by Alan Simpson, the president of Vassar College; "The Lord is my external, internal, integrated mechanism; I shall not be deprived of gratifications for my visceral generic hungers or my need dispositions. He motivates me to orient myself toward a nonsocial object effectiveness significance. He positions me in a nondecisional situation. He maximizes my adjustment." I read somewhere that Buster Keaton was asked by a sociologist in rotund polysyllabic language a question which in brief was whether his films tried to depict the plight of the little man in a bewildering world: said Keaton, after due reflection, "Well, we thought of a gag, and then we thought of another gag." For an early example of deflation we might go back to Chaucer's Franklin, who disclaimed any knowledge of "Colours of rethoryk": "For th'orisonte hath reft the sonn his lyght,— / This is as muche to seye as it was nyght!"

We have noticed only a few examples of the misuse of words and of the varieties of jargon that increasingly debase current English. We have not touched the abundance and vitality of clichés, which will not wear out "in the foreseeable future"; but this piece must "grind to a halt." For a final reminder of the illustrious past, we might recall Spenser's eulogy of "Dan Chaucer, well of English undefyled"; Mr. Auden was quoted at the outset; and there is T. S. Eliot's echo of Mallarmé "To purify the dialect of the tribe" (*Little Gidding*). Language must be protected not only by poets but by the saving remnant of people who care—even though, as the flood rises, their role may be nearer King Canute's than Noah's.

The Language of the Election
and Watergate Years

Mario Pei

Before entering upon my main topic, it may be worthwhile to record a few samples of what less indulgent critics would style "Crimes against the Language"—the customary crop of accidental misspellings, misusages of grammar, erroneous interpretations of our vaunted linguistic heritage.

There is, for instance, a *Newark Star-Ledger* editorial (March 24, 1973) which speaks of a judiciary concerned with "meeting out justice"; and the description vouchsafed by the Aerospace editor of *Los Angeles Times* (Oct. 23, 1972) of the SR-71 as a "thoroughly honest and docile airplane in normal traffic pattern flight," which makes one wonder how a dishonest plane would behave. Elsewhere, the spelling "tripulets" for "triplets" leads one to surmise that "quadruplets" might be reincarnated as "quadrupeds." The *Graffiti* editor characterizes the popular "You know—" as "words used by people who don't." Author Lawrence Schoonover offers the case of the labor leader who complains that certain politicians change their position all the time, "now here, now there, like Willie the Wisp"; along with that of the lady evangelist who asks: "Are you convicted that Jesus came to save you?" and when she gets an affirmative reply goes on to add: "Just wonderful! Wish we were all convicted!" followed up by the sportscaster who asserts: "We will go over and over our shortcomings until we have perfected them." He bemoans the loss of distinction between initial *w* or *wh*, as in "wet" and "whet," or "wail" and "whale," and advocates the addition of Chinese-style classifiers of the "look-see" type, such as "wet-water" *vs.* "whet-sharpen," or "wail-bemoan" *vs.* "whale-fish." Columnist O'Brian remarks that "Godspell" is so clean that it has been renamed "Goshspell," and adds a case of words that fall into desuetude and oblivion, illustrated by the little girl who asks her father "Who was Rudy Vallee?" When he replies that he was somebody who used to sing through a megaphone, she goes on to inquire: "What's a megaphone?"

Columnist James Kilpatrick reports that in papers prepared by applicants for grants to professional journalists one applicant came up with "similiar," "knowlingly," "in-laid," and "effecting" for "affecting," a second "comperability," "numberous," and "Louisana," a third with "elegible," "jockying," "supercede," "thru," and "franchize."

It is not too often that we hear a complaint about the misuse of a slang form, but Mike Royko protests against the general use of "clout" in the sense of having the power to strike a stout blow in a given cause ("He's got lots of clout"), and claims not only that the expression originated in Chicago, but also that it has strayed from its primitive use, which he equates with political pull, or even the wielder thereof. Examples: "My tax bill is only $1.50. I got clout in the assessor's office." "Who's clouting for you?" "My clout wrote to the mayor." I have sought confirmation in vain in the various dictionaries, including those of slang; but Royko is a native speaker of Chicagoese, and I feel inclined to accept his authority.

Before leaving the topic of English usage, I have a poser of my own. It was stressed in the press and on TV that the midwife's profession should be pronounced "midwif(f)ery," with a short second *i*, following a purely British usage, unrecognized by any major American dictionary. How then should we pronounce "housewifery," for which even the British Oxford prefers the pronunciation that is normal to us? With a full rather than a half wife?

Crimes against foreign languages come into play as well; but these are of the oft-repeated type, such as pronouncing Paola, Kansas, like "Payola," or Conigliaro's name as koh-nig-lee-AH-roh instead of koh-nee-LYAH-roh, or feminizing French *employé, fiancé* into employee, fiancee in spelling, and *Canadiens* into *Canadiennes* in pronunciation. At any rate, the majority come under the heading of advertising. But one that is particularly striking, going with AMGOT and CON EDISON in producing abbreviations that arouse laughter abroad is the recently abbreviated COCU for Consultation on Church Union, an organization that aims at promoting unity among Protestant denominations totaling twenty million members. Did no member of the board know any French?

In retaliation, the French government has launched a crusade to purge French of recent popular additions from the tongue of the Anglo-Americans. Among terms singled out for extinction are "flashback," "one-man show," "hit parade," "features," "zoning," "jumbo jet," "show business," "scoop," "space craft," "kitchenette," "know-how." Their replacements are *rétrospectif, spectacle solo, palmarés* (literally "honor list"), *variés, zonage, gros-porteur* (literally "big carrier"), *industrie de spectacle, exclusivité, aéronef* (literally "airship"; would not *astronef* have served the purpose better?), *cuisinette, savoir-faire.* If I may be permitted one observation on *savoir-faire,* which has to do with personality, likability, diplomacy, getting along with people: this had previously been borrowed from French by English, and altogether lacks the mechanical-industrial connotations of "know-how." It will confuse French speakers rather than help them.

1972 was a presidential election year; 1973 may be described as the Year of Watergate, even though Watergate's events began while the campaign was still in progress.

Sideshows in weasel wording, before, during, and after both facts are exemplified by Governor Reagan's creation of "Teddycare" for the all-comprehensive Medicare-Medicaid program proposed by Senator Edward Kennedy; a similar coinage of "Educare" for a program designed to extend the blessings of higher education to retirees; "Demogrant" to describe McGovern's proposal of one thousand dollars a year to every man, woman and child in the United States; Vice-President Agnew's "radiclib," merging radical and liberal, and his earlier alliterative description of Mayor Lindsay, then beset by presidential ambitions, as the "fumbling flugelman of Fun City." In the 1973 New York primaries, a slogan about "making waves" if he got elected may or may not have been instrumental in carrying candidate Goldin to the post of Chancellor the the Exchequer of that same city.

More specific to the campaign was McGovern's slogan about "taxing the same way money made by money and money made by man," outstripped only by his "Come home, America!" and his radio-TV description as "McGovern—Democrat—for the people." Some had the effrontery to inquire "What people?" in view of Democratic primary principles which included the winner-take-all of California and the proportional representation on the various delegations by sex and color (but not by ethnic groups), invoked against Daley's duly elected Illinois delegation. McGovern's long-haired yippee followers, whom the Republicans had called "creeps," were described as sensitive to that appellation, and were rebaptized "non-delegates." "Chairperson" and "chairpeople" were created at the 1972 Democratic convention to replace an insufficient "chairman" and an awkward "chairwoman." It was my own suggestion that these new terms be further abbreviated into "C.P." (or "SEEPEE") on the analogy of "M.C." ("EMCEE") and the older "C.B." ("SEABEE"), with the further possibility, through functional change, of turning "C.P." into a verb ("to C.P. a meeting").

The two candidates shared certain linguistic formations. "Nixonomics," coined by the Democrats, was extended to "McGovernomics" by the *New York Times* financial editor, while columnist Peter Lisagor in his May 16, 1972, column offered "Nixon Watchers," "Nixonology," and even worked his way back to "Lyndonology." McGovern was given personal credit for having playfully told some pro-Muskie hecklers "Hush, you Muskies!" while one of his followers seemingly created the fake slogan "Trusk Mustie!" "Govern for McPresident!" and "The cities are not unMcGovernable" may have come from either friend or foe. Vice-President Agnew came in for a few cracks: "an Agnewesque game of golf" is attributed to Muskie, while James Reston of the *New York Times* is the source of "Agnewsticism," a new Washington cult to the effect that the truth is safer in the hands of the politicians than in those of the new media, and that the administration is always right, especially when it's wrong.

On the Republican side, the President himself is credited with "governess government" and the "Spirit of Apollo," replacing the earlier Spirits of Camp David and Glassboro, along with the later modest, yet ambitious "Generation of Peace." "Southern Strategy" may have originated with John Mitchell. Then there was the "economic game plan," probably coined by Nixon, who is an inveterate football fan, and the "open-mouth policy," deplored by his opponents, which soon gave way to Phases One, Two, Three, Three and a Half, and Four, still deplored by his opponents. Less jocular were descriptions of Nixon's personal entourage as the "German Mafia" (but President Kennedy had previously been charged with having an "Irish Mafia"), and "All the King's Krauts." There was a Jewish joke about good chicken soup being renamed "Nixon Soup," because "it's all perfectly clear."

Washington Post cartoonist Herbert Block (Herblock), who is not a Nixon admirer, offered in his book *The State of the Union* a term, "the New Prolitics," which has to do with changes in word-meanings insinuated into the public consciousness by public relations ("PR") men and by slick PR television techniques. "Whiter than the White House" is offered to the advertising world. Other innovations, according to Herblock, are the "preventive event" (widespread heralding of a forthcoming but delayed presidential activity); the "non-event" (such as the Vice-President telling the President and his cabinet what a wonderful job they are doing); the "world-shaking event" (moon landing, reshuffling of departments, China-Russia visits, wage-price freezes); the "misspoke ploy" (an occasional slip of the presidential tongue). Typical of the Herblock technique is a cartoon in which Nixon addresses a press conference and makes two things perfectly clear: 1. the country is in fine shape, and 2. Congress is to blame for the mess we're in.

Even Nixon's foreign policy of rapprochement with China and Russia did not escape criticism. Starting with the tour of a Chinese Ping-Pong team in the United States, it was at once noted that the President no longer referred to "Red China," or even "Mainland China," but to the "People's Republic of China." As the plot thickened, critics began to talk of "Ping-Pong" or "Chow Mein Diplomacy," forgetting that the first term had been heralded in 1901 by a *Punch* cartoon which showed Britannia and China playing Ping-Pong over table labeled "diplomacy." Full accord with the People's Republic of China was retarded by the question of what to do with the Republic of China we had sponsored in Taiwan. Our "Two-China Policy" was quickly satirized into a "One and a half-China Policy" (this antedates Phase Three and a Half of the economic game plan by a full year). But the UN General Assembly, with or without our connivance, soon ended that.

Of paramount importance since the beginning of 1973 was the Watergate incident, still unresolved as I write. To be sure, it had occurred in 1972, but at that time few took notice of it. Its first name was the "Watergate caper," a sort of political prank played upon the opposition, much in the same fashion as one football team kidnapping the ram which is the mascot of the opposing team on the eve of the game. McGovern tried to make it an issue during the final phases of the presidential campaign, but to no avail. Then press, TV, the Senate, and the judge who tried the men caught at Watergate converged their efforts to bring it into the public consciousness. The public shrugged, both here and abroad. Politics, after all, is politics, and dirty politics is an ancient and time-honored phenomenon. "So what else is new?" was the comment of an Italian newspaper. "We have a bigger bugging and wire-tapping scandal of our own." East of the Iron Curtain, where government "controls" are part of everyday life, there wasn't even a ripple. Many Americans wondered why, in a society that tolerates attempts by subversives to paralyze the life of the nation's capital, burn and bomb government and university buildings, break into government offices, pilfer and destroy government documents, so much attention should be devoted to what seemed at first an episode of nonviolent lawlessness committed by individuals.

It was only after the administration made the monumental blunder of calling off Phase Two of the economic program, causing prices to rise to unprecedented heights and the dollar to fall to unprecedented depths, that the people really became Watergate conscious, very possibly by reflex action. What had been a caper worthy of schoolboys now became, in the words of columnist Joseph Alsop, the "Watergate horror" (he used the term five times in a single column). Others picked up the new expression, to the point where even Claire Boothe Luce used it in a *New York Times* article of June 3, 1973, which was a strong defense of the administration. Alsop later retreated from his extreme position and spoke instead of the "Watergate obsession," while Ernest Cuneo called it the "Watergate joggle." But Representative H. Runnel of New Mexico came out with the statement that henceforth tourists to Washington would be interested in three things: the Washington Monument, the Lincoln Memorial, and the "Tomb of the Unknown Burglar." As for popular consciousness, *Parade* for June 17, 1973, informs us that American youths have turned "Watergate" into a verb and integrated it into their lexicons, using such phrases as "Don't Watergate me!" ("Don't compromise or involve me!"), "Don't Watergate my cigarette lighter!" ("Don't swipe it!"), "Are you pulling a Watergate on me?" ("Are you trying to involve me in something illegal?"). Obviously, "Watergate" as a part of the language is here to stay.

It is not for me, especially at this point, while both Senate and Grand Jury investigations are in progress, to pass judgment on what columnist Carl Rowan calls "the most sinister political crimes in the nation's history," forgetting that the Warren whitewash to the contrary notwithstanding, there still remains unsolved the mystery of President Kennedy's assassination and who may have been involved in it over and above the Communist-trained man who fired the fatal shots (Leo Janos, a former Johnson aide, in the July 1973 *Atlantic Monthly* describes Lyndon Johnson's strong suspicions on that score). If President Nixon was reluctant to believe in the involvement of some of his closest associates, it is true that President Truman also described the Alger Hiss case as a "red herring" before the full facts came out.

The purely linguistic outcroppings of Watergate are numerous. When some of those involved stated that they were not going to be scapegoats for the higher-ups, they were humorously described by one columnist as unwilling to "scape their goats." Senator Adlai Stevenson said that we had passed from the New Deal to the Fair Deal, and now to "The Deal" pure and simple. Irving Janis described the participants in the affair as victims of "Groupthink," elaborating this concept about a cohesive group that fosters the shared illusion of invulnerability and tends to minimize the risks of an enterprise with further examples from the Bay of Pigs episode, and even the Vietnam war, which everyone, from President Johnson down, encouraged everyone else to think we were going to win. Don Bacon stated that the Nixon campaign aides who monitored the activities of McGovern and Shriver styled themselves the "Response Mechanism," while their opponents called them the "Attack Group." The men delegated to break into the office of Ellsberg's psychiatrist were called the "Plumbers," seeking to repair real or fancied security leaks (in this connection, E. Howard Hunt, who wrote some whodunits and had them published under a *nom-de-plume*, later had them reissued under his own name, which Jack O'Brian styled his "nom-de-plumber"). In the course of the Senate hearings, the statement "when the going gets tough, the tough get going" was attributed to John Mitchell. "Caught with their trousers at half-mast" was the colorful expression coined by Carl Rowan for some of the accused, while Vice President Agnew described the Senate hearings as a "political beauty contest," with "Perry-Masonish features." Walter Cronkite, describing the missing witness Segretti, stated that his name meant "secrets" in Italian, which was an error (*segreti* is the term for "secrets," and the single or double *t* gives the two words different pronunciations and derivations). There appeared in a memo circulated by the Office of Information a recommended shift from "the President" to "President Nixon" when referring to Mr. Nixon (possibly because the first term was reminiscent of the "Campaign to reelect the President").

The display of mingled glee and sanctimoniousness on the part of those who do not like Nixon continues and will continue, even though a Gallup Poll conducted in June, 1973, and reported by CBS-TV, indicated that if the election had been held again at that time, approximately the same percentage of voters would have preferred Nixon to McGovern and, by lesser majorities, even to Humphrey and Muskie. This percentage changed in an August poll to indicate a very slight edge for McGovern over Nixon, but since the poll coincided with the Great Beef Shortage and a further drastic rise in food prices, and the question "Why?" is never asked in these polls, one may wonder whether the drop in the President's popularity was due to Watergate or to dissatisfaction with economic happenings that reflected the sale of our vast grain surpluses to the U.S.S.R. What remained unchanged was the over-whelming percentage of people who said Nixon should neither resign nor be impeached.*

The Senate hearings brought out other interesting linguistic points. There was the coming into vogue of the expression "at this point in time." There was the learned discussion of the term "misprision of justice, if any ("misprision" is an archaic legal term that goes back to the sixteenth century in the sense of "scorn," "contempt," retaining the older French meanings, which have been modified in modern French, where *méprendre* is "to make a mistake," and *méprise* a misunderstanding).

The learned Senators and witnesses took some liberties with English pronunciation and syntax, as when, on July 29, Senator Baker used "vestigal" for "vestigial," and Senator Ervin used "rout" for "route," while Ehrlichman on July 30, referring to two stories circulated by Deane, stated that "neither one of them are true." This apart from the Chairman's statements that Watergate is a greater tragedy than the Civil War, and that failure to submit the tapes means the end of the Republic; or Senator Inouye's audible "What a liar!" which brought the retort from Attorney White that the Senator was a Jap. For this there was a precedent in Vice-President Agnew's description of one of his friends as a "fat Jap" and brings up the question whether the mere abbreviation of a national designation should be considered derogatory or insulting. Lastly, there is President Nixon's reference to people who want to "wallow in Watergate," and Evans and Novak's description of the "Watergate atrocities" (August 10), which goes Alsop's "Watergate horror" one better.

Next to politics in weasel-word interest is the 1972–1973 language of advertising. Among the dozens of striking items is the continued use of "save," something you are said to do when you buy an item that is either on special "sale" or which one firm supposedly sells at a lower price than its competitors. This usage even led to a TV satire, where a giddy wife comes

---

* Dr. Pei wrote this article well in advance of the dismissal of Special Prosecutor Archibald Cox, the related resignation of Attorney General Elliot Richardson and dismissal of his assistant William Ruckelshaus, and the strong public reaction against these events—which, characteristically of the spirit of the time, were all subsumed under the journalistic shorthand term "the Cox firing."—Ed.

home with a three hundred dollar fur stole and explains to her distraught husband that she bought it with the money she had "saved" by buying three separate household appliances, each for one hundred dollars less than granny had paid for them. Hand-in-hand goes the "WEEE-O!" of a food chain, followed by "How–prices have changed!" But they don't tell you in which direction they have changed. Perhaps "WEEE-O! should be replaced by "We know!" Then there is that thirteenth month of the year, "Junuary," coined by a firm that offers you in January what might be offered in June; but what's the advantage? "Inscrutably delicious" is the way a Chinese restaurant advertises its cuisine, overlooking the double meaning in the first word.

As a linguist, I particularly detest two things: the mishandling of foreign languages for advertising purposes, and the use of phony accents, both native and foreign. Why should Chef Boyardee (boh-YAR-dee) come out as boy-ar-DEE, or Gino be spelt Jeno? Why "Cotto Salami" for what should be "Salame Cotto"? Why should Jean-Pierre Aumont mispronounce his own language and say ZEE-zah-nee for zee-zah-NEE? Why should a *sangria* said to be made in Spain be spelled "Sant'gria," as though it were the name of a female saint, when the word comes from *sangre* "blood"? Then there is that ad that tells you that man is what he eats. This, of course, is not true, and may even be offensive (you eat pork chops, therefore you are a pig?); but in German, where the saying originated, it happens to be a pun on words (*Mann ist was er isst,* with *ist* ["is"] and *isst* ["eats"] pronounced exactly alike); but this is altogether lost in English. Aumont's French accent is authentic, save for his deliberately misplaced accent on one word; so is the Spanish accent of the characters who advertise a Spanish dry sherry. But what shall we say of the German accent of Mad King Ludwig of Bavaria as he proclaims the beer-fest that made Munich famous?

Worst of all are the phony native accents that offend the ear: the toothless pseudo-New Englander who advertises an otherwise excellent bread; the phony Italian-American of Jimmy Durante or, worse yet, Rocky Graziano; the phony western tones of Johnny Cash with his concluding "like they say"; and what about the low-pitched, apologetic girl who identifies herself as "the voice of your friendly transmission," and bemoans your neglect of her needs for greasing and repairs?

Of course, the criticism does not apply where the intention to spoof is obvious, as in *Hee Haw*'s Tennessee portrayal, or those Alka Seltzer Jewish gems that have become proverbial ("Do yourself a favor!"; "Try it! You'll like it!"; "Not a little bit of everything; everything!"). What can be done with the human voice and its tones in the way of arousing a favorable impression for the product is demonstrated by the girl who is told by her mother to do a little dusting of the furniture with a polish before the guests arrive: "Lemon Pledge?!?!"

This could go on and on.* The Committee for the Rejection of Obnoxious Commercials (CROC) has seen fit to offer a CROC award for the year's worst commercials. Their suggestions include Mr. Whipple and his Charmin; Pristene's stimulating discussion of deodorant sprays between a mother and daughter; Wisk's "Ring Around the Collar!"; Playtex's Cross Your Heart bra. But there are many, many other candidates one could mention ("Fly me!"; "Sorry, Charlie!"; "Bullish on America"; "It's the real thing!"; "the Uncola").

Commercialism in advertising is, of course, a bane of our capitalistic society. But it is spreading to Communist countries. The label of a Chinese wine designed for export to the English-speaking market says in part: "Nutritious and roborant; promoting the brain and recovering the memory; strengthening the organs and systems of generations"; further on, it is described as good for "general weakness, untimely senility, kidney trouble, neurasthenia, sores, dizziness, anemia, poor memory, involuntary perspirations, insomnia, palefaces, poor appetites." Can it be that once our Commu-competitors get going they'll beat us at our own game?

Closely linked by a web of publicity to the world of advertising is the realm of stage and screen. Here we find creations galore: the brand-new "Obie" award suggested for Off-Broadway (O.B.) productions (as though we didn't have enough of these mutual admiration society celebrations); Jack O'Brian's *stripteuse* for a female devotee of strip-teasing (with *stripteur* for the male of the species, we presume?); such choice expressions as "Dingbat," "Meathead," and "Lovable Bigot" from TV's most popular program, *All in the Family*. There are, too, ancient bloopers of usage that are revived with ancient pictures, as when Charlton Heston, playing Moses in the 1956 *Ten Commandments*, is immortalized in the phrase "This is the road that I must trod!" New York's Philharmonic is said to be facing a "desperation gap" between intake and deficit spending. "One bean" is the expression for one hundred dollars

---

* We are moved to nominate all "mini-" compounds for early retirement. An ad in *New York* (11/26/73), for instance, calls a Judith Crist Film Weekend a "minivacation."–Ed.

introduced by the rock-and-roll industry (but this word, according to Wentworth and Flexner, has shifted its monetary symbolism from an archaic five dollar gold piece, or a British pound [1859] to one dollar [1941], and now again). "Money in the bank" is the graphic term used in Hollywood for such hardy perennials as *Sound of Music, Mary Poppins, Snow White* and *Bambi*, which are resurrected every eight or ten years.

There are also startling shifts in permissible vocabulary. John O'Connor reminds us in the *New York Times* that in 1960 WNBC censored the use of "WC" on the Jack Paar Show, while today we have *V.D. Blues*, with such songs as "Don't give a dose to the one you love most!" Young audiences, says a WCBS vice-president, have forced us into being more candid.

On the truly arty stage, we have progressed from the "Cult of the Absurd" of Ionesco to Beckett's *Breath*, which requires no actors and lasts 35 seconds, yet is described as a play. "As Close to Silence as a Man Can Get" comments reviewer A. Alvarez. I would substitute "inanity," or even "insanity," for "silence."

Pari passu with stage and screen in creativeness goes journalism. Jack O'Brian in rapid succession not only contributes "smutacular," "jazzcotek," "pesterazzi" (the American version of the Italian *paparazzi*), "croupiess" for a female croupier, "she nonchalanted," "Rhonda Fleming flamored into the Casino Russe," "a rose is a rose is an itch" (this for a flower allergy), and a perhaps over-familiar "Dickieburt" for Richard Burton; he also suggests *S-sssss* as the title for a King Cobra movie, and reminds us that it was commentator Paul Harvey who in 1961 devised the term "skyjacking" after being among the victims of the first such crime.

"Ganglord" is coined by an editor for the Costello of Kefauver Investigation fame; "blood doning" by WCBS News; "beautility" (combining beauty and utility in architecture) by Ada Huxtable; "dystopia" (the opposite of "utopia") by Lyman Sargent in *The Futurist* (he describes it as negative, pessimistic pictures of the future, mainly in science fiction); "paramedic" by Ann Landers for a male nurse. "The Emmigrants" is coined by Roger Ebert, who apparently can't make up his mind whether they are immigrants or emigrants (they can, of course, be both, from the standpoint of two different countries). Stanley Davis attributes to Mayor Lindsay an attempt to improve the Fun City image by calling muggings and police crime reports "Manhattan acupuncture." From Britain, Eric Partridge gives us "to stormy-petrel with éclat." I am not certain who created "confortability," "approbate," and "momarchy" ("She ran her household as though it was a momarchy"). "Gazatka" sounds Russian, and is described as "a rough time." "Honcho" sounds Spanish, but where does it come from, and precisely what does it mean? "Maven," a cross between a fan and a kibitzer, is said to come from Hebrew. And why "cold duck" for a type of wine?

The swift changeability in the language of youth was vividly brought out in a news item about a Pentagon language guidebook for returning POW's, designed to bring them up to date on all they had missed during the years of their captivity, which, after all, did not average more than five. Yet the introduction to the guidebook says "During your long absence, the language of the youth has changed in somewhat the same way as the language you used differed from that of your parents during your younger years."

I have not been fortunate enough to view a copy of the guidebook, but abundant samples are forthcoming from other sources. Jon Horn, in his *New York Times* article *Glomming the Apple* (the "Big Apple" is an old slang nickname for New York), offers such gems as "bagel babies" (Jewish girls); "glom" (to take in, digest; earlier it was a noun and meant "hand"); "grotty" (gritty, seamy; at an earlier period, it was occasionally used as a term of admiration); "hang tough" (to persevere); "punched out" (mugged, beaten up); "taken off" (robbed); "The Scene" (where it's at; but this goes back to at least 1957). In response to a request for information from columnists Helen and Sue Bottel, the following changes were volunteered by young readers: "groovy" to "gravy baby"; "right on" to "right there" or "left arm"; "out of sight" to "out of state"; "scram" to "make like a banana and split." Additional contributions: "crunchy" for "great"; "tuff tootie" for "too bad!"; "baddest" for "the best." Favorite interjections for various occasions range from "Oh, peanut butter!" "Fudgecycle!" and "Son of a Pickle" (or "Son of a Biscuit") to "oof," "doof," and "skidoop." "Peanuts!" is said to have replaced the old "Wow!"; the imported "poco loco" describes a dumb action, and "cootie" means "derrière," in "Get your cootie off the table!"

Daniel Yankelovitch, a social researcher, gives a list of counterculture aversions (words that get them up tight) that includes "professional," "system," "planning," "organization," "technology," "mechanization," "institutions," "determination," "programming," "achievement." It figures.

On the drug addiction scene, Carl Rowan gives the following names of barbiturates: "downers," "goofballs," "red devils," "yellow jackets," "blue angels," "Christmas trees" (the last four refer, specifically, to seconal, nembutal, amythal, and tuinal). "Sunshine" and "sopors" are presented elsewhere; the first is described as a "superior" type of LSD, the latter as non-barbiturate sleeping pills. For cocaine, we have the following alternatives: "snow," "flake," "girl," "her lady," "happy trails," "nose-candy," "star-spangled powder," "gift of the sun god," "heaven-leaf," "rich man's drug."

As Eve said to her despondent spouse as they left the Garden of Eden: "Adam, we are living in an age of transition!" Yet Socrates, in the fifth century B.C., complained of the children of his day, who loved luxury, showed contempt for authority and disrespect for their elders, chattered incessantly, ate too much, and tyrannized their teachers. So why complain?

The vocabulary of Women's Liberation has been pretty thoroughly explored. Most of the recent items are in the nature of puns and jokes. There is, for instance, the spurious report that while California and Iowa were considering nominating the ladybug as the official state insect, Women's Rights advocates insisted that it be renamed the "personbug." In this connection, Roderick Nordel in the *Christian Science Monitor* offers a list of ingenious suggestions: "the League of Person Voters," "the Persons' Aid Society," "the Person Scouts of America," "the Persons of the American Revolution," "Old Person Time," "Person Machree," "the Person I Love," "a mailperson," "personfingers," and even an affectionate diminutive, "Perssy." The suggestion that "history" be reshaped into "herstory" runs into etymological difficulties, while Ann Landers reports a case of a waitress who met with reproof when she asked some middle-aged women tourists from England "What will you girls have?" on a rather flimsy ground that "girl" has a cheap connotation in England; "madam" was suggested as a replacement, but "What will you madams have?" runs into one of the American connotations of "madam."

On the more authentic side, we have the establishment of WITCH (Women's International Terrorist Conspiracy from Hell), an extremist feminist movement, plus the coining of "Nasties" for the Libbers by their avowed enemies, the "Pussycat League." "Daughter-of-a-Bitch" is suggested as the appropriate replacement for "S.O.B." when circumstances warrant, and "jockette" for lady jockey has also been reported, now that the item is available. The coinage of matronymics used as family names, such as "Franchild," "Velmadaughter," and "Silverwoman" rounds out the current crop.

In the field of sex, there is the Schulz book title *Snoopy, the Sensuous Dog*; "The Wonderful World of Flesh" used in connection with *Love American Style*; the highly scientific *Torschlusspanik* ("Closing Door Panic"), reported in *National Observer* as the label given by psychologists to the phenomenon of older men chasing younger women because time is running out on them. From Australia comes a cute "a naughty" to betoken sex relations out of wedlock. Ann Landers is responsible for "sex as a contact sport," "dancing as the vertical expression of a horizontal idea," and the resurrected, but also reversed French saying "There are no frigid wives, just lousy lovers." Jack O'Brian contributes "Filth Estate" for pornography, "incumbent companion" for an actress' male partner without benefit of clergy, and informs us that director Bertolucci taught Marlon Brando the obscene vocabulary for *Last Tango in Paris* which Brando included in his "Sintax." James Bacon quotes Russ Meyer, King of the Nudies, to the effect that when it comes to giving a film a rating, "north and south pelvic movements rate an X—east and west an R".

More melancholy is the lexicon of homosexuality, which Mike Nichols defines as "once the love that dare not speak its name; now it won't shut up." Here we find "herosexual" and "hobosexual," "Mother" (the dominant partner), "Hildaboopsie," combining "Hilda," the homosexual term for horrible, with "boopsala," a Yiddish term of endearment; and "AC-DC" for a double homosexual. The use of butter in *Last Tango* has led European viewers to relabel it *The Butter Film*, and a Paris promoter wanted to use Maria Schneider's picture on butter packets, but was turned down.

The black language includes "dapping," the practice of slapping and grasping one another's hands in a complicated greeting symbolic of racial solidarity; "blackonomics," possibly on the analogy of "Nixonomics"; "tricknology," said to be what the whites practice on blacks; "blackthink," one whose thinking is oriented along black lines. "Blacula" is the black take-off on Dracula, but "blacksploitation" has been coined to describe films produced by whites and designed to appeal to blacks and their money.

Roderick Nordell, with tongue in cheek, reports an interview with Rennie Fairweather, described as the author of *How to Be Nice to White People* (subtitle: *White on White*). Whites, he implies, may be offended by such terms as "Ruddy Rex," "Gray Eddie," and "Sallow Susie" or "Pale Joey." In addition, he points out that while "black" may be associated with some unpleasant connotations, "white," too, has its drawbacks: "white with fear," "white as a ghost," "pasty-faced," "white-livered," "showing the white feather," "waving the white flag," and, of course, "whitewash."

Not to be outdone, militant Indians have expanded "Uncle Tom" into "Uncle Tom-Tom," for an Indian who collaborates with Palefaces. They have also protested against the use of "Indian" or "Redskin" as the name of a team, bringing about the replacement of the Dartmouth Indians with "Big Green," and of the Massachusetts Redmen with "Minutemen." The Indian pictured on pennants and soft drink containers, according to the University of Massachusetts Student Senate, connotes a "false, distorted and racist picture of our Indian heritage." Perhaps so.

The vocabulary of crime and illegality has had some recent additions; "cycle-jacking" for the stealing of bicycles; "drugola" as payola in drugs, usually made to disc jockeys; "whirligig" for police helicopter; "shorting the pot" for holding back the full assessment on the "pot," amassed from income from illicit activities; this is a "crime against crime," and is punishable by the customary "enforcers." From Britain comes a new term, "Granny Bashers," to describe teen-age London girls armed with knives who prey on old women.

The field of labor relations has contributed the term "father-and-son union" for the closed-corporation, or even hereditary aspect that often prevails in some union organizations, precluding access to outsiders, particularly minority groups. Then there is the newly discovered "job alienation," where the worker gets tired of going through the same motions eight hours a day; the cure for this is said to be "job redesigning," permitting him to go through different motions. There is also "flextime," where you come in when you like, and adjust your working day to suit yourself. This system is said to have been imported from Europe, and to have been used to good advantage by Lufthansa and Nestlé. You come in any time between 8 and 9:30 a.m., take a half-hour lunch break somewhere between 12 and 1:30, and quit somewhere between 4 and 6. This may function well where the work is not coordinated, and one person's work does not hinge on another's. Cheating is presumably prevented by punching a time clock.

From the side of capital come an interesting noun and an equally interesting verb: the first is "oligopoly," a semi-monopoly conducted by a few leading firms in a given field (drugs and gasoline come to mind). How they get around anti-trust laws is their own business. The second is "to satisfice": here a big corporation allows small competitors to compete, so as to ward off government, consumer and competitor complaints, but at the same time show a substantial profit to its own shareholders. The two seem to go hand in hand. From engineering circles in Ohio we get an interesting expression with sexual overtones: "to go to bed with," meaning to agree to a contract.

The vocabulary of high finance is satirized in what is supposed to be a wife's complaint: "Our marriage started out as an equal partnership; now I'm a wholly-owned subsidiary."

The language of science has brought us a recent creation, "neutercane," said to be intermediate between the hurricane and the frontal storm, and developing where the tropical and temperate climate zones meet. There is also the suggestion to replace our familiar "speedometer" (which goes back to 1904) with "tachometer," making the compound entirely Greek instead of a hybrid. "Tachometer," which first appeared in 1810, was originally used in connection with the velocity of machines of all kinds; an alternative "tachymeter," appearing in 1860, was at first used in connection with surveying instruments, later with speed, and Webster III equates it to "speedometer." "Odometer" (or "hodometer") measures distances only.

Scientific and pseudo-scientific gobbledegook is criticized by Stanislav Andreski in his book *Social Science as Sorcery*. He speaks of "quantified trivialities," "pseudo-mathematical decorations," and the "hallucinogenic letter *n*" (for "need"), used as a symbol in formulas ("n Aff"–the urge to affiliate; "n Ach"–the urge to achieve; he adds "n Bam"–the urge to bamboozle). *How to Speak like an Educator without being Educated* is the contribution of Barbara Stover and Ilva Walker, who cite administrative circulars with phrases such as "Flexible ontological productivity will implement control group and experimental group"; or "adaptable and reciprocal nuclei will terminate in total modular exchange."

But Gobbledegook has numerous facets. To cite from the invocation of a minister who opened a legislative session: "Oh Lord, keep us from the sin of administrivia!" The law brings us "constitutional bricolage," the art of making do with the tools on hand (in this case, our somewhat outworn Constitution), through a system of interpretations. From the Pentagon come "managing assets" (the art of leading troops in an artificial *Kriegsspiel*); "ticket punchers" (officers interested only in promotions based on one step at a time); the description of the POWs' return as "Operation Egress Recap"; the definition of "tunnel" as a "metaphorical subterranean connector system linking hypothetical ingress and egress channels," and of the "light at the end of the tunnel" as an "increased capability of luminescent egress visibility." There is also "cubic random numbers generators" for dice, but I will not swear to its military origin. From the general ranks of bureaucracy come "undefinitized," the definition of "ongoing" as "moving, no matter how slowly," an "affirmative action program" designed to make possible the hiring of more blacks, the abbreviation "S.O.B." not in its customary acceptance, but for "Superior Official Bureaucrat"; there is the distinction between "conference" (something you have to fly to to get results), "meeting" (something held in the home office), and "symposium" (either of the foregoing, but with no results); the distinction between "bureaucrat-lifers" and "bureaucrat-politicians"; "Siberia" (being exiled from a job you like to one you don't like). This from the U.S. Department of Labor: "The occupational incidence of the demand change is unlikely to coincide with the occupational profile of those registered at the employment office," which is translated by "The jobs may not fit the people." Business offers "personalized recreational eco-unit" for garden, "dinette unit" for table, "involuntarily leisured" for unemployed, "arrested increases in personal income" for wage freeze.

In view of all the foregoing, why should we doubt the statement made by Senior Editor Stuart Flexner of Random House Dictionary: "If Shakespeare were to materialize today in London or New York, he would be able to understand only five out of every nine words in our vocabulary."

Words from
Watergate

STEFAN KANFER

Wilson: *How do you know that, Mr. Chairman?*
Ervin: *Because I can understand the English language. It is my mother tongue.*

Y ES, BUT LAWYER John Wilson's clients, John Ehrlichman and H. R. Haldeman, are also children of that mother tongue. And so are Caulfield and Dean, Odle and Porter, Mitchell and Magruder, and virtually every other Watergate witness. Those witnesses are a peculiar group of siblings, obedient to every authority except that of their parent language.

Even with the admission of tapes no one will ever master the entire vocabulary or thought processes of the Nixon Administration. But tantalizing glimpses are possible through the aperture of the Ervin hearings. By now of course, the Nixonian cadre has turned a few phrases to bromides, notably the sci-fi sounds "At that point in time," and "In that frame." Still these clichés are excellent indicators of the Administration's unwritten laws of language: 1) never use a word when a sentence will do; 2) obscure, don't clarify; 3) Humpty Dumpty was right when he said to Alice: "When I use a word . . . it means just what I choose it to mean."

Most of the Watergate witnesses prefer not to answer with a simple yes or no. The vagueness shown last week by H. R. Haldeman has been the motto of the month: "I am not sure whether I was or not. I may very well have been." Other witnesses felt the truth was illusory; facts could only be construed "in their context." The quibbling over nuances would do credit to Henry James—as when Ehrlichman vainly tried to distinguish between "literal" and "actual."

Perhaps because Haldeman has been characterized as a former ad man, he has avoided any run-it-up-the-flagpole chatter. Still he introduced some collector's items: "Zero-defect system," for perfection; "containment" for the witholding of information. Throughout the hearings, where precision would help, a file of worn metaphors and similes appears. Usually the phrases smack of the military or sports—two arenas for their threadbare lexicons. Porter thought of himself as "a team player," Dean as a soldier who had "earned my stripes." Ehrlichman considered himself proficient at "downfield blocking." J. Edgar Hoover was "a loyal trooper." Mitchell football-coached, "When the going gets tough, the tough get going"; and everybody worried about the chief "lowering the boom."

Responsibility was obviously diffused; in the New Nixon years, power no longer seems to emanate from persons but from real estate. The President rarely appears in testimony. The word comes from "the Oval office." When Caulfield carried the fragile promise of Executive clemency, said McCord, he spoke of "the very highest levels of the White House"—perhaps the first times that favors were to be dispensed by architecture.

Euphemisms are to the tongue what novocain is to the gums. In the hearings, criminality is given scores of numbing disguises. For "intelligence-gathering operations" read "breaking and entering," for "plumbers" read "burglars," for "stroking" read "cheap flattery," for "puffing" read "expensive flattery," for "White House horrors" read "Government-sponsored crimes." The roster seems endless: "dirty tricks," "laundered money," "telephone anomalies"—all perform the same function: the separation of words from the truth.

Sometimes the resonances are poignant: McCord's use of the familiar "game plan" or young Odle's attempt to "make a couple of things perfectly clear." Occasionally they are mystifying, as in the characterization of CBS Newsman Daniel Schorr as "a real media enemy"—as opposed, perhaps, to an unreal media enemy. Often, however, they are terrifying because they illuminate just how much ignorance the functionaries had—not only of the law but of themselves.

To the Ervin committee, for example, Ehrlichman released a clandestine tape recording of a conversation he had with Herbert Kalmbach. It contains a dazzling example of self-deception. Kalmbach is asked to testify that he spoke to Ehrlichman in California, when in fact the conversation took place in Washington. "I wouldn't ask you to lie," says the former presidential aide.

It was this recording that prompted Mary McCarthy to speculate in the London *Observer*: "[The tape] shows Ehrlichman demanding that his friend commit perjury. That is the only way it can be read. Perhaps this is illuminating. If Ehrlichman cannot realize what his taped voice says in plain English, perhaps Nixon cannot either, and so his own battery of tapes may be produced after all."

Whether or not the President can comprehend plain English, it is certain that many on his staff could not or would not. In their obfuscations they were not alone. Long before the Nixon Administration took office, the military had its "pacification" and "fragging." Radical critics led their own assaults on the English language with the substitution of "offing" for killing, the prating of "fascism" every time an obstacle was encountered. At the same time, business gave its own donation at the office, with the computer talk of "inputs," "software" and "print-outs."

Indeed, every sector has its private jargon meant to mystify the outsider, frequently at the cost of undermining the speaker. Yet all these linguistic abuses have paled beside the rhetorical revelations of Watergate. With that special gift of hindsight so praised by committeemen and witnesses, the spectator can now perceive that the seeds of the affair were planted long ago, in the first days of Nixon's tenure. Once upon a point in time, Administration spokesmen instructed commentators: "Don't judge us by what we say but by what we do." As the world now realizes, verb and act are in the deepest sense inseparable.

In his classic essay, *Politics and the English Language,* George Orwell spoke for all time: "If thought corrupts language, language can also corrupt thought." Yet even with his innate pessimism, Orwell offered a solution—a method more applicable today than it was in the holocaust of the '40s. "One ought to recognize," he wrote, "that the present political chaos is connected with the decay of the language, and that one can probably bring about some improvement by starting at the verbal end."

It takes no feminist to see how much the nation owes its mother tongue. If that tongue is to speak again with clarity and force, alterations have to begin, not in the spirit of litigation but in its opposite: the defense of values. The Watergate evasions will have to be swept away with those who mouth them. Honest politics will not miraculously reappear. But in the absence of bromides and shibboleths, Americans may once again be able to put in some good words for their Government. And vice versa.

New Peak
for Newspeak

NEWSWEEK

AFTER A RECENT Vietnam bombing mission, a B-52 pilot summed up the day's work as an "effective ordnance delivery" (translation: target demolished). When George Romney abruptly exited from the Presidential race, his New Hampshire campaign manager explained that the candidate believed he lacked "a positive reference input" (translation: a good image). In its January letter to shareholders, Litton Industries attributed declining stock profits to "volume variances from plan" (translation: strikes).

Once confined to Mad Ave and Foggy Bottom, euphemisms, circumlocutions, jargon and other high-flown forms of linguistic obfuscation have now become as pervasive as pollution. From San Antonio (where the sidewalks at HemisFair are called "people expressways") to New York City (where a garage mechanic advertises himself as an "automotive internist"), the word is out that anything goes, verbalizationwise.

Physicians are starting to call pep pills "activity boosters." A Milwaukee brokerage house recently touted a certain stock because it has "a small downside risk with a worthwhile upside potential." Preschoolers are now enrolled in "early learning centers," where they orbit between their "pupil stations" (desks) and the "instructional materials resource center" (library).

This election year will witness its share of confrontations, accommodations and reconciliations. "You have to watch the words that are being tossed around these days," observes Sen. Eugene McCarthy. "You never know what you're getting into." Even superliterates like William Buckley, Jr. occasionally contribute to the mess. During a TV appearance, Buckley closed a 176-word answer to a question by observing " . . . and this seemed to me a centrifugalization, a social centrifugalization which would cut the whole energy circuit of civilizations."

Sugar Coating

Much of the word pollution results from a tropistic reaction to a disagreeable truth. As the problems of Vietnam, race and poverty grow more complex and pressing, the need for sugar-coated palliatives grows more insistent. Vietnam has popularized "gradualism," "infrastructure" and "defoliation," while prompting one State Department official to suggest that U.S. bombing pressure on the enemy "should be mainly violins, but with periodic touches of brass" (more selective than massive). Such gibberish, observes Yale professor of psychiatry Robert Lifton, "helps psychically numb people to what's happening on the other side of the weapon."

Sometimes, of course, military euphemisms are designed to conceal reality as well as to soften it. British satirist David Frost is a veteran observer of the genre. As he humourously sees it, the term "strategic withdrawal" usually means a rout; "a phased withdrawal" is a rout with insufficient transport; a "deliberate, unprovoked act of aggression" is the other side starting a war; and a "pre-emptive air strike" is our side starting a war. (Even military leaders in Hanoi display a fondness for wordsmanship; a recent visitor to North Vietnam's capital reported that U.S. B-52 attacks were scornfully referred to as the "U.S. Civic Action Fishpond and Well-Digging Program.")

By the same sugar-coating process, the residents of America's inner cities (slums) have been subjected to a bewildering array of euphemisms, perhaps to justify the increasing incidence of civil disorders (riots). As a forlorn slum-dweller in a Jules Feiffer cartoon put it: "First I was poor. Then I became needy. Then I was underprivileged. Now I'm disadvantaged. I still don't have a penny to my name—but I have a great vocabulary."

Thanks partly to the hegemony of the computer, bureaucratic gobbledygook is more obtuse than ever (box). According to lexicographer Theodore M. Bernstein, former Defense Secretary Robert McNamara is responsible for introducing technical jargon to the brass hats at the Pentagon—and by osmosis, to most of Washington's speech- and memo-writing corps. "McNamara is one of the few men alive who uses computerisms properly," says Bernstein, as assistant managing editor at The New York Times. "But now that they've filtered down, they've come to mean nothing."

HOW TO WIN AT WORDMANSHIP

After years of hacking through etymological thickets at the U.S. Public Health Service, a 63-year-old official named Philip Broughton hit upon a sure-fire method for converting frustration into fulfillment (jargonwise). Euphemistically called the Systematic Buzz Phrase Projector, Broughton's system employs a lexicon of 30 carefully chosen "buzzwords."

Column 1	Column 2	Column 3
0. *integrated*	0. *management*	0. *options*
1. *total*	1. *organizational*	1. *flexibility*
2. *systematized*	2. *monitored*	2. *capability*
3. *parallel*	3. *reciprocal*	3. *mobility*
4. *functional*	4. *digital*	4. *programming*
5. *responsive*	5. *logistical*	5. *concept*
6. *optional*	6. *transitional*	6. *time-phase*
7. *synchronized*	7. *incremental*	7. *projection*
8. *compatible*	8. *third-generation*	8. *hardward*
9. *balanced*	9. *policy*	9. *contingency*

The procedure is simple. Think of any three digit number, then select the corresponding buzzword from each column. For instance, number 257 produces "systematized logistical projection," a phrase that can be dropped into virtually any report with that ring of decisive, knowledgeable authority. "No one will have the remotest idea of what you're talking about," says Broughton, "but the important thing is that they're not about to admit it."

DIRECTIVE

Indeed, the spread of "technalese" prompted Robert Wood, Under Secretary of the Department of Housing and Urban Development, to issue a tongue-in-cheek directive to all HUD divisions. Henceforth, announced Wood, continued use of technical jargon would result in "a quarterly reduction in personnel ceiling of the offending unit at the rate of 5 per cent." Perhaps Wood should have pretended he meant it. Shortly after his directive, a report by a HUD division called for "action-oriented orchestration of innovative inputs generated by escalation of meaningful indigenous decision-making dialogue."

Jargon is also being incorporated into administrative titles. An educator in Binghamton, N.Y., for example, identifies herself as an Associate for Institutional Relations and Title III Schedules of the Upper Susquehanna Regional Supplementary Educational Services.

Nowhere has the art of obfuscation been more refined than in the drawing up of administrative proposals. Lloyd Kaplan, a 33-year-old information officer for the New York City Planning Commission, has made a hobby of analyzing the technique. "Proposals," he reports, "are habitually placed in *frameworks* so they can be viewed from the proper *perspective*. Looking through the framework, it is easy to chart appropriate *guidelines*. Such guidelines are *flexible* and handy for making *bold thrusts, dramatic approaches* and *pioneering breakthroughs*.

"Money," continues Kaplan, "is never mentioned. *Resources* is the prime substitute, although *expenditures, allocations, appropriations* and *funds* are also popular. Resources is also esthetically pleasing because it brings to mind the act of digging up and forms a truly Miltonic phrase when preceded by 'overburdened municipal'."

John Hightower, executive director of the New York State Council on the Arts, is another perceptive student of proposal-making. In requesting money, says Hightower, the cardinal rule is to never employ the word "subsidy," since it implies one is asking for complete funding. In place of subsidy, inventive politicians like New York Sen. Jacob Javits have taken to using "subvention."

TECHNIQUE

A second rule is to fluff up a proposal with the sort of euphemisms that bestow an aura of importance without revealing anything specific. An application for a Federal grant from a small southern California college illustrates the technique. Describing a proposed project, the applicant states: "It is not simply a cross-disciplinary venture or an interdisciplinary venture; it is a pan-disciplinary venture and this, of course, is in the nature of all real experience."

Such grotesqueries might be expected to spew from the bureaucratic sector, but it is a singularly depressing fact that those who should know better seem just as culpable. A hospital physician advises the new lab assistant to "participate in the orientation process" when what he really means is "move around until we find something for you to do." The university dean boasts that the "interface" between his departments is "kinetic" when all that he has noticed is that the sociology chairman has bought the zoology chairman a drink. Even the high priests of the new-time religion play the game, especially when they are called on for personal commitments. As theologian Robert McAfee Brown notes, leading statements like "I believe . . . " have given way to the more anonymous "The Judeo-Christian tradition affirms . . . "

Only the Supreme Deity knows where it will all be finalized – or for that matter, what it all means. Until He chooses to speak, the task of translation falls to such guardians of the language as Lloyd Kaplan, who is now laboriously compiling a definitive study called "Newspeak Made Simplifax." "If I move right along with it," says Kaplan, "I should have it finished by 1984."

The Forked-Tongue
Phrase Book

RUSSELL BAKER

How to translate our campaigning politicians:

"My fellow Americans."–"Anybody who switches to the channel showing the movie is unpatriotic."

"It's wonderful to be back in the American heartland."–"What's the name of this dump?"

"Let's look at the record."–"Let's not."

"Peace with honor."–"War."

"Never has democratic government been more gravely endangered." –"My polls show I am likely to get beaten."

"These zealots of the radical left."–"Put me down as a champion of motherhood."

"Without regard to race, creed or color."–"Ho hum."

"Many people have asked me to spell out my position on American policy toward subsidies for the rectified juice industry."–"My ghost writer thinks there's some political mileage in this, so I agreed to try it."

"Let us remember that these young people are the citizens of tomorrow."–"At present, however, they are still just kids."

"On the way over here a little girl came up to me and said . . . "–"This isn't really true, of course, but my television adviser says it is good for my image to tell anecdotes like this."

"I will never stoop to smear and innuendo."–"The polls show I have it won if I play it cool."

"Let us not judge a man by the way he cuts his hair."–"I trust everyone has noticed that my opponent has not cut his for more than a year."

"My opponent's religion should not be an issue in this campaign, and I will never heed the advice of those who urge me to make it an issue."–"In case it has not been generally observed here, I would like to point out that he adheres to a minority sect with extremely odd views on transubstantiation."

"And standing there in that kibbutz, I said . . . "–"No Arab, I."

"My opponent has sought to sell himself as though he were a powder for the relief of acid indigestion, through use of the most expensive campaign of television huckstering in the history of American government. This crass commercial cheapening of public office is a vice in which I shall never indulge."–"I am in desperate need of funds to purchase television time."

"As Walter Bagehot once said of politics . . . "–"Will any intellectuals in the audience please note that I have a ghost writer who knows who Walter Bagehot is and will tell me if I want to know."

"The disgruntled young must learn to work effectively within the system for the reforms they so ardently desire."–"Do as I say and in time you may be elected to public office to do as I do."

" . . . and I pledge myself to the defense of the Constitution of the United States."–"Upon being elected, I shall immediately offer six amendments to the Constitution to do away with certain unconstitutional provisions now embedded in that document, and to make constitutional certain practices which it now, unfortunately, forbids."

"How wonderful it is to get away from Washington and be back here with the people!"–"At least it gives my liver that rest the doctor ordered."

"Now, I'm going to be perfectly honest about this."–"Oh no I'm not."

6
THE LANGUAGE OF
THE BLACKS

The subject of "black English" is currently much debated in academic circles, in the press, and elsewhere. The controversy focuses on such points as the validity of black English, the extent to which black students should be taught and should be expected to use black English or standard English, and whether or not blacks should be encouraged to use each form according to the circumstances. In the first article, Dorothy Seymour discusses this subject.

The chapter concludes with an article on the subtle and often inadvertent "racist" language used by whites.

Black English

DOROTHY Z. SEYMOUR

IN THE CLASSROOM they made for their desks and opened their books. The name of the story they tried to read was "Come." It went:

Come, Bill, come.
Come with me.
Come and see this.
See what is here.

The first boy poked the second. "Wha' da' wor'?"

"Da' wor' is, you dope."
"Is? Ain't no wor' is. You jivin' me? Wha' da' wor' mean?"
"Ah dunno. Jus' is."

To a speaker of Standard English, this exchange is only vaguely comprehensible. But it's normal speech for thousands of American children. In addition it demonstrates one of our biggest educational problems: children whose speech style is so different from the writing style of their books that they have difficulty learning to read. These children speak Black English, a dialect characteristic of many inner-city Negroes. Their books are, of course, written in Standard English. To complicate matters, the speech they use is also socially stigmatized. Middle-class whites and Negroes alike scorn it as low-class poor people's talk.

Teachers sometimes make the situation worse with their attitudes toward Black English. Typically, they view the children's speech as "bad English" characterized by "lazy pronunciation," "poor grammar," and "short, jagged words." One result of this attitude is poor mental health on the part of the pupils. A child is quick to grasp the feeling that while school speech is "good," his own speech is "bad," and that by extension he himself is somehow inadequate and without value. Some children react to this feeling by withdrawing; they stop talking entirely. Others develop the attitude of "F'get you, honky." In either case, the psychological results are devastating and lead straight to the dropout route.

It is hard for most teachers and middle-class Negro parents to accept the idea that Black English is not just "sloppy talk" but a dialect with a form and structure of its own. Even some eminent black educators think of it as "bad English grammar" with "slurred consonants" (Professor Nick Aaron Ford of Morgan State College in Baltimore) and "ghettoese" (Dr. Kenneth B. Clark, the prominent educational psychologist).

Parents of Negro schoolchildren generally agree. Two researchers at Columbia University report that the adults they worked with in Harlem almost unanimously preferred that their children be taught Standard English in school.

But there is another point of view, one held in common by black militants and some white liberals. They urge that middle-class Negroes stop thinking of the inner-city dialect as something to be ashamed of and repudiated. Black author Claude Brown, for example, pushes this point of view.

Some modern linguists take a similar stance. They begin with the premise that no dialect is intrinsically "bad" or "good," and that a nonstandard speech style is not defective speech but different speech. More important, they have been able to show that Black English is far from being a careless way of speaking the Standard; instead, it is a rather rigidly constructed set of speech patterns, with the same sort of specialization in sounds, structure and vocabulary as any other dialect.

Middle-class listeners who hear black inner-city speakers say "dis" and "tin" for "this" and "thin" assume that the black speakers are just being careless. Not at all; these differences are characteristic aspects of the dialect. The original cause of such substitutions is generally the carry-over from one's original language or that of his immigrant parents. The interference from that carry-over probably caused the substitution of /d/ for the voiced *th* sound in this, and /t/ for the unvoiced *th* sound in *thin*. (Linguists represent language sounds by putting letters within slashes or brackets.) Most speakers of English don't realize that the two *th* sounds of English are lacking in many other languages and are difficult for most foreigners trying to learn English. Germans who study English, for example, are surprised and confused about these sounds because the only Germans who use them are the ones who lisp. These two sounds are almost nonexistent in the West African languages which most black immigrants brought with them to America.

Similar substitutions used in Black English are /f/, a sound similar to the unvoiced *th*, in medial word-position, as in *birfday* for *birthday*, and in final word-position, as in *bruvver* for *brother*. These sound substitutions are also typical of Gullah, the language of black speakers in the Carolina Sea Islands. Some of them are also heard in Caribbean Creole. Another characteristic is the lack of /l/ at the end of words, sometimes replaced by the sound /w/. This makes a word like *tool* sound like *too*.

One difference that is startling to middle-class speakers is the fact that Black English words appear to leave off some consonant sounds at the end of words. Like Italian, Japanese and West African words, they are more likely to end in vowel sounds. Standard English *boot* is pronounced *boo* in Black English. *What* is *wha*. *Sure* is *sho*. *Your* is *yo*. This kind of difference can make for confusion in the classroom. Dr. Kenneth Goodman, a psycholinguist, tells of a black child whose white teacher asked him to use *so* in a sentence—not "sew a dress" but "the other *so*." The sentence the child used was "I got a *so* on my leg."

A related feature of Black English is the tendency in many cases not to use sequences of more than just one final consonant sound. For example, *just* is pronounced *jus, past* is *pass, mend* sounds like *men* and *hold* sounds like *hole*. *Six* and *box* are pronounced *sick* and *bock*. Why should this be? Perhaps because West African languages, like Japanese, have almost no clusters of consonants in their speech. The Japanese, when importing a foreign word, handle a similar problem by inserting vowel sounds between every consonant, making *baseball* sound like *besuboru*. West Africans probably make a simpler change, merely cutting a series of two consonant sounds down to one. Speakers of Gullah, according to one linguist, have made the same kind of adaptation of Standard English.

Teachers of black children seldom understand the reason for these differences in final sounds. They are apt to think that careless speech is the cause. Actually, black speakers aren't "leaving off" any sounds; how can you leave off something you never had in the first place?

Differences in vowel sounds are also characteristic of the nonstandard language. Dr. Goodman reports that a black child asked his teacher how to spell rat. "R-a-t," she replied. But the boy responded, "No ma'am, I don't mean rat mouse, I mean rat now." In Black English *right* sounds like *rat*. A likely reason is that in West African languages, there are very few vowel sounds of the type heard in the word *right*. This type is common in English. It is called a glided or dipthongized vowel sound. A glided vowel sound is actually a close combination of two vowels; in the word *right* the two parts of the sound "eye" are really "ah-ee." West African languages have no such long, two-part, changing vowel sounds; their vowels are generally shorter and more stable. This may be why in Black English, *time* sounds like *Tom, oil* like *all,* and *my* like *ma.*

Black English differs from Standard English not only in its sounds but also in its structure. The way the words are put together does not always fit the description in English grammar books. The method of expressing time, or tense, for example, differs in significant ways.

The verb *to be* is an important one in Standard English. It's used as an auxiliary verb to indicate different tenses. But Black English speakers use it quite differently. Sometimes an inner-city Negro says "He coming"; other times he says "He be coming." These two sentences mean different things. To understand why, let's look at the tenses of West African languages; they correspond with those of Black English.

Many West African languages have a tense which is called the habitual. This tense is used to express action that is always occurring, and it is formed with a verb that is translated as *be.* "He be coming" means something like "He's always coming," "He usually comes," or "He's been coming."

In Standard English there is no regular grammatical construction for such a tense. Black English speakers, in order to form the habitual tense in English, use the word *be* as an auxiliary: *He be doing it. My Momma be working. He be running.* The habitual tense is not the same as the present tense, which is constructed in Black English without any form of the verb *to be: He do it. My Momma working. He running.* (This means the action is occurring right now.)

There are other tense differences between Black English and Standard English. For example, the nonstandard speech does not use changes in grammar to indicate the past tense. A white person will ask, "What did your brother say?" and the black person will answer, "He say he coming." "How did you get here?" "I walk." This style of talking about the past is paralleled in the Yoruba, Fante, Hausa, and Ewe languages of West Africa.

Expression of plurality is another difference. The way a black child will talk of "them boy" or "two dog" makes some white listeners think Negroes don't know how to turn a singular word into a plural word. As a matter of fact, it isn't necessary to use an *s* to express plurality. For example, in Chinese it's correct to say "There are three book on the table." This sentence already has two signals of the plural, *three* and *are*; why require a third? This same logic is the basis of plurals in most West African languages, where nouns are often identical in the plural and the singular. For example, in Ibo, one correctly says *those man*, and in both Ewe and Yoruba one says *they house*. American speakers of Gullah retain this style; they say *five dog*.

Gender is another aspect of language structure where differences can be found. Speakers of Standard English are often confused to find that the nonstandard vernacular often uses just one gender of pronoun, the masculine, and refers to women as well as men as *he* or *him*. "He a nice girl" and even "Him a nice girl" are common. This usage probably stems from West African origins too, as does the use of multiple negatives such as "Nobody don't know it."

Vocabulary is the third aspect of a person's native speech that could affect his learning of a new language. The strikingly different vocabulary often used in Negro Nonstandard English is probably the most obvious aspect of it to a casual white observer. But its vocabulary differences don't obscure its meaning the way different sounds and structure often do.

Recently there has been much interest in the African origins of words like *goober* (peanut), *cooter* (turtle), and *tote* (carry), as well as others that are less certainly African, such as *to dig* (possibly from the Wolof *degan*, "to understand"). Such expressions seem colorful rather than low class to many whites; they become assimilated faster than their black originators do. English professors now use *dig* in the scholarly articles, and current advertising has enthusiastically adopted *rap*.

Is it really possible for old differences in sound, structure and vocabulary to persist from the West African languages of slave days into present-day inner-city Black English? Easily. Nothing else really explains such regularity of language habits, most of which persist among black people in various parts of the Western Hemisphere. For a long time scholars believed that certain speech forms used by Negroes were merely leftovers from archaic English preserved in the speech of early English settlers in America and copied by their slaves. But this theory has been greatly weakened, largely as the result of the work of a black linguist, Dr. Lorenzo Dow Turner of the University of Chicago. Dr. Turner studied the speech of Gullah Negroes in the Sea Islands off the Carolina coast and found so many traces of West African languages that he thoroughly discredited the archaic-English theory.

When anyone learns a new language, it's usual to try to speak the new language with the sounds and structure of the old. If a person's first language does not happen to have a particular sound needed in the language he is learning, he will tend to substitute a similar or related sound from his native language and use it to speak the new one. When Frenchman Charles Boyer said "Zees ees my heart," and when Latin American Carmen Miranda sang "Souse American way," they were simply using sounds from their native languages in trying to pronounce sounds of English. West Africans must have done the same thing when they first attempted English words. The tendency to retain the structure of the native language is a strong one, too. That's why a German learning English is likely to put his verb at the end: "May I a glass of beer have?" The vocabulary of one's original language may also furnish some holdovers. Jewish immigrants did not stop using the word *bagel* when they came to America; nor did Germans stop saying *sauerkraut*.

Social and geographical isolation reinforces the tendency to retain old language habits. When one group is considered inferior, the other group avoids it. For many years it was illegal to give any sort of instruction to Negroes, and for slaves to try to speak like their masters would have been unthinkable. Conflict of value systems doubtless retards changes, too. As Frantz Fanon observed in *Black Skin, White Masks,* those who take on white speech habits are suspect in the ghetto, because others believe they are trying to "act white." Dr. Kenneth Johnson, a black linguist, put it this way: "As long as disadvantaged black children live in segregated communities and most of their relationships are confined to those within their own subculture, they will not replace their functional nonstandard dialect with the nonfunctional standard dialect."

Linguists have made it clear that language systems that are different are not necessarily deficient. A judgment of deficiency can be made only in comparison with another language system. Let's turn the tables on Standard English for a moment and look at it from the West African point of view. From this angle, Standard English (1) is lacking in certain language sounds; (2) has a couple of unnecessary language sounds for which others may serve as good substitutes; (3) doubles and drawls some of its vowel sounds in sequences that are unusual and difficult to imitate; (4) lacks a method of forming an important tense; (5) requires an unnecessary number of ways to indicate tense, plurality, and gender; and (6) doesn't mark negatives sufficiently for the result to be a good strong negative statement.

Now whose language is deficient?

How would the adoption of this point of view help us? Say we accepted the evidence that Black English is not just a sloppy Standard but an organized language style which probably has developed many of its features on the basis of its West African heritage. What would we gain?

The psychological climate of the classroom might improve if teachers understood why many black students speak as they do. But we still have not reached a solution of the main problem. Does the discovery that Black English has pattern and structure mean that it should not be tampered with? Should children who speak Black English be excused from learning the Standard in school? Should they perhaps be given books in Black English to learn from?

Any such accommodation would surely result in a hardening of the new separatism being urged by some black militants. It would probably be applauded by such people as Roy Innis, Director of C.O.R.E., who is currently recommending dual autonomous education systems for white and black. And it might facilitate learning to read, since some experiments have indicated that materials written in Black English syntax aid problem readers from the inner city.

But determined resistance to the introduction of such printed materials into schools can be expected. To those who view inner-city speech as bad English, the appearance in print of sentences like "My mama, he work," can be as shocking and repellent as a four-letter word. Middle-class Negro parents would probably mobilize against the move. Any stratagem that does not take into account such practicalities of the matter is probably doomed to failure. And besides, where would such a permissive policy on language get these children in the larger society, and in the long run? If they want to enter an integrated America they must be able to deal with it on its own terms. Even Professor Toni Cade of Rutgers, who doesn't want "ghetto accents" tampered with, advocates mastery of Standard English because, as she puts it, "If you want to get ahead in this country, you must master the language of the ruling class." This has always been true, wherever there has been a minority group.

The problem then appears to be one of giving these children the ability to speak (and read) Standard English without denigrating the vernacular and those who use it, or even affecting the ability to use it. The only way to do this is to officially espouse bidialectism. The result would be the ability to use either dialect equally well—as Dr. Martin Luther King did—depending on the time, place, and circumstances. Pupils would have to learn enough about Standard English to use it when necessary, and teachers would have to learn enough about the inner-city dialect to understand and accept it for what it is—not just a "careless" version of Standard English but a different form of English that's appropriate at certain times and places.

Can we accomplish this? If we can't, the result will be the continued alienation of a large section of the population, continued dropout trouble with consequent loss of earning power and economic contribution to the nation, but most of all, loss of faith in America as a place where a minority people can at times continue to use those habits that remind them of their link with each other and with their past.

The Language
of White Racism

HAIG A. BOSMAJIAN

THE ATTEMPTS TO eradicate racism in the United States have been focused notably on the blacks of America, not the whites. What is striking is that while we are inundated with TV programs portraying the plight of black Americans, and with panel discussions focusing on black Americans, we very seldom hear or see any extensive public discussion, literature or programs directly related to the source of the racism, the white American. We continually see on our TV sets and in our periodicals pictures and descriptions of undernourished black children, but we seldom see pictures or get analyses of the millions of school-age white suburban children being taught racism in their white classrooms; we see pictures of unemployed blacks aimlessly walking the streets in their black communities, but seldom do we ever see the whites who have been largely responsible, directly or indirectly, for this unemployment and segregation; we continually hear panelists discussing and diagnosing the blacks in America, but seldom do we hear panelists diagnosing the whites and their subtle and not so subtle racism.

Gunnar Myrdal, in the Introduction to his classic *An American Dilemma*, wrote that as he "proceeded in his studies into the Negro problem [an unfortunate phrase], it became increasingly evident that little, if anything, could be scientifically explained in terms of the peculiarities of the Negroes themselves." It is the white majority group, said Myrdal, "that naturally determines the Negro's 'place.' All our attempts to reach scientific explanations of why the Negroes are what they are and why they live as they do have regularly led to determinants on the white side of the race line." As the July 1966 editorial in *Ebony* put it, "for too long now, we have focused on the symptoms of the disease rather than the disease itself. It is time now for us to face the fact that Negroes are oppressed in America not by 'the pathology of the ghetto,' as some experts contend, but by the pathology of the white community." In calling for a White House Conference on Whites, the *Ebony* editorial made the important point that "we need to know more about the pathology of the white community. We need conferences in which white leaders will talk not about us [Negroes] but about themselves."

White Americans, through the mass media and individually, must begin to focus their attention not on the condition of the victimized, but on the victimizer. Whitey must begin to take the advice of various black spokesmen who suggest that white Americans start solving the racial strife in this country by eradicating white racism in white communities, instead of going into black communities or joining black organizations or working for legislation to "give" the blacks political and social rights. This suggestion has come from Floyd McKissick, Malcolm X, and Stokely Carmichael. McKissick, when asked what the role of the white man was in the black man's struggle, answered: "If there are whites who are not racists, and I believe there are a few, a very few, let them go to their own communities and teach; teach white people the truth about the black man." Malcolm X wrote in his autobiography: "The Negroes aren't the racists. Where the really sincere white people have to do their 'proving' of themselves is not among the black *victims*, but out on the battle lines of where America's racism really *is*—and that's in their own home communities; America's racism is among their own fellow whites. That's where the sincere whites who really mean to accomplish something have to work." Stokely Carmichael, writing in the September 22, 1966 issue of *The New York Review of Books*, said: "One of the most disturbing things about almost all white supporters of the movement has been that they are afraid to go into their own communities—which is where the racism exists—and work to get rid of it."

A step in that direction which most whites can take is to clean up their language to rid it of words and phrases which connote racism to the blacks. Whereas many blacks have demonstrated an increased sensitivity to language and an awareness of the impact of words and phrases upon both black and white listeners, the whites of this nation have demonstrated little sensitivity to the language of racial strife. Whitey has been for too long speaking and writing in terminology which, often being offensive to the blacks, creates hostility and suspicions and breaks down communication.

The increased awareness and sensitivity of the black American to the impact of language is being reflected in various ways. Within the past two years, there have been an increasing number of references by Negro writers and speakers to the "Through the Looking Glass" episode where Humpty Dumpty says: "When I use a word it means just what I choose it to mean—neither more nor less." "The question is," said Alice, "whether you can make words mean so many different things." "The question is," said Humpty Dumpty, "which is to be master—that's all." The "Through the Looking Glass" episode was used by Lerone Bennett, Jr. in the November 1967 issue of *Ebony* to introduce his article dealing with whether black Americans should call themselves "Negroes," "Blacks," or "Afro-Americans." In a speech delivered January 16, 1967 to the students at Morgan State College, Stokely Carmichael prefaced a retelling of the above Lewis Carroll tale with: "It [definition] is very, very important because I believe that people who can define are masters." Carmichael went on to say: "So I say 'black power' and someone says 'you mean violence.' And they expect me to say, 'no, no. I don't mean violence, I don't mean that.' Later for you; I am master of my own terms. If black power means violence to you, that is your problem. . . . I know what it means in my mind. I will stand clear and you must understand that because the first need of a free people is to be able to define their own terms and have those terms recognized by their oppressors. . . . Camus says that when a slave says 'no' he begins to exist."

This concern for words and their implications in race relations was voiced also by Martin Luther King, who pointed out that "even semantics have conspired to make that which is black seem ugly and degrading." Writing in his last book before his death, *Where Do We Go From Here: Chaos or Community?*, King said: "In Roget's Thesaurus there are some 120 synonyms for 'blackness' and at least 60 of them are offensive—such words as 'blot,' 'soot,' 'grime,' 'devil,' and 'foul.' There are some 134 synonyms for 'whiteness,' and all are favorable, expressed in such words as 'purity,' 'cleanliness,' 'chastity,' and 'innocence.' A white lie is better than a black lie. The most degenerate member of the family is the 'black sheep,' not the 'white sheep.' "

In March 1962, *The Negro History Bulletin* published an article by L. Eldridge Cleaver, then imprisoned in San Quentin, who devoted several pages to a discussion of the black American's acceptance of a white society's standards for beauty and to an analysis of the term "black" and the positive connotations of the term "white." Cleaver tells black Americans that "what we must do is stop associating the Caucasian with these exalted connotations of the word *white* when we think or speak of him. At the same time, we must cease associating ourselves with the unsavory connotations of the word black." Cleaver makes an interesting point when he brings to our attention the term "non-white." He writes: "The very words that we use indicate that we have set a premium on the Caucasian ideal of beauty. When discussing inter-racial relations, we speak of 'white people' and 'non-white people.' Notice that the particular choice of words gives precedence to 'white people' by making them a center—a standard—to which 'non-white' bears a negative relation. Notice the different connotations when we turn around and say 'colored' and 'non-colored,' or 'black' or 'non-black.' "

Simon Podair, writing in the Fourth Quarter issue, 1956, of *Phylon* examines the connotations of such words as "blackmail," "blacklist," "blackbook," "blacksheep," and "blackball." The assertion made by Podair that it has been white civilization which has attributed to the word "black" things undesirable and evil warrants brief examination. He is correct when he asserts that "language as a potent force in our society goes beyond being merely a communicative device. Language not only expresses ideas and concepts but it may actually shape them. Often the process is completely unconscious with the individual concerned unaware of the influence of the spoken or written expressions upon his thought processes. Language can thus become an instrument of both propaganda and indoctrination for a given idea." Further, Podair is correct in saying that "so powerful is the role of language in its imprint upon the human mind that even the minority group may begin to accept the very expressions that aid in its stereotyping. Thus, even Negroes may develop speech patterns filled with expressions leading to the strengthening of stereotypes." Podair's point is illustrated by the comments made by a Negro state official in Washington upon hearing of the shooting of Robert Kennedy. The Director of the Washington State Board Against Discrimination said: "This is a black day in our country's history." Immediately after uttering this statement with the negative connotation of "black," he declared that Robert Kennedy "is a hero in the eyes of black people—a champion of the oppressed—and we all pray for his complete recovery."

Although King, Cleaver, and Podair, and others who are concerned with the negative connotations of "black" in the white society are partially correct in their analysis, they have omitted in their discussions two points which by their omission effect an incomplete analysis. First, it is not quite accurate to say, as Podair has asserted, that the concepts of black as hostile, foreboding, wicked, and gloomy "cannot be considered accidental and undoubtedly would not exist in a society wherein whites were a minority. Historically, these concepts have evolved as a result of the need of the dominant group to maintain social and economic relationships on the basis of inequality if its hegemony was to survive." This is inaccurate because the terms "blackball," "blacklist," "blackbook," and "blackmail" did not evolve as "a result of the need of the dominant group to maintain social and economic relationships on the basis of inequality if its hegemony was to survive." The origins of these terms are to be found in the sixteenth and seventeenth centuries in England where the origins of these terms were mostly based on the color of the book cover, the color of printing, or the color of the object from which the word got its meaning, as for instance the term "to blackball" coming from "the black ball" which centuries ago was a small black ball used as a vote against a person or thing. A "black-letter day" had its origin in the eighteenth century to designate an inauspicious day, as distinguished from a "red-letter day," the reference being to the old custom of marking the saints' days in the calendar with red letters.

More important, the assertion that the negative connotations of "black" and the positive connotations of "white" would not exist in a society wherein whites were a minority is not accurate. Centuries ago, before black societies ever saw white men, "black" often had negative connotations and "white" positive in those societies. T. O. Beidelman has made quite clear in his article "Swazi Royal Ritual," which appeared in the October 1966 issue of *Africa*, that black societies in southeast Africa, while attributing to black positive qualities, can at the same time attribute to black negative qualities; the same applies to the color white. Beidelman writes that for the Swazi "darkness, as the 'covered' moon, is an ambiguous quality. Black symbolizes 'impenetrability of the future,' but also the 'sins and evils of the past year. . . .' " Black beads may symbolize marriage and wealth in cattle, but at the same time they can symbolize evil, disappointment, and misfortune. "The word *mnyama* means black and dark, but also means deep, profound, unfathomable, and even confused, dizzy, angry." To the Swazi, "that which is dark is unknown and ambiguous and dangerous, but it is also profound, latent with unknown meanings and possibilities." As for "white," *mhlophe* means to the Swazi "white, pale, pure, innocent, perfect, but this may also mean destitute and empty. The whiteness of the full moon, *inyanga isidindile*, relates to fullness; but this term *dinda* can also mean to be useless, simply because it refers to that which is fully exposed and having no further unknown potentialities."

What King, Cleaver, and Podair have failed to do in their discussions of the negative connotations of "black" and the positive connotations of "white" is to point out that in black societies "black" often connotes that which is hostile, foreboding, and gloomy and "white" has symbolized purity and divinity. Furthermore, in white societies, "white" has numerous negative connotations: white livered (cowardly), white flag (surrender), white elephant (useless), white plague (tuberculosis), white wash (conceal), white feather (cowardice), *et cetera*. The ugliness and terror associated with the color white are portrayed by Melville in the chapter "The Whiteness of the Whale" in *Moby Dick*. At the beginning of the chapter, Melville says: "It was the whiteness of the whale that above all things appalled me."

What I am suggesting here is that the Negro writers, while legitimately concerned with the words and phrases which perpetuate racism in the United States have, at least in their analysis of the term "black," presented a partial analysis. This is not to say, however, that most of the analysis is not valid as far as it goes. Podair is entirely correct when he writes: "In modern American life language has become a fulcrum of prejudice as regards Negro-white relationships. Its effect has been equally potent upon the overt bigot as well as the confused member of the public who is struggling to overcome conscious or unconscious hostility towards minority groups. In the case of the Negro, language concepts have supported misconceptions and disoriented the thinking of many on the question of race and culture." Not only has the Negro become trapped by these "language concepts," but so too have the whites who, unlike the blacks, have demonstrated very little insight into the language of white racism and whose "language concepts" have "supported misconceptions and disoriented the thinking of many on the question of race and culture."

The Negroes' increased understanding and sensitivity to language as it is related to them demands that white Americans follow suit with a similar understanding and sensitivity which they have not yet demonstrated too well. During the 1960's, at a time when black Americans have been attempting more than ever to communicate to whites, through speeches, marches, sit-ins, demonstrations, through violence and non-violence, the barriers of communication between blacks and whites seem to be almost as divisive as they have been in the past one hundred years, no thanks to the whites. One has only to watch the TV panelists, blacks and whites, discussing the black American's protest and his aspirations, to see the facial expressions of the black panelists when a white on the panel speaks of "our colored boys in Vietnam." The black panelists knowingly smile at the racist phrasing and it is not difficult to understand the skepticism and suspicion which the blacks henceforth will maintain toward the white panelist who offends with "our colored boys in Vietnam." "Our colored boys in Vietnam" is a close relation to "our colored people" and "our colored," phrases which communicate more to the black American listener than intended by the white speaker. John Howard Griffin has pointed out something that applies not only to Southern whites, but to white Americans generally: "A great many of us Southern whites have grown up using an expression that Negroes can hardly bear to hear and yet tragically enough we use it because we believe it. It's an expression that we use when we say how much we love, what we patronizingly call 'our Negroes.' " The white American who talks of "our colored boys in Vietnam" offends the Negro triply; first, by referring to the black American men as "our" which is, as Griffin points out, patronizing; second, by using the nineteenth century term "colored"; third, by referring to the black American men as "boys."

Most whites, if not all, know that "nigger" and "boy" are offensive to the Negro; in fact, such language could be classified as "fighting words." But the insensitive and offensive whites continue today to indulge in expressing their overt and covert prejudices by using these obviously derogatory terms. Running a series of articles on racism in athletics, *Sports Illustrated* quoted a Negro football player as saying: "The word was never given bluntly; usually it took the form of a friendly, oblique talk with one of the assistant coaches. I remember one time one of the coaches came to me and said, '[Head Coach] Jim Owens loves you boys. We know you get a lot of publicity, but don't let it go to your head.' Hell, when he said 'Jim Owens loves you boys,' I just shut him off. That did it. I knew what he was talking about." An athletic director at one of the larger Southwestern universities, discussing how much sports have done for the Negro, declared: "In general, the nigger athlete is a little hungrier and we have been blessed with having some real outstanding ones. We think they've done a lot for us, and we think we've done a lot for them" (*Sports Illustrated*, July 1, 1968). One of the Negro athletes said of the coaching personnel at the same university: "They can pronounce Negro if they want to. *They can pronounce it.* But I think it seems like such a little thing to them. The trouble with them is they're not thinking of the Negro and how he feels. Wouldn't you suppose that if there was one word these guys that live off Negroes would get rid of, one single word in the whole vocabulary, it would be *nigger?*" (*Sports Illustrated*, July 15, 1968). When a newspaperman tried to get the attention of Elvin Hayes, star basketball player at the University of Houston, the reporter shouted, "Hey, boy!" Hayes turned to the reporter and said: "Boy's on *Tarzan*. Boy plays on *Tarzan*. I'm no boy. I'm 22 years old. I worked hard to become a man. I don't call you boy." The reporter apologized and said: "I didn't mean anything by it" (*Sports Illustrated*, July 1, 1968).

Whites who would never think of referring to Negroes as "boy" or "nigger" do, however, reveal themselves through less obviously racist language. A day does not go by without one hearing, from people who should know better, about "the Negro problem," a phrase which carries with it the implication that the Negro is a problem. One is reminded of the Nazis talking about "the Jewish problem." There was no Jewish problem! Yet the phrase carried the implication that the Jews were a problem in Germany and hence being a problem invited a solution and the solution Hitler proposed and carried out was the "final solution." Even the most competent writers fall into the "Negro problem" trap; James Reston of the *New York Times* wrote on April 7, 1968: "When Gunnar Myrdal, the Swedish social philosopher who has followed the Negro problem in America for forty years, came back recently, he felt that a great deal had changed for the better, but concluded that we have greatly underestimated the scope of the Negro problem." Myrdal himself titled his 1944 classic work *The American Dilemma: The Negro Problem and Modern Democracy*. A book published in 1967, *The Negro in 20th Century America*, by John Hope Franklin and Isidore Starr, starts off in the Table of Contents with "Book One: *The Negro Problem*"; the foreword begins, "The Negro problem was selected because it is one of the great case studies in man's never-ending fight for equal rights." One of the selections in the book, a debate in which James Baldwin participates, has Baldwin's debate opponent saying that "the Negro problem is a very complicated one." There are several indications that from here on out the black American is no longer going to accept the phrase "the Negro problem." As Lerone Bennett, Jr. said in the August 1965 issue of *Ebony*, "there is no Negro problem in America. The problem of race in America, insofar as that problem is related to packets of melanin in men's skins, is a white problem." In 1966, the editors of *Ebony* published a book of essays dealing with American black-white relations entitled *The WHITE Problem in America*. It is difficult to imagine Negroes sitting around during the next decade talking about "the Negro problem," just as it is difficult to imagine Jews in 1939 referring to themselves as "the Jewish problem."

The racial brainwashing of whites in the United States leads them to utter such statements as "You don't sound like a Negro" or "Well, he didn't sound like a Negro to me." John Howard Griffin, who changed the color of his skin from white to black to find out what it meant to be black in America, was ashamed to admit that he thought he could not pass for a Negro because he "didn't know how to speak Negro." "There is an illusion in this land," said Griffin, "that unless you sound as though you are reading Uncle Remus you couldn't possibly have an authentic Negro dialect. But I don't know what we've been using for ears because you don't have to be in the Negro community five minutes before the truth strikes and the truth is that there are just as many speech patterns in the Negro community as there are in any other, particularly in areas of rigid segregation where your right shoulder may be touching the shoulder of a Negro PhD and your left shoulder the shoulder of the disadvantaged." A black American, when told that he does not "sound like a Negro," legitimately can ask his white conversationalist, "What does a Negro sound like?" This will probably place the white in a dilemma for he will either have to admit that sounding like a Negro means sounding like Prissy in *Gone With the Wind* ("Who dat say who dat when you say dat?") or that perhaps there is no such thing as "sounding like a Negro." Goodman Ace, writing in the July 27, 1968, issue of the *Saturday Review* points out that years ago radio program planners attempted to write Negroes into the radio scripts, portraying the Negro as something else besides janitors, household maids, and train porters. Someone suggested that in the comedy radio show *Henry Aldrich* Henry might have among his friends a young Negro boy, without belaboring the point that the boy was Negro. As Mr. Ace observes, "just how it would be indicated on radio that the boy is black was not mentioned. Unless he was to be named Rufus or Rastus." Unless, it might be added, he was to be made to "sound like a Negro."

Psychiatrist Frantz Fanon, who begins his *Black Skin, White Masks* with a chapter titled "The Negro and Language," explains the manner of many whites when talking to Negroes and the effects of this manner. Although he is writing about white Europeans, what Fanon says applies equally to white Americans. He points out that most whites "talk down" to the Negro, and this "talking down" is, in effect, telling the Negro, "You'd better keep your place." Fanon writes: "A white man addressing a Negro behaves exactly like an adult with a child and starts smirking, whispering, patronizing, cozening." The effect of the whites' manner of speaking to the Negro "makes him angry, because he himself is a pidgin-nigger-talker." "But I will be told," says Fanon, "there is no wish, no intention to anger him. I grant this; but it is just this absence of wish, this lack of interest, this indifference, this automatic manner of classifying him, imprisoning him, primitivizing him, decivilizing him, that makes him angry." If a doctor greets his Negro patient with "You not feel good, no?" or "G'morning pal. Where's it hurt? Huh? Lemme see—belly ache? Heart pain?" the doctor feels perfectly justified in speaking that way, writes Fanon, when in return the patient answers in the same fashion; the doctor can then say to himself, "You see? I wasn't kidding. That's just the way they are." To make the Negro talk pidgin, as Fanon observes, "is to fasten him to the effigy of him, to snare him, to imprison him, the eternal victim of an essence, of an *appearance* for which he is not responsible. And naturally, just as a Jew who spends money without thinking about it is suspect, a black man who quotes Montesquieu had better be watched." The whites, in effect, encourage the stereotype of the Negro; they perpetuate the stereotype through the manner in which they speak about and speak to Negroes. And if Fanon is correct, the whites by "talking down" to the Negro are telling that black American citizen to "remember where you come from!"

Another facet of the racism of the whites' language is reflected in their habit of referring to talented and great writers, athletes, entertainers, and clergymen as "a great Negro singer" or "a great black poet" or "a great Negro ball player." What need is there for whites to designate the color or race of the person who has excelled? Paul Robeson and Marian Anderson are great and talented singers. James Baldwin and Leroi Jones are talented writers. Why must the whites qualify the greatness of these individuals with "black" or "colored" or "Negro"? Fanon briefly refers to this predilection of whites to speak with this qualification:

> ... Charles-André Julien introducing Aimé Césaire as "a Negro poet with a university degree," or again, quite simply, the expression, "a great black poet."
>
> These ready-made phrases, which seem in a common-sense way to fill a need—for Aimé Césaire is really black and a poet—have a hidden subtlety, a permanent rub. I know nothing of Jean Paulhan except that he writes very interesting books; I have no idea how old Roger Caillois is, since the only evidence I have of his existence are the books of his that streak across my horizon. And let no one accuse me of affective allergies; what I am trying to say is that there is no reason why André Breton should say of Césaire, "Here is a black man who handles the French language as no white man today can."

The tendency to designate and identify a person as a Negro when the designation is not necessary carries over into newspaper and magazine reporting of crimes. There was no need for *Time* magazine (July 19, 1968) to designate the race of the individual concerned in the following *Time* report:

"In New York City, slum dwellers were sent skidding for cover when Bobby Rogers, 31, Negro superintendent of a grubby South Bronx tenement, sprayed the street with bullets from a sawed-off .30 cal. semi-automatic carbine, killing three men and wounding a fourth." *Time*, for whatever reason, designated the race of the person involved in this instance, but the reports on other criminal offences cited by *Time*, on the same page, did not indicate the race of the "suspects." As a label of primary potency, "Negro" stands out over "superintendent." The assumption that whites can understand and sympathize with the Negro's dismay when black "suspects" are identified by race and white "suspects" are not, is apparently an unwarranted assumption; or it may be possible that the whites *do* understand the dismay and precisely for that reason continue to designate the race of the black criminal suspect. To argue that if the race is not designated in the news story then the reader can assume that the suspected criminal is white, is not acceptable for it makes all the difference if the suspect is identified as "a Negro superintendent," "a white superintendent," or "a superintendent." If we were told, day in and day out, that "a *white* bank clerk embezzled" or "a *white* service station operator stole" or "a *white* unemployed laborer attacked," it would make a difference in the same sense that it makes a difference to identify the criminal suspect as "Negro" or "black."

If many Negroes find it hard to understand why whites have to designate a great writer or a great artist or a common criminal as "colored" or "Negro," so too do many Negroes find it difficult to understand why whites must designate a Negro woman as a "Negress." Offensive as "Negress" is to most blacks, many whites still insist on using the term. In a July 28, 1968 *New York Times Magazine* article, the writer, discussing the 1968 campaigning of Rockefeller and Nixon, wrote: "A fat Negress on the street says, passionately, 'Rocky! Rocky!' " As Gordon Allport has written in *The Nature of Prejudice*, "members of minority groups are often understandably sensitive to names given them. Not only do they object to deliberately insulting epithets, but sometimes see evil intent where none exists." Allport gives two examples to make his point: one example is the spelling of the word "Negro" with a small "n" and the other example is the word "Negress." "Sex differentiations are objectionable," writes Allport, "since they seem doubly to emphasize ethnic differences: why speak of Jewess and not of Protestantess, or of Negress, and not of whiteness?" Just as "Jewess" is offensive to the Jews, so too is "Negress" offensive to the Negroes. "A Negro woman" does not carry the same connotations as "Negress," the latter conveying an emotional emphasis on both the color and sex of the individual. *Webster's New World Dictionary of American Language* says of "Negress": "A Negro woman or girl: often a patronizing or contemptuous term."

When the newspaper reporter tried to get the attention of twenty two year old basketball star Elvin Hayes by shouting, "Hey boy!" and Hayes vigorously objected to being called "boy," the reporter apologized and said: "I didn't mean anything by it." In a few cases, a very few cases, white Americans indeed "didn't mean anything by it." That excuse, however, will no longer do. The whites must make a serious conscious effort to discard the racist clichés of the past, the overt and covert language of racism. "Free, white, and 21" or "That's white of you" are phrases whites can no longer indulge in. Asking white Americans to change their language, to give up some of their clichés, is disturbing enough since the request implies a deficiency in the past use of that language; asking that they discard the language of racism is also disturbing because the people being asked to make the change, in effect, are being told that they have been the perpetrators and perpetuators of racism. Finally, and most important, calling the Negro "nigger" or "boy," or "speaking down" to the Negro, gives Whitey a linguistic power over the victimized black American, a power most whites are unwilling or afraid to give up. A person's language is an extension of himself and to attack his use of language is to attack him. With the language of racism, this is exactly the point for the language of white racism and the racism of the whites are almost one and the same. Difficult and painful as it may be for whites to discard their racist terms, phrases, and clichés, it must be done before blacks and whites can discuss seriously the eradication of white racism.

7

THE LANGUAGE OF WOMEN'S LIBERATION

During the past few years, the women's liberation movement has been warmly debated by both sexes. Women are habitually relegated to a secondary place in society. In the first article presented here, the author discusses the changes that women liberationists would like to see effected in the English language.

The article is answered by Stefan Kanfer, who examines the pros and cons of the efforts of women liberationists to "unsex" the English language. In such an attempt there is the danger, Kanfer declares, for much that is of value in the language to be lost.

Finally, in an amusing satire on the language of "male chauvinism," a woman liberationist exposes "male villainy."

Is It Possible for
a Woman to Manhandle
the King's English?

ISRAEL SHENKER

W HEN THE 79TH annual convention of the American Psychological Association opens in Washington Sept. 3, the most astonishing psychological phenomena will be the presiding officers. Instead of turning up as chairman or chairlady, each will have been transmuted into a sexually obscure "chairperson."

This is the way the language rumbles in deference to women's liberation. The leader of the attack is Varda One, publisher of a Los Angeles underground newspaper, who complained in an interview that the English language has forced women to see themselves "through a male mirror which distorts and insults them."

In every issue of "Everywoman" she shatters another bit of the mirror she calls Manglish. Varda One (this is what she calls "a liberation name"—others have opted for such as Betsy Warrior, Ann Fury and Dair Struggle) is high on the uses of "Person" as substitute for Mister, Missus and Miss.

Since "Mr." conceals man's marital state, many women would congeal Mrs. and Miss into like neutrality. Representative Bella S. Abzug, Democrat of New York, has opted for Ms. (pronounced ms). Varda One says Congressperson Abzug misses the point: "We don't go around addressing persons by their race, height or eye color. Why should we identify them by sex?"

Varda One favors a Nabokovian pninvention—"Pn," (short for Person). "I'd be Person Varda One," she said. Person H. W. Fowler, of English Usage fame, put the case flagrantly by saying "a female is, shortly put, a she, or put more at length, a woman-or-girl-or-cow-or-hen-or-the-like."

Women liberationists do not like it at all. The very term "women's lib" is unpopular in some circles which prefer "womankind."

"How can a woman MAN the barricades?" asks Emily Toth of Baltimore, writing in "Women—A Journal of Liberation."

In one English town recently, the town fathers (mothers?) could not decide what to label the municipal conveniences: Gents? Men? Ladies? Women? The doors stayed locked until the issue could be resolved.

As far as many women liberationists—members of womankind—are concerned, the issues have not only been joined, but also resolved. Words ending in "-mistress," such as postmistress and headmistress, offend womankind by laying undue stress on the female element. Great old paintings are meanwhile old masters, never old mistresses, masterpieces, never mistress-pieces.

On the ashheap of herstory (a word Everywoman has embraced) are antique splendors such as doctress, inventress, paintress, presidentess and professoress. Negress and Jewess survive, but not in acceptable speech. Increasingly unpopular with Varda One and others are authoress, poetess, sculptress.

As patters now stand, artisans defying the preferences of the militants say "she" (never he) needs a new coat of paint, "she" (not he) needs new spark plugs. "Thar she blows!" they will say of a gusher, and advice for recalcitrant machinery is "Give her a good kick."

It is, however, the huMAN race to which we all belong, in a word: MANkind. MAN discovers fire, invents the wheel, and is the measure of all things. Great thinkers are seminal, and even NON-thinkers enter the race as Homo Sapiens.

In the menagerie of metaphor, as women have discovered, the male is lion-hearted, never woman. She must twitter her life away as a bird, chick or magpie, though Detroit's "Fifth Estate" warns that it will refuse to publish such terms. Anyone can be a silly goose, but never a silly gander. (Among animals the singularly ideal collective is probably "fish—neutral as to gender, confusing as to number.)

Distasteful words formerly applied indifferently to female or male have come to stigmatize only the former: harlot, whore, wench. Some liberationists—such as Ethel Strainchamps, writing in "Woman in Sexist Society"—are upset that homosexual refers only to man.

People still speak of girl Friday and career girl, but not career boy. "Man alive!" is a respectable cry, but never "Woman alive!" "O boy!" never "O girl!" A Harvard man, but a Radcliffe girl.

In her book "After Nora Slammed the Door," Eve Merriam complains that "being called a girl when one is well past the age of consent (or dissent) makes me feel that I do not have to act as a responsible adult—not yet, anyway."

Varda One has found an appalling richness of words to describe women who nag, including beldame, fishwife, henpecker, shrew and virago. But no tag for male nags. "Penis envy" is in good psychological standing, she notes but who ever heard of womb envy?

In "The Growth and Structure of the English Language," Otto Jesperson wrote that English is "the most positively and expressly masculine of the languages" he knew. When there are feminine as well as masculine forms, the masculine is listed first—man, woman; male, female; husband, wife.

Varda One would drop husband and wife in favor of "partner" (never abbreviated to its first two letters). To reduce confusion in phrases like "he or she," "his or her," Pn. Varda One invented "ve" for the nominative, "vis" for the possessive and "ver" for the objective. A typical Varda version: "A teacher must learn to listen. Ve must respect vis students' opinions. They must be important to ver."

Up against this veil of meaning in the doctoral dissertation she will defend tomorrow at Northeastern University, Virginia V. Vallan uses "she" as generic pronoun. A typical Valian effort: "The psychological operations a language user performs as a listener are the reverse of those she performs as a talker."

Liberationist writer Mary Orovan suggests that "co" replace "he or she," with "cos" for possessive, "co" for objective, and "coself" for "himself or herself." Dana Densome, writing in the Boston periodical "The Female State," feels "she" should replace "he or she" since the word "he" is in "she." "Woman" would stand for man as well as woman. For the objective case, Pn. Densome suggests "herm" ("her" plus "him"), as in hermaphrodite.

The question bothering some is whether one herms the language by proliferating confusion while man decays. When Norman Mailer, chairperson of a debate on womankind, used the word "lady" he was roundly upbraided by the women present, though he was only trying to pay a compliment.

Surnames themselves—e.g., Mailer, Miller, Tiger—are excessively masculine. Robertson means son of Robert, and the name Lucy Johnson is now widely proposed as an example of how ridiculous English can get.

Even God has been put in Her place. "Trust in God, She will provide," is old liberationist coinage, and pleased Clare Boothe Luce. "In Goddess We Trust" has now revalued the currency.

In England, My Lord may still be addressed to a woman judge, but what to do about a governor who is a woman? One can hardly call her a governess.

With many words, the masculine form does double duty: secretary, solicitor, councillor. At the White House, women serve as "White House Fellows." Carol Greitzer, elected to New York's City Council, let it be known she wanted to be known as Councilman, then changed her mind—which is a Person's privilege.

Convinced that the dictionary is the most prejudiced book in the language, Varda One is preparing a Dictionary of Sexism. Alas, this is the King's English, not the Queen's. The very alphabet is man's province, and usually replies to his names: Abel, Baker, Charlie, all the way through Roger and out.

Sispeak:
A Msguided Attempt
to Change Herstory

STEFAN KANFER

As THE CHAIRPERSON of Senator McGovern's task force on the environment," begins Robert N. Rickles' letter to constituents. Chairperson? The title is no partisan issue: the G.O.P. also had a chairperson in Miami Beach. Thus another label comes unglued. The man and his woman are Out; the neuter "person" is In–and only the chair is allowed to linger undisturbed. Chairperson is just the latest exchange in that great linguistic bazaar where new terms are traded for old. The elderly "Mrs." and the shy "Miss" now curtsy to the crisp, swinging "Ms." "Congressone" has been suggested in federal corridors to replace the Congressman-woman stigma.

Lexicographers Ms. Casey Miller and Ms. Kate Swift recently amplified the Women's Lib party line: men have traditionally used language to subjugate women. As they see it, William James' bitch-goddess Success and the National Weather Service's Hurricane Agnes are products of the same criminal mind, designed to foster the illusion of woman as Eve, forever volatile and treacherous. The authors therefore suggest the elimination of sexist terms. "Genkind," they think, would provide a great encompassing umbrella under which all humanity could huddle, regardless. Varda One, a radical philologist, asks for the obliteration of such repugnant pronouns as he and she, his and hers. In place she offers ve, vis and ver. "We don't go around addressing persons by their race, height or eye color," says One. "Why should we identify them by sex?" Unfortunately, such designations tend to remove rather than increase an individual's sense of self. "Personalized" Christmas cards are about as personal as a paper cup.

Through the echoes of the new verbalism, one can sense the distress of that crystal spirit, George Orwell. In *Nineteen Eighty-Four* he posited the principles of a new tongue. "In Newspeak," wrote Orwell, "words which had once borne a heretical meaning were sometimes retained for the sake of convenience, but only with the undesirable meanings purged out of them." "Goodsex" meant chastity; "crimethink" suggested equality. "The greatest difficulty facing the compilers of Newspeak," continued Orwell, "was not to invent new words, but, having invented them, to make sure what they meant: to make sure what ranges of words they canceled by their existence."

Certainly the compilers of the new Sispeak have no such totalitarian purposes. Big Sister is not yet watching, and from the beginning the feminist wordsmiths have had to endure mockery and ridicule. Cartoonists and satirists have suggested that the ladies were Libbing under a Msapprehension. Their inventions were Msanthropic and Msguided attempts to change herstory. The *Godmother* was to be Mario Puzo's new Mafia novel; Womandarin Critic Susan Daughtertag was the new bottle for the old whine. Shedonism, girlcotting and countessdowns were to be anticipated in the liberated '70s. As for the enemy, he could expect to be confronted by female belligerents inviting him to put up his duchesses. He would find, in short, that his gander was cooked. All flagrantly gendered words would be swiftly unsexed. The ottoman would become the otto-it, the highboy would metamorphose into the highthing, and ladyfingers would be served under the somewhat less appealing name of person-fingers.

Yet beyond the hoots and herstrionics, the feminists seemed to have reason on their side. Tradition does play favorites with gender. Man, master, father are the commonplaces of theological and political leadership. Who, for example, could imagine the Four Horsepersons of the Apocalypse or George Washington, first in the hearts of his countrypeople? Even the literature of equality favors the male: Robert Burns sang "A man's a man for a' that!" *"Mann ist Mann,"* echoed Brecht. "Constant labor of one uniform kind," wrote Karl Marx, "destroys the intensity and flow of a man's animal spirits." The U.N. Charter speaks of the scourge of war, which "has brought untold sorrow to mankind." It is pathetically easy to spy in this vocabulary a latent slavery, a cloaked prejudice aimed at further subjugating women in the name of language.

No wonder, then, that the movement has set out to change the dictionary. With a touching, almost mystical trust in words, it seems to believe that definition is a matter of will. And indeed sometimes it is. The change from Negro to black has helped to remake a people's view of itself. But it is a lone example. Far more often, words have been corrupted by change. The counterculture's overuse of "love" has not resulted in a lessening of hostilities; "heavy" has become a lightweight adjective. The abuse of the word media has resulted in a breakdown of intelligence; invitations have even been sent out to "Dear media person." For the most part, the new lexicographers behave like Humpty Dumpty in *Through the Looking Glass*: a word may mean whatever they want it to mean. Naturally, said Humpty, "when I make a word do a lot of work, I always pay it extra." One wonders what Women's Lib's new words will be paid. They are, after all, working overtime, and against immense cultural and sociological odds.

In the philosophy of semantics there is a standard rhetorical question: Is it progress if a cannibal eats with a knife and fork? Similarly, if society is sexist, is it altered when its language is revised? Or do its attitudes remain when its platitudes change? The prognosis is not good. Words, like all currency, need to be reinforced with values. Take away the Federal Reserve and its dollar bill is waste paper. Take away meaning and a word is only noise. Changing chairman to chairperson is mock doctrine and flaccid democracy, altering neither the audience nor, in fact, the office holder. Despite its suffix, chairman is no more sexist than the French designation of "boat" as masculine, or the English custom of referring to a ship with feminine pronouns. Chairman is a role, not a pejorative. Congressman is an office, not a chauvinist plot. Mankind is a term for all humanity, not some 49% of it. The feminist attack on social crimes may be as legitimate as it was inevitable. But the attack on words is only another social crime—one against the means and the hope of communication.

For *A Clockwork Orange*, Anthony Burgess created a wall-to-wall nightmare in which society dissolves into violence and repression. The condition is reflected in the breakdown of language into "nadsat," a jumble of portmanteau constructions ("He looked a malenky bit poogly when he viddied the four of us"). To Burgess, language is the breath of civilization. Cut it short and society suffocates. That is an insight worth pondering. For if the world is to resist the nadsat future, readers and writers of both sexes must resist onefully any meaningless neologisms. To do less is to encourage another manifestation of prejudice—against reason, meaning and eventually personkind itself.

A Women's Lib Exposé
Of Male Villainy

ANN BAYER

I WAS MEETING my friend Hyperia Smith for a drink the other day and could tell from the agitated stride of her well-shaped legs and the high color in her pleasant face that she was furious. "Guess what a couple of male chauvinists just did," she burst out. "One of them said, 'Take a look at that dish!' and the other said, 'Yeah, a real tomato!' Those sexual oppressors!"

Before going any farther perhaps I should explain who Hyperia is. I knew her when she was just like any other downtrodden female living a perfectly contented enslaved life. Then one day while she was putting her husband's clothes in the washing machine, she had an awakening, and the next thing I heard she'd joined the women's liberation movement. Now one of its most vociferous and farsighted leaders, she is so conscious of the sexism rampant in our society that she finds it in the most outlandish places, and she has also gained an excellent command of the fem lib vocabulary.

"Gee," I said to Hyperia, "I wish someone would call *me* a tomato."

"That kind of statement," snapped Hyperia, "explains why you will always be caught in the bonds of male servitude."

She paused to order a bloody mary and went on, "Apparently you still can't recognize a devious paternalistic device when you hear one. When men act as if they are flattering us, what do they call us? Cookie, or gumdrop, or sugar, honey or cheesecake. What's so flattering about being looked on as something to be devoured? You'd think they were cannibals. Or they keep saying, 'Hey, chick!', 'Hi there, kitten!' Just a plot to remind us that we're weak and keep us in a subservient role. And when they really get generous with their compliments, we're an instrument of war, like a bombshell."

"Or an act of violence," I said, bringing up a fond memory. "A New York construction worker once called me a knockout. I've never forgotten it."

"Exactly," she agreed, missing my point entirely. "It's all part of the ideology of masculine superiority. But look how close their insults are to their compliments. If you're not a bombshell, what are you? A battle-ax. If we're not chicks, we're dogs, or cows or—ugh—bats. And when we're not fauna, we're flora: clinging vines, shrinking violets, wallflowers."

She shuddered—and went on: "Men see women not as human beings but as things. And even more, they see things as women. The most horrible things."

"Like what?"

"Like cataclysms. Who do you think has been threatening life and property in the Caribbean this year?"

I couldn't guess.

"Alma and Becky. And waiting off the coast somewhere are Celia, Dorothy and Ella. What sort of meteorologists do you think plotted to identify hurricanes by using girls' names? Male meteorologists.

"And who else but a man would name the deadliest insect in the whole country after a bereaved woman? Did you know—" she leaned across the table and lowered her voice "—that the female black widow has a habit of killing the male after mating? I can just imagine what that poor lady spider has to contend with to make her get so worked up.

"And," she said, her voice rising again, "who do you think they name a carnivorous plant after? The goddess of love."

"Oh," I said brightly, "the Venus's-flytrap."

"Tell me," she went on, "what is the very cruelest instrument of torture ever devised?"

"The iron maiden," I shot back.

"Right. And it's no accident either that the vehicle for hauling hardened criminals off to prison is called—

"A Black Maria," I interrupted.

Hyperia doesn't like to be upstaged and looked a little annoyed. I pointed out meekly that many wonderful things also have feminine names: lazy Susans, blue jeans, ladybugs, brown betty. . .

"I don't happen to think brown betty is all that wonderful," sniffed

Hyperia. "But there's something even worse than name-calling. Think of the indignities we women suffer in ads. How would a man like it if, right in the middle of a sonata, he was grabbed up from the keyboard by a lustful violinist who nearly breaks his back with passion? Or if he were barred from smoking a cigarette designed exclusively for rugged cowgirls? Or suppose it was men who had to have those embarrassing fantasies: 'I dreamed I was a toreador in my boxer shorts.' " Hyperia's face lighted up with liberated glee. "Now that would strip the male arrogance from those sexual supremacists."

8

THE LANGUAGE OF SCIENCE AND SPACE

The great advances in space exploration during recent years and the continued explosion of scientific knowledge have both contributed to a rapid growth in technological vocabulary and expression. The following articles are devoted to the language of science and space. The chapter opens with a linguistic analysis of aerospace English.

This is followed by a partial transcript of talk between Houston Control Center and American astronauts during one of their moon walks.

Other articles discuss space terminology and the "extensive linguistic and syntactical changes wrought in our language by science and technology."

A Linguistic Look
At Aerospace English

Donald A. Sears and Henry A. Smith

There has been extremely little written on the subject of this paper.[1] None of the standard technical writing books deals with language as affected by aerospace science and technology. Linguists, except for the few referred to and the mathematical/electronic communication specialists, have not treated aerospace or scientific English.

Yet some of the linguistic aspects of aerospace English are both interesting and worthy of study for the light they shed on broader problems of language. In order to clarify our approach to these problems, it is first necessary to distinguish levels of aerospace English.

One level is that found in the usage guides and technical writing handbooks employed within the industry. They are concerned strictly with written language in its final printed form. The scientific language reflected in them is "concrete, specific, simple, direct, precise, generally more active than passive, concise, clear, and readable."[2]

Another level is that of the raw, crude language of a rough draft reflecting "birdworks"[3] conversation. This paper is a consideration, from the standpoint of linguistics, of birdworks prose of this unedited sort. Specifically we wish to investigate the words and the language patterns peculiar to aerospace technology in order to discover to what extent the evolution of aerospace technology has influenced the language generally. Has the hardware affected the words; have the programs, with all of their economic, political, and cultural implications, affected American language patterns?

THE WORDS

Imbedded in our everyday speech are words that evidence the once pervasive influence of the predecessor of modern astronomy, astrology. The extent of these vestiges of old astrology is greater than we usually realize. The heavenly bodies have caused us to be *jovial, mercurial, saturnine, martial, and venereal* (an ironic tribute to the goddess of love). Something of the original "value" of some astrological terms is still maintained: *disaster* (an evil star) retains a superlative graveness, and *consider* (to be with the stars) still denotes a very high form of mental deliberation.*

Well may we ask, then, if modern aerospace technology exerts such an etymological influence. And if so, what effect does such a vocabulary have on American speech? The American linguist Leonard Bloomfield has stated:

> The connotation of technical forms gets its flavor from the standing of the trade or craft from which they are taken. Sea terms sound ready, honest, and devil-may-care: *abaft, aloft, the cut of his jib, stand by*; legal terms precise and a bit tricky: *without let or hindrance, in the premesis, heirs and assigns.* . . . [4]

Similarly, aerospace terms have a confident devil-may-care tone from historical air-force sources (the mission is *A-OK*), but there is an added tinge of mystery drawn out of the deep, adventurous, and unknown "space" which we are approaching: *space probe, acculation, neutrosphere, primary body, translunar, weightlessness, earth-escape trajectory.*

Economy of effort is a strong influence on aerospace words, and it can be seen in the tendency to abbreviate (*recirc* is widely used for *recirculation, conbud* is official for *contractural budget*) and in the tendency to make new words from the abbreviations, as in the case of acronyms. *NASA/næsə/* started as *The National Aeronautics and Space Administration,* then became *The N-A-S-A,* then *the NASA,* and finally *NASA.* Problems arise: one company which has two large NASA contracts uses both LOX and LO$_2$ in written reports as abbreviations for *liquid oxygen* depending on which program is being reported

---

* The asterisk is also an astrological effect.

because of the preferences of the particular NASA project managers. All engineers, of course, say *LOX*. Editors in the Publications Department, of course, say *LOX* or *LO₂* as a matter of habit, depending on which program group they are in, since it is their duty to maintain the integrity of final report language. (The last three words themselves form part of the jargon of the trade.)

Some acronyms have strange histories and also exert an interesting influence. For example, a Saturn booster rocket must be tested and checked before it is delivered to NASA. However, such a rocket is a rather complex set of systems encased in an aerodynamic structure, and the testing and checking process involves the performance of some 30 to 40 separate and combined tests, which have to be reported in written form to NASA. In the original contract, these reports were originally referred to as *system test and checkout reports*. Soon an abbreviation arose, but it was phonetically clumsy: *STCR*. It then became redundantly an *STCR report*. Eventually, just as if *STCR* were a Hebrew tetragrammaton, the engineers added vowel points, and the word *streetcar* emerged as a reference for *system test and checkout report*. It proves that words are arbitrary. Once in a while an engineer from another part of the program will ask in complete puzzlement: "What the hell is a streetcar?" However, this problem has had the good effect of causing more careful linguistic planning by the people who control acronyms in additions to the contract. Some of the latest are the *failure effect analysis report (FEAR), special materials and special handling (SMASH),* the *electronic ground automatic destruct sequencer (EGADS) button.*

A few words, of course, are not arbitrary. An editor recently encountered a *POGO* program and could not figure out the acronymic referents. It turned out that *POGO* was not an acronym even though it had been capitalized. *POGO* is the accordion-like squeeze and stretch oscillation that occurs along the central axis of a launch vehicle during lift-off and flight. The expression was meant to be the same as for the movement involved in using a pogo stick. This type of cultural reference could have unfortunate consequences, since it is idiomatic and confusing to a non-American audience. It proves that language is better left alone to be arbitrary so that it can be understood by all.

Sometimes a word resists being stretched to fit an expanded meaning. Until recently, the verb *slave* was used for one unit being *slaved* (or tied into the function of) another mechanically (in the manner of gears) and also, in an extended meaning, for gyros being *slaved* to electrical potentials in closed loop systems. However, the latter was a new concept, and *slaving* was not really meant. The verb *slew* has now replaced *slave* for gyros or for gears electrically *slewed* to each other.

The level of usage of words used in space technology is in an unusually chaotic state, mainly because there is never sufficient time for usage to settle into a stable body of "Standard Aerospace English." To start with, English is a highly assimilative language; aerospace English, because of its encounter with new scientific concepts and technical possibilities, becomes radically assimilative. As a result, "standard" is hard to find; "correct" usage is often impossible. Language purists who find themselves in aerospace organizations can never completely adjust to the situation. Numerous lists and documents of "preferred" usage are issued, but these are seldom followed and often not even read by technical writers. Most competent writers see an allomorphic range of intelligible forms (e.g., *LOX* and *LO*$_2$), make selections, and use them consistently within specific areas of documentation.

When a piece of equipment is delivered to NASA, the first information reported back to the contractor is *squawks*. These are not *complaints*, which would be a word too strong in connotation; not *discrepancies*, which is too weak and concerned mainly with basic design problems of principal interest to the contractor before the item has completed its manufacturing cycle; and certainly not *mistakes*, the contractor, by means of advanced inspection techniques, already knowing about them. They are simply *squawks*. Purists have tried for years to find a succinct but pure alternative to this word, but have so far been unsuccessful, and the term has become standard aerospace English. Other examples of standard slang are *debugging* and *boilerplate* (used in regard to formula-type language standard for all reports), both of which are also examples of transferred meaning.

Taboo Words

A technical aerospace editor was asked what he felt his main job to be. He replied facetiously, "When I edit a report, my first job is to change all of the *errors* to *malfunctions* and all of the *failures* to *partial successes*." This was a standard practice and the editor was the official keeper of the euphemisms. The reliability engineers, on the other hand, did not want to avoid taboo words; they were chiefly interested in alarming the program to potential failures. To alarm, of course, they needed to use taboo words, like *dangerous* and *catastrophic failures*, which the good editor would, in turn, change to *catastrophic partial successes*. During the early stages of a large booster-rocket contract, all of the companies serving as subcontractors had to be referred to as *suppliers* rather than as *vendors*, because *vendor* implied a poor, blind beggar *vending* pencils. Editors were expected to correct all deviations. Eventually, according to linguistic laws, the disyllable won out, and the trisyllabic *supplier* was eliminated, except when used in the alliterative phrase *supplier support*.

THE PATTERNS

The physicist Percy Bridgman has said that on the printed page, he was

> . . . compelled to express . . . nonverbal emergence in verbal terms. The words in which the physicist defined the meaning of such concepts as "length" must be of the type that have non-verbal referents–no more can be demanded. We have to get back onto the verbal level if we wish to communicate the results of our nonverbal operations.[5]

Bridgman basically wanted *verbalized* language in order to avoid metaphysical and moral problems in expression of reality as seen by science.

In everyday aerospace English, there are two areas of "reality" that the writer must verbalize:

1. Technical facts
2. The meaning (often nontechnical) he wishes the reader to draw from the facts

The communication in writing of these two items is the problem of the aerospace writer. The patterns of aerospace English result from the linguistic encounter with this problem. Engineers often say and believe that the meaning is more important than the English. To the extent that it is true, the hardware and the programs have influenced the language for their own purpose. Also, to the extent that it is true, there are specific patterns of aerospace English.

Technical Factors

The aerospace writer sits down before an accumulation of data. He must present the data verbally and give it meaning in a report. Is his problem one of merely choosing the correct, the preferred words and in making his language "concrete, specific, simple, direct, precise, generally more active than passive, concise, clear, and readable?" Or must he pattern his language in certain ways? Benjamin Lee Whorf, an engineer and a linguist said,

Reference is the lesser part of meaning, patternment the greater. . . . It is certain that scientific terms like "force, average, sex, allergic, biological" are . . . no more certain in reference than "sweet, gorgeous, rapture, enchantment, heart and soul, stardust."[6]

If Whorf's thesis be true, we should expect pattern to supersede reference (or words) as the determiner in aerospace English.

One example of this is the use of redundancy and exaggeration. There are such word groups as the *Specific Specification Control Board* and documents such as the *Logistics Support Plan*. For years, all revisions of reports of a large booster program carried a notice on the cover: "This reissue completely supersedes and replaces all previous issues of this document." The "pattern" of this notice resulted from the strong desire to prevent anyone from using outdated information. Rocket boosters must contain, by pattern of design, hundreds of redundant systems to preclude failure and to provide reliability; they are overdesigned, well beyond what is necessary for normal function. The same overdesign appears in much of the prose. The following sentence, taken from a printed document, is a good example:

The reliable acquisition of accurate biomedical data on animals has become increasingly important with the use of animals in space flight programs.

It is a long way of saying that measurements must be more accurate and reliable for biomedical data than for other data. "Acquisition of data" should be understood to involve reliability and accuracy. The *degree* of reliability and accuracy is something else. And "biomedical data" on something besides animals would constitute some kind of radical breakthrough worthy of a book of its own.

This type of making assurance doubly sure through redundancy is, of course, never recommended in style guides and should not appear in final printed form. Nevertheless, it does appear often enough in rough copy to be no accident but the manifestation of the techniques of over-design on language.

The popular concept of a *countdown* being merely a "count" like "one, two, three, go" was changed as the public witnessed actual countdowns on television. The real meaning or referent of the word is a long, difficult, technical checkout with many *holds* and frequent *postponements*. The obvious referent was the wrong one. Now the public language has adjusted itself to the real pattern. Words like *hold* instead of *stop* or *pause* and even *GO/NO GO* have entered the language. Similar qualifications are *memory* (often a device), *noise* (to include nonsounds), the verb *optimize*, and new concepts of measurement such as *g's* (gravities) and *Machs* (times the speed of sound).

Paradoxically, *quality* is now measured *quantitatively*. NASA defines *quality* as

> A measure of the degree to which it conforms to specification or workmanship standards. Its *numerical rating* (our italics) is obtained by measuring the percentage defective of a lot or population at a given time.[7]

Aerospace English does not distinguish between *quality* and *quantity* in the same way that standard English does.

Since our national space program is tied in with our economy and with international and domestic politics, scheduling is an everchanging thing. The shifting nature of schedules influences the pattern of language. A plan of action for a program change contained the following order:

> Reconfigurate equipment container base drawing to reflect new insert requirement at vehicle 5.

Vehicle 5 is the fifth production model of a booster rocket. The prepositional phrase *at Vehicle 5* would normally terminate an action: *Look at Vehicle 5* for example. But here it is used as a time reference because of the ever-changing schedule. Other usages stemming from the flexible nature of aerospace schedules are *critical path* (the sequence of events on a charted schedule which will take the longest and ultimately govern the accomplishment of other phases of the overall schedule), and *PERT* (and the verb *perted*, from *program evaluation review technique*, a scheduling system).

The verb *reconfigurate* from the aforementioned order is also a term of aerospace writing. A nonengineer might be satisfied with "Change the base drawing," but since the engineer knows that the drawing is a *configuration*, any modification to it is naturally a *reconfiguration*. In this case, there could be too strong an emphasis upon the referent rather than the meaning intended; *change* certainly supplies the pattern, does not curtail the meaning, and is much more economical.

Another aspect of pattern of aerospace English can be seen in the same order in the phrase *equipment container base drawing*. Noun clusters such as this appear frequently enough in aerospace language to constitute a pattern. They are caused by the necessity to describe complicated equipment, and they cause aerospace English to be more agglutinative in certain respects than is standard English. Other noun clusters are *explosive devices simulator set, net positive suction head,* and *stage systems design parameters.* From two of these, the "galloping plural," a technical-age phenomenon, can also be observed. In the last example, singular *system* would suffice; but there are many *systems,* so that the plural must be *built into* the phrase. This technical pattern, a mechanistic result of engineer-built language, is gaining wider usage, into popular technical language, as in *sports* car.

Another minor type of patterning is observable in the use of adjectival subordinate elements as adverbial modifiers.

> Acoustic testing on the forward skirt was accomplished during the first two weeks of December, which completes all testing on the forward skirt.
> Also, this addition allows the facility recorders and cameras to be slaved to the countdown programmer, thereby preventing a premature run out of paper or film during critical firing times.

This practice serves to control the level of reference just because it is not too precise.

Aerospace writing is free, in a sense, of some inhibitions, and often the exigencies of pattern bring to life ancient meanings and produce new meanings. The phrase,

> Responsibility for safing the camera capsule for all pyrotechnics prior to departure from the recovery ship. . . .

was taken from a plan of action for correct processing of cameras recovered after the flight of a large booster rocket. The cameras were ejected from the booster by means of an explosive wire, and they were picked up in the ocean. To avoid having any unused explosive going off in the faces of members of the post-recovery team, the capsule must be disarmed or *safed.* Webster's *Third New International,* liberal and up-to-date as it is, still calls *safed* obsolete. But the word is quite handy and economical for the space program (similar to the slang *debug* and *squawk*). *Pyrotechnics* is really the art of making firecrackers or even an eloquent display of wit. In this case, it is something that, through error or failure (*partial success*), could cause a delayed explosion. The assimilation of new meanings and the renascence of obsolete terms allows great elasticity of expression for conveying specifically chosen levels of technical meaning: in this case, the company was not to be blamed for anyone's getting injured by leftover explosives on the ejected camera.

Nontechnical Factors

The language generally has had its own impact on the patterns of aerospace communications. This can be seen in the romantic tendency to name every rocket or spacecraft after a Greek or Roman god (*Jupiter, Atlas, Hercules, Saturn, Apollo, Thor* [Norse], *Mercury, Gemini,* etc.). These names seem to connote a secular or pagan overseriousness regarding man's ability to conquer the unknown universe by means of "godlike" man-made vehicles, sort of a heresy of technique. Such naming breeds an overconfidence, a sign of which is the gravity of disappointment and the serious economic implications of failure or even poor performance. But it is hard to believe that a "god" could die, even a god of technology. Therefore, the "answer" to any problems of failure always seems to be with the "organization" or the "management" of the program. There seems to be no room for what the poet Paul Roche has called "the rank obstinacy of things." We seem more to be following the thought that Norbert Wiener was so fond of, "God may be subtle, but he is not plain mean," and that might be an example of scientific heresy caused by our linguistic overconfidence.

Confidence in the face of the reality of failure and hardship as seen, for instance, in the military linguistics of World War II:

> Though there's one motor gone
> We will still carry on
> Coming in on a wing and a prayer

and of such realistic names as *The Ruptured Duck* as opposed to *Apollo* or *Jupiter* is a sharp linguistic contrast to the present mentality. If there is one motor gone from a major space vehicle and the astronaut comes in "on a wing and a prayer," someone will be in serious trouble.

The international and domestic political aspects of the *race for space* bring about a linguistic atmosphere of "hard sell." By means of the space program, the United States can make a favorable impression on the "uncommited" nations; the Democrats could win votes; California representatives want to bring more money into the state in the form of more big contracts; individual companies want the contracts. Consequently, there is a lot of selling, and the language tends to be persuasive, overpositive, and rigged, much like the language and art of socialist realism in which nothing ever really goes wrong and certain negative facts or realities are nearly hidden in the positive perspective. "Factual" data must always be interpreted in the right light. In a program in which an expensive experimental package was placed in a space pod and put into orbit, the costly pod and package failed to separate from the spacecraft and was destroyed upon reentry. In the final report to the customer, the opening paragraph read like a bulletin from *Pravda*:

> The objectives of this program were accomplished. The test results demonstrated that such experiments are feasible for use in space flight research. Sufficient information was obtained to permit recommendations to be made for future efforts.
>
> All equipments functioned properly with the exception of the scientific pod, which failed to eject from the missile prior to reentry. Thus, the pod and experimental package were not recovered.

Note the *positive* tone given to the conclusion. Objectives were accomplished. All *equipments* (the galloping plural) functioned properly, except. . . . The linguistic-semantic (meaning control) communicative necessities override any dry, objective listing of the simple facts. The taboo notion of the failure of the expensive recovery system was euphemized: "The . . . package was *not recovered.*" This positive *pattern* or *stylistic* is seen in many aerospace reports; there is a high frequency of positive words (*accomplished, successful, on-schedule, functioned properly, partial success*) and a tabooing of negative words (*failure, error,* etc.)

CONCLUSION

One might compare the linguistic aftermath of the Biblical effort to step beyond our sphere by means of a tower with the linguistic effects of the similar contemporary efforts at Cape Kennedy. In the first case, the result is best described by the etymological depth of the very name of the effort. The United States' space program is no legend, however, and the linguistic *spin-off* from it can be more accurately defined than that of Babel. It seems that when the engineers use English, they change it to suit their advantage. But that is really the same thing as using English, assimilative and adaptable as it is. Where English cannot be used, other languages are developing.[8]

The engineer who said that the meaning is more important than the English still had to make his meaning meaningful (control its loss) to an English-speaking readership. Perhaps we should say that the meaning (or the language) is more important than the preferred usage.

In a recent, nationally televised lift-off, the smooth, articulated voice from mission control said, in a relaxed Southern dialect, "The pitch and roll program are in." Not many listeners know what the pitch and roll program is, and the speaker does not know that the program *is in*. There is a language gap between advanced technical aerospace English and the standard language of the common man.

There is a semantic problem. For instance, *input* has replaced *put into* in computer parlance; the noun has become the verb again. But the preposition has been retained, and many computer documents now contain *input into*. (The data were input into the program.) The strictly technical computer man is not affronted by this: the "field" of language in which he moves will provide him with the basis for satisfactory comprehension; *input into* forms part of the area of his meaning. This is a sign of a language gap.

The existence of the gap is further verified by the fairly recent development in the aerospace industry of a high-priced group of technical editors (not writers). This field is new, and its personnel are drawn mainly from other language-related fields: journalism, teaching, advertising, the ministry. The race for space has created an urgency in aerospace technical development which has to be reported to nontechnical industrial executives and government officials. At its root the problem may be an educational one. In many universities, engineering majors are required to take few English or foreign language courses; therefore, they do not develop competence in formal composition even though some might be gifted at self-expression. But, in today's communicative world, they have to write; they have to report to the nontechnical sponsoring community. In the current moon project, it is estimated that the paperwork, if put in a stack, would reach deeper than the space probe itself.

As the paper mounts, technical editors are astounded, day after day, as they labor through reams of rough copy. They rewrite; they interview the engineer-writers; they key in references to illustrations and tables; they have the book typed and printed nicely, with a well-designed cover. Then a copy is sent to the engineer and he reacts like the actor quoted by H. Allen Smith: "My God, what a swell book I've written!"

---

[1] Alfred M. Bork, *Science and Language* (Boston, 1966), Walker Gibson, ed., *The Limits of Language* (New York, 1962), and Mario Pei, *Language of the Specialists* (New York, 1966) are perhaps the most useful.

[2] These possibly redundant terms are taken from Theodore A. Sherman, *Modern Technical Writing* (New Jersey, 1966). He says, "Our style becomes readable when we choose our words intelligently, write sentences of suitable length, develop such qualities as simplicity and directness and conciseness—in fact do all the things that have been recommended" (p. 23). This approach to language is something like that of a foreign-traveling English lady quoted by H. Allen Smith, *How To Write Without Knowing Nothing* (New York, 1950): "I don't see why, if one speaks slowly and distinctly, English should not be understood by everybody."

[3] *Bird* is "a colloquial term for a rocket, satellite, or spacecraft." (Mario Pei, *Language of the Specialists*, p. 375). A *birdworks* is an aerospace corporation.

[4] Leonard Bloomfield, *Language* (New York, 1933), p. 152.

[5] Percy W. Bridgman, "Words, Meanings, and Verbal Analysis," in Bork's *Science and Language*, pp. 23–43.

[6] Benjamin Lee Whorf, *Language, Thought, and Reality* (Cambridge: MIT Press, 1956), p. 261.

[7] NASA, *Apollo Terminology* (Washington, D.C., 1963).

[8] For nonverbal communication, see, for instance, J. R. Pierce, *Symbols, Signals, and Noise* (New York, 1961).

Walking –
and Talking –
on the Moon

NEW YORK TIMES

*Following are conversations between controllers in Houston and Comdrs.
Charles (Pete) Conrad Jr. and Alan L. Bean, who made their first moon
walk yesterday after landing the lunar module, Intrepid, in the Ocean of
Storms. The conversations were transcribed by* The New York
Times. *All times given are Eastern Standard.*

CONRAD (6:39 A.M.): I'm headed down the ladder.

BEAN: O.K., wait. Let me get the old camera on you, Pete.

CONRAD: Man, is that a pretty-looking sight, that LM [landing
module].

BEAN: O.K., O.K., got the old camera running.

CONRAD (6:45 A.M.): Down to the pad. . . . Whoopie, man, that may
have been a small step for Neil, but that's a long one for me. I'm going to step
off the pad. Right. Up. Oh, is that soft. Hey, that's neat. I don't sink in too far.
I'll try a little–boy, that sun's bright. That's just like somebody shining a
spotlight in your hands. I can walk pretty well, Al, but I've got to take it easy
and watch what I'm doing. Boy, you'll never believe it! Guess what I see
sitting on the side of the crater. The old Surveyor!

BEAN: The old Surveyor, yes, sir.

CONRAD (laughter): Does that look neat. It can't be any further than 600 feet from here. How about that?

HOUSTON: Well planned, Pete.

CONRAD: I have the decided impression I don't want to move too rapidly. But I can walk quite well. The Surveyor really is sitting on the side of a steep slope. I'll tell you that.

BEAN: Boy you sure are lean forward, Pete.

CONRAD: Hey, lean forward, I feel like I'm going to fall over in any direction.

BEAN: You're leaning—

CONRAD: Hey, Houston, one of the first things that I can see, by golly, is little glass beads. I got a piece about a quarter of an inch in sight and I am going to put it in a contingency sample bag.

CONRAD: O.K., I got the table out, testing the MESA [Modularized Equipment Storage Assembly] . . . Very nice. Very nice. Hey, Al.

BEAN: Yep.

CONRAD: I could work out here all day, just take your time . . . Dum de dum dum dum. Dum de dum dum dum.

CONRAD: I've got both canisters, Al, both batteries. As soon as I get them in here, I got to pack the contingency samples.

BEAN: O.K., but just—I tell you, you just can't move as fast as I thought you could. You got to take it real easy.

CONRAD: O.K. That a boy. You look great. Welcome aboard.

BEAN: You hop a little bit—

CONRAD: If you turn around and walk over to your right and look over that crater, you're going to see our pal sitting there. That's one steep slope it's on.

BEAN: O.K., here we go.

CONRAD: That a boy.

BEAN: There that thing is. Look at that!

CONRAD: Look how close we almost landed to that crater!

BEAN: Beautiful, Pete.

CONRAD: Look at the descent engine. It didn't even dig a hole.

BEAN: O.K., Houston; I'm going to do the TV camera now.

HOUSTON: Roger, Al.

BEAN: Hey, it's real nice moving around up here. You don't seem to get tired. You really hop like a bunny. Where is earth? There it is. You can look at TV.

HOUSTON: Al, we copy your comment on insertion on that into the ground. How far in are you?

BEAN: Oh, I pounded it in over a foot I'd say and it didn't look like it was any harder toward the end than right at the beginning. It's there. . . . O.K., Houston, I'm going to move the focus a bit and see what happens.

HOUSTON: Roger, Al, don't spend too much time on it; you're running a tad behind.

BEAN: O.K. Well, I'll tell you what. I can feel that the wheels, when I hold the end of the lens, I can feel the wheels running because I can feel something in motion inside. O.K., now, I just changed completely the settings I had before.

HOUSTON: O.K., Al, we see no change down here.

BEAN: O.K., let me try another F stop, the other way. How's that?

HOUSTON: There's no change down here; Al . . . What change did you make?

BEAN: I hit it on the top with my hammer. I figured we didn't have a thing to lose.

HOUSTON: Skillful fix, Al.

BEAN: I hit it on the top with this hammer I've got. Yes, that's skilled craftsmanship.

HOUSTON: Al, we're still not getting a good picture. Why don't you press on and we'll try to get back to it later if we have time.

BEAN: O.K., I'll pound it a little bit. There you go. . . . That ought to give you some sort of a picture that you can think about. Be glad to come back on work on it. Got to go to work again.

CONRAD: Al?

BEAN: Yes sir.

CONRAD: What I need is a piece of cake.

CONRAD: There's all kinds of cake around here.

HOUSTON: Pete, go ahead.

CONRAD: O.K., the flag is up.

HOUSTON: Roger, copy, the flag is up. We show you are very close to the nominal timeline.

CONRAD: We have the flag up like I said; hope everyone down there is as proud of it as we are to put it up.

HOUSTON: Affirmative, Pete; we're proud of what you're doing.

CONRAD: Al, how was the LM inspection?

BEAN: I'm working on it right now.

CONRAD: Taking a look at that Surveyor, Al, I suspect we ought to be able to get there quite readily. I'm going to head over there by the crater a little bit, but instead of—whoop!

BEAN: Watch yourself, it's easy to slide.

CONRAD: You can say that again. I know that you've been over here, haven't you.

BEAN: Uh, uh.

HOUSTON: Al, do you have any comments on the foot pad interaction with the surface?

BEAN: Yes I do. Actually we—Pete's pads went in a little but further than did Neil's. Most of the pads are in about an inch and a half and it sort of looks like we were moving lightly forward and that pretty well killed off our left, right velocity when we touched down.

HOUSTON: Roger, Al. Do you see anything on the surface from the DPS?

BEAN: No, I don't. The surface under there is interesting . . . it doesn't have the loose dust particles as does the rest of the lunar surface about here. It also has a number of small round dirt clods, if you want. They seem to be strolling off in a radial direction from underneath the skirt of the engine. I'll take a couple of pictures. Shots about 8 inches or so off the ground.

HOUSTON: Roger, Al, it's a good description.

BEAN: Oh, there it is; I can see it. Hello there, earth. Where is it?

BEAN: Hey, you can see some little shiny glass, yeah, glass in these rocks.

CONRAD: Yeah, I reported that.

BEAN: You can also see some pure glass if you look around.

CONRAD: You can jump in the air.

CONRAD (7:41 A.M.): Houston, how long we been up?

HOUSTON: Pete, you've been out 1 hour and 2 minutes and you're both running about 2 minutes nominal behind.

BEAN: Looks like a good place for the solar wind collector, Pete. I think I'll stick it right here.

CONRAD: O.K.

BEAN (9:02 A.M.): O.K., Houston. The magnetometer is deployed. It's level and it's pointed exactly east and the little black do is right in the middle. What are you mumbling about over there?

CONRAD: I just don't like all that dirt on it. I don't know what we can do though . . . all you can do is tap it a little bit and hope some of it falls off.

INTREPID: Does that antenna look like it's pointed at earth? It looks close. That's it. [Pete Conrad and Al Bean talking to each other while setting up: the ALSEP.]

CONRAD: Say, are you dirty. I'm just as dirty . . . I can't believe it. . . . Houston, how long we've been out?

HOUSTON: Pete you've been out 2 plus 40 and . . . you're running around 20 minutes behind.

CONRAD: O.K. That American flag sure looks pretty back there next to the LM, doesn't it?

BEAN: Boy, do I like to run up here. This is neat. The first thing we're going to do is run over to that volcano-looking thing or whatever that little jobberdoo is.

HOUSTON (9:21 A.M.): Pete now, Pete, now Houston, looks like you did the job. We're getting data back.

CONRAD: Hey, you don't know how happy I am. . . . How long are you going to let us stay out?

HOUSTON: Pete, you'll be extended 30 minutes so you're out for a total of four hours . . . and you've got about one hour left. We have some words on the traverse [walk] back.

BEAN: We're standing over at the head crater. Why don't we start picking up some rocks, Pete, while we're waiting. Yeah, yeah.

HOUSTON: Pete, now two things we'd like you to do on the traverse on the way back. One is to get samples and some documentation of those mounds and secondly, if you can get over to the thousand-foot crater which is northwest of the ALSEP and get samples and documentation from there.

CONRAD: Thousand-foot crater . . . you don't mean the head crater, do you? Let's get some of this mound, Al.

HOUSTON: Pete, Houston. The crater which we speak of is about 300 feet northwest of head crater.

CONRAD: Oh, I see it. You mean the breat big one. . . . Yeah, we can go over there.

CONRAD: We're almost over to the thousand-foot crater. Got about another 200 feet to go. . . . We're in an area right now which looks like it had a fresh impact not too long ago. It doesn't have that old look like all the rest of them do. . . .

HOUSTON: Roger, Pete, now we copy that. And we'd like you back to the LM to start the closeout in 10 minutes.

CONRAD: O.K. Holy Christmas. We're going to have to smoke there, Houston.

HOUSTON: That's affirmative.

Space Language
Is Out of Sight

Nicholas C. Chriss

THE APOLLO 15 astronauts spotted some unsymmetrical dimethyl hydrazine this week. Mission Control, however, said it is storable and hypergolic.

The event reportedly occurred in aeropause, near the aerothermodynamic border and during an anomalistic period.

Everyone knows the people in the space program march to the beat of a different drum. This is most readily seen in their language, which is made up of strange-sounding words with obscure meanings.

The people are obscure, too. When the Americans first got their hands on Werner von Braun and asked him about his V-2 rockets, he smiled and said, "Why don't you talk to Dr. Robert Goddard?"

As it turned out, Goddard was an American, virtually unknown in his own country, the father of modern rocketry, a man who was accused of trying to perpetrate a fraud when he said rockets could travel in a vacuum. The language may be one reason why people find the space program hard to understand. And that's understandable.

Unsymmetrical dimethyl hydrazine is a component of fuel. Hypergolic means it is self-igniting. Aeropause is not something you get when you pass the age of 40, rather it is the level above the earth's surface where the atmosphere becomes ineffective for human functions and fades off into space. The aerothermodynamic border is where the atmosphere becomes too thin to generate much heat.

An anomalistic period is the time between a spacecraft's arrival at perigee in one orbit and perigee on the next.

AND A PERIGEE . . .

And everyone should know by now what a perigee is.

There are a lot of words in space language that you would think mean one thing, but actually mean something else. This doesn't make it any easier.

For example, any normal person would know that a "specific impulse" is something a man feels when he sees Raquel Welch get out of a car in a miniskirt.

In space jargon it means "an expression of the performance limit of rocket propellants arrived at by dividing the thrust in pounds by the weight flow rate in pounds per second."

As if the terminology weren't bad enough, with words like reticle, rotary hydraulic actuator, hypergolic and so forth, the space people abbreviate them, or use acronyms.

ALWAYS IN A HURRY

This may be because people in the space program are always in a hurry. They don't have time to say rate gyro assembly. They say RGA.

They don't say separation. They say "sep." They don't say revolution. They say "rev." They don't say rough order of magnitude, they say ROM. They don't say pound per square inch. They say PSI.

They don't say program zero-zero. They say POO.

They don't say the rocket engine fired. It "burned."

And if this isn't bad enough, they toss in German words like "gegenschein" and "brennschluss."

The former means a "faint light area in the sky," the latter, the "end of rocket firing."

WHAT'S A BURP?

But just words in English are bad enough. Anyone would know what you meant if you said, "burp." But if you say, "BURP" to a space type he thinks you are talking about the backup rate of pitch.

In normal English you'd think an "afterbody" was someone coming up behind you. Not in space talk. There, it means "a companion body that trails a spacecraft in orbit, anything from a discarded clamp ring to a spent launch vehicle stage."

Everybody on the ground knows what an ACE is. But in space talk it is attitude control electronics. And any person with his feet on the ground would know that ACME means Acme Cement Co., or Acme Car Wash or some such thing.

But to space people it means attitude control and maneuverable electronics.

Space people never say something is all right, or going well. They say it is "nominal." If something is wrong, they wouldn't be caught dead saying it that way. Instead they call it an "anomaly."

The thing the astronauts put on they call a pressure garment assembly, which is their way of saying spacesuit. And how about this dialog between astronauts David R. Scott and James B. Irwin as they set off to explore the moon:

SCOTT: Yeah, I'm right behind you.
IRWIN: Oh, you are?
SCOTT: Yeah, go slow.
IRWIN: Let's go. I'm ready to configure you.

Irwin didn't mean any harm by this statement. He merely meant that he was ready to follow Scott. And that's the way you talk in the world of space.

Some Effects of
Science and Technology
Upon Our Language

W. Earl Britton

A LANGUAGE MUST be stable to provide a reliable means of precise communication yet dynamic in order to accommodate itself to change. These requirements are contradictory and therefore not easily brought into phase.

The difficulty of the task becomes evident in view of the extensive linguistic and syntactical changes recently wrought in our language by science and technology, changes dictated by the scientist's urgent need of a medium for communicating complex and difficult concepts. In this brief examination of these developments, I want to commend the scientists for their contribution to our diction but express some reservations about their influence upon our syntax.

Estimates suggest that during the past twenty-five years advances in technology and communications media have produced a greater change in our language than in any similar period in history.[1] Even the *Little Oxford Dictionary of Current English* introduced into its 1941 edition twenty-five, two-column, closely packed pages of words not there in 1937. A large number of these were technical, like *A-bomb, antibiotic, automation, chain-reaction, crash dive, electronics, microwave, scan,* and *trailer.* In the same year *Webster's Collegiate Dictionary*, in addition to most of the new entries in the *Little Oxford*, added among others *panel discussion, motorcade, microfilm, mesotron, knee action, escalator clause, preview,* and *monitor.*

NEW SCIENTIFIC TERMS

Many of the new scientific terms have remained in their specialized fields, as one can see by examining the 640 expressions in AEC's *Nuclear Terms* and the 6000 in NASA's *Dictionary of Technical Terms for Aerospace Use.* What is surprising is the large number of scientific words that have spread over into the general vocabulary. People only vaguely acquainted with computers refer to *input* and *output*; a non-technical article on methods of learning contains *interface, capsule description, pay-off, payload,* and *feedback*; and an English professor completely ignorant of electronics remarks, "Our committee is not locked in on this program." But general terms of scientific origin are not peculiar to the twentieth century; widely used words like *eliminate, acid test, potential,* and *ultimate analysis* were originally technical expressions in the vocabulary of physics and astronomy.[2]

In science, new words normally emerge in response to the need for novel, precise, and economical communication. The expressions *experimentally doable* and *capsulate* must be such responses. Recently our office received a call from industry for a generic term to cover all types of machines like fork-lifts and hydraulic excavators that multiply and manipulate the power of man. There seems to be no such word, but one will emerge if the demand is sufficient.

The sources of new words are often unknown. There are guesses, for instance, about *jalopy* and *bulldozer*, but no one is sure. In most cases, though, words are formed by well-established means. Here there is time only to remind ourselves of the most common ones:

1. Borrowing from Greek and Latin, our earliest sources, but less commonly employed by the newer sciences, except for proper names like Mercury, Saturn, and Apollo.
2. Extension or alteration of the meanings of extant words, as in *jet, beach-head, take-off,* and *space.*
3. Combinations of established words like *television, astronaut,* and *supersonic.* Especially interesting is the combination of non-technical words to form a technical term like *feedback, countdown,* and *airtight.*
4. Addition of prefixes like *mini-* in *minicircuit,* and suffixes like *-ize* in *optimize, -ate* in *automate, -able* in *weldable,* and *-ity* in *criticality.*
5. Use of proper names like *Masonite* and *Sanforize.*
6. Use of terms suggested by the action or appearance like *breakthrough* and *solid state.* The expression *black box* is noteworthy because it originates perhaps in the appearance of a housing, but, more impor-

tantly, enables the scientist to by-pass, at least temporarily, a detailed description of a device.

7. Abbreviation or shortening of words in a compound like *mascon* (mass concentration) and *selsyn* (self-synchronous).

8. Finally, and perhaps most exciting, the development of the acronym. Obviously resulting from the need for economy and convenience of expression, the acronym is usually formed from the initials of a phrase name. Uncommon in business, despite names like *Texaco* and *Sunoco*, which may not be true acronyms, it is now commonplace in science, as in *radar, NASA, sonar,* and *napalm.* Sometimes acronyms develop almost by accident, as Sears and Smith explain in their account of *streetcar.* The original phrase, *system test and checkout report,* was reduced for brevity to *STCR,* but this was not easy to say. Hence, it became an *STCR* report, and eventually, by the addition of vowels, *streetcar.*[3]

More careful planning now avoids such trouble. Some of the later and more amusing examples are *failure effect and analysis report* (FEAR), *special materials and special handling* (SMASH), and the *electronic ground automatic destruct sequencer* button (EGADS). Sears and Smith go on to explain the confusion that can be caused if a word is printed in capitals so that it can be incorrectly interpreted as an acronym. This happened to the word POGO, though it was being used in its basic sense to describe the "accordian-like squeeze and stretch oscillation that occurs along the central axis of a launch vehicle during liftoff and flight."[4] Of course, when an acronym becomes part of the regular vocabulary, it usually loses its capitals.

Diction

All that has been said here about diction naturally leads to the fundamental problem of how far one should go in accepting new combinations and creations. The question poses real difficulty for English teachers and editors, caught as they are in the cross fire between the old and the new, and yet asked for rulings on usage.

Their position is not unique, though. As long ago as 1619 an Englishman by the name of Alexander Gill cried out:

O harsh lips, I now hear all around me such words as *common, vice, envy, malice*; even *virtue, study, justice, mercy, compassion, profit, commodity, colour, grace, favor, acceptance.* But whither, I pray in all the world, have you banished those words which our forefathers used for these new-fangled ones? Is the new barbaric invasion to extirpate the English tongue?[5]

The British fear of linguistic invasion from outside is still present. A purist as recently as 1959 objected to the use of meaningless prepositions in the American manner, citing cases like "Meeting up with one's girl" and "Testing out a car."[6] A similarly nationalistic view was expressed by a Fiat engineer, who proudly explained the obvious superiority of Italian over other languages; then, with a twinkle, admitted that Italy had had to import the word *automotive* because Italian neither possessed nor could create its equivalent. Even the French, so committed to preserving the purity of their language, have found their Academy unable to stem the in-roads from other languages and, for that matter, to block changes within. In 1959 a member of their Office of French Vocabulary explained that they did not seek to ostracize foreign words, but merely to regulate their entry. "The object," he continued, "is to guard against words that are used through ignorance and snobbishness when adequate French equivalents are available."[7]

Such historical resistance to change would seem absurd were it not for the outcries that greeted *Webster III* from such eminent publications as *The New York Times* and *The New Yorker* magazine. And the battle between current usage and historical tradition has not ceased, as every editor, writer, and teacher so well knows. They also know that in this age of vocabulary explosion and dynamic syntax, especially in science, a stand must be taken, however difficult and sometimes distasteful the task.

I

If one is compelled to take a stand, he might appeal to reason and logic for assistance, despite his personal preferences. It would seem that the evaluation of a new coinage might be made on the criteria of need, clarity, and efficiency. There is little point to a new term if one already exists; there is little point in adopting a word or phrase unless it is clear and meaningful; and certainly there is no point in adopting the word or phrase if there are more efficient ways of communicating the same information.

Appraisal of the word *ruggedize* by these criteria would lead to acceptance because it is useful, clear, and efficient. To object to it because of its sound or to label it as crude is to ignore parallel forms like *summarize* and *minimize*. On the other hand, *finalize*, though apparently of British origin, has disturbed many observers because of the defect E. B. White complained of: one is not sure at times whether it means *terminate* or *put into final form. Weatherwise* and *dollarwise* are simply tautological, as in the radio announcer's "Weatherwise, it's going to rain" and the businessman's "Dollarwise, it's expensive." But what of *equipments* in the plural? Isn't the engineer seeking brevity and directness by employing the word in place of *the various pieces of equipment?* There is logic here, despite the offense to our sensibilities. And all of us need to remember that every word was new once.

I do not want to leave the impression that all contemporary scientific language is good, but I do feel that, by and large, it is fresh, efficient, and often exciting. And certainly the scientist has added enormously to our stock of words. On the other hand, he may have exerted an even greater influence upon our syntax. The changes in diction we see about us daily; the changes in syntax are not always so apparent.

To recognize these changes, we need to recall the principal features of scientific style, described in detail by Harold Simpson. Among science writers, the subject-verb-object, simple sentence is a six-to-one preference over compounded forms; the mean sentence length twenty-six words. Even more characteristic is the heavy dependence upon nouns—25% more common in scientific writing than in general writing. Adverbs are used infrequently; the impersonal *it* and the vague *this* are plentiful; the passive voice is favored over the active; phrasal constructions are popular, especially the prepositional; and the loosely attached participle abounds.[8]

These features seem bland enough; then why the wholesale criticism of scientific writing, both here and abroad? One significant cause is the scientist's tendency to overdo what is otherwise acceptable. In his effort to be clear, he may overdesign; in his effort to be brief, he may overcompress. Both efforts may lead to the structural complexity and redundancy that have come to be widely regarded as professional style, as illustrated in the sentence cited by Sears and Smith, "This reissue completely supersedes and replaces all previous issues of this document."[9]

Excess causes the scientist trouble especially in his use of nouns. When he permits nouns to replace verbs and *makes decisions* rather than *decides,* he wastes words and sacrifices the force and vigor of the single-word verb. When he assembles before a headword numerous nouns as modifiers in an effort to be clear, he may grow wordy and sometimes confusing. Professor John R. Baker has observed that "it would never enter anyone's head to say a 'tea-containing cup'; one would naturally say a 'cup containing tea.' Yet in scientific journals one will find 'iron-containing globules' when what is meant is 'globules containing iron.' "[10]

This departure from normal sentence patterns, especially in very long collections of modifiers like "All the training equipment analysis contains data directly relevant to realistic technical manual preparation" is annoying but nothing like so disturbing as the collection of modifiers that puzzle the reader because he does not discover until the end of the sentence what they modify. The ultimate in this sort of construction is the statement, "The engine front support stiffening bolt retaining nut attaching weld fractured." Such sentences are not easily comprehended. Just as bad is the pile-up composed of several pairs of modifiers which are not hyphenated to guide the reader, as in the statement, "Fuel, selected on the basis of the best metallurgical information available in 1953, was unalloyed alpha rolled, beta heat treated, metallic uranium slugs enriched to 2.778 a/o (atom percent) U^{35}."

II

These constructions may well result from the scientists' effort to be brief. Yet the same scientists, ironically enough, often resort to wordy and needless phrases after nouns. Simpson cites *specimens in the form of sheet* as an instance of the wordy way of saying *specimens in sheet form*. The scientists also violate their principle of terseness in their use of phrasal modifiers like *by a factor of* and *of the order of*, though the meaning of each can be put more simply, and in their fondness for phrases like *large in size* where *large* would do. Even worse, scientists often inject these expressions into general writing and speaking.

Though the scientist may overdo, not all that he does is bad. Certainly he has contributed to the widespread use of the adverbial participle, a construction long needed in our language. Insistence upon detachment has led the scientist to omit the personal pronoun or noun after a participial phrase, thereby arousing the ire of the grammarian, who denounces him for dangling a modifier. But in a sentence like "Assuming that the meter is accurate, the computation can be based on its reading," modern linguists generally accept the participle as an adverb modifying the main clause and therefore not requiring a headword. Anyone who has tried to edit out of a scientific manuscript all such adverbial modifiers is well aware of the resulting absurdities. Though he did not originate it, the scientist, by extensive use of this construction, has contributed notably to our syntax.

Unfortunately he doesn't always differentiate between an adverbial participle and a true dangler, that is, an adjectival participle without a head-word. Consequently, the reader often is left unsure of the meaning. Even worse, the scientist depends unduly upon the participial phrase that is loosely attached to the end of a sentence or clause. Though it does not dangle, the phrase is obscure, for there is no way of knowing whether it expresses cause, result, or simply additional information. In the sentence, "The casting is cooled rapidly, preventing primary graphite from forming," only the reader who already understands the process knows whether the cooling is designed to prevent the formation of graphite, or produces the result incidentally. If purpose is meant, the infinitive would be more precise. And how would you interpret the statement, "The film can be fabricated on bag machines using glue type seals"? The careless reader can easily miss the two potentially different meanings because of the tacked-on participial phrase.

In conclusion, let me restate my thesis in slightly altered form: despite some unfortunate effects, science has done extremely well by our diction; on the other hand, despite some good effects, science has not improved our syntax.

---

[1] Thomas Long, "Tek-nol'o-ji and Its Effect on Language," *Space Digest*, March, 1969, p. 87.

[2] *Ibid.*

[3] Donald A. Sears and Henry A. Smith, "A Linguistic Look at Aero-space English," *Word Study*, No. 4 (April, 1969), p. 2.

[4] *Ibid.*

[5] Alexander Gill, *Logonomia Anglica* in *English as Language*, ed. Charlton Laird and Robert M. Gorrell (New York, 1961), p. 2.

[6] Reuters dispatch from London, August 10, 1959, in *English as Language*, p. 4.

[7] Joseph Wechsberg, "Is French Knockouté?" *New York Times Magazine*, June 28, 1959, p. 44.

[8] Harold B. Simpson, "A Descriptive Analysis of Scientific Writing" (Unpublished diss., University of Michigan, 1965), p. 34.

[9] Sears and Smith, p. 4.

[10] John R. Baker, "English Prose Style in Scientific Papers," *Nature*, 176 (1955), 851.

9

ACADEMIA
AND ITS JARGON

The specialized language of one branch of learning often seems to be a closed book to persons in other areas. Thus it is that Andrew Halpin pleads in the first article of this section for the scientist, for one, to write so clearly that the layman can understand scientific writing without the help of a middleman.

The next article, by Herman A. Estrin, tells what college newspapers across the country are writing about in the 1970s.

This is followed by an article explaining what public school teachers' euphemistic reports to parents about their children in one New Jersey city really mean. Another Time *essay, entitled "Right You Are If You Say You Are—Obscurely," is a parody of the arcane jargon used by professors of sociology, theology, medicine, and philosophy.*

Jargon . . .
Sacred and Profane

ANDREW W. HALPIN

THESE REMARKS ABOUT the dissemination of research findings in education would not be complete without comment about a popular suggestion that has been offered as a solution to our dilemma: that we develop "middlemen" who will function between the scientist and the practitioner and who will "translate" the findings of the scientist into a form more comprehensible to the practitioner. This is, indeed, a tempting idea. There is only one thing wrong with it. It won't work.

The advocates of this idea gloss over the fact that nothing remotely similar exists in other professions. The physician, in his training, must learn to read and understand medical research; he is trained to draw upon primary sources. Popular opinion notwithstanding, I must denounce as a canard the suggestion that the *Reader's Digest* functions as the middleman for the medical profession. The lawyer, too, must deal with the precedents of prior cases and must be equipped to function without an interlocutory middleman. Likewise, the engineer must have sufficient knowledge of physics and structural mechanics to apply new research findings to the practical tasks with which he deals from day to day. Indeed, in proposing that educational middlemen be trained to function between the scientist and the practitioner we admit to a failing that—at least in this respect—disqualifies education as a profession. The core of this failing is not hard to find. We need only look at our undergraduate programs for teachers (and, sadly, even our graduate programs) to see how seldom our students are required to deal with primary sources. This is in marked contrast to what takes place in such disciplines as psychology and biology. To spare our students from effort and "boredom," the material in education textbooks is presented to them in the form of predigested pap. Indeed, some of the textbooks seem to be at such a remove from primary sources that one surmises that they have been "written" by applying scissors, Scotch tape, and a table of random numbers to the ten most popular books previously published on the same subject.

The notion of the educational middleman is based upon another fallacy: that the ideas of the research man can, or even need to be, translated into another language. To some extent, the scientist himself is at fault in failing to communicate effectively, and I do not intend to exculpate him for this. When his jargon blocks communication he must be condemned. But here I believe that we must take into account a point that often is disregarded: There are two kinds of jargon—sacred and profane. Let me deal with these in reverse order.

Profane jargon is composed of clichés, half-formulated concepts, slogans, loaded words, and parades of abstract terms for which there are no clear referents. Jargon of this kind usually results from the infrangible fact that the author's ideas are not clear; because his ideas are not clear he covers his bed of imprecise ideas with a blanket to match—a patchquilt of fuzzy language. This jargon is marked by a dearth of concrete images; by an array of inert, passive verbs; and by nouns that have been converted, willy-nilly, into new, grotesque verbs. In these instances, the scientist is inclined to invent new words simply because the poverty of his own language and his cursory acquaintance with literature prevent him from recognizing that most of his ideas could be expressed in simple, and often vigorous, English. This type of bafflegab must be condemned because it fails to communicate even what few clear ideas it may contain. But even more, profane jargon must be denounced on aesthetic grounds. It is ugly.

THE MEANING OF SACRED JARGON

"Jargon" may also mean the technical language of a science. Because science must be conceived, in large part, as a special language, and because the syntax of science is as important as its content, we cannot eliminate the use of special language and special concepts in scientific writing. This jargon results not from fuzzily conceived ideas but from ideas that have been defined operationally and usually with devastating clarity. This is sacred jargon, and it is not to be defiled for the blandishment of the popularizers.

Now here is where we run into a refractory problem. The scientist's critic feels uncomfortable in the presence of new concepts and concludes that the author's technical terms are just new words for old ideas; he then summarily condemns as jargon not only the words but the concepts themselves. This allegation misses the point that the scientist has created, in fact, not just new words but new ideas. In creating new ideas the scientist classifies phenomena into fresh categories—boxes that do not always coincide with the categories presented by naive experience. These new categories cannot always be described in orthodox, everyday language. Faced with this contradiction, the critic, speaking to the scientist, resorts to the gambit, "Can't you use ordinary words to say what you mean? Don't you *really* mean . . . ?" In short, the critic tries to force the scientist's concepts into the structure of his own verbal categories. The only answer the honest scientist can give is, "No, I don't *really* mean that at all. I mean precisely what I have said." The critic bristles, for he considers his own categories inviolate. To understand what the scientist is saying, the critic must now relinquish his preconceived categories, for in order to understand any single concept in the scientist's language the critic must first understand the total theoretical context within which each concept is imbedded. This requires greater effort than the critic is willing to expend; it is easier for him to ridicule the scientist's legitimate use of jargon than for him to exert the energy necessary to understand it. The scientist's own abusive use of "profane jargon" allows the critic to justify his own unfounded attack upon the scientist's use of "sacred jargon." Unfortunately, many scientists make themselves easy victims for such attacks.

Misunderstanding on both sides arises out of inertia or sheer laziness Profane jargon impedes communication; and here the blame must be placed on the scientist's slothful attitude toward clear writing. The critic's resistance to sacred jargon equally hinders communication; and here the blame rests with the critic's failure to differentiate between the language of science and the language of everyday life.

These obstacles to the success of the middleman proposal are formidable enough, but typical attempts to follow through on this proposal are quickly grounded by another starkly practical problem: Where do we find competent middlemen? I can only writhe as I watch the fatuous and condescending attitude of both the scientist and the educational practitioner toward prospective middlemen. Even the advocates of the middleman plan imply that the middleman should serve as a type of editorial assistant, at a status level only slightly above that of the average secretary and certainly below that of the research technician. The men who hold to this view then become chagrined when they discover that they cannot locate a suitable candidate for the job. I have known only two or three people who could qualify. Although these people were interested in this work and had been interviewed for such jobs, in every instance they could only reject with contempt the niggardly salary offered. Nor were they willing to be treated as sub-professional lackeys. I think that we had better face up to an uncomfortable truth: A competent middleman must possess skills of a different and possibly higher order than those of either the scientist or the practitioner. The middleman jobs are top-level positions that should command salaries commensurate with the skills demanded. But I know of no college of education, and certainly of no school system, that has budgeted enough funds for a skilled middleman. Further, I do not believe that the ego of either the scientist or the practitioner will permit him to be gracious in granting a middleman the status he deserves. I repeat: This is not a job for a young manuscript editor or a part-time employee of the English department; and it is not a job for an indigent but well-intentioned doctoral student in education. If the middleman proposal is to work at all—and I am not sure that it will—then we would have to create a new occupation. We would have to budget ample funds for the men and women who fill this role and would have to devise a rich program for training a new professional breed. If this were done, and were done with sufficient support, perhaps the effort would pay off. But we had better realize at the outset how enormous a task it will be.

Yet please note that even if we should be able to persuade legions of top-quality middlemen to devote themselves to the dissemination task in educational research, their work would be futile unless we can simultaneously reach four other objectives:

1. Raise the standards of research so as to produce a professional corps which can understand, respect, and act upon research findings.
2. Recruit for the profession, *and retain in it*, young men and women who possess strong achievement-motivations, conjoined with the intellectual and creative capacities required for research careers.

3. Strengthen teachers' motivation to do research by rewarding such efforts and by developing within our schools an organizational climate that encourages creative inquiry.
4. Incite competition among the schools and ruthlessly publicize not alone those schools that are doing exemplary work but also those that merit only a bar sinister on their coats of arms.

I am mindful that my views can be construed as so gloomy that, by contrast, I make Cassandra sound like Pollyanna. Yet you must understand, too, that I could not be so scathing in my indictment of the present situation in educational research did I not trust in the ultimate victory of rationality and possess deep faith in the future of American education. To save the patient, a surgeon sometimes must cut deep. Yet a responsible physician will not even bother to operate unless he believes that there are greater than chance possibilities that the patient will survive, and unless he knows, too, that the risk of the operation is a lesser evil than are the imminent and certain ravages of the disease itself. Analogously, in the surgical role that I have taken toward the "culture" of education, I, too, take risks. But I take these risks not because I despise the patient but because I love and respect him and because I am gravely worried about his welfare.

The Collegiate Press:
Irresistible, Irreverent, but Relevant

HERMAN ESTRIN

THE COLLEGIATE PRESS is irresistible because students as well as faculty and administrators read the student newspapers upon their date of publication avidly and at times omnivorously; it is irreverent because in its reporting it sometimes shows a lack of awe or a lack of what the "older generation" would call respect; it *is* relevant because it reflects the hopes, the anger, the joys, the fears, the anxieties, the accomplishments, and the frustrations of the collegians. During 1972, the college editors, regardless of the size or background of their college or university, wrote about these concerns.

This writer perused over two hundred college newspapers from all over the country; analyzed the news stories, features, and editorials; and found ten major items which most concerned the college editors and their staffs.

These concerns are as follows:

1. A COMMITMENT TO THE COMMUNITY

More than ever before, collegians are surely involved in the community to tackle the problems which surround them. Many students have accepted a personal commitment and responsibility for helping to create an environment in which new attitudes, concepts, and ideas can emerge and develop.

What specifically have the collegians done for the community? Let's read these headlines from their newspapers:

Vets to Hold Christmas Party for Kids
    (Crippled Children's Hospital)
Bona students participate in 'labor of love'
    Aid mentally retarded children
Tau Delts Start a Scout Troop at Cerebral Palsy Center
One hundred Students Donate Blood for Boys Suffering Hemophilia
Students Help Kids 'Experience'
IFC Collect 167 Pints of Blood
Stevens Involved in Hoboken
    The primary service is the teaching of reading and language skills to
    Hoboken's large Spanish-speaking population; yet the course offerings
    have included landscaping and dramatics.

The Interfraternity Council Report of Newark College of Engineering stated:

    Today's active college students seek involvement with contemporary
    problems such as drug abuse and urban education, planning, and recreation.
    We must direct the efforts of fraternity members toward these areas of
    concern, with the purpose of aiding the educational system in developing
    today's college students into better students.

To be specific:

    Black Studies Class Helps Convicts
    Black studies 195 is working on a project to set up a halfway house for
    federal and state ex-cons. Sponsored by interested people from San Francisco to
    Los Angeles, the halfway house would provide drug rehabilitation, housing, and
    jobs for its residents.

                                                                    —UCSB News

2: A PERMISSIVENESS REGARDING SEX

The '72 newspapers have *no* hang-ups concerning sex. Sex is treated
casually, frankly, and relevantly. Some papers run syndicated columns of "Hip
Pocrates", "The doctor is IN", and "The Doctor's Bag", which consist of
questions and answers about sex and incidentally about drugs and alcoholism.
Specifically, these columns discuss masturbation, breast size, venereal diseases,
abortions, douching, contraception, male and female homosexuality, and
sexual intercourse and its problems as youth see them.
    One college has established a "Center for Human Sexuality," designed
for contraceptive and abortion referral.

Another college has a "Human Sexuality Center" to increase student awareness in all areas of human sexuality including birth control, abortion, homosexuality, marriage and family planning, general body hygiene, and venereal diseases. (*Rider News*, 3/10/73)

Collegians have found that Sex Forums draw SRO-crowds. The crowds exhaust the topics of abortions, birth control methods, veneral diseases, "virginity-hunting" when men look for prospective wives, and sexually aggressive women. (*Metropolitan*, 4/9/72)

One college headline reads: *Intervisitation Rules Approved by Senate*, and this text copy follows:

> The official definition of cohabitation for the College now is: A state of existence between two or more parties when one or more parties is illegally inhabiting another party's dormitory room.

At the University of California at Santa Barbara, *Nexus*, the university paper, presented a frank account of venereal diseases as seen in such heads as:

V.D.—how to make sure if you think you've got it
The V.D. fight; is Isla Vista turning the tide?
Gonorrhea seems milder than it is
Syphilis gets worse as it stays longer

The Word, the student newspaper of Burlington County College (N.J.) had a page devoted to V.D. treatment, written factually by a female reporter.

A candidness concerning homosexuality on the campus is evidenced in such headlines as:

Love is Gay Experience for Everyone
—*Rider News*, 4/8/72
Gays, straights discuss love
—*Daily Nexus*, 5/3/72
Social Oppression of Lesbians
—*Daily Nexus*, 5/3/72

Thanks were given by the *Argo* staff of Richard Stockton State College to the Committee for Abortion Information and Referral of Ventnor, N.J., for *Nine Methods of Birth Control*. This information listed in columnar form the method, the effectiveness, its cost, the side effects, the doctor's involvement, and the manner in which the method is used.

In collegiate newspapers the topic of abortion is discussed in feature articles, in questions and answers form in "The Doctor's Bag" and "Hip

Pocrates" and in paid advertisements. However, the *Bona Venture* of St. Bonaventure U., ran this story:

> *Right to life group conducts drive*
> Controversy surrounding an anti-abortion display placed in the window of the University Center Book Store by the Olean Right-to-Life Committee.
> The display, part of an anti-abortion drive which included a march and rally in Olean, featured color photographs of aborted fetuses.

Another unusual feature story in the Bona Venture (4/28/72) was:

> *How to be raped without really trying*
> The lecture was one of the best attended all year. The two-hour lecture combined humorous anecdotes with the serious subject of how to handle yourself when you are being attacked.

3: A BOLDER USE OF ADVERTISEMENTS

In the advertisement section, students included such ads as abortion information and assistance, male contraceptives, alcoholic anonymous, narcotic addicts rehabilitation, precana conferences, GROPE (Gay Rights of People Everywhere), Tampax tampons, term papers researched and professionally typed, wine, beer, draft counseling, pregnancy counseling, among others. One newspaper ran this ad:

> It is no longer necessary to read your textbooks! We have prepared synopses of a large number of textbooks that eliminate the need for reading the books. Our files are continually growing. The cost of each synopsis is $3.50. All areas are covered except economics, science, language and law. If we do not have a synopsis of the book you order on file we will do one. Orders take one to two weeks to process.

and then added this disclaimer:

> (Improper use of termpapers is strongly condemned by the faculty and administration and may result in academic dismissal.)

The philosophy of Women's Liberation is exemplified by this ad:

> TOMBROCK GIRLS
> NEED GUYS!
> Tombrock College, an all girls' school in West Paterson, is having its first dance this semester on Saturday—TOMORROW!! SAC has decided to run a FREE

BUS up to the event but we need at least FIFTY GUYS!! If you want to go, sign the poster on the activities board by the Center Desk. COME!!

—Vector, 2/4/72

4: A Concern about the Security on Campus

The college campus is definitely concerned about the thefts, assaults, vandalism, and even murders on the campus. Editorials and headlines have the following titles:

Security: What You Should Do
Lights, Ambulance Head Security List
Security—Another Look

The following is an excerpt from an article which appeared in the *Independent* of Newark State College:

> This campus is not an Ivy Tower. As seen by the number of thefts, robberies, and assaults, we are subject to the same problems as outside communities. Realizing this, don't invite trouble. One's own personal safety is of paramount concern:
>
> 1. Never walk alone at night—this is a good practice to follow regardless of your sex.
> 2. Keep away from wooded and shrubbery-filled areas while walking—they make perfect hiding places for a would-be assailant or purse snatcher.
> 3. Walk along well-lighted paths and sidewalks at night, even if it means giving up the "short-cut" route.
>
> The parking lots have been defined as our "high crime" areas. So-ooo . . .
>
> 1. Always lock your car and roll up all windows.
> 2. Remove any "tempting" valuables from sight—put tape decks, etc. in your trunk.
> 3. Always check your car inside, front and back, before entering.
> 4. At night, always be ready with your key in hand while approaching your car or residence door. Don't fumble around for it.
> 5. At night, park in well-lighted areas, as close as possible to your destination.

5: Students' Evaluation of the Faculty

One of the major points of controversy in many college communities is the question: To what degree should students regulate the substance and the quality of their educations? The answer to this question is a faculty and course evaluation by the students.

Concern for these evaluations is evidenced by these headlines:

Humanities Program to be Evaluated by Students
Academic Affairs Board Wants to Evaluate Faculty
New Faculty Evaluation Questionnaire in Works
Tau Beta Pi Evaluate Instructors: Program to Improve Teaching Techniques

Many students published the results of the faculty evaluation and set forth these goals of the publication:

A. To provide the students with a guide to the teaching methods of the faculty.
B. To provide the faculty with objective feedback of student opinion regarding their teaching methods.
C. To stimulate the discussion of teaching methods between faculty and students.
D To promote faculty-student relationships.

6. Job Security

Almost all collegians want a job after graduation. In some professions, namely engineering and teaching, jobs were scarce this year. As a result, newspapers featured such articles as:

Top Starting Salary $12,605
Teacher Demand in Australia
Engineering Week . . . Job Opportunities in Jersey
Don't Wait for Jobs to Come to You
Job Placement Survey of May Graduates Shows That 51% Have Found Jobs

Another prominent vocational feature was the Recruitment Schedule for the week. The items included the date, the agency, the specific time and the place for the interview.

7: A Commitment to Peace

Student editors spoke out against the war in Vietnam and deplored its continuance. Some of the headlines indicate this commitment to peace:

Jane Fonda Shows One of Her Souvenirs from North Vietnam

Students Work for End to Asian Wars
Marches Fill Streets
War Against War
War and People March On

One editorial read:

> ... each of us is partly responsible for the actions of our government in Southeast Asia. Had we awakened to the horror of this war sooner, and protested more vigorously, perhaps bombs would not be falling on civilians in Hanoi this moment. The weight of the dying and the dead rests on all our shoulders. We must act. WE MUST ACT NOW!

8: A CONCERN FOR RELEVANT COURSES IN THE CURRICULUM

In response to the students' cry for reform in the curriculum and for "relevance," colleges are experimenting more and are introducing new and unusual courses. Subjects like weaving and yoga have crept into curriculums. At many colleges, students have selected, prepared, and even taught some of these courses—on prisons, ecology, peace, and women's liberation.

At an engineering college a headline read:

Alumni Ass'n Offers Free Courses in Social Competence:
Conversation, Dancing, Speed Reading, Tennis, and Horseback Riding

9: A CONCERN FOR THE RIGHTS OF STUDENTS AND OTHERS

The campus newspapers through the years have championed students' rights and the rights of others. The following heads indicate the kinds of rights which they have advocated:

Lettuce Boycott Continues on Campus
The Felon's Right to Vote
The Right to Divorce
The Berrigan Case
The Returning Vet
The Black Artist Strangled in America
Diejueno Indians are Vanishing
Wanted: Black Teachers for Rider

10: AN INTEREST IN THE ARTS

Some papers presented an entire supplement called "The Arts". However, most papers had a single page devoted to the arts. Students wrote reviews and reactions to the latest records, provocative motion pictures, operas, ballets, books, concerts, television, and radio attractions, and even belly dancing.

In a review of the controversial film, "Deep Throat," a student wrote:

> The visual effect of the movie is unbelievable. I have never been exposed to so much of so many kinds of sex in so short a span of time in so much detail.
>
> If you have a deep yearning to view sex instead of performing on your own, this movie is for you. Sex is what this filmy film is all about.
>
> Don't see this film if you are squeamish or have any hang-ups about sex. It will only hang you up further.
>
> And please, don't tell my mother that I told you about it.

Or, what about this "provocative" headline—that is, if nudity is an art!

> *Nude Beach Here? IVCC's All in Favor*
> After many months of arrests and court proceedings, the issue of nude bathing has finally been seriously taken up by the Isla Vista Community Council. Since the Sheriff's Summerland beach arrests of last spring and the popular use of Devereaux Beach for nude bathing by I.V. residents, the IVCC has proposed a nude beach area for Isla Vista for those who wish to soak up some sun in the nude.
>
> —*UCSB Nexus*, 10/11/72

Four other areas of concern are noticeable in the collegiate press in '72:

- *The many facets of counseling.*
  In their columns, many papers offered counseling services, which included personal, vocational, alcoholic, medical, drug, academic, sexual, draft, and term paper counseling.

- *A movement towards ecology.*
  In their papers, students advanced their ideas concerning ecology and discussed noise and water pollution, recycling, food facts, food fraud, herbicides, and soil and beach erosion.

- *A presentation of women's liberation movement on campus.*
  Many newspapers wrote articles reacting to women's liberation:

Faculty women discuss sexism
Career Woman vs. Marriage: Which is the Good Life?
Kotex, Crotch Spray Become Feminist
Women's Changing Roles
Panel Discussion—Hoboken Feminism
What is the Women's Movement?

• *A decline in the use of obscenities.*
During this year the use of obscenities in campus newspapers declined. Most upset by their use was the faculty, not the students. Many editors admitted that the obscenities have lost their shock value. Others claimed that the use of obscenities in the collegiate press indicated immaturity of the writer.

In addition to these popular concerns of the collegiate press, college newspapers wrote about more effective teaching, tenure of professors, salaries of staff and professors, parking problems, pass-fail grades, the "new religion," and students' participation in curriculum planning and in college governance.

In summary, the collegiate press in the seventies is producing a forthright, candid approach to the real problems, concerns, and interests of its readers—the student body. College editors—responsible, sophisticated, knowledgeable, provocative, and at times, irreverent and daring—offer their readers an informative, stimulating, timely press.

Woodbridge Seeks
to Better Image
of School System

Campbell Allen

NEW JERSEY'S FOURTH largest school system is beginning to use parent-teacher relations as a vehicle for bettering its image and, hopefully, reversing a long history of budgetary setbacks.

The township's 405 elementary school teachers have been instructed in writing, in effect, to be extra nice to parents, and to use "positive" euphemisms on children's progress in an effort to keep parents "satisfied and encouraged."

Kits given to teachers include a list of 35 "negative expressions," such as "lazy," "stubborn" and "rude" and the "more positive expressions" the school administration recommends they use when conferring with parents.

The administration's purpose is clearly stated in one of the instruction sheets accompanying the kit.

The first paragraph says, "The parent-teacher conference is a sound foundation for good human relations, constructive school support and evaluation. The parent who is 'sure' of his child's teacher is a booster for our school and our educational program."

PRACTICAL SUGGESTIONS

Under the heading, "some practical suggestions," Item 2 advises the teacher to "start conversation (with parents) on child's strongest traits and abilities and introduce weakest ones carefully."

Item 5 says, "open the door to future conferences by leaving something to talk about," while Item 8 advises the teacher to "plan ways of concluding conference so parents will leave feeling satisfied and encouraged."

Critics within the school system, while convinced of the value of parent-teacher conferences and the use of tact with parents, believe the administration has gone too far.

Describing a child as stupid, a liar and a dumbell is brutal and unnecessary, but some principals and teachers feel the administration's list of alternative words and phrases goes to the opposite extreme and really amounts to misleading double-talk.

CRITICS' STAND

Critics contend this may win friends for the school system but is not in the interest of children because euphemistic jargon may blind parents to genuine problems.

"Parents," one teacher commented, "should not be sent away from conferences satisfied and encouraged when their children are behaving badly or doing really poor work."

For instance, if the teacher (following the administration's guide to words and phrases) says, "Johnny sometimes depends on others to do his work," parents may miss the point—that Johnny sometimes cheats in class.

Or, using the same guide, how about this mild-sounding report: "Well, Johnny is capable of doing better, that is he can do better work with help, although he insists on having his own way and has a tendency to stretch the truth. Despite not being physically coordinated and being an outspoken boy who tries to get attention, Johnny could do neater work and has a chance of passing if. . . "

Johnny's parents had better prepare for the worst, because the teacher is really saying Johnny is a clumsy, stupid, stubborn, sloppy, and an insolent liar, who is bound to fail as all dumbells do.

Below is the Woodbridge school administration's list of "negative expressions" with their "more positive" counterparts. Note that words and phrases do not always correspond and some are not even synonymous (list headings are ours):

If Teacher Says This:	She May Mean This:
Should	Must
Can do more when he tries	Lazy
Disturbs class	Trouble maker
Should learn to work with others	Uncooperative
Depends on others to do his work	Cheats
Can do better work with help	Stupid
Can learn to do the right thing	Never does the right thing
Working at his own level	Below average
Absent without permission	Truant
Discourteous	Impertinent
Takes without permission	Steal
Poor habits	Unclean
Capable of doing better	Dumbell
Cooperation	Help
Handicapped	Poor
Lost opportunity	Calamity
Complacent, not challenged	Disinterested
Investment	Expense
Invest in	Contribute to
Insists on having his own way	Stubborn
Outspoken	Insolent
Tendency to stretch the truth	Liar
Could make better use of time	Wastes time
Could do neater work	Sloppy
Failed to meet requirements	Incurred failure
Difficulty in getting along with others	Mean
Usually	Time and again
Uncertain	Dubious
Below his usual standard	Poor grade of work
Not physically coordinated	Clumsy
Seldom shares with others	Selfish
Inconsiderate of others	Rude
Reserved	Bashful
Tries to get attention	Show-off
Has a chance of passing if	Will fail him

Right You Are
If You Say You Are
– Obscurely

TIME

The scene is the office of the dean of admissions at Instant College. A pale adolescent approaches the dean, who is appropriately clad in flowing white memos.

STUDENT: Y-you sent for me, sir?

DEAN: Yes, my boy. We've decided to accept you as a student here at Instant.

STUDENT: Sir, I can't tell you how pleased I am. I mean, my high school average is 65, I got straight Ds in mathematics, confuse the Norman Conquest with D-day, have a sub-average IQ, and got turned down by every other college in America. Yet in spite of all of this, you've accepted me.

DEAN: Not in spite of it, boy! Because of it!

STUDENT *(dimly)*: Sir?

DEAN: Don't you see? You're a challenge. We're starting with nothing—you. Yet before we're through, corporations will seek your advice, little magazines will print your monographs on such arcane subjects as forensic medicine and epistemology, newspapers will publish your utterances as you enplane for conferences abroad.

STUDENT: Me?

DEAN: You. Because you will be an Expert.

STUDENT: An expert what?

DEAN: Just an Expert.

STUDENT: But, sir, I don't know anything and I can't learn much. Not in four years, anyway.

DEAN: Why, my boy, we'll have you out of here in an hour. All you need is the catalyst that instantly transforms the lowest common denominator, you, into an Expert.

STUDENT: Money? Power? Intellect? Charm?

DEAN: No these things are but children's toys compared to Jargon.

STUDENT: Jargon?

DEAN *(turning to his textbook)*: The dictionary calls it "confused, unintelligible language: gibberish, a dialect regarded as barbarous or outlandish." But we at Instant call it the Expert's Ultimate Weapon. In 1967, it will hypnotize friends, quash enemies and intimidate whole nations. Follow me.

A school bell rings, and the entire faculty enters: Dr. Gummidge, professor of sociology; the Rev. Mr. Logos, head of the theological seminary; Dr. Beazle, head of the medical school; Mr. Flap, instructor in government; and finally, General Redstone, chief of the ROTC. Dr. Gummidge steps forward, conducts the student to an uncomfortable chair, mills about him like a lonely crowd, and begins.

GUMMIDGE: Remember Gummidge's Law and you will never be Found Out: The amount of expertise varies in inverse proportion to the number of statements understood by the General Public.

STUDENT: In other words?

GUMMIDGE: In other words, never say "In other words." That will force you to clarify your statements. Keep all pronunciamentos orotund and hazy. Suppose your mother comes to school and asks how you are doing. Do I reply: "He is at the bottom of his class—lazy and good-for-nothing"?

STUDENT: Why not? Everyone else does.

GUMMIDGE: I am not everyone else. I reply: "The student in question is performing minimally for his peer group and is an emerging underachiever."

STUDENT: Wow!

GUMMIDGE: Exactly. If you are poor, I refer to you as disadvantaged; if you live in a slum, you are in a culturally deprived environment.

STUDENT: If I want to get out of a crowded class?

GUMMIDGE: You seek a more favorable pupil-teacher ratio, plus a decentralized learning center in the multiversity.

STUDENT: If I'm learning a language by conversing in it?

GUMMIDGE: That's the aural-oral method. Say it aloud.

The student does and is completely incomprehensible. A cheer goes up from the faculty.

GUMMIDGE: From now on, you must never speak; you must verbalize.

STUDENT: Must I verbalize Jargon only to my peer group?

GUMMIDGE: Not at all. You can now use it even when addressing preschoolers. In his book *Translations from the English*, Robert Paul Smith offers these samples: "He shows a real ability in plastic conception." That means he can make a snake out of clay. "He's rather slow in group integration and reacts negatively to aggressive stimulus." He cries easily. And "He does seem to have developed late in large-muscle control." He falls on his head frequently.

STUDENT (*awestruck*): I'll never be able to do it.

GUMMIDGE: Of course you will. The uninitiated are easily impressed. It's all rather like the ignorant woman who learns that her friend's son has graduated from medical school. "How's your boy?" she asks. The friend clucks sadly: "He's a practicing homosexual." "Wonderful!" cries the first. "Where's his office?" Do I make myself clear?

STUDENT: No, sir.

GUMMIDGE: Fine. Now open your textbook to the David Riesman chapter. Here is the eminent sociologist writing about Jargon: "Phrases such as 'achievement-oriented' or "need-achievement' were, if I am not mistaken, invented by colleagues and friends of mine, Harry Murray and David C. McClelland .... It has occurred to me that they may be driven by a kind of asceticism precisely because they are poetic men of feeling who ... have chosen to deal with soft data in a hard way." Now then, my boy, is there any better example of flapdoodle than that?

STUDENT: Well, how about these samples from Harvard Sociologist Talcott Parsons: "Adaptation, goal-attainment, integration and pattern maintenance."

GUMMIDGE: Yes, first rate. Even I practice them, just as Horowitz plays the scales. Try them in a sentence. Two men open a store. Someone provides the cash. What's that?

STUDENT: Adaptation?

GUMMIDGE: And then they entice customers—

STUDENT: Goal-attainment.

GUMMIDGE: They set up a sales staff—

STUDENT: Integration.

GUMMIDGE: And they don't steal from the cash register.

STUDENT: They agree to maintain the wider values of the culture. That's pattern maintenance.

GUMMIDGE: Perfect. See how complicated you can make things? Imagine what damage you can wreak in the schools where a situation is no longer practical, it is viable; where a pupil is no longer unmanageable, but alienated. Get it?

STUDENT: Got it.

GUMMIDGE: Do books have words and pictures?

STUDENT: No, sir, they have verbal symbols and visual representations.

GUMMIDGE: You're on your way. For your final exam, read and commit to memory the 23rd Psalm Jargonized by Alan Simpson, president of Vassar College.

STUDENT (*droning*): "The Lord is my external-internal integrative mechanism, I shall not be deprived of gratifications for my viscerogenic hungers or my need-dispositions. He motivates me to orient myself towards a nonsocial object with effective significance."

The student falls into a dreamlike trance during which Professor Gummidge tiptoes off and is replaced by the Rev. Mr. Logos, who continues the psalm.

LOGOS: "He positions me in a nondecisional situation. He maximizes my adjustment. . . " (*As the student wakes up*): I'm the Reverend Mr. Logos. Bless you, my son.

STUDENT: I see you're wearing a turned-around collar and a *yarmulke.* Just what is your religion?

LOGOS: I am a theologian. Does that answer you?

STUDENT: No.

LOGOS: Splendid. How would you refer to a priest disagreeing with a minister?

STUDENT: As two guys arguing?

LOGOS: No, no, no! Religious leaders never argue, they have dialogues, or I-Thou relationships.

STUDENT: If their studies are mainly about Jesus?

LOGOS: They are Christocentrically oriented. If they are interpreting the Bible, hermeneutics is the term.

STUDENT: Can you predict what words will be In for the theological year ahead?

LOGOS: Certainly. demythologizing, optimism, theology of hope, *engagé* and commitment.

STUDENT: I like dialectic theology and conceptualism.

LOGOS: Forget them. They're all Out. Concentrate on phenomenology, sociological inspiration, ethical activism, crisis of authority.

STUDENT: Suppose someone realizes that I don't have the faintest idea what I'm talking about?

LOGOS: Then accuse him of objectification. If he doesn't go away, ask him what he did before he got religion, before his ultimate faith-concern, or better still, *Selbstverständnis.*

STUDENT: But that's not even English.

LOGOS: All the better. Many influential theologians wrote in German—Bultmann, Bonhoeffer, Barth—and German not only offers us a chance to obfuscate, it adds a tangy foreign flavor. For instance, there is *Historie,* meaning bare facts, *Geschichte,* meaning interpretive history.

STUDENT: Sort of like the difference between *The World Almanac* and Toynbee.

LOGOS: Remember Gummidge's Law: don't clarify!

STUDENT: Sorry.

LOGOS: Don't let it happen again. *Vorverständnis* is one of my favorites. It means presupposition. *Wissenschaft* is far better than saying simply discipline or science, and anxiety sounds much deeper if you say *Angst.* If you grow weary of German, there is always Greek—almost everyone has seen *Never on Sunday*—with such splendid specimens as *kerygma* (message of the Scriptures) and *agape* (divine love).

STUDENT (*writing furiously*): Are you sure Jargon really works? In religion, I mean?

LOGOS: Does it? I quote from a distinguished cleric: "I can't make heads or tails out of a great deal of what Tillich says." The confessor is Dr. Billy Graham himself.

At this, the Rev. Mr. Logos is borne away by the laity to edit a book of his sermons entitled Through Exegesis and Hermeneutics We Arrive at Kerygma. *In his place steps Dr. Beazle, who takes the student's blood pressure, temperature, hemoglobin count and wallet.*

BEAZLE: Now what kind of medical career do you want, physical or psychiatric?

STUDENT: I don't know. I never thought about it.

BEAZLE: That's a good start. Suppose we begin with plain everyday medicine. Was it not Herman Melville who wrote: "A man of true science uses but few hard words, and those only when none other will answer his purpose; whereas the smatterer in science thinks that by mouthing hard words he proves that he understands hard things." Now you don't want to be an ordinary man of true science when you can be a full-fledged Smatterer, do you?

STUDENT: I guess not.

BEAZLE: Very well, remember never to let the patient be fully aware of what is wrong. Even tonsillitis can be described as a malign hypertrophied condition that affects nares and pharynx and may result in paraphonia clausa. It was I, you know, who wrote the sign seen in hospitals: "Illumination is required to be extinguished on these premises on the termination of daily activities."

STUDENT: Which means—

BEAZLE: Put out the lights when you leave.

STUDENT: Marvelous.

BEAZLE: It was nothing, really. We medical men have been confounding patients for years. As far back as 1699, the physician and poet Samuel Garth wrote: "The patient's ears remorseless he assails / Murders with jargon where his medicine fails." Still, physical medicine is nothing compared with psychiatry. There's where we Jargonists truly have our day. Suppose a man loses his wife and is unable to love anyone because he is sad. What do I tell him?

STUDENT: Cheer up, there are lots of fish in the—?

BEAZLE (*interrupting*): Of course not. I intone: You have suffered an object loss in which you had an over-cathesis of libido and have been unable to decathect the libido and invest it in a new object. Do you follow me?

STUDENT: I think so.

BEAZLE: Then be warned: the public is on our trail; they now have learned the meanings of the "oses" and the "itises." You had better replace them with "inadequacies," and "dependencies," tell the man who acts out fantasies that he is "role playing," speak of the creation of a child as "exclusive electivity of dynamic specificity."

STUDENT: And when the child is born?

BEAZLE: His development proceeds through "mutual synthesis carried on through a functional zone of mutuality."

STUDENT: In short, he grows up.

BEAZLE: In long, he proceeds in a continuous unidirectional ever-varying interplay of organism and environment.

STUDENT: If a patient is unhappy?

BEAZLE: He is having an identity crisis.

STUDENT: But suppose he's just unhappy?

BEAZLE: No one is just unhappy. Psych harder!

STUDENT: I'll start immediately. I will follow Lionel Trilling's dictum: no one will fall in love and get married as long as I'm present.

BEAZLE: What will they do?

STUDENT: Their libidinal impulses being reciprocal, they will integrate their individual erotic drives and bring them within the same frame of reference. How am I doing?

BEAZLE: Not badly, but I can still understand you.

STUDENT: Sorry. Day by day I will grow more obscure, until my patients and I completely fail to communicate.

BEAZLE: Oh, if only I could believe that! Smog, confuse, obfuscate! *He exits, to invent a cure for clarity and lucidity which he will sell to nine leading pharmaceutical firms. Mr. Flap and General Redstone come forward.*

FLAP: Order of magnitude, expedite, implement, reorient, interoccupational mobility, mission oriented—

REDSTONE: Component forces, readiness levels, destruct—

STUDENT: Excuse me—

REDSTONE (*ignoring him*): Credibility, paramilitary department—wide contingency plans, pre-emptive war, scenario, remote area conflict . . .

FLAP: Expedite, channels, maximize, bureau potential—

STUDENT: Gentlemen, please, I—

DEAN: It's no good, son. Once the civilian and the military start arguing, it can go on for years.

REDSTONE: Circular error probability, target systems, pipeline requirements, deterrent gaps . . . counterinsurgency . . . soft target . . . *The general grinds to a halt. Two enlisted men enter, paint him a neutral olive drab and carry him off to the Pentagon, where he will replace a computer.*

FLAP (*running down*): Extended care facilities . . . oligopoly . . . input . . . phasein . . . interlocking intervention . . . (*He creaks, coughs and crawls into a filing cabinet.*)

DEAN (*handing the student a diploma printed on sheep-like vinyl*): We've done all we can for you, son. In George Orwell's paraphrase: "The race is not to the swift—nor the battle to the strong . . . but time and chance—"

STUDENT: I know. "Objective considerations of contemporary phenomena compels the conclusion that success or failure in competitive activities exhibits no tendency to be commensurate with innate capacity, but that a considerable element of the unpredictable must be taken into account."

DEAN: Exactly. (*Moist of eye, he pats the new graduate on the head.*) You can now take your pick of careers in medicine, religion, business and geopolitics—as well as wine-tasting and art criticism. And if you fail at everything, there's a job for you at Instant College. (*Calling after him as the student exits.*) And remember, it is better to curse one candle than to light the darkness . . .
He extinguishes the lights, leaving the audience in blackness as

THE CURTAIN FALLS

10
THE ARTS
AND THE MASS MEDIA

The language of the rapidly changing fields of the arts and the mass media is the subject of this chapter. The chapter opens with Richard Kostelanetz's brief critical survey of contemporary literature, and Robert Christgau ranges widely over rock lyrics.

Drama critic Marilyn Stasio offers an amusing satire on the clichés and opportunism of the New York theatre, and Time *editors write about the "quiet revolution" in television.*

Contemporary
Literature

RICHARD KOSTELANETZ

Despite scattered opinion to the contrary, there exists, let me suggest, a contemporary literature that is worth the most serious attention. Not only does this Post-World War II writing offer a wide spectrum of numerous important works, but several recent writers, such as Samuel Beckett, Albert Camus, Ralph Ellison, Jean Genet, Alberto Moravia, and Jean-Paul Sartre, have produced some of the most significant literature of the twentieth century. Like their predecessors, the great moderns of forty years ago, the best contemporary writers critically engage the continuous upheavals in both society and literary form that define the culture of the twentieth century. Though their style and subjects are as pertinent as the morning news, their purposes remain as traditional as writing itself. Through literature, they strive to understand the radical nature of the present, both in its content and form, and to show how the eternal in man and the legacy of history fare in the world today. To do this, they have largely resisted the efforts of conservative critics to make them toe the line of the "rules" for their art. Rather, contemporary writers, particularly the best of them, continue to reject forms and subjects they feel are archaic and to create original vehicles to carry their awareness of the unprecedented modern situation. The best of this recent literature, because of its pertinence, excellence and difficulty, merits the most conscientious analysis and delicate appreciation a reader or critic can give.

Like the masters of all twentieth century art, contemporary writers express their oppressive awareness of the predicament of the times. Though maǹ has achieved extraordinary material and technological progress, the greatest literature of the past forty-five years tells us over and over again that the quality of his life has not improved apace, for he is the victim, rather than the beneficiary, of the advances of history. In depicting modern life, individual writers choose to concentrate upon various aspects of the total situation. Albert Camus and Jean-Paul Sartre in their fiction emphasize that modern man who would isolate himself from society is not only psychologically alienated but potentially capable of denying his moral responsibility, and Saul Bellow and Boris Pasternak insist that the institutions of modern society inevitably frustrate human wants. Totalitarian methods of control, so George Orwell and Norman Mailer tell us, infiltrate democratic societies as well as dictatorial, and more recently Anthony Burgess sees that life in our time is so horrendously violent that the lone individual can do little to defend himself against its unexpected onslaughts. Alberto Moravia and others dramatize that true human relations are made impossible both by biological needs and the selfishness of man isolated in mass society; and Eugene Ionesco and Samuel Beckett demonstrate that contemporary man, who has neither a universally accepted explanation for the mysteries nor an ethical system universally observed, faces an existence which is fundamentally absurd. James Purdy and Ralph Ellison emphasize that although man is terribly alone and incapable of overcoming his isolation, he still asserts his right to exist. Many of these themes, it is true, characterized the major writings of forty years ago. The rootlessness and *anomie* of twentieth century man were, of course, felt and explored by Eliot and Joyce as well as by Mann and Kafka, all profoundly aware of the contagious malaise of the age.

However, this literary image of the modern world has recently undergone a slight, but perceptible, shift. A comparison of the major themes of T. S. Eliot and Samuel Beckett, both among the most eminent and most representative writers of their respective generations, illustrates the change. In *The Waste Land,* Eliot emphasized intellectual disillusion and despair, historical disintegration from stability into anarchy, and the decline of religious faith. In his portrait of the modern situation, he generally opposes the present to the past. Beckett, however, discards all sense of linear history in order to focus upon the eternity of individual isolation. He suggests that man is doomed to recognize that systematic beliefs and concerted actions are impotent before the metaphysical absurdity that has always been his fate. Unlike Eliot, whose pessimism was so thorough he could envision redemption only in a *return* to the past, Beckett believes in the ontological indomitableness of the human spirit. In his recent novel, entitled with the pun *Comment C'est* (How It Is, or To Begin), Beckett's Pim, the prototypical man, struggles through limbo, crawling *forward* at an excruciatingly slow pace, his face always down in the mud. Despite all obstacles and with no discernible reason for being or going on, Pim continues to move.

The shift in emphasis from Eliot to Beckett epitomizes other changes in literature's view of man's existence. For one contrast, what separates the best contemporaries from the generation of Faulkner and Hemingway is the former's refusal to let their sensitive protagonists escape into death. Bellow's Tommy Wilhelm, Ellison's Invisible Man, the narrator of Jean Genet's prose, J. D. Salinger's Holden Caulfield, Michael Butor's Jacques Revel, Günter Grass's insane narrator, and Sartre's Roquentin are all faced with the possibility of death, but their awareness of their possible extinction only inspires them to draw strength from their deepest sources of resilience and to salvage their lives. This refusal to retreat into history or death signifies, I think, that the best writers *accept* modern existence, with all its horror and absurdity, as an incontrovertible fact. From this straight-forward acceptance comes a more affirmative attitude, albeit very tentative, towards man's destiny. Despite the most adverse of situations, despite incessant failures and indignities, and despite an oppressive sense of impotence, humankind in recent writing continues to crave life, even a partial existence in a cave or in limbo, to affirm at all costs the passionate desire merely to exist.

Likewise, writers today observe the modern decay from a different perspective. Whereas Eliot and Mann, as ultimate authorial voices, seem aloof from the modern chaos, the voices of, say, Beckett, William Burroughs, Ellison and Genet are clearly in the midst of it; not even the privileges of literature afford an outpost of retreat. This transition emerges from these passages of poetry. The first is a translation from the Spanish of Rafael Alberti's *Castigos (Punishments)* of 1929:

> I did not know that the doors changed their places,
> That souls could blush at their bodies,
> Nor that at the end of a tunnel light brought death.
>
> (Trans. J. M. Cohen)

The same alienation and despair are expressed in these famous lines from "The Fire Sermon" section of *The Waste Land*:

I can connect
Nothing with nothing.

In both passages, the narrator is an outsider, supposedly a more sensitive being, cut off from the world around him. In recent poems by the Frenchman Jean Laude, the Rumanian Paul Celan and Samuel Beckett, the narrator makes his own predicament that of Everyman:

> The words sink in the sand. Surrounded by eggs, the numbers rot and the pendulum goes wild in the dead zone where the body of a new day takes form. Everything is a sign. On the ground strewn with bodies, clenched hands point in opposite directions, but I am the crossroad, the confluence where threats find their source.
>
> (Jean Laude, trans. Jean Paris)

In his "Todesfuge" (Death Fugue), one of the greatest contemporary poems, Paul Celan, a Rumanian-born Jew who lives in Paris and writes in German, makes "black milk" his symbol for the quality of life after the atrocities of Hitler:

> Black milk of morning we drink you at dusk
> we drink you at noontime and dawntime we drink you at night
> we drink and drink. . . .
>
> (Trans. Jerome Rothenberg)

The following passage is from "Dieppe," which Beckett first wrote in French and then translated into English:

> What would I do without this world fearless incurious
> where to be lasts but an instant where every instant
> spills in the void of ignorance of having been
> without this wave where in the end
> body and shadow together are engulfed.

In Beckett's poetry, as in his later fiction and much other recent writing, there is in essence no difference between the experiences of the narrator and the world at large.

Contemporaries eschew the historical and religious contrasts that were plentiful in the literature of the 1920's and 1930's. In an earlier time, the protagonist of Hemingway's "A Clean Well-Lighted Place" substituted "nada" for every important word in the Lord's Prayer, a symbolic way of saying that for him each of these phrases means "nothing." Beckett's protagonists, in contrast, have moved beyond nothingness, which depends upon an awareness of possible significance, to a further point, which we call absurdity. "For to know nothing is nothing, not to want to know anything likewise, but to be beyond knowing anything," concludes Beckett's Molloy, "it is then the true division begins, of twenty-two by seven for example, and the pages fill with the true ciphers at last." Since twenty-two divided by seven, or Pi, produces a number without final limits, an indefinite answer, it, along with permutations that signify that all is possible and nothing meaningful, becomes Beckett's paradigm for an existence "beyond knowing anything." Through vignettes and symbolic musings like these, Beckett demonstrates that the first mark of the more extreme condition of absurdity is the recognition that traditional codes of value are not just meaningless but that they are so irrelevant as to be forgotten. In this respect, the symbolic likenesses of decaying tradition, such as falling church steeples, dirty rivers, decrepit mansions, dissonant music, and ineffectual men of the cloth—so abundant in the writings of a generation ago—are largely absent from major contemporary works. The literary careers of Joyce and Eliot themselves foreshadowed this change. In their early works, they used mythological and historical parallels to contrast the present with the past, or the probable past; however, in their later work, they largely omitted such comparisons. In *Finnegans Wake*, Joyce sees human history as circular—the book ends with the same sentence with which it began; and Eliot turned from modern life to the ahistorical purity of traditional religion.

Following the most important writers since 1920, the major contemporaries have continued the revolt against literary realism in favor of more imaginative ways of rendering human existence. The realist writer exemplified by Emile Zola believed he could best evoke reality through the accumulation of accurate details, as though his point would not be convincing unless it was supported by verifiable data; and though this tradition has influenced writers as diverse in talent, intelligence and seriousness as C. P. Snow and Herman Wouk, Vasco Pratolini and Françoise Sagan, Philip Roth and Augus Wilson, it is distinctly separate from the dominant tradition of modern narrative literature. Rather, the key recent writers attempt to describe a large group of people or even the modern human condition by isolating the *essence* of its existence. Through a sensitive portrait of the resonant microcosm, they illuminate the macrocosm. In early modern literature, Joyce's Leopold Bloom took on universal dimensions, as did Thomas Mann's sanitarium in *The Magic Mountain*. In contemporary writing, just as Orwell's Winston Smith represents Every Englishman confronting a society that suppresses his humanity and the plague of Camus' Oran represents the sickness of modern life, so Vladimir and Estragon in their waiting for Godot take on the dimension of modern man confronting a world without discernible meaning, and Joseph Heller's Yossarian, *un homme moyen sensuel*, recognizes there is today no justification for violence and death.

In addition to adopting, with slight modification, their predecessors' picture of the world, most of today's significant writers have absorbed the major stylistic revolutions of modern literature by employing the advances of their elders for their own purposes. As Joyce in *Finnegans Wake* coined a new prose, a blend of many languages, to express his particular message about the universality of the basic familial pattern, so Anthony Burgess devised "Nadsat," an English heavily infused with Russian, to enrich his fictional vision of life in the near future. Exemplifying the same fusion of language and content, the eloquent repetitions that flood Samuel Beckett's prose evoke his special sense of life, as the adjectiveless, unmetaphoric prose of Alain Robbe-Grillet matches his emotionless, super-objective view of the human scene. Following Henry James and Faulkner, contemporary writers as different as J. D. Salinger and Doris Lessing, as Nathalie Sarraute and Lawrence Durrell, have shifted the narrative voice from one character to another to reveal more of the situation than we would learn from just a single point-of-view. Likewise, just as poets from Rimbaud to Theodore Roethke have tried to depict the depths of the human unconscious, so novelists from Henry James to the present have attempted to penetrate and describe the subtleties of consciousness and modes of perception, an effort developed by Marcel Proust and Virgina Woolf and continued by Jean-Paul Sartre in *Nausea* and, with especial success, by Nathalie Sarraute in *The Planetarium*. Here the voices are not characters in the traditional sense but participating consciousnesses spinning free and deflecting like objects in a planetarium.

Intrinsic in this is the desire to capture time and objects not as they are in natural fact but as we subjectively perceive them. To achieve this experiential fidelity, contemporary novelists often discard conventional methods of describing time and space. Instead, they create a fiction in which the original technique itself, rather than what it describes, becomes the center of interest. In confronting this kind of work, then, the reader first must perceive the writer's particular style rather than, as he did with conventional fiction, first comprehending the natures of the various characters.

Just as composers, dancers and painters exhibit the modern impulse to explore the possibilities of their arts, so writers have pursued several paths of experiments which have increased the alternatives of literary reality and our range of perception. One line leads toward a fiction where time ceases to have any existential significance for its characters, as in Beckett's last novels; or where time, individually and thus subjectively perceived, becomes the central issue in the novel, a preoccupation mastered by Faulkner in *The Sound and the Fury* and continued by Claude Simon in his several novels and Lawrence Durrell in *The Alexandria Quartet.*

Similarly, whereas we once witnessed the characters and the scene emerge from pertinent details, now some novelists have pushed the visual content of fiction to two opposite extremes. First, through an excess of visual facts, as in the fiction of Alain Robbe-Grillet, the narrator's eye becomes a movie camera that is obligated to report all that it sees. At the other limit, the author compresses his visual material, painting a character with a single idiosyncratic detail; and to evoke his presence later in the novel, the writer needs only to mention that essential detail. This technique was used successfully by F. Scott Fitzgerald and Nathanael West in the twenties and thirties, and James Purdy and John Hawkes have employed it more recently. Likewise, playwrights from Strindberg to Genet have tried to invert and distort our normal perceptions of illusion and reality, often, as in Pirandello, making the ambiguous relation between the two the central issue of a play.

For all these reasons, form in all modern literature, pre-Second World War as well as post, tends to be, in Joseph Frank's incisive dichotomy, spatial rather than narrative, or lyric rather than dramatic. That is, what ties a book together is not its developing action, which focuses our interest on what happens next; but its vision, which is generally conveyed by resonant images, by fragmented characterizations, by telling juxtapositions, by a disordered arrangement of the scenes and by haphazard glimpses into human states of consciousness and mood. All these elements, if the literary work is successful, coalesce into a coherent whole which we perceive as we see a painting— visually, at once, rather than temporally, in time. To effect this change, modern writers have eliminated certain devices and patterns which have been the skeletal bones of traditional narrative literature–expository structure, climaxes, turning points, and symmetrical plot.

Therefore, with spatial form comes a distortion of traditional lines of emphasis. The sort of small aspect that might be of secondary interest in a traditional work can, in a modern piece, take on a special symbolic significance. In classic modern works, examples include the birds and trees of Yeats' poetry, Benjy's wrong turn around the village circle at the end of *The Sound and the Fury,* and the soap and potted meat in Joyce's *Ulysses*; in recent literature, writers continue to infuse significance into seemingly trivial things–the sucking of stones in Beckett's *Molloy*, the tin drum in Günter Grass's novel, and the contents of the Invisible Man's suitcase. Our interest in these books comes from recognizing the important details, discovering their significance, and piecing them together into a whole.

Contemporary poets, too, have accepted the modern revolutions. First, the spatial organization of long poems as diverse as Alexander Blok's "The Twelve" and Eliot's *The Waste Land* has been also employed in recent long poems, such as Yves Bonnefoy's *Douve* and Kenneth Koch's *Ko*, and, as before, in most major short poems. From this follows the destruction of traditional syntax in favor of other systems for structuring the lines of poetry, a change that occurred in all the languages of poetry early in the twentieth century. In place of traditional connectives, poets today depend upon non-expository kinds of relations, such as the repetition of emotional states, patterns of images, suggestive contrasts, a consistent range of suggestion, and a coherent symbolic or metaphoric dimension, to unify their poems. Recent poetry does not directly tell or argue but rather evokes and suggests; likewise, it presents not a clear, sequential development but one that is distorted, multiple and ambiguous. To put it another way, modern poets have shifted away from a poetry of concrete images and relations as well as an easily identifiable meaning to a more abstract poetry in which relations are tenuous and elliptical, comparisons more often implied than stated, and, in more extreme cases, both intention and final meaning sometimes undiscernible. Such poetry has a compositional logic of its own; and by reading and re-reading the poem, particularly concentrating on its vital elements, one can discern an organizing principle in what at first and even second glance seems chaos. As Joseph Frank put it, "The meaning relationship is completed only by the simultaneous perception in space of word-groups that have no comprehensible relation to each other when read consecutively in time." In prose, the most ambitious and interesting experiment in this direction is Michel Butor's travelogue of America, *Mobile* (1962); in theatre, Beckett's *Play* (1963) exhibits a similar achievement. They are, perhaps, the forerunners of a thoroughly spatial novel and drama.

In addition to assimilating the key formal developments of modern literature, contemporaries have added their own lines to the chart of literary possibility. Since, after Hitler, after the extermination of captive peoples and the bombing of civilian cities in World War II, after the fact of atomic war and the threat of a thermonuclear war that could end all human history, the world *felt* considerably different from an earlier generation, post-war writers recognized the need first to understand precisely how life today is different and then to devise new forms that could match their awareness. Since Ionesco, so he said, felt that, "Cut off from his religious, metaphysical and transcendental roots, man is lost; all his actions become senseless, absurd, useless," he was forced to reject the going theatrical guidelines in order to find an absurd form, one heavily imbued with nonsensical and ludicrous images, that would match the disorder and madness he saw around him. The idea of human life as absurd had, of course, been espoused by earlier writers; but where the characters of Camus' and Sartre's plays argue about it or discover it in the course of action, Pinter's and Ionesco's people present it in absurd language, absurd situations, and absurd conflicts until the vision of absurdity encompasses both the detail and the totality. Just as Ionesco's lecturer in *The Chairs* when assigned to deliver Ultimate Truth speaks gibberish, so Pinter's dumbwaiter, which is man's only contact with the Mysterious Above, sends down incomprehensible messages. This literature embodies the most representative form of contemporary writing; and to judge by the widespread admiration for the plays of Ionesco, Beckett, Pinter, N. F. Simpson, Jack Gelber and the fiction of Heller and John Barth, readers today find in absurd literature a most thoroughly appropriate image of the contemporary predicament.

After absurdity, the second most pertinent trend in contemporary writing includes those writers who with an unprecedented force have uncompromisingly damned the events of recent history, the worth of conventional ideas of normalcy, and the pretense that modern man has progressed from the savages. True, these themes permeated most modern literature, but what distinctly separates the contemporaries from the earlier writers is the intensity, both in style and vision, of the works that embody these themes. In dealing with the Nazi atrocities, André Schwarz-Bart in *The Last of the Just* ties the extermination of European Jewry, particularly the death of "the just men," to the disintegration of all modern life, all told in a prose that sings hysteria on every page; in the same way, the protagonist of Elie Wiesel's *Night*, written in French by an Israeli, evokes the incredible horror of a Nazi concentration camp, while Paul Celan captures in "The Death Fugue" the tone of the mechanized humanity that performed such horrors. In these works, the ferocious strength of the writer's negation makes earlier works of protest seem faintly tame.

Throughout modern literature, the image of the modern world as hell is evoked likewise with a violence and intensity equally unprecedented. The unrelieved terror and depravity of William Burroughs' *Naked Lunch* strikes me as more frightening than Celine's visions, for Burroughs succeeds in repudiating Celine's boast that only he could sustain intense negation for the length of a novel. This kind of extreme dissent illuminates a wide variety of contemporary works—the novels of the Spaniard Camile José Cela; the poetry of Allen Ginsberg; in a slightly different guise, the plays (not the novels) of Jean Genet; Anthony Burgess' best fiction; and Ralph Ellison's *Invisible Man*. Perhaps the final touch to this theme of rejection is provided by the closing lines of the "Soliloquy of the Individual," a stunning history of mankind by the Chilean poet, Nicanor Parra:

> Perhaps I'd better return to that valley,
> To that rock which once was home,
> And start to engrave again,
> From end to beginning,
> The world in reverse.

(Trans. Jorge Elliott)

Just as these negative modern writers have often, but not always, achieved comedy in the ferociousness of their rejection, so absurd writers accomplish the same fusion by creating terror at the heart of their comedy. In this respect, too, contemporary literature contrasts with earlier modern. If the dominant tone of the most penetrating works of Eliot and Hemingway is a humorless despair, Beckett, again the epitome, creates an air of tragi-comic finality—under each moment of terror lies the joke of our existence and under each joke a grim terror. More specifically, the writer may start with a comic sequence that eventually takes on the dimensions of terror, as Joseph Heller or Ionesco do; or he may open with an image of terror that eventually becomes funny, as in, say, James Purdy's *Malcolm* or William Burroughs' *Naked Lunch*.

In contrast to writers who indirectly engage the contemporary situation, others demonstrate a retreat into the most private kind of experience, particularly man's perception of himself, nature and others; the writers who pursue this path generally employ rather traditional forms. This response to the present, perhaps better understood as an anti-response, presupposes a distinct contradiction between modern life and the "art" of literature and, it follows, the feeling that the purity of the second must be salvaged from the terrors of the first. This retreat defines the work of two important poets: Theodore Roethke, whose "Words for the Wind" opens "Love, love, a lily's my care," and René Char, whose characteristic moment is, "The stride of the girl / Has caressed the lane / Has passed through the gate." In fiction, the comparable response characterizes most of the recent American gothic novelists ranging from Flannery O'Connor to Truman Capote, the work of the English "New University Wits," the novels of Françoise Sagan and their imitations—in general, books by novelists who cultivate an accuracy of detail rather than a pervasive and resonant vision. Retreat into private perception is probably the privilege of the poet; but such an inclination in novelists, though their talents and techniques may be prodigious and fine, produces essentially minor works, for their books will lack the scope and urgent contemporaneousness that are the prime characteristics of truly significant contemporary writing. The major authors of our time have looked unflinchingly at our condition; and out of its anti-poetic ugliness, they have fashioned works of an original, compelling and relevant form, a literature illuminating and more profound than "beautiful," which at its best perceives some of the contemporary reality that evades our limited perspective.

Just as it is naive to condemn contemporary writers for having too bleak a view of the human condition or for presenting their vision in too difficult a form, it is useless, I think, to speak, as is often done, of absurd theatre as "anti-theatre" and, say, the objectivist French novel as "anti-fiction." Both are simply new forms of each genre. Neither repudiates all the conventions of that genre as much as the "anti" prefix suggests. Rather, each draws selectively upon certain trends in each genre (Martin Esslin has traced the genealogy of absurd theatre; the new novel has a comparable one); and in using the tradition with discrimination, the author fuses the possibilities of the genre with his awareness of the specialness of the present.

While the literature of the last twenty years has included several great works which are important to us today, I do not think literary historians of the future will look upon 1944–1964 as comparable to the twenty years between the First and Second Wars, which witnessed the appearance of the best writings of Eliot, Yeats, Joyce, Mann, Proust, and Faulkner. Nonetheless, it is foolish to write off, as some pessimistic critics have done, the past twenty years as insignificant, for in that time appeared the flowering of the absurd theatre, the beginnings of the absurd novel, a variety of propitious experiments in fiction, the development of the first substantially modernist British theatre, the major works of Sartre, Camus and Beckett, Pasternak's great novel, the poetry of John Berryman, Yves Bonnefoy and Robert Lowell, Moravia's psychologically incisive fiction, and the novels of Ralph Ellison, Alain Robbe-Grillet, and John Barth. Moreover, through the efforts of those who have refused to accept the "rules" of literature and, instead, seem to follow Claude Levi-Strauss' dictum that, "Truth lies in the progressive expansion of meaning," the range of what is possible in literature has continued to enlarge, so that the young and unborn will be able to confront a greater variety of usable forms and viable attitudes than has ever been available in the past.

Rock Lyrics
Are Poetry (Maybe)

ROBERT CHRISTGAU

UNTIL IT NARROWED its programming, there was one hip radio station in New York, the station of the college kids and the bright suburban adolescents and the young professionals and the hippies—your station, if you're within range: WOR-FM. Not that there was much choice—AM radio in New York is antediluvian. But for a while, WOR-Stereo did seem to try. Its playlist was flexible and enormous and its deejays enjoyed much freedom. WOR was the home of the born-again Murray the K, with his "attitude music" and his tell-it-like-it-is (baby) cool, and coming up strong behind was the latetime (ten-to-two) jock, a spade named Rosko. Rosko emcees at the Village Theater, which is a story in itself, but not this one. This one is about Rosko and Kahlil Gibran, now-deceased author of a dozen or so quasi-poetic, pseudo-religious texts, the most famous of which is *The Prophet*.*

Rosko quit WOR when the station decided to chase after the post-adolescent AM audience with a tight oldies playlist, but he had more in

---

* Already I can hear the screaming. You *like* Kahlil Gibran, right? So let's have it out. A critical essay—consider yourself forewarned—illumines nothing so much as the prejudices of its author. My tastes in music derive largely from Alan Freed and Thelonious Monk, but my tastes in poetry and philosophy were pounded into me by a phalanx of Ivy League professors. I think Kahlil Gibran is the worst kind of trash, much worse than Harold Robbins, say, because good people take him seriously.

common with all the screaming-meemies than he probably suspected. Just like Cousin Brucie or B.M.R., he did not so much announce a show as preside over a ritual. Cultism is not confined to teeny-boppers. All four jazz fans out there should remember Symphony Sid, who played virtually the same cuts night after night for literally years, announcing the same Stan Getz / Oscar Brown, Jr. / Nina Simone / Willie Bobo / Miles Davis in the same throat-cancer growl. Rosko did Sid one better. He played the same stuff every night, Beatles / Stones / Dylan, plus hip hits and various cult heroes—Richie Havens, Vanilla Fudge, Jimi Hendrix, Big Brother, Judy Collins. Then, to ice the cake, he would climax his show with a reverent reading from Kahlil Gibran. "And he who has deserved to drink from the ocean of life deserves to drink from your little stream"; "The soul unfolds itself, like a lotus of countless petals"; "Vague and nebulous is the beginning of all things, but not their end, and I would fain have you remember me as a beginning," et cetera. In the background was poor Ravi Shankar, who hadn't been so ill-used since fans loved it. They flooded the station with requests for printed versions, which Rosko answered with the sweet suggestion that they buy the book. A Gibran boomlet—you may even have been part of it.

I hope not. Admirers of books like *The Prophet* crave the enthrallment of poetry without the labor. For poetry—the Greek *poiein* means to construct or make—involves labor, in the creation and the understanding. Perhaps even too much so. Ever since the Industrial Revolution moved art out of the mainstream and produced the artistic rebel, whose avant-garde art comprises virtually all the good work in this century and much in the last, the arts have moved slowly and sadly beyond ordinary people. Artists have turned inward and concerned themselves with form. Not without superb results, either—whatever disservices they are done in the classroom, Proust, Yeats, Pollock, Stravinsky, and all the others have produced work which is not only marvelous technically, but very real emotionally, to those who know the language. The problem is, not many do—art is still not very respectable, and it's a lot more trouble than it used to be. What's worse, many who take the trouble succeed imperfectly, and turn to mass art or kitsch.

I want to say right now that none of the categories I'm going to be using are worth much. All but a few artists resist categories; the good ones usually confound them altogether. So a term like "rock" is impossibly vague; it denotes, if anything, something historical rather than aesthetic. "Mass art" and "kitsch" are pretty vague as well. Let's say that mass art is intended only to divert, entertain, pacify—Mantovani, Jacqueline Susann, *Muscle Beach Party*, etc. Kitsch is a more snobbish concept, and a more sophisticated product. It usually has the look of slightly out-of-date avant-garde in order to give its audience the illusion of aesthetic pleasure, whatever that is. An important distinction, I think, is that many of the craftsmen who make kitsch believe thoroughly in what they are doing. That may be true of the creators of mass art, too, but their attitude is more businesslike—they don't worry about "art," only commercial appeal.

I think it is just because they didn't worry about art that many of the people who ground out the rock-and-roll of the fifties—not only the performers, but all the background people—were engaged (unconsciously, of course) in, making still another kind of art, folk art. If longevity is any criterion, then I say the Five Satins will be remembered longer than the Weavers, because consciousness tends to kill what is vital in folk art. Like any rule, this one is far from perfect. Paul Anka's songs were horrible even though he didn't worry about art; Pete Seeger did, and his stuff was good. Or take a better example. In 1944, James Agee wrote an essay called "Pseudo-Folk" that deplored contemporary jazz; Duke Ellington was marvelous in his way, Agee argued, but he was also effete, and gimme that Jelly Roll. Like everything Agee wrote, "Pseudo-Folk" was sensible and heartfelt. But as it was written a young alto-sax played named Charlie Parker was creating jazz that had all the vitality of folk art plus all the complexity and technical inventiveness of the "higher" arts. You never can tell.

The same kind of transformation may be occurring right now in what used to be called rock-and-roll. It is certainly fashionable to think so. But despite all the happy praise, no one really seems to understand what is going on. Here is Robert Shelton of the New York *Times*: "More than a few conservatives in and out of the academy will be quick to dismiss serious writing by pop stars as commercial gimmickry, box-office ploys and faddist ephemera. Time, I submit, will strain out the worthless and leave us with some valuable creative works, in music and in literature, by a wholesome group of new writers." Shelton's facts are okay, but there is something dreadfully wrong about his tone—wholesome indeed. Does time really "strain out the worthless," or is it merely that we judge what is present and what is past by two entirely different and entirely proper standards? Does Shelton want to imply that "commercial gimmickry, box-office ploys and faddist ephermera" are necessarily inconsistent with "valuable creative works"? The Beatles have long since pulverized that cliché. Another example comes from Leonard Bernstein, who told a nationwide TV audience, "Many of the lyrics, in their oblique allusions and wayout metaphors, are beginning to sound like real poems." In a way Bernstein was right. Many rock lyrics sound like poems, especially to those who don't read poetry, which is almost everyone. But then, so does Kahlil Gibran.

The songwriter who seems to sound most like a poet is Bob Dylan. Dylan is such an idiosyncratic genius that it is perilous to imitate him–his faults, at worst annoying and at best invigorating, ruin lesser talents. But imitation is irresistible. Who can withstand Paul Nelson of *Little Sandy Review*, who calls Dylan "the man who in every sense revolutionized modern poetry, American folk music, popular music, and the whole of modern-day thought"? Or Jack Newfield of the Village Voice, wandering on about "symbolic alienation ... new plateaus for poetic, content-conscious songwriters ... put poetry back into song ... reworks T. S. Eliot's classic line ... bastard child of Chaplin, Celine and Hart Crane," while serving up tidbits from Dylan's corpus, some of which don't look so tasty on a paper plate? However inoffensive "The ghost of electricity howls in the bones of her face" sounds on vinyl, it is silly without the music. Poems are read or said. Songs are sung.

Dylan gets away with it simply because there is so much there. The refrain of "My Back Pages," his renunciation of political protest–"I was so much older then, I'm younger than that now"–may be the finest line he has ever written. Its opening–"Crimson flames tied through my ears"–may be the worst. The song bulges with metaphors and epithets, some apt, some stuck in to fill out the meter. The tired trick of using a noun for a verb to spice things up reaches an all-time low with the word (?) "foundationed." Dylan's obsession with rhyme (which he has lately begun to parody: "Hear the one with the mustache say, jeeze / I can't find my knees") compels him to match "now" with "somehow" three times in six stanzas. Twice this is totally gratuitous. But the third time–"Good and bad, I define these terms, quite clear no doubt somehow"–"somehow" becomes the final qualification in a series of qualifications, and works perfectly: a typical hit among misses.

"My Back Pages" is a bad poem. But is a good song, supported by a memorable refrain. The music softens our demand, the importance of what is being said somehow overbalances the flaws, and Dylan's delivery–he sounds as if he's singing a hymn at a funeral–adds a portentous edge not present just in the words. Because it is a good song, "My Back Pages" can be done in other ways. The Byrds' version depends on intricate, up-tempo music that pushes the words into the background. However much they mean to David Crosby, the lyrics–except for that refrain–could be gibberish and the song would still succeed. Repeat: Dylan is a songwriter, not a poet. A few of his most perfect efforts–"Don't Think Twice," or "Just Like a Woman"–are tight enough to survive on the page. But they are exceptions.

Such a rash judgment assumes that modern poets know what they're doing. It respects the tradition that runs from Ezra Pound and William Carlos Williams down to Charles Olson, Robert Creeley, and perhaps a dozen others, the tradition that regards Allen Ginsberg as a good poet, perhaps, but a wildman. Dylan's work, with its iambics, its clackety-clack rhymes, and its scattergun images, makes Ginsberg's look like a model of decorous diction. An art advances through technical innovation. Modern American poetry assumes (and sometimes eliminates) metaphoric ability, concentrating on the use of line and rhythm to approximate (or refine) speech, the reduction of language to essentials, and "tone of voice." Dylan's only innovation is that he sings, a good way to control "tone of voice," but not enough to "revolutionize modern poetry." He may have started something just as good, but modern poetry is getting along fine, thank you.

It is fortunate that Dylan's most prominent disciple, Donovan, is not an imitator. His best stuff crosses Dylan's surrealist bent with the jazzy cleverness of thirties' songwriters like Cole Porter. Donovan makes demands on his listeners (tossing off an elliptical image like "To a leopard's you've been changin' " or devoting whole songs to his medieval fetish) and he delights in obscurity (everyone loves "Mellow Yellow" and "Sunshine Superman," but no one understands them–and don't tell me about bananas, but once again he is a songwriter, and in a much less equivocal way than Dylan. With a few tricks so well tried that they are legitimate *lingua franca*, at least for his special audience (that is us), he is working to deliver songwriting from superannuated sentimentalists like Johnny Mercer and shrewd camp followers like Tommy Boyce and Bobby Hart. In another way, Mick Jagger and Keith Richard are doing the same thing. They began by writing pungent pseudo-blues from their peculiar, ironic vantage–"Heart of Stone," "The Last Time," etc. Now, while sticking to old forms, they have allowed their sense of themselves to dominate their sense of blues tradition, producing a body of work that is as consistent and various as anything this side of Lennon-McCartney, but still song, not poetry. In the atmosphere that they and Donovan and especially Dylan have created, dozens of intelligent crafts-men–from folk-rockers like Marty Balin and John Sebastian to commercial talents like Neil Diamond and Mike Nesmith–are working down below to return popular songwriting to the honest stature it had in the thirties and beyond. The new songwriters are sentimental, not about the way the world is, but about their feelings toward it. That is a great step forward.

Dylan's influence has not always been so salutary. Lennon-McCartney and Jagger-Richard would have matured without him. But had there been no Dylan to successfully combine the vulgar and the felicitous, would we now be oppressed with the kind of vague, extravagant imagery and inane philosophizing that ruins so much good music and so impresses the Kahlil Gibran fans? I doubt it. Gary Brooker and Keith Read of Procol Harum, for an instance, obviously have a lot of talent. The opening of "Homburg" ("Your multilingual"–piano chord–"business friend") is my choice for line of the month, and the transformation of Bach in "A Whiter Shade of Pale" was brilliant and well executed. But is "A Whiter Shade of Pale" poetry? From the ads London placed in the trades, you might assume it was Shakespeare, newly unearthed. In fact there is a rumor that it was adapted from an Elizabethan poem. No matter. Full of obscure clichés ("skipped the light fandango"; "sixteen vestal virgins") with a clever (admittedly) title phrase and refrain, the overall archaic feel reinforced by literary reference ("the miller told his tale"), it sold because it did such a successful job of sounding like poetry, which, as we all know, is obscure, literary, and sort of archaic. Pure kitsch. Not much better is the self-indulgence of the Doors' Jim Morrison. "Twentieth Century-Fox," "Break on Through," "People are Strange" and "Soul Kitchen," listed in ascending order of difficulty, all pretty much succeed. But Morrison does not stop there. He ruins "Light My Fire" with stuff like "our love becomes a funeral pyre"–Ugh! what does that mean? Nothing, but the good old romantic association of love and death is there, and that's all Morrison wanted–and noodles around in secondhand Freud in "The End." Morrison obviously regards "The End" as a masterwork, and his admirers agree. I wonder why. The music builds very nicely in an Oriental kind of way, but the dramatic situation is tedious stuff. I suppose it is redeemed by Morrison's histrionics and by the nebulousness that passes for depth among so many lovers of rock poetry.

The Doors and Procol Harum are good groups. Each has given me much pleasure. But I don't think "The End" and "A Whiter Shade of Pale" are just bad tries. I think they grow out of a bad idea, the idea that poetry–a concept not too well understood–can be incorporated into rock. This idea is old fashioned and literary in the worst sense. But young rock groups write "symbolic" lyrics that they like only because they wrote them, and they set them to music, and the cycle starts again. In a sense Morrison and Brooker-Reed are responsible for these kids in the same way Dylan is for them.

This phenomenon obviously has limitless depths (though in fairness it should be said that most groups—most of the ones you hear, anyway—avoid them), but I think its heights have been reached by a songwriter who has in abundance the one quality that Dylan, Morrison, and all their lessers lack. The songwriter is Paul Simon, and the quality is taste. Simon is so tasteful the media can't help but love him. Even Richard Goldstein has guessed that "chances are he's brought you closer to the feel and texture of modern poetry than anything else since the big blackout." Goldstein does pin down the reason for Simon and Garfunkel's popularity, though: "They don't make waves."

Paul Simon's lyrics are the purest, highest, and most finely wrought kitsch of our time. The lyrics I've been putting down are not necessarily easy to write—bad poetry is often carefully worked, the difference being that it's easier to perceive flaccidly—but the labor that must go into one of Simon's songs is of another order of magnitude. Melodies, harmonies, arrangements are scrupulously fitted. Each song is perfect. And says nothing.

What saddens me is that Simon obviously seems to have a lot to say to the people who buy his records. But it's a shock. Like Kahlil Gibran all he's really doing is scratching them where they itch, providing some temporary relief but coming nowhere near the root of the problem. Simon's content isn't modern, it is merely fashionable, and his form never jars the sensibilities. He is the only songwriter I can imagine admitting he writes about that all-American subject, the Alienation of Modern Man, in just those words. His songs have the texture of modern poetry only if modern poetry can be said to end with early Auden—Edwin Arlington Robinson is more like it. Poets don't write like Robinson any more because his technical effects have outlived their usefulness, which was to make people see things in a new way. And even in such old-fashioned terms, what Simon does is conventional and uninspired. An example is "For Emily, Wherever I May Find Her," in which "poetic" words—organdy, crinoline, juniper (words that suggest why Simon is so partial to turn-of-the-century verse) and "beautiful" images (softer-than-the-rain, wandered-lonely-streets) are used to describe a dream girl. Simon is no dope; he knows this is all a little corny, but that's okay because Emily is an impossible girl. Only in order for the trick to come off there has to be an ironic edge. There isn't, and "For Emily" is nothing more than a sophisticated popular song of the traditional-fantasy type.

This kind of mindless craft reaches a peak in Simon's supposed master-piece, "The Dangling Conversation," which uses all the devices you learn about in English class–alliteration, alternating concretion and abstraction, even the use of images from poetry itself, a favorite ploy of poets who don't know much of anything else–to mourn wistfully about the classic plight of self-conscious man, his Inability to Communicate. Tom Phillips of the New York *Times* has called this song "one of Paul Simon's subtlest lyrics . . . a pitiless vision of self-consciousness and isolation." I don't hear the same song, I guess, because I think Simon's voice drips self-pity from every syllable (not only in this song, either). The Mantovani strings that reinforce the lyric capture its toughness perfectly. If Simon were just a little hipper, his couple would be discussing the failure of communication as they failed to com-municate, rather than psychoanalysis or the state of the theatre. But he's not a little hipper.

Still, maybe he's getting there. A new album should be out shortly (there is one more track to record at this writing) and could be a surprise. Simon is going through changes. He has released almost nothing new since *Parsley, Sage, Rosemary and Thyme*, which contains "For Emily" and "Dangling Conversation." Last winter's "At the "Zoo" is more concrete and less lugubrious than his other work, just a whimsical song about Central Park Zoo, and despite an occasional kernel of corn ("It's a light and tumble journey"), the metaphors work because they are fun: "Zebras are reac-tionaries / Antelopes are missionaries." "Fakin' It" is more serious, but the colloquial diction that dominates the song–in the first, third, and fifth sections, there is no word that isn't among the most common in the language: "The girl does what she wants to do / She knows what she wants to do and I know I'm / Fakin' it / I'm not really makin' it"–adds a casual feel; even when the verbiage becomes more Simonesque, it is seasoned with a dash of the colloquial: "A walk in the garden wears me down / Tangled in the fallen vines / Pickin' up the punch lines." In addition, the song contains an ex-traordinarily subtle switch. "I own a tailor's face and hands / I am the tailor's face and hands." No image-mongering there, just one little changeover, from a clever metaphor to a painful identification.

In an oblique and probably unconscious way, I think "Fakin' It" is true rock poetry, an extension of a very specific tradition. The pop that preceded rock, and still exists today, was full of what semanticist S. I. Hayakawa has listed as "wishful thinking, dreamy and ineffectual nostalgia, unrealistic fantasy, self-pity, and sentimental clichés masquerading as emotion." The

blues, by contrast, were "unsentimental and realistic." Rock-and-roll combined the gutless lyrics of pop with the sexual innuendo of blues music and
delivery. What this meant in practice was that it had no lyrics at all. Most rock
fans just ignored what inane content there was in favor of the sound and the
big beat. So rock diction became imbecilically colloquial, nonsense syllables
proliferated, and singers slurred because nobody cared. Be-bop-a-lula, you can
really start to groove it, caught Aunt Mary something and she ducked back in
the alley. In "Fakin' It," the basic-English diction, the eleven repetitions of
the title, and that almost inaudible changeover not only avoid Simon's usual
pretensions; combined with the big-beat arrangement, they create a mood that
asks "Why should this mean anything?" Only it does.

It is by creating a mood that asks "Why should this mean anything?"
that so-called rock poets can really write poetry—poetry that not only says
something, but says it as only rock music can. For once Marshall McLuhan's
terminology tells us something: rock lyrics are a cool medium. Go ahead and
mumble. Drown the voices in guitars. If somebody really wants to know what
you're saying, he'll take the trouble, and in that trouble lies your art. On a
crude level this permits the kind of one-to-one symbolism of pot songs like
"Along Comes Mary" and "That Acapulco Gold." "Fakin' It" does other
things with the same idea. But the only songwriters who seem really to have
mastered it are John Phillips and Lennon-McCartney.

Phillips possesses a frightening talent. "San Francisco—Flowers in Your
Hair," catering to every prurient longing implicit in teenage America's
flirtation with the hippies without ever even mentioning the secret work, is a
stunning piece of schlock. A song like "Once Was A Time I Thought" (as if
to say to all those Swingle Singer fans, "You thought that was hard? We can
do the whole number in fifty-eight seconds") is another example of the range
of his ability. You have the feeling Phillips could write a successful musical, a
Frank Sinatra hit, anything that sells, if he wanted to.

Perhaps you are one of those people who plays every new LP with the
treble way up and the bass way down so you can ferret out all the secret
symbolic meanings right away. Personally I think that spoils the fun, and I
suspect any record that permits you to do that isn't fulfilling its first function,
which pertains to music, or, more generally, noise. The Mamas and Papas'
records are full of diversions—the contrapuntal arrangements, the idiot
"yeahs," the orchestral improvisations, the rhyme schemes ("If you're entertaining any thought that you're gaining by causin' me all of this pain and
makin' me blue, the joke's on you") and Phillips' trick of drawing out a few

words with repetitions and pauses. Perhaps this isn't conscious. In songs like "California Dreamin'," "12:30" and many others, Phillips is obviously just a good lyricist (with a lot of tender respect for the fantasy world of pure pop that critics like Hayakawa derogate so easily). But his lyrics are rarely easy to understand. Maybe it's just me, but I wonder how many of you are aware that a minor track on the second album, "Strange Young Girls," is about LSD. No secret about it – there it is, right out in the open of the first stanza: "Strange young girls, colored with sadness / Eyes of innocence hiding their madness / Walking the Strip, sweet, soft, and placid / Off'ring their youth on the altar of acid." But you don't notice because there's so much else to listen to.

My favorite Phillips song is "Straight Shooter." By now, everyone knows "Straight Shooter" is about drugs. They printed it right in the *Times* and everything. But its genius is that it doesn't have to be – it works equally well as one of those undefined, meaningless love songs that have always been the staple of rock. Oh, there are a few little aberrations – baby is suspected of holding anything, not anyone, and the "half of it belongs to me" doesn't make sense. But this is rock-and-roll. It doesn't have to make sense. Even the "just get me high" has all sorts of respectable precedents, like the "I get highs" in "I Want to Hold Your Hand," which may be about spiritual high but is no drug song. In addition there is the irony of this bright, bouncy melody being all about some needle freak. It's a characteristic trick – Phillips likes to conceal the tone of a lyric in a paradoxical melody (the perfect example being the gentle-sounding "Got a Feelin' "). Every level of uncertainty makes the song more like the reality we actually perceive. Yet the whole effect occurs within a strict rock framework.

Phillips achieves rock feel with his arrangements. The lyrics themselves are closer to traditional pop – Rodgers and Hart's "My Heart Stood Still," on the second album, sounds less out of place than Bobby Freeman's "Do You Wanna Dance?" on the first. Lennon-McCartney do it with diction. Their early work is all pure rock – the songs are merely excuses for melody, beat and sound. Occasionally it shows a flash of the subtlety to come, as in the sexual insinuation of "Please Please Me" or the premise of "There's A Place" ("There, there's a place / Where I can go / When I feel low, when I feel blue / And it's my mind"). More often it is pure, meaningless sentiment, couched in the simplest possible terms. By the time of *A Hard Day's Night* the songs are more sophisticated musically, and a year later, in *Help!*, the boys are becoming pop songwriters. *Help!* itself is a perfect example. Words like "self-assured" and "insecure" are not out of rock diction, nor is the line: "My independence seems to vanish in the haze." This facet of their talent has culminated (for the moment) in songs like "Paperback Writer," "A Little Help from My Friends," and "When I'm Sixty-four," which show all the verbal facility of the best traditional pop and none of the sentimentality, and in deliberate exercises like "Michelle" and "Here, There and Everywhere," which show both.

Other songs like "Norwegian Wood," "Dr. Roberts," "Good Morning, Good Morning" are ambiguous despite an unerring justness of concrete detail; little conundrums, different from Dylanesque surrealism because they don't fit so neatly into a literary category (Edward Lear is their closest antecedent). Most of the songs since *Rubber Soul* are characterized by a similar obliqueness. Often the Beatles' "I" is much harder to pin down than the "I" in Donovan or Jagger-Richard, a difficulty that is reinforced by their filters, their ethereal harmonies, and their collective public identity. This concern with angle of attack is similar to that of poets like Creeley.

Lennon and McCartney are the only rock songwriters who combine high literacy (as high as Dylan's or Simon's) with an eye for concision and a truly contemporary sense of what fits. They seem less and less inclined to limit themselves to what I have defined as rock diction, and yet they continue to succeed—the simultaneous lushness and tightness of "Lucy in the Sky with Diamonds," for instance, is nothing short of extraordinary. They still get startling mileage out of the banal colloquial—think of the "oh boy" in "A Day in the Life," or the repeating qualifications in "Strawberry Fields Forever." But they have also written two songs which are purely colloquial—"She Said She Said," and "All You Need Is Love."

"She Said She Said" is at once one of the most difficult and banal of Beatle songs. It is a concrete version of what in "The Dangling Conversation" (despite all those details) remains abstract, a conversation between a hung-up, self-important girl who says she knows "what it's like to be dead" and her boy friend, who doesn't want to know. (If Simon had written it, the boy would have argued that he was the one who knew.) The song uses the same kind of words that can be found in "She Loves You" (the quintessential early Beatles song), yet says so much more. Its conceit, embodied in the title, is meaningless; its actuality is a kind of ironic density that no other songwriter (except Dylan at his best) approaches. One of its ironies is the suggestion that callow philosophizing is every bit as banal as the most primitive rock-and-roll.

"All You Need Is Love," deliberately written in basic English so it could be translated, makes the connection clearer by quoting from "She Loves You" while conveying the ironic message of the title. Is love all you need? What kind of love? Universal love? Love of country? Courtly love? "She Loves You" love? It's hard to tell. The song employs rock-and-roll—dominant music, big beat, repeated refrain, simple diction—and transforms it into something which, if not poetry, at least has a multifaceted poetic wholeness. I think it is rock poetry in the truest sense.

Maybe I am being too strict. Modern poetry is doing very well, thank you, on its own terms, but in terms of what it is doing for us, and even for the speech from which it derives, it looks a bit pallid. Never take the categories too seriously. It may be that the new songwriters (not poets, please) lapse artistically, indulge their little infatuations with language and ideas, and come up with a product that could be much better if handled with a little less energy and a little more caution. But energy is where it's at. And songs—even though they are only songs—may soon be more important than poems, no matter that they are easier too.

Once there were bards and the bards did something wondrous—they provided literature for the illiterate. The bards evolved into poets and the poetry which had been their means became their end. It didn't seem to matter much after a while, since everyone was literate anyway. But semiliteracy, which is where people go when they're not illiterate any more, is in some ways a worse blight.

The new songwriters think there should be bards again and they're right, but the bardic traditions are pretty faint. Too many of them are seduced by semiliteracy—mouthing other people's ideas in other people's words. But they are bards, and that is very good. Maybe soon it will be a lot better.

This essay was written (too fast, like most journalism) in the early fall of 1967 for *Cheetah*, now sadly departed. Though I haven't been able to resist a few stylistic fixes, I have left it mostly as is. If the piece seems dated to me now, in the fall of 1968, then any revisions would no doubt seem dated by the time they appeared. Journalism ought to survive with its limitations of time and place intact.

Nevertheless, I feel compelled to put things in some small perspective and right a few wrongs. I'm probably guilty of overkill on Paul Simon, who has since gone on to his just reward as the writer of a Number One filmscore, but when I wrote this he was still taken seriously by people who deserved better. And though I love "Mrs. Robinson" and consider *Bookends* S&G's finest album, I don't think Simon has lived up to the promise I discerned in

"Fakin' It." As for John Phillips, I am now convinced the Mamas and the Papas are destined to become high camp, but that doesn't change what they were and sometimes still are for us, and I stand by my praise.

What I describe as the poetry of rock has to do with surprise, and it is still relevant: the effect of a lyric by John Kay of Steppenwolf, say, or even Gerry Goffin and Carole King, is frequently enhanced by indirection. But since last fall there have been only two completely successful examples of this tradition, the ultimate test being how broadly they sold: Lennon-McCartney's "Hello Good-bye" and Peter Townshend's "I Can See for Miles." I am beginning to think such specimens will become increasingly rare. The technique is based on one overriding assumption: that no one takes rock seriously. It can only survive as long as that assumption is viable, if not as a present truth then as a living memory. But even the memory seems to be dying. It may be that the most lasting verbal effect of what I can only call the rock ambience may be a new eloquence in popular songwriting, typified by a figure like Randy Newman, whose work has little to do with rock per se.

The key figure in all this is Bob Dylan, who as a vocalist and a writer has pointed out all sorts of new directions for song. I think I misunderstood what Dylan did for those of us who always knew he was a rotten "poet." It was his very badness that attracted us. His overwriting was the equivalent in folk music of the happy energy of the Beatles. He loved language enough to misuse it. Of course, if he hadn't had the genius to use it brilliantly as well, that would hardly have been a virtue. But he did, and so revitalized areas of language that had seemed exhausted. The songwriter who has learned most from this is Leonard Cohen, with his wry exultation in silly rhymes and inconsistent or overly consistent images. It may be, by the way, that poets have learned something from Dylan's freedom as well. In any case I know now that the work of poets like Robert Creeley was no longer really central when I wrote this. Anyone who would like to sample what has replaced it should refer to *Bean Spasms*, by Ted Berrigan and Ron Padgett.

Stasio
On Theatre

MARILYN STASIO

ANTICIPATION, AS EVERY staunch theatre-lover knows, is part of the ritual of theatregoing. One anxiously scans the theatre forecasts for driblets of news about the upcoming shows, savoring the while each morsel of gossip, each tidbit of information about theatres signed, stars contracted, directors fired, play "doctors" hastily engaged, producers filing for bankruptcy—all the happy signs of artistic creation in gestation. Unfortunately, from past experiences one also learns to sight theatrical trouble spots, those *déjà vu* signs of overly familiar plots, directorial gimmicks, ritual formats, and human foibles which serve warning when we are in for a resurrection of much of the same garbage which we thought had been safely buried. So, in anticipation of this season's theatrical abortions, I submit herewith a list of *things I can live without, thanks anyway, fellas:*

- Musical adaptations of successful movies which were themselves comedy remakes of prizewinning stage dramas which originated as French novels baséd on 18th-century Austrian operettas suggested by by old Germanic folk legends.
- Mae West in "Hello, Dolly!"
- Rampant, sticky-poo cutesiness in Off Broadway program biographies. "Sondra Starlet was born under the sign of Taurus the Bull; is wild, smoky and mysterious, all fire and ice; loves wild horses, making

love on a trampoline, and freedom" or, "Johnny Juvenile made his debut in Backwater Country Day School at the age of six, in the role of a dancing carrot." These merely tell me that little Sondra and Johnny are a couple of no-talents without enough professional credits to fill out the paragraph.

● Emotional-Blackmail Broadway comedies about singing nuns, brave dogs, or blind kids. Blind dogs, brave nuns, singing kids. Brave kids, blind nuns, singing dogs.

● Homosexual *Sturm-und-Drang* Drama. The new sexual freedom in the theatre has produced a rash of dramas about the homosexual experience which are positively saturated in sloppy sentimentality. Among the deluge of soap-opera weepers, expect: "John's Other Husband," "That Boy," "Search for Last Night," "Henry Trent," "Our Guy Sunday," "Stanley Dallas," "John Loves Larry," and perhaps a new interpretation of "Barefoot in the Park."

● Liberace in "Hello, Dolly!"

● Stoned Theatre. This is an Off Off Broadway phenomenon. Stoned theatre is written by stoned playwrights and performed before stoned audiences by stoned casts. By its nature, stoned theatre is inaccessible to the straight critic, who finds it thoroughly incomprehensible. The critic, of course, always has the option of entering into the spirit of stoned theatre. However, this may result in another problem: he may never reach the theatre, but get sidetracked by an interesting blank wall. Searchers might find him, three days later, still riveted to that wall, happily reviewing the graffiti.

● Impassioned love letters from enamored fans who finally reveal, in the last flaming paragraph of their empurpled prosody, that they are struggling playwrights who just happen to have a new play opening next week in East Orange, New Jersey, and wouldn't I just love to come and review it.

● Raquel Welch and/or Rex Reed in "Hello, Dolly!"

● Who-Dat? biography musicals. Broadway seems to have an unquenchable penchant for elevating the most obscure, or simply just the most improbable characters to musical-theatre prominence. Save us from: "Zasu!," "The Life of Faye Emerson," "The Millard Fillmore Story."

● Gabrielle Chanel in "Hello, Dolly!"

● Generation-gap comedies on Broadway. In which the parents are martyrs who heroically endure the anti-social boorishness of their Now-generation offspring. The climax comes when the parents lovingly help the kids to see themselves as they really are—selfish, boring, humorless, tyrannical, bratty little monsters.

- Generation-gap comedies Off Broadway. The same William Ritman set may be used, but in this version the kids are the martyrs who heroically endure the injustice of their Establishment-spokesmen parents. The climax comes when the kids lovingly help their folks to see themselves as they really are—corrupt, insensitive, fascistic, war-mongering, uptight, spineless, money-mad, tranquilizer-popping Liberals.

- Generation-gap comedies Off Broadway. In which teenaged radicals heroically working for the Revolution endure the compromising tactics of an older, apologist generation of 20-year-olds. The climax comes when the Liberationists bomb the headquarters of the pacifist sell-outs and expose them for what they really are—old.

- The *New* generation-gap comedies. In this most recent and most sophisticated manifestation of the genre, the older generation goes to bed with the younger generation and, if their astrologers approve, may even marry them.

- The Duchess and/or Duke of Windsor in "Hello, Dolly!"

- Intimidation Theatre. In which the grundgy-looking Love-Generation cast crawls among the audience, plucking the least responsive-looking members from their seats and hauling them up on the stage to participate in a naked group-grope. Those uptight, buttoned-down fascisti redneck honkie pigs who politely demur are mugged on the spot for their unloving attitude.

- Theatre of Self-Righteousness. A variant of Intimidation Theatre. Also known as Pure-in-Heart-Theatre, or Better-Not-Knock-It-Baby-If-You-Know-What's-Good-For-You Theatre. Included in this genre are plays exuding such lofty ideals or promoting such noble causes that their creators feel exempt from being professionally criticised on such mundane grounds as literary merit or production values.

- Emasculated Classics. "King Lear" in the nude. "Hedda Gabler" in drag. "Long Day's Journey into Night" with a rock score. And absolutely any adaptation which claims to be "a brilliant reinterpretation bringing new contemporary relevance to this great masterpiece and revealing with blinding clarity the similarity of the two eras—8th century Tibetan monastic life and the commune culture of Avenue B."

- Shows which tout themselves in any of the following terms: "a today musical ... mind-bending ... speaks for our time ... with-it ... something else ... freaky ... cool ... right-on ... together ... groovy ... outtasight ... ultimate turn-on ... ultimate trip ... hottest new ... wild new ... irrepressible new ... revolutionary new ... dirty."
- David Merrick in "Hello, Dolly!"

... And Now
a Word about Commercials

TIME

COMMERCIALS ARE INFURIATING. They are also irresistible. Commercials are an outrageous nuisance. They are also apt to be better than the programs they interrupt. Commercials are the heavy tribute that the viewer must pay to the sponsor in exchange for often dubious pleasure. They are also an American art form. A minor art form, but the ultimate in mixed media: sight, sound and sell.

Commercials—or a great many of them—are better than ever. How and why this came about is one of the more fascinating phenomena in television. They are part of the background music, as it were, of the American scene. Hardly anybody pays total attention to them; hardly anybody totally ignores them. Many, the very good and the very bad, force or insinuate themselves into the imagination. Even a reluctant viewer cannot quite resist the euphoria induced by airline ads that waft him up up and away, or travel spots, island-hopping in a wink of quick cuts, that drop him on a sun-splashed beach. Even while grumbling, he marvels at the dexterity, not to say ludicrous imagery, of a white tornado suddenly swirling through an untidy kitchen. He wakes up singing "You can take Salem out of the *country*, BUT ... " His kids, riding shotgun on the shopping cart, may not know a stanza of *The Star-Spangled Banner*, but they can rap out several verses of "To a Smoker, It's a Kent."

With their vast and relentless power of amplification, the writers of commercials sprinkle more tag lines and catch phrases into the conversation than the poets, fettered to their paper and print, can ever hope to put into the American idiom. "A little dab'll do ya," "Fly the friendly skies," and "Leave the driving to us," are in fact a kind of pop poetry.

Commercials also have deeper, more serious impact. In a discussion of last year's ghetto riots, the Kerner Report suggested that the enticements of TV commercials, "endlessly flaunted before the eyes of the Negro poor and the jobless ghetto youth," were an important inducement to the state of unrest. Opinion Researcher Mervin Field goes so far as to suggest that commercials constitute "a looter's shopping list."

Whether or not that analysis is correct or fair, commercials obviously represent the American materialist vision of the good life—all the shiny possessions and luxuries that people want, or are supposed to want.

CONVENIENTLY DEAF

TV pushes this vision to an overwhelming degree. Empires have been built on commerce, trade has opened up frontiers, but nothing like the TV sales pitch has ever existed before. Despite the genuine entertainment that so many of the good commercials afford, television still succeeds in crushing its viewers with ads that are too annoying, too loud, too often and just too much. Roughly 20% of TV air time is given over to commercials. This year 2,000 advertisers will pour $3.1 billion into television advertising—twice the budget of the poverty program—reaching 95% of the nation's homes. What's more, the TV spieler has a unique license. He doesn't have to stick his foot in the door. He's already in the living room, chattering away from *The Farm Hour* right through *Sermonette*. Conveniently deaf, he just smiles and hammers home his quota of 600 "brief messages" a day.

Worse yet, he seems to catch his second breath always at the wrong time. He cuts into the movies just when things are getting interesting, or links three, four or five commercials in a row during the station breaks. Even the war news suddenly comes to an abrupt halt for the sake of sell. The bloody events in Viet Nam, incongruously flanked with sales messages glorifying the good life at home, leave the viewer with the inexplicable sensation that the commercials and the war are one and the same: Which is the more real?

And what are the limits? On the day Robert Kennedy died, Walter Cronkite no sooner wrapped up the latest bulletins on the killing than the screen cut cold to a mouthwash ad. Later, during the funeral, commercials were dropped. The television industry, which devoutly believes in commercials, pays its highest tribute by forgoing them. That is the first grand gesture (the second gesture is a reminder detailing how much money the network relinquished in the public service).

INTERPLAY

The money alone that goes into commercial production is stupefying. Film Director Stanley Kubrick, himself something of a big spender (*2001: A Space Odyssey* cost $11 million), observed recently that "a feature film made with the same kind of care as a commercial would have to cost $50 million." As it is, the cost of a one-minute commercial—rehearsals, filming, reshooting, dubbing, scoring, animation, printing—runs to an average of $22,000 or about five times more than a minute of TV entertainment.

For that kind of money, the mini-moviemakers command top talent. Frank Sinatra sells Budweiser beer. Sid Caesar does a comedy routine for Sperry Rand, while José Ferrer supplies the voice-over continuity. Edward G. Robinson poured for Maxwell House coffee. Jack Benny promotes Texaco gasoline. George Burns puffs El Producto cigars. Sometimes the process is reversible. Actress Barbara Feldon was a sexy slink of a salesgirl for Top Brass hairdressing ("Sic 'em, tiger") before she went big on legit TV as co-star of *Get Smart!* Pam Austin, the original Dodge girl, is now a member of the cast of *Rowan and Martin's Laugh-In.*

Off the screen, the roster of professionals is equally impressive. Hollywood Cameraman George Folsey, who has been nominated for an Oscar 13 times, now trains his lens on Miller High Life beer and Sanka coffee. Composer Mitch Leigh, who wrote the music for *Man of La Mancha*, is a top jingle writer for commercials. Dress Designer Bill Blass does the wardrobe for the models who are nuzzling up to the Princess telephone.

The men who put it all together, the directors, may one day be hailed as true innovators in film—it is they who pack a succinct story into a few seconds—and in the process produce many new cinematic ideas. The work of such directors as Michael Cimino for Kodak, Howard Zieff for Benson & Hedges and Mike Elliott for Rheingold has precipitated an interplay of ideas that flows freely between Madison Avenue and the conventional movie set. The directors dabble with Fellini-like stream-of-consciousness techniques. Hollywood copies TV's fast cuts and odd-angle perspectives. The quality of Richard Lester's movies—*A Hard Day's Night, Petulia*—reflects his experience as director of more than 300 commercials.

CEBUS

This refreshing infusion of talent came just in time; the old sock-it-to-'em pitch was making a lot of people punchy. The only way to sell certain analgesics was to make the viewer queasy just watching: faucets dripped acids into the stomach, hammers clanged on anvils in the head. It was getting increasingly difficult to tell whether the little old winemaker was getting tanked on Drano, or pushing Ken-L Ration for hungry Living Bras. Gradually, after 20 years of hard-sell harangue, viewers developed a kind of filter blend up front. They did not turn off their sets; they turned off their minds. Admen refer to that phenomenon as the "fatigue factor," but their research departments know it by the more ominous name of CEBUS (Confirmed Exposure but Unconscious). In one recent survey, 75% of the viewers tested had no recollection of what products they had just seen demonstrated.

These audiences have been joined by the Pepsi generation, which sees but does not believe. Raised on the tube, these young people have heard and seen all the obvious plays on insecurity and are unimpressed by all the weaseling statements that sound impressive but mean nothing. Marshall McLuhan (who else?) has observed that future historians will find in advertising "the richest and most faithful daily reflections that any society ever made of its entire range of activities."

If so, the reflections derived from the old, hard-sell commercials will be rather odd. In the typical American family, Mom is obviously a nut. Every blessed washday, she is seen running around the backyard with wild, passionate abandon, embracing her laundry and squealing, "It even smells clean!" That's more than can be said for Sis. Poor kid, her best friend just told her she's got rotten armpits. As for Dad, he keeps getting punched in the eye because he won't switch his brand of cigarettes. So he asserts his virility by barreling around mountain roads in his wide-track, fast-back, four-on-the-floor Belchfire with the racer's edge. And Junior, well, the sudden joy of discovering that he's got 27% fewer cavities has apparently unhinged him. Now he stands in front of the mirror all day and counts his pimples. And after dinner, the whole family gathers at the hearthside, unwraps their Wrigley's and, with a hi ho and a hey hey, chews their little troubles away.

REAL PEOPLE

This kind of pitch, with its view of the consumer as saphead, is still all too prevalent. But, increasingly, as admen are trying to break through the

CEBUS barrier, the old commercial is being replaced with the truly new brand of ad with miracle ingredients—some honesty, some humor, packaged with meticulous care. It might be called the uncommercial, and it has transformed the viewer into a consumer of the pitch as much as of the product.

He identified with the characters who for once look almost like real people—fat, scrawny, drab, sassy, ordinary. He is caught up in a Jell-O ad, in which a snatch of conversation and a glimpse of beaming faces around the dinner table capture the mood and moment of a young soldier home on furlough. He is washed in nostalgia as a Kodak spot scans a lifetime by focusing on a greying couple as they rummage through old snapshots. Says Adman David Ogilvy: "The consumer isn't a moron—she is your wife." Adwoman Mary Wells, president of Wells, Rich, Greene, sounds the credo of the new uncommercial makers: "You have to talk person to person with people, use people words and people terms. You have to touch them, show humanness and warmth, charm them with funny vignettes. You have to make them feel good about a product so they'll love you."

LOVABLE TUMMY

One of the first breakthroughs in uncommercial making came in 1964 in a new Alka-Seltzer series. For years, "Speedy Alka-Seltzer," the cartoon imp with a tablet for a hat, insulted audiences by pushing the fizz as though he were conducting a *Romper Room* class. Then the Jack Tinker agency took over the account and decided to try for a touch of wit and realism: a film showing nothing more than a quick succession of people's midriffs being prodded and pushed, or just merrily jouncing along. The message was: "No matter what shape your stomach's in, when it gets out of shape, take Alka-Seltzer." Along Madison Avenue, the film became an instant classic. Among Alka-Seltzer's latest, and best, is the cartoon of a man and his disgruntled but lovable-looking tummy seated in separate chairs, hashing out their troubles before an unseen marriage counselor. It ought to be revolting, but it isn't. The drawing style has some of the wonderful, way-out whimsy of Thurber and the deceptive, squiggly-line bite of Jules Feiffer, while the dialogue is reminiscent of an Elaine May–Mike Nichols routine.

Along with Alka-Seltzer, Volkswagen, Avis, and Chun King chow mein pointed the way. If critics were to categorize commercials in the manner of plays or films (and why not?), they would find a variety of styles and sub-styles. For a start, one can discern:

● THEATER OF THE ABSURD. A beautiful girl gets into the back seat of a Rolls-Royce, takes off her clothes and climbs into a bathtub brimming with Calgon bath oil. The Dash soap man butts into conversations and flings laundry at innocent people. "Louise Hexter," he commands, "start wearing cleaner blouses!" The shaming, the touch of half-suppressed hysteria, is unsettling. Another instance of the absurd involves the flamenco dancer who stomps the living daylights out of a Bic ballpoint pen that has been attached to his heel. Here the effect is different. One remembers all the other similar nonsense—the pen that writes under water, the watch that survives a trip on the rudder of an ocean liner—and one inevitably begins to speculate in grudging fascination about what they might try next.

● THEATER OF CRUELTY. To demonstrate a new type of insulating foil, Union Carbide places a baby chicken in a small foil-lined metal box and then lowers it into a beaker of boiling water. Several long moments later, out pops the chick, frisky and unfried. The initial plunge is not exactly Grand Guignol, but it does provide a bit of a shock. A recent spot for American Motors shows a gang of men demolishing a competitor's car with sledge hammers. Who would admit to hating autos? Still, there is a certain undeniable thrill in seeing all that shiny metal crumple.

● SURREALISM. This is usually mixed with metaphors come to life: the real dove that turns into a bottle of Dove liquid soap, the Ultra Brite girl who brands strangers with long-distance kisses. There is also an element of "I can do anything you can do"—worse. Thus when Aerowax ricochets machine-gun bullets off its "jet-age plastic," another brand looses a stampede of elephants to trample over its "protective shield." The surrealistic approach often has a certain childish charm at first, but with repetition it quickly palls.

● EXISTENTIAL SLAPSTICK. The genre seems to mix Mack Sennett and Samuel Beckett. A woman, responding to the call, "Where's the Open Pit?" dashes across the lawn with a bottle of Open Pit barbecue sauce—and disappears into an open pit. A baker, having carelessly forgotten his Vicks Cough Silencers, tosses pizza dough into the air, coughs and catches it—splat—in the face. Splat again, as the Pond's girl gets schlopped in the eye with cold cream. And whack! umph! and aaagh! as a mousy little guy, sploshed with Hai Karate after-shave lotion, brutally chops down a scent-crazed female on the make. Nothing like a little good-natured sadism to punch home a point.

- FUN SEX. Currently the best example of this type is the ad in which a blonde looks straight through the camera and coos, "Take it off. Take it off. Take it *all* off!" while the music rips through a bump-and-grind melody. Of course she is really talking to some guy shaving with Noxzema, and she is referring to his beard. At first it seems wrong. Isn't it the man who is supposed to shout: "Take it off"? But in an instant, the reversal of roles becomes rather charming and even sexy, which is more than can be said for shaving. The girl, incidentally, is Gunilla Knutsson, Miss Sweden of 1961, but her heavy accent still sounds like a put-on.

- LOW SATIRE. Some commercials kid themselves, some razz the production style of various other products. A Jeno's pizza skit kids the halitosis hucksters. Marilyn says: "I'll tell you what your problem is, Gloria. You have bad pizza. Bad pizza!" After Gloria switches to Jeno's, Marilyn tries another tack: "Now I'd like to talk about your deodorant." Gloria: "Marilyn, how would you like a nice belt in the mouth?" A small masterpiece, worthy of Jonathan Winters or the late Ernie Kovacs.

- HIGH SATIRE. Relatively high, anyhow. Benson & Hedges gets a lot of laughs as it demonstrates the disadvantages of smoking its longer cigarette: a jewel thief hides behind the drapes, but his B & H sticks through and gives him away; a girl writes in to thank B & H for the extra length, since it comes in handy on her job—she sticks it in her mouth while a marksman flicks it with his bullwhip.

HOW MANY MILLIMETERS?

Good gags, as any adman knows, stick in the mind. And so do successful commercials, so much so that they keep coming back like a bad memory. Shell once got good mileage out of a spot in which a driverless car went rolling off to a Shell station to lap up some gas with TCP. So now Sinclair shows an auto deserting a pair of newlyweds to get a quick belt of KRC. A few years ago, Chevrolet displayed a car atop a spirelike butte in the Mojave Desert. Ah so, said the Toyota people, and right away they airlifted their sedan to the top of Fujiyama. Now in what promises to become the acrophobia sell, there is a new hair-coloring ad showing a girl atop another outcropping in the Colorado high country declaring to the world that "New Dawn sets you free."

But when it comes to out-Heroding Herod, nothing can match the great millimeter mania. It is not enough that cigarette ads, which seem to be one endless round of jingle-jangle whoop-de-do by a babbling brook or out there in Marlboro Country, are among the more mindless on TV.* Now they are engaged in a dreary interior dialogue. In reply to Chesterfield's joshing boast that its 101s are "a silly millimeter longer," Winston Super Kings scoff: "It's not how long you make it." Right, says Pall Mall 100s. What counts is whether you're "longer at both ends." Going everybody one less, Player's cigarettes is currently marketing a new brand in Canada that is "five millimeters shorter" than regular size, which means that "you smoke a little less, you pay a little less." If that doesn't make it, there is always Armour Bacon Longs, which are "a couple millimeters bigger" because they "shrink a little less." Sighing, the Camel filters man shows an 18-inch-long cigarette and wonders, "Where will it all end?"

YELLOW MENACE

Not, it is hoped, with victory for the ugh plugs, which fall under the heading of the Dreadful D's: drugs, dentifrices, deodorants, detergents and dandruff removers. They all deal in intensively competitive products, and their problem is the kind of problems they treat. Stuffed sinuses, after all, are not exactly a popular subject, but that does not stop the admen from hawking some nasal spray as if it were the greatest breakthrough since the Salk vaccine.

Strategies vary, but basic to every Dreadful D campaign is the oldest device of all: crisis-making. Thus by sheer repetition, the hawkers suggest that the primary cause of air pollution is bad breath and that the real yellow menace is not Red China but stained teeth. And judging by Katy Winters' early-warning nose, half the nation needs to be told an Ice Blue Secret.

If the Dreadfuls seem to be deliberately outrageous, it is because they are.

---

* In a report to Congress, the Federal Trade Commission recommended by a 3-to-1 vote that cigarette ads be altogether banned from radio and TV. The Commission specifically objected to ads that equate smoking with good times, and noted that in January alone, viewers between twelve and 17 were exposed to a total of 60 cigarette commercials, mainly on such favorite teenage shows as the *Smothers Brothers Comedy Hour* and *The Wednesday Night Movie*.

The gimmick game is called "brand recall," and the ground rules dictate that the only ads that anybody remembers are the very good—and the very bad. Pretty good does not count. Quick: Which airline promotes its baggage service by shipping its pitchman in a crate with his head sticking out? Everybody remembers greasy kid stuff, but what stuff is supposed to be superior? Which TV manufacturer, to prove that all its money has been poured into developing a better set, shows its board of directors in their undershirts? If a viewer can unhesitatingly answer Braniff, Vitalis and Sylvania, then he is watching too much TV.

According to one school of thought (which is not to be encouraged), people may buy certain kinds of products even though they hate the commercial. The axiom drawn from all this is that contempt breeds familiarity, and familiarity breeds sales. The recently retired White Knight (for Ajax cleanser) was the most ridiculed horseman since Don Quixote. He galloped so many laps around the plains of suburbia—1,000,000 in five years—that after a while, he became a rather endearing symbol of camp. What is more, according to one claim, his magic lance added a not-so-subliminal phallic meaning.

PROMISES, PROMISES

That particular revelation came during one of the "depth interviews" conducted in the name of motivational research, the wayout wing of advertising in which the Freudian sell is rudimentary. As all admen know, people don't buy products, they buy psychological satisfaction: the promise of beauty, not cosmetics; oral gratification, not cigarettes. Depthwise, baking a cake is supposedly a reenactment of childbirth and shaving a form of castration. Speed and performance, or a sense of male power, are blatantly stressed in automobile commercials. Cars become wild animals or fish—Wildcat, Impala, Cougar, Stingray, Barracuda. When a man slips behind the wheel humming "Only Mustang makes it happen," he, too, becomes a big ripsnorting stud. Ridiculous? Well, whoever heard of a car called the Aardvark or the Pussycat?

Actually, most admen use this sort of motivational psychology the way Roman emperors used auguries or modern politicians use religion: they don't necessarily believe in all that stuff, but they invoke it when it seems useful. Often, motivational research merely boils down to an inspired hunch. The elaborate process of commercial making begins in earnest with an agency brainstorming session. Once the slant of a campaign is determined, writers and artists then work up rough drawings of the ads in comic-strip form.

Ideally, these "story boards" will have a "hooker opening" or an intriguing scene-setter, plus a memorable catch phrase or two that dramatizes the need, say, for Murine to cure "eye pollution" or for Wizard air freshener to wipe away "house-itosis."

PRESTIGE SOUND

The script is then delivered to a production group–usually an independent agency. In the casting process, actors are chosen for the "authentic look," Jack Gilford, for instance, seems typecast as the conniving Cracker Jack addict, and Lou Jacobi looks every bit the beleaguered traveling salesman in a Hertz ad. Narrators Ed Herlihy for Kraft Foods and Alexander Scourby for Eastern Air Lines are prized for their ability to project "appetite appeal" and a "prestige sound." Just as important is the preparation of catchy music, which may even become a bestseller on the pop charts, as was the good fortune of Benson & Hedges' *Disadvantages of You* and Polaroid's *Meet the Swinger.*

At length, a small army of actors, makeup men, hairdressers, set designers, wardrobe people, technicians and directors head out to make their film, and act out the admen's fantasies. Perhaps they will alight in an ancient West German castle, which was the setting for a recent Volkswagen commercial. Maybe the cameraman will strap himself to the back of a speeding motorcycle or scoot around in an electric wheelchair to achieve new whirling, eye-catching effects.

SATURDAY JUNGLE

While a TV series films an average of ten minutes worth of script in one day, the shooting of a 60-second commercial often takes two or three days and can run through 25,000 ft. of film to get the final, worthy 90 ft. For an ad introducing Mattel Toys' new Bathhouse Brass line, a film crew covered 1,000 miles to shoot in eight different locations. The spot shows a parade of kids cavorting across sand dunes and careering down slides while madly blasting away on their plastic "brassoons," "toobas" and "flooglehorns." A kind of psychedelic version of the Pied Piper, the ad is typical of the wild, hyped-up pitches aired in the "Saturday morning jungle."

Except for time and expense, few if any campaigns can match the series of Shell ads that were an endurance test in more ways than one. To demonstrate Platformate, Shell's "extra mileage ingredient," the Ogilvy & Mather agency set up an endurance contest between cars containing Shell gasoline with the Platformate additive, and others without. Then they filmed the cars as they raced across the Bonneville salt flats; the Platformate cars always won. The films were two years in the making and cost an estimated $300,000. Even so, one ad in the series had to be junked. Some Negro viewers, led by Comedian Dick Gregory, complained that the film showing five white Platformate cars outdistancing five black cars was a demeaning insult. Nowadays, Shell is phasing out its endurance-test ads and, like most of its competitors, is running coupon contests on TV.

PUPIL RESPONSE

Admen go to extraordinary lengths in trying to determine whether the result of all their efforts is effective or not. Prior to launching a commercial, agencies screen it before test audiences and run a series of checks and quintuple checks that are as elaborate as those for a space shot. Lie detectors, word association, sentence completion and the Minnesota Multiphasic Personality Inventory are among a few of the methods used. Foote, Cone & Belding lugs rearview projectors to homes to get verdicts. Kenyon & Eckhardt plays TAG (Target Attitudinal Group), a method of extensive indirect questioning.

Leo Burnett's Creative Research Workshop uses the "galvanic skin-response test," which measures the perspiration level—and thus interest—of volunteers through electrodes clamped to their hands. Another device is the "pupillary-response camera." It records the dilations of the viewer's pupils as he watches a test commercial. If the subject likes what he sees, his pupils widen: if not, he can catch a little nap time.

Yet for all the probings and brain-candling, TV ads fail with reassuring regularity—reassuring because it means that the masses are still beyond manipulation. Indeed, owing to what the researchers call "the fluid, ever-changing force of subcultures," the viewers are still downright unpredictable.

Manhattan's Rheingold beer people learned this when they went after the "ethnic market" with a $300,000 series of beautifully filmed ads, each showing a group of Greeks, Negroes, Jews, Puerto Ricans, Irish or Japanese partying it up with Rheingold. The mock-modest point was that the sponsor really didn't know why his beer was so widely loved, but "We must be doing something right." Wrong. Research later showed that no minority group wanted to drink a beer that could be so popular with other minority groups. As a result, Rheingold switched to a more forceful, if simple-minded pitch proclaiming the "ten-minute head."

DELIVERY SERVICE

Despite such evidence of consumer independence, some critics believe that TV commercials, along with all advertising, have a seductive effect upon the population, compelling it to overconsume its own overproduction. Even John Kenneth Galbraith, who has referred to advertising as "organized public bamboozlement," points out that the picture is not quite so simple and that advertising is an inevitable part of the U.S. economy. Harvard Sociologist Chad Gordon observes: "We are a materialistic culture, and material acquisitions came before the first commercial was ever made. Commercials did not create status envy or the desire for increased status"—even though they can overstimulate those desires, and many others as well.

The more immediate question is not what commercials do to the economy, but what they do to TV. Obviously, they will not go away—much as one would like them to at times. But must they dominate the channels quite as much as they do? Sometimes it appears that all TV fare is one supercommercial, with entertainment simply an extension of the sales pitch. The networks become, in effect, just audience-delivery services. It is not that they are influenced by advertisers—they are psyched by them. In a classic episode, Chevrolet once changed the script of a western to read "crossing" instead of "fording" a river.

Such an incident is less likely now than it used to be (a recent Chevy commercial actually mentioned Ford by name). But it still remains indicative of a certain way of thinking by sponsors. With the exception of a few enlightened companies—among them Xerox, Hallmark, Bell Telephone and Western Electric—most advertisers still prefer to avoid controversial or special-interest programs, and are happily led to the kind of show that provides the best frame for a sales pitch. Sometimes the frame and the picture merge completely, as when Clairol builds a beauty pageant around its commercials.

What can be done? Chances are that if everyone keeps his fingers crossed and buys the right products, the lighthearted uncommercials will spread and increasingly crowd the ugh-plugs off the air. But that is not enough. Another prospect is that the networks, goaded by viewer resentment, will move closer to the European scheme by having fewer but slightly longer commercial breaks. At present, with 9,000 new items appearing on the supermarket shelves each year, sponsors have started "clustering"—cramming more but shorter messages into the same time space. In the past two years alone, the number of products shown on TV has increased by about one-third, most of them in ten-, 20- and 30-second shots. There will also be more "piggybacking": promoting two unrelated products in one ad. "Triggerbacking" and "quarterbacking" are just a station break away.

GLORIOUS HOURS

Humorist Stan Freberg, a freelance commercial producer who created the Sunsweet prune and Jeno's pizza ads for TV, is pushing another possible cure. It is frankly utopian. He calls it "The Freberg Part-Time Television Plan: A Startling but Perfectly Reasonable Proposal for the De-escalation of Television in a Free Society, Mass Media-wise." The plan calls for a week like this:

Monday. Television as usual.

Tuesday. The set goes black, but one word shines in the center of the screen: Read!

Wednesday. Television as usual.

Thursday. The set goes black again, but this time we see the word Talk!

Friday. Television as usual.

Saturday. The words Unsupervised Activity.

And *Sunday?* Says Freberg: "We have to have somewhere to lump all those leftover commercials, don't we? Think of it! Twenty-four glorious, uninterrupted hours of advertising!"

It might just work—and it could be worse.

SPITBALLING WITH FLAIR

Spitballing, or brainstorming, is something like a group-therapy session in which the patient is the product and the doctors are the admen. Recently, *Time* Correspondent Edgar Shook sat in on a brainstorming meeting at Chicago's North Advertising Inc. The patient: Flair, a new Paper Mate pen with a nylon tip. Among the doctors: North President Don Nathanson, Creative Director Alice Westbrook, Copy Chief Bob Natkin and Copywriters Steve Lehner and Ken Hutchison. The dialogue, somewhat condensed:

NATKIN: We have what I think must be the first graffiti advertising campaign, which we've been running in teen-age magazines. The reason I bring this up is that it could be translated into TV and could be very arresting.

WESTBROOK: I love graffiti.

NATKIN(*reading from graffiti ads*): "Keep America beautiful. Bury a cheap ugly pen today. Buy a Paper Mate." Some research has been done on this and it looks like it's working. "Draw a flower on your knee with a Paper Mate Flair."

WESTBROOK: Why not "navel"?

NATKIN: They wouldn't let us say it. We are going to compromise. It was going to be "Draw a flower around your genitals with a Paper Mate Flair." Then they'd say "knee" and we'd say "navel," and we'd meet in the middle.

WESTBROOK: Body paint is going to get hotter and hotter.

NATHANSON: Did you read that memo I sent out about the bosoms? God, I think bosom makeup is going to be big.

WESTBROOK: I do too. I know just the color for it too.

NATHANSON: You know, you can do a fantastic industrial campaign on the idea of a silent pen. Because just think of the noise level. I mean, nothing is noisier than these competitor's pens. Everybody quiet. Just listen. (*He scratches first with the competitor's pen, then with a Flair.*)

WESTBROOK: Boy, that really moves me.

LEHNER: Picture the kind of thing you would get if you were awarded the Legion of Honor. Real parchmenty, with a great big heraldry and wax and stamps. And on the certificate it says, "The American Anti-Noise League." And you hear the announcer say with great . . .

HUTCHISON: Flair.

LEHNER: . . . "From the American Anti-Noise League, for exceptionally smooth writing without scratching or squeaking." You hear a trumpet. Tah-Tah! We dissolve to another document. "To Flair from the United Cap Forgetters Council: for having a new kind of ink that won't dry out if you leave the cap off overnight." And a couple of trumpets. Bum-Bum! And on to a third document. "To Flair from the National Pen Pounders Association: for having a smooth, tough, nylon point that won't push down." And you've got three trumpets going, and an announcer comes back in and says, "Flair even looks like a better way to write." We would play it very straight. Very pompous. Like Robert Morley's voice when he says these words. You get a kind of electricity between the silliness.

WESTBROOK: Let's face it. People just don't get emotionally involved with their pens. I think there's the danger of taking yourself too seriously when you're talking about a thing like that.

LEHNER: We have other ideas that we think would be stronger at this point in time. For instance, one thing that we're playing with now is a guy sitting at his desk . . .

WESTBROOK: A big, snappy executive.

LEHNER: And his secretary is with him and this guy is making notations like a guy would. Writing. "Yeah." "No." "See me . . . "

WESTBROOK: "You're fired." Stuff like that.

LEHNER: And when this girl goes out of the room, he takes a leather portfolio, looks around, opens it up and starts doodling some very silly, funny little things. And the announcer says: "Introducing a new executive status symbol—Flair. To the casual observer, Flair is a dignified, serious executive pen. But when you're alone, Flair reveals its true identity as the executive play pen. The greatest doodler in the world. This Christmas give him the executive play pen. Flair."

WESTBROOK: That's a great line! I think we ought to pretend like we got some new colors and see what we can do with it.

NATHANSON: What a television color commercial it could be, with fuchsias and, oh, I don't know, you name them. You know, orchid colors. You'll get women to write letters with orchid . . .

WESTBROOK: You could have a black pen with white ink or a white pen with black ink. Sort of an integrated pen, you know. (*Laughter.*) It could be called "the soul pen."

NATHANSON: Black paper!

WESTBROOK: With white ink! That's groovy!

NATHANSON: With blue paper!

WESTBROOK: Purple paper with pink ink! Pink paper with purple ink!

NATHANSON: Brown ink! We present them with a whole slew of marvelous ideas. Sealskin and alligator pens!

WESTBROOK: Phony fur pens! Wouldn't you love a fur pen? a mink pen? How about a tiger pen? Or a leopard pen? Would you believe an alligator pen?

NATKIN: How about a grey flannel pen?

WESTBROOK: Grey flannel is out. How about a turtle neck pen?

(To learn what, if anything, resulted from this meeting, watch your TV set.)

11

CENSORSHIP
AND PORNOGRAPHY

Following Supreme Court decisions during the past decade, the United States has witnessed a great increase in freedom of expression of once-taboo subjects on the stage, in films, and on television and in the press. This newly won freedom has at the same time been much debated in the press, in the courts, and by the public. Much of the debate has centered on the issue of "pornography." Exactly what is pornography? Can it be satisfactorily defined from a legal point of view? Where and to whom should pornography be available? How can it be controlled? As the question of censorship is frequently raised in connection with pornography, this chapter opens with an article on various aspects of censorship.

The chapter continues with a Time *essay on the "new" pornography, especially in books and literature.*

The chapter concludes with a sequel to this essay: "Pornography Revisited: Where to Draw the Line." In this article Ruth Brine discusses the impact of the flood of pornography in recent years and the possibility of restraining this flood.

Censorship

Henry J. Abraham

CENSORSHIP IS ESSENTIALLY a "policy of restricting the public expression of ideas, opinions, conceptions and impulses which have or are believed to have the capacity to undermine the governing authority or the social and moral order which that authority considers itself bound to protect" (Lasswell 1930, p. 290). Censorship usually takes two forms: prior, which refers to advance suppression; and *post facto*, which involves suppression after publication or pronouncement has taken place. Although it is more frequently practiced under autocratic regimes, it is also present, in varied forms, in those states normally viewed as Western liberal democracies; and its execution is as variegated as are the states and governments involved. Broadly speaking, however, those who favor and those who oppose censorship normally bracket themselves with one of two approaches to society as represented by great names of the past. The former agree with Plato, St. Augustine, and Machiavelli that those who are qualified to identify evil should be empowered to prevent its dissemination. The latter, siding with Aristotle, Oliver Wendell Holmes, Jr., and John Dewey, maintain that a man is free only so long as he is empowered to make his own choices.

In its contemporary form, censorship is exercised both by public and by private authorities. Although it is still predominantly associated with governmental (public) action, its exercise by private groups—with religious as well as secular interests—is becoming more common. In the United States, since the end of World War II, the rise of private vigilante groups in a number of areas of everyday life clearly indicates this trend. The erstwhile dichotomy

(Lasswell 1930, p. 291) of either political or religious censorship no longer suffices. Today, censorship, both public and private, may be generally grouped into four categories: political censorship; religious censorship; censorship against obscenity, i.e., censorship of morals; and censorship affecting academic freedom. It is important to remember, however, that these are merely categories of convenience and that a given act of censorship may, of course, embrace more than one category. Thus, the Tridentine Rules (formulated at the Council of Trent in 1564 under the guidance of Pope Pius IV) were religious in origin, but to some extent they were involved with obscenity; their enforcement was political; and there was then no academic freedom as we know it today. The investigations of alleged subversive influences in American schools, colleges, and universities in the years following World War II had political, as well as educational, overtones.

HISTORY

The history of censorship, so closely linked with a basic sense of insecurity, represents a continuum of the battle between the individual and society and can be sketched only briefly here. Turning first to the Bible (Jer. 36.1-26), we find that the prophet Jeremiah encountered censorship when the book he had dictated to Baruch was mutilated by King Jehoiakim. During classical antiquity, censorship was sporadically applied. In the fifth century B.C., Sparta placed a ban on certain forms of poetry, music, and dance, because its rulers believed, or wished to believe, that these cultural activities tended to induce effeminacy and licentiousness. For their liberal thoughts on religious matters, Aeschylus, Euripides, and Aristophanes felt the censor's sting. Republican Rome considered itself devoted to virtue and assumed the right to censor any citizen who did not embrace that concept in the cultural realm. The theater was banned by the censor, except on the occasion of certain games (where tradition bestowed upon dramatic art a degree of license in both gesture and speech). Although there is no conclusive evidence of literary censorship either in Rome or Greece, the famed poet Ovid was banished to the Black Sea area by Emperor Augustus, allegedly because of his "licentiousness" but more likely because of his political views.

In the era of the Christian church, the earliest and most extreme manifestation of censorship is found in the Apostolic Constitutions, said to have been written in A.D. 95 by St. Clement of Rome at the dictates of the apostles. The constitutions forbade Christians to read any books of the gentiles, since it was thought that the Scriptures were all a *true* believer need read. There then followed a long series of prohibitions issued by the early church fathers, among them the death penalty edicts of the Council of Nicaea and the Emperor Constantine against the pens of Arius and Porphyry in 325; the decree of 399 by the Council of Alexandria under Bishop Theophilus, forbidding the Origens to read and own books; the stern punitive measures, akin to the book burning days of the Hitler era, by Pope Leo I in 446; and the first papal Index, which made its appearance in 499 under Pope Gelasius. The concept of the Index, which was formalized by the amended Tridentine Rules, embracing a list of proscribed books for Roman Catholics, is still in existence today (see Gardiner 1958, pp. 51–54).

During the Middle Ages a new version of prior censorship commenced: the submission of manuscripts by writers to their superiors, both as a matter of courtesy and as a prophylactic against subsequent censure. But with the advent of printing and with steady cultural growth, the ecclesiastic authorities insisted upon formal, organized censorship. In 1501 Pope Alexander VI issued his famous bull against printing of books, which was designed to protect the vast domain of the Church of Rome against heresy. Even more drastic measures were taken by the Scottish Estates in 1551. By 1586, all books printed in England had to be read and approved by the Archbishop of Canterbury or the Bishop of London prior to publication. But the written word was not all that felt the censor's power in England; it was extended to drama by the public authorities, once religious drama, always under the control of the church, had become obsolete.

In 1693, England substituted *punitive* for *prior* censorship of printing. This form essentially exists in many lands now and is generally much preferred to prior censorship, if there must be censorship. Probably the best-known illustration of this type of censorship is the John Peter Zenger case in 1735, often referred to as the birth of freedom of the press; for New York Governor William Cosby was unsuccessful in his gross attempt to silence and punish the courageous printer (see Zenger 1957, pp. 3–131).

It should be noted here that the triumph of Protestantism, and the subsequent rise of the nation-state, had brought about a significant switch in emphasis in the employment of censorship. Practically speaking, the monarchs became separated from the church, and to a considerable extent their interests in censorship no longer coincided. Thus, the compelling force necessary to sustain censorship was no longer concerned with religious beliefs. In those instances in which a state still guarded against blasphemy or heresy, it was from the conviction that these were often antecedent steps to sedition and treason, especially where the authority for the monarch's position came from the doctrine of the divine right of kings. Censorship was still aimed at beliefs and facts, but the orientation had switched from the religious to the political arena.

The seventeenth and eighteenth centuries were the transition years in the development of the freedoms and rights of men, which we value so much. Here the first voices began to ring out for the rights of the individual against the state, so that by 1695 the last formal governmental restraint upon literature in England had been withdrawn. Among the voices who made themselves heard in those centuries were Milton, Spinoza, Voltaire, and Locke.

Prior to this transition period, sundry intriguing devices had been employed to look after the interests of the monarch. King Henry VIII had entrusted the control of books to the infamous Court of Star Chamber. Queen Elizabeth maintained control by giving the Stationers' Company monopoly on printing, for which they reciprocated by hunting out all undesirable books. Coincident with this she granted powers of suppression to the archbishops of Canterbury and York.

The Stuarts brought with their rule even more severe censorship, allowing their bishops control over the importation of books. The first breakthrough for free thought came in 1640 when the Long Parliament abolished the Court of Star Chamber. This brief respite lasted until 1643, when Parliament reintroduced licensing. This was the specific act that resulted in Milton's eloquent plea for free speech, his *Areopagitica*. In this work, he exposes the many absurdities, anomalies, and tyrannies inherent in literary censorship. During the Restoration, the devices of censorship employed by the former monarchs were maintained with the passage of the Licensing Act of 1662, which was aimed at "heretical, seditious, schismatical or offensive books or pamphlets."

The move toward individual rights being generated in England at this time reached its culmination in 1695, when the Licensing Act was not renewed, and governmental censorship temporarily disappeared from the English scene. Although the English had gained their freedom, in those nations where Catholicism still held sway, there was very little freedom to express ideas that would offend the church. This tradition has lasted even into the modern era in such nations as Spain.

The eighteenth century is conspicuous in historical perspective because of the freedom of expression that it attained. Even in the colonies, with the spread of the Great Awakening (dating from about 1740), the growth of freedom from the chains of Puritan control was evident. By 1789, the freedoms of the bill of rights were accepted as the natural heritage of all men. The remarkable feature of this phenomenon, both in England and America, was that it was a reality, not just an idea on a piece of paper.

It is in the field of morals—the area of censorship commonly classified as that of obscenity—that not the most widespread but the most extreme forms of censorship and attempted censorship have transpired during the past two or three centuries. This censorship has been both on a public and private level, the former chiefly by virtue of a host of defense-against-obscenity statutes and ordinances, the latter by pressure groups, chief among them the Catholic church, whose emphasis in the realm of censorship has perceptibly changed from the old preoccupation with heresy to one that emphasizes morals, although the religious overtones are understandably present. But public and private aims and designs again merge here.

. Although in certain types of censorship the political authority is concerned with defending the *status quo* and its position in it, this is not true of censorship of morals. More often than not, state action is not in defense of itself but in the form of a service to some influential members of the polity, in ridding the society of certain ideas that are considered offensive by these influential members. The common method of achieving these ends is the formation of watchdog groups that comb the arts and letters and upon finding works—books, plays, movies, etc.—that they consider obscene strive either for their official suppression or for private boycotts. The first of these societies, the English Society for the Suppression of Vice, appeared in London in 1802. It was to be the forebear of such American vigilante groups as Anthony Comstock's New York Society for the Suppression of Vice and the New England Watch and Ward Society (Craig 1962, pp. 138–139).

The effectiveness of these groups in the United States is evidenced by the vast amount of obscenity legislation that has been passed in the last century. Beginning with the clause in the Tariff Act of 1842 that barred the importation of obscene matter, American legislatures have produced a multitude of statutes designed to protect the minds and morals of both children and adults in our society. The 1920s through the 1940s marked the height of the moralistic legislation.

In England, the single most important piece of censorship legislation was the famous Campbell Act of 1857 (the Obscene Publications Act of 1857), named for its proponent, who was the lord chief justice. There was a great cry against it in Parliament, because in Campbell's attempt to strike down the sale of obvious hard-core pornography from the shelves of the bookstores of Holywell Street in London, he had left few safeguards to defend against similar attacks upon all literature that dealt with sex. The act was finally passed when Campbell defined an obscene work as written for the single purpose of corrupting the morals of youth, and of a nature calculated to shock the common feelings of decency in any well-regulated mind.

However, his successor, Lord Cockburn, in the grasp of the Victorians, did not so limit the obscene. In the famous Hicklin case he said, "the test of obscenity is this, whether the tendency of the matter charged as obscenity is to deprave and corrupt those whose minds are open to such immoral influences, and into whose hands a publication of this sort may fall" (L.R3/QB/371, 1868). Using standards such as this, the Comstocks on both sides of the Atlantic–indeed throughout the world–infiltrated various boards of censorship, and by the turn of the century succeeded in reducing "acceptable" literature to that fit for reading by children. At that time, more than one author was endangering his chances of publication if he referred to a leg as a "leg," rather than calling it a "limb." Starting in the late 1920s, however, American federal courts have been instrumental in salvaging some semblance of reasonableness in these matters.

In a series of opinions, the most important of which were the combined 1957 cases *Roth* v. *U.S.* and *Alberts* v. *California* (354 U.S. 476), the Supreme Court both defined the obscene and detailed the protections to which literature accused of being obscene was entitled. Associate Justice William Brennan, in his opinion, made clear that "obscenity is not within the area of constitutionally protected speech or press," because it is "utterly without redeeming social importance" (354 U.S. 484, 485). However, he cautioned that "sex and obscenity are not synonymous," and the portrayal of sex, for example, in art, literature, and scientific works, "is entitled to constitutional protection as long as it is not obscene." But his judicial test is not entirely helpful: Material is obscene when "to the average person, applying contemporary community standards, the dominant theme of the material taken as a whole appeals to prurient interest" (354 U.S. 487). This standard, and its later application by the courts to specific works, seems to indicate that the Supreme Court's view of what literature is obscene in modern America is limited to that genre of literature generally known as hard-core pornography. But the need to define hard-core pornography reintroduced the basic dilemma of drawing lines.

A categorized, comprehensive list of works censored in the United States was compiled in 1940 by Morris Ernst, one of the foremost crusaders against censorship. It includes some of the world's greatest classics, for example, works by Homer, Shakespeare, Whitman, and Darwin (Ernst & Lindey 1940, pp. 228–230).

The history of censorship in France and the other European nations has an amazing historical similarity to that of America. The giants of French literature, such as Baudelaire, Hugo, Verlaine, and Zola, have felt the same stings of censors as their counterparts in English. The modern laws regarding obscenity in France, Italy, Belgium, Germany, and the Netherlands, roughly parallel those of America; whereas those of the Scandinavian nations are a little more lenient. This is probably a reflection of the different attitudes toward sex prevailing in those nations.

Censorship in the world of dictatorships must be viewed from a different perspective, of course. Essentially, the rights of individuals in these nations are at a pre-Renaissance level in terms of the Western world. Consequently, censorship there is designed to propagandize as well as to forbid. This has been especially true in the totalitarian dictatorships, where complete control of the mind is a prerequisite for complete control of the society.

CRITIQUE

In its most general form, censorship is involved with the realm of ideas, ideas that naturally must take the form of something written or spoken in order to be censorable. Censorship implies that certain ideas are not only invalid, but that they should not be presented; that they constitute a genuine danger. In Lasswell's terms of "who gets what, why and how," censorship is thus concerned with controlling "dangerous" expression of ideas. It follows, then, that those who have been most successful in controlling ideas that endanger their interests are those who already possess authority. Hence, the most successful practitioners of censorship through the ages have been the authority figures themselves—church, monarchs, dictators. Those in non-public positions, who desire the suppression of certain ideas but do not of themselves have the necessary official authority to do so, will thus endeavor to enlist the aid of whatever authority may be promising. Because this is often difficult, if not impossible, private groups in today's Western democracies then resort to personal pressure tactics, designed to intimidate those who have influence over, or who are in command of, channels of communication. A pertinent illustration of this technique, very successfully employed in the United States since the 1940s and 1950s (particularly during the McCarthy era), has been the so-called blacklisting of controversial literary figures as well as performing artists, thus blocking their employment in certain media of communication, notably and the movies, radio, and television–the live stage having more successfully resisted that type of pressure (see Cogley 1956, *passim*).

Far less successful, especially in the United States, however, have been attempts to censor the press, which has enjoyed a unique position of communication freedom, even more so than in traditionally censorship-leery Britain. Although press censorship has continued in many lands even in the 1960s, not excluding certain Western democracies (France, for example), the Supreme Court of the United States again made quite clear in 1964 that the press is not only not censorable by way of prior restraint but that it cannot even be sued for allegedly libelous statements unless deliberate malice is proved conclusively in a court of law (*The New York Times Co.* v. *Sullivan*, decided March 9, 1964, 84 U.S. Sup. Ct. 710).

The bases of censorship are themselves largely repugnant to the ideas of Western liberal tradition, yet even the West must comprehend the three possible rationalizations that seem to exist for censorship.

The first rationalization is that ideas presented, or about to be presented, are "false" and/or "dangerous" by the standards of the authorities in power and that they must hence be suppressed or punished.

Related to this is the second rationale for censorship, equally obnoxious to Western traditions, that of elitism, the justification of which goes back to Plato and the *Republic*. Here, the belief is that the minds of those who would be subjected to the ideas to be censored are not capable of seeing the "falsity" and would hence be led astray. Western political tradition rejects this notion, but many a private pressure group in the West does not, as the persistent attempts by them, and at times by public authorities, to censor school textbooks demonstrate to this day. Yet any historical investigation will quickly prove that those who have set themselves up as being uniquely qualified to ferret out the truth have been no more capable of doing so than their adversaries.

The third rationale for censorship seems to be the one that stands on strongest grounds. Ideas that lead to "antisocial action"–for example, hard-core pornography–may be censored. Here, however, a crucial distinction enters: We are no longer so much in the realm of ideas as in the realm of overt action, and it is here that even the West may wish to, indeed may have to, draw a line between the cherished freedom of expression and the right of society to establish a modicum of standards of overt behavior. How, where, and by whom such a line is to be drawn is the peculiar dilemma of those who love and cherish the precious tradition of ordered liberty.

The New Pornography

TIME

JOHN CLELAND WAS a luckless little hack who in 1748, destitute and desperate, scribbled *Fanny Hill* or *Memoirs of a Woman of Pleasure* for a flat fee of 20 guineas. He went on to become an inept philologist, ducked creditors much of his life, and died aged and unsung. If the poor fellow were only alive today, he could be a Big Writer, for critics on both sides of the Atlantic have acclaimed his ability to describe repetitive fornication with elegance and grace. He could wear hand-sewn Italian loafers, sell his still unwritten books to the paperbacks and the movies for a cool million, and lecture at progressive colleges on "Erotic Realism in the Novel."

But he would have to work hard, very hard, to keep up with the competition. For just about anything is printable in the U.S. today. All the famed and once hard-to-get old volumes are on the paperback racks, from the *Kama Sutra* to the Marquis de Sade's *Justine*. Henry Miller's *Tropic of Cancer*, once the last word in unprintable scatology, can often be picked up in remainder bins for 25¢. Miller has almost acquired a kind of dignity as the Grand Old Dirty Man of the trade, compared with some of the more current writers. Krafft-Ebing's *Psychopathia Sexualis* is out in two new editions, which for the first time render all those horrendous Latin passages in English—and, surrounded by the author's quaint 19th century moralizing, they seem tame alongside *Candy* or Norman Mailer's *An American Dream*.

Maurice Girodias, the shy little Parisian who was the world's foremost publisher of English-language pornography until tightening French censorship put his Olympia Press out of business, often talks about setting up shop in the U.S., but it is difficult to see what he could peddle. Barney Rosset,

279

publisher of Grove Press and in a sense the American Girodias, is way ahead of him. Says Rosset hopefully: "Who knows if the limits have been reached? Just because the scientists split the atom, did they sit back and say, "Well, that's it?" The pioneering publisher could always push the limits a little farther by trying the notorious *Story of O. or The Debauched Hospodar*. But one of these days even Rosset may run out of material.

The avowed professional pornographers face a related dilemma. The fact is that all kinds of respectable hardcover books now contain subject matter and language that would have brought police raids only a few years ago "is really killing us," says a West Coast practitioner. Far from giving up, the cheap paperback pornographers are diversifying by expanding their old preoccupation with lesbianism and sado-masochism, while searching for ever more bizarre combinations and settings. Still, it is tough trying to stay ahead of the avant-garde.

With everyone so afraid of appearing square, the avant-garde is obviously trying to determine just how far things can be pushed before anyone will actually admit to being shocked. New York now exports to various other centers of culture a mimeographed magazine whose title is somewhat stronger than *Love You, A Magazine of the Arts*; its pages are filled by some certified avant-garde writers, many homosexuals, who mostly write *pissoir* poetry.

While cheap "nudie" movies are branching out into torture and lesbianism in a desperate attempt to keep a few steps below Hollywood, the far-out new wave in New York and San Francisco is also creating a cinema of sorts; such "underground" films as Jack Smith's *Flaming Creatures* and Andy Warhol's *Couch* feature transvestite orgies with masturbation and other frills—although they seem even more concerned with an almost narcotic attack on the concept of time, since most of them are interminable.

After a visit to the U.S., Malcolm Muggeridge, onetime editor of *Punch*, complained: "I'd have joined a Trappist order rather than take more. All those ghastly novels—sex is an obsession with the Americans." Besides, adds Muggeridge, "if the purpose of pornography is to excite sexual desire, it is unnecessary for the young, inconvenient for the middle-aged, and unseemly for the old."

RETREAT OF CENSORSHIP

Unnecessary or unseemly, or just unpleasant, what young and old may now read or see is part of the anti-Puritan revolution in American morals.

The Greek term *pornographos*, meaning literally "the writing of harlots," has always been relative and subjective. As D. H. Lawrence put it, "What is pornography to one man is the laughter of genius to another." Until the 1930s, U.S. courts generally followed a celebrated 1868 ruling of Britain's Lord Chief Justice Sir Alexander Cockburn, whose test for obscenity—used more or less interchangeably with pornography—was the effect any material might have on a hypothetical schoolgirl, or its tendency to "deprave and corrupt those whose minds are open to such immoral influences." This ruling, which bedeviled and outraged the literary world for some 65 years, ignored the overall literary or educational merit of a book for the adult reader.

The schoolgirl test began to crumble in 1933 with the famed ruling by the U.S. Circuit Court of Appeals in New York, which held that James Joyce's *Ulysses* was not obscene—despite its impudent pudendicity and ovablastic genitories—since the "proper test" is a book's "dominant effect." In 1957, in decisions that upheld the conviction of two mailorder pornography dealers, the U.S. Supreme Court finally defined its own views on the matter. First, it flatly denied the smut peddlers' contention that the 1st and 14th Amendments guaranteeing freedom of speech and press gave them a right to sell obscene material. Second, the court held that the Constitution does guarantee freedom for ideas "having even the slightest redeeming social importance—unorthodox ideas, controversial ideas, even ideas hateful to the prevailing climate of opinion." The court defined obscenity as material "utterly without redeeming social importance," and set up as its test "whether to the average person, applying contemporary community standards, the dominant theme of the material taken as a whole appeals to prurient interest."

This does not establish a uniform permissiveness across the U.S. Each city, county and state can bring actions that publishers or distributors must defend individually, at sometimes prohibitive costs. But in general, what constitutes "redeeming social importance" is endlessly arguable, and even plainly unredeemed "hard-core" pornography is easier than ever to buy, particularly since the Supreme Court ruled that allegedly obscene books or movies cannot be seized by police until they have been so adjudged in the courts.

MATTER OF TASTE

Lately, a distinct reaction against permissiveness has begun. Pressure is increasing from citizens' organizations such as the Roman Catholic National

Organization for Decent Literature, the Protestant Churchmen's Committee for Decent Publications, and Citizens for Decent Literature, a nonsectarian organization that now has 300 chapters around the country. These groups are shrill, sincere, and sometimes self-defeating. When a Chicago court ruled three years ago that Henry Miller's *Tropic of Cancer* could be sold locally, the C.D.L. flooded Chicago with excerpts of outrageous passages in the book, undoubtedly giving them wider circulation than they had ever before enjoyed in the city.

Miller, for one, considers such alarms trivial in the light of the Bomb. "We are now passing through a period of what might be called 'cosmic insensitivity,' " he says, "a period when God seems more than ever absent from the world and man is doomed to come face to face with the fate he has created for himself. At such a moment, the question of whether a man be guilty of using obscene language in printed books seems to me inconsequential. It is almost as if, while taking a walk through a green field, I espied a blade of grass with manure on it, and bending down to that obscure little blade of grass I said to it scoldingly, "Naughty! Naughty!' "

Not everybody can be as cosmically insensitive as that, particularly when, as it sometimes appears, there is so much manure and so little grass. Actually, there is relatively less indignation from the pulpits of any denomination than one might expect. Says Harold Bosley, pastor of Manhattan's Christ Church Methodist: "The new license in the arts is one of the major problems in the church today. But none of us are interested in rigorous public censorship. We must help create an attitude of self-censorship and responsibility, otherwise we're dead ducks." And Baptist Minister Howard Moody of the Judson Memorial Church in New York's Greenwich Village feels that a new Christian definition of obscenity should not concentrate on sex or vulgar language alone, but on anything, particularly violence, whose purpose is "the debasement and depreciation of human beings."

As for psychiatrists, they are great believers in the Jimmy Walker dictum that no girl was ever ruined by a book, asserting, in effect, that no one is harmed by pornography who is not sick to begin with. The young, it is widely conceded, are more vulnerable, but no one has yet devised a practical way of keeping books from the young by law without also keeping them from adults—which would mean a return to the Cockburn rule.

Perhaps beyond questions of law, even beyond concern for morals, the problem is one of taste.

An open mind toward the new, the shocking, even the intolerable in art is an intellectual duty, if only because so many great and shocking artists from Swift to Joyce were so vehemently condemned at first. It hardly follows that any writer who manages to shock is therefore automatically entitled to respect as a worthy rebel. Yet this is how their followers regard the heroes of today's avant-garde, notably Jean Genet (*Our Lady of the Flowers*) and William Burroughs (*Naked Lunch*). "The new immoralists" is what they are labeled by *Partisan Review* Editor William Phillips, who is anything but a literary reactionary. He adds: "To embrace what is assumed to be beyond the pale is taken as a sign of true sophistication. And this is not simply a change in sensibility; it amounts to a sensibility of chaos."

AGAINST MORALISTS & HEDONISTS

Genet, Burroughs and other chroniclers of fagotry and fellatio are different from the realists of sex like Zola, the sentimentalists of sex like D. H. Lawrence, the poetic demons of sex like Baudelaire. They are different from the good old-fashioned pornographers like *Fanny Hill's* Cleland or the masters of bawdry from Ovid to Aretino, Rabelais, Boccaccio and (in an off moment) Mark Twain. However unconventional, these writers found delight in sex; however critical of human folly, they were partisans of mankind. The new immoralists attack not only society but man and sex itself. Their writings add up to homosexual nihilism, and what Fanny Hill would have thought of them is made clear by her "rage and indignation" when she observed a pair of "male-misses, scarce less execrable than ridiculous."

Writing in *Commentary*, William Phillips nails the whole genre by devastatingly describing Burroughs' *Nova Express* as "the feeding almost literally of human flesh and organs on each other in an orgy of annihilation. The whole world is reduced to the fluidity of excrement as everything dissolves into everything else.." And Critic John Wain adds: "A pornographic novel is, in however backhanded a way, on the side of something describable as life. *Naked Lunch*, by contrast, is unreservedly on the side of death."

In their defense it is often said that the new immoralists merely seek to show the world as they see it, in all its horror and lovelessness; but that is simply the old error of confusing art with event, a propagation of the notion that a novel trying to convey dullness must be dull. Sheer nightmare does not redeem a book any more than sheer pollyannaism. The Genet-Burroughs crowd, including such lesser sensationalists as John Rechy (*City of Night*) and Hubert Selby (*Last Exit to Brooklyn*), are not pornographers, if pornography is defined as arousing sexual excitement. These writers have created a por-nography of nausea, which if anything has the opposite effect. They are thus the enemies of the hedonist almost more than the enemies of the moralist.

SEX AS IDEOLOGY

Apart from making sex hideous and inhuman, the new pornographers also make it hopelessly dull. They should have learned from Sade, who used sex to assert the impossible—the totally unlimited freedom of man—and pushed the concept into insanity. Along the way Sade desperately tried to force his imagination beyond human limits by inventing inhuman horrors, but he only managed to make his compilation shatteringly dreary. Toward the end of his *120 Days of Sodom* he was no longer really writing, but simply setting down long lists of neatly numbered and tersely outlined enormities—the effect being ludicrous and totally unreal. Much of the current writing on sex approaches this quality of mechanical repetition and unreality.

For one thing, the constant use of the limited four-letter vocabulary tends to rob the words of what legitimate shock effect they used to have. "Powerful words should be reserved for powerful occasions," says Novelist Philip Toynbee. "Words like money can be devalued by inflation." Stuart B. Flexner, co-author of the authoritative *Dictionary of American Slang*, believes that this is already happening. "The next step is to find a new crop," he says, "but I don't know yet what these will be."

Secondly, it is becoming ever clearer that, as Novelist Saul Bellow said not long ago, "polymorphous sexuality and vehement declarations of aliena-tion are not going to produce great works of art." The vast majority of writers, publishers and critics rejoice over the decline of censorship. While it permits the emergence of much trash, they feel that this is the necessary price for the occasional great work that might otherwise be taboo—for example, Nabokov's *Lolita*, a brilliant *tour de force*. But they concede that the new permissiveness paradoxically imposes a more difficult task on the writer; in a way it is harder to work without than within limits. Says Critic-Author Leslie Fiedler: "We've got our freedom. Now the question is what do we do with it."

Joseph Heller, author of the far from prudish *Catch-22*, adds: "Now that we have established more dirty talk and more promiscuity in literature, we've established the obvious. What is accomplished by being specific? A reader's imagination is a more potent descriptive power than any author has. When everything is told, what you're left with is pretty crude and commonplace. The love scenes in *Anna Karenina* are infinitely more intimate than any explicit sex scene I can recall."

Besides, Tolstoy did not suffer from the pathetic phallacy according to which all existence revolves around sex. Many authors today treat sex the way Marxists treat economics; they see it at the root of everything, and daydream about sexual triumph the way revolutionary writers daydream about power. Thus in the tirelessly explicit writing of Norman Mailer, sex is a personal boast, a mystique and an ideology—and, in all three capacities, solemn and unconvincing.

Sex has, of course, infinite variants and imposes many compulsions. There will always be cheap pornography, and in a permissive age it will flourish openly and, perhaps, eventually fade; in a restrictive age, it will live clandestinely and, probably, remain a hardy growth. The purpose of sex in serious literature is to help convey the feeling and meaning of life as it is. Thus literature neither denies the existence of the wildest aberrations nor the use of the most clinical or bawdy language—but does not celebrate them as norms.

In the long run a sense of humor may be far more effective against the new pornography than censorship ever could be. "A return to ribaldry would be a very good thing," says Methodist Minister Tom Driver. "People ought to laugh in bed, and at some of the current writing about bed." There are signs that some are indeed laughing—and laughing at the authors of pornography. For sex is far too important a matter to be left merely to writers.

Pornography Revisited:
Where to Draw the Line

RUTH BRINE

MANHATTAN NEWSSTANDS ARE so crowded with displays of *Call Girl*, *Gay Party, Ball and Desire* that it is sometimes the New York *Times* that is sold under the counter. The situation is similar in many big cities. Detroit newsstands even have dildos and whips for sale, bestselling books vie with each other in sexual explicitness and vulgarity and there are no off limits at all in the theater. Around Times Square, exhibitions of simulated intercourse can be seen afternoons and evenings for $5 and up. Skin flicks and their ilk, which used to be limited to a few hundred city theaters, are now shown in about 2,000 moviehouses, many of them in suburbs and small towns, while the criteria by which commercial films are rated are flickering rapidly skinward. What was once R is now GP, and what was X only a year ago is now R. As such ratings and audience thresholds change, so does the borderline of legal obscenity, which is partially defined by "contemporary community standards" that are constantly getting lower.

The national Commission on Obscenity and Pornography recommended—for a variety of reasons—the repeal of dozens of anti-obscenity laws. Judging by the violent reactions that the report provoked, its recommendations are not likely to be widely adopted; on the contrary, signs of a new restrictive mood toward pornography have begun to appear. The publishers of an explicitly illustrated edition of the pornography commission's report itself were indicted by grand juries in Dallas and San Diego. The New York City

Criminal Court convicted the editor and publisher of *Screw*, the nation's No. 1 underground sex tabloid, of publishing obscenity. In San Francisco, where everything conceivable has been seen for several years, the D.A. recently got convictions against three porno film-house proprietors, one of them for showing a movie in which a woman had intercourse with a dog, a stallion and a hog. The Supreme Court split 4 to 4 in a decision on the obscenity of the film *I Am Curious (Yellow)*, which had the effect of upholding the ban on the film in Maryland. Although legal sophisticates realized that this was due to the abstention of Justice William Douglas, some of the more censorious nevertheless took heart.

Meanwhile, a new round of discussion has opened, much of it in favor of some sort of censorship.

QUESTION 1: DOES PORNOGRAPHY REALLY DO ANYONE ANY HARM?

The liberal position, of course, is that "no girl has ever been seduced by a book." That statement is erroneous, according to Poet-Librarian Felix Pollak–or at least he hopes it is: "For the saying doesn't do the cause of literature any good, or the intellectual cause in general. If one denies the power of the word to do evil, one denies the power of the word to do good. In effect, one denies the power of the word. I prefer the healthy fear and awe of the written and spoken word, evidenced by censorious zealots, to the wishy-washy neutralism of the liberalist anti-censors."

But how can one prove the evil effects of words or pictures? Never had there been such a concerted effort to answer this question as was made by the pornography commission with its $2,000,000 budget. In one study that became notorious, measuring devices were attached to 23 penises while the owners were exposed day after day to erotica. The resulting data proved only what one might suspect: that men can become satiated. According to the majority report, pornography cannot be proved to cause crime, sexual deviancy or severe emotional disturbances. This is a conclusion somewhat at odds with that reached by the national Commission on the Causes and Prevention of Violence, whose behavioral studies indicated that exposure to violence does cause harm. The violence commission therefore recommended more restraint, while the pornography commission recommended less.

A dispassionate look at the tangle is provided by Harvard Government Professor James Q. Wilson in the quarterly *The Public Interest*. Wilson found the obscenity studies "unexceptionable within their limited framework." But, he said, "one cannot simulate in the laboratory the existence or nonexistence of a lifelong exposure to or preoccupation with obscenity, any more than one can simulate a lifelong exposure to racist or radical opinions." His major thesis is that proof of harm is largely beside the point. Even if behavioral studies could not prove that individual Negroes are harmed by being denied access to public facilities, reasons Wilson, he would still want them to have that access. Violence and obscenity are moral issues, he believes, and judgments about them must rest on political and philosophical, not utilitarian considerations.

Question 2: Does Pornography Have A Deleterious Effect Upon The Moral Climate As A Whole And On Values Generally?

A highly theoretical argument for censorship is made by University of Toronto Government Professor Walter Berns. Democracy, more than any other form of government, requires self-restraint by its citizens, he maintains, and self-restraint can be partially achieved by laws governing public amusements. Pornography makes people shameless, he believes: "Those who are without shame will be unruly and unrulable; having lost the ability to restrain themselves by obeying the rules they collectively give themselves, they will have to be ruled by others." Therefore pornography leads to tyranny, Berns concludes.

Whatever else it does or does not do, pornography makes strange bedfellows. New Left Philosopher Herbert Marcuse is as censorious of it as is Berns. While Berns fears that pornography makes men unrulable, however, Marcuse thinks that it makes them tame. Marcuse objects to sexual permissiveness because he thinks it is a safety valve that keeps people from exploding and breaking up the System. To him, the relaxation of sexual taboos is a sort of capitalist plot. "Desublimation," as he calls it, is therefore repressive.

Many observers are most concerned about the sadistic component of much current pornography. "No civilization, with the possible exception of the Aztec, could produce an art whose sexual ferocity would rival that of the West," according to Mexican Poet-Diplomat Octavio Paz. In Western pornography, "death spurs pleasures and rules over life. From Sade to the *Story of O*, eroticism is a funeral chant or a sinister pantomime." Reading about sadism can have a cumulative effect, according to Psychoanalyst Ernest van den Haag.

Der Stürmer, a Hitlerite journal that mixed anti-Semitism and sex, contributed to the general atmosphere that made it possible to slaughter Jews, Van Den Haag believes. Similarly, he says, today's sadistic pornography contributes to a general atmosphere in which sadism becomes generally permissible.

There is, however, the question of what comes first. Maybe pornography circulates freely because public standards have already changed; maybe people read about sadism because they are already sadistic. Political Scientist Wilson Carey McWilliams argues this point well: "Degeneracy becomes socially visible, emerging from underground, only when it has reason to expect a welcome. Certainly this is the case in relation to sexuality. Our verbal sexual morals had become nothing more than cant some time ago. Worse, they were a form of hypocrisy which discouraged respect for law."

QUESTION 3: DOES THE FIRST AMENDMENT, WHICH GUARANTEES FREE SPEECH, PROTECT OBSCENITY?

Not until 115 years after the first federal obscenity law was passed did the Supreme Court address itself directly to the constitutionality of such laws. Then, in the Roth case of 1957, it held them, in general, to be constitutional. "Obscenity is not within the area of constitutionally protected speech or press," the majority decided. And what is obscenity? A three-part test soon evolved: 1) the dominant theme of the material taken as a whole must appeal to a prurient interest in sex; 2) the material must be patently offensive because it affronts contemporary community standards; 3) the material must be utterly without redeeming social value.

Whereas the Roth decision generally upheld anti-obscenity laws, the succeeding interpretations of it usually knocked them down. They have, for the moment at least, virtually abolished literary censorship. A further liberalizing decision was made two years ago in *Stanley* v. *Georgia*. The court concluded that obscenity, when it is read or viewed at home, is protected by the Constitution. This decision, it is now argued, implies the right to buy or receive obscenity. In short, decision after decision has opened wider the umbrella of the First Amendment.

However, at the same time, a few cases snapped that umbrella shut again—under specific circumstances. One involved sales to minors. In *Ginsberg* v. *New York*, the court held that states may make it a crime to sell "to minors under 17 years of age material defined to be obscene to them whether or not it would be obscene to adults." The court's reasoning was that "the well-being of

its children is a subject within the state's constitutional power to regulate."
And *Ginzburg* v. *United States* makes it possible to prosecute publishers for
"pandering to the widespread weakness for titillation by pornography," even
if the obscenity of the material being pandered is in doubt.

Thus the law on obscenity is bewildering, even to many lawyers,
though some are gamer than others in defending it. "The landmark case of
Roth," wrote Earl Warren Jr. recently, "is still valuable, and in fact has gained
viability with each succeeding interpretation, even though it now bears little
resemblance to what we originally thought it to be."

QUESTION 4: CAN OBSCENITY LAWS BE ENFORCED?

Stanford Law Professor Herbert Packer declares flatly that a vigorous
campaign of law enforcement against pornography "would involve costs in
money, manpower and invasions of privacy that we as a society are unwilling
to pay." One of the pornography commission's best arguments for repealing
many existing laws was that they have not worked. The trouble begins with
definitions. Justice Potter Stewart says that he cannot define hard-core pornography, but he knows it when he sees it. This is understandable, but is
scarcely a practical basis for criminal indictments.

Nor has the courts' three-part test been much help. How big is the
community? A town, a state, the nation? What is prurient interest? What
about "utterly without redeeming social importance"? Even if something is of
value only to masochists, asks Justice Douglas, how can it be said to be utterly
without social importance? Others argue, in effect, that no law is perfect;
society must do the best it can. "The Sherman antitrust law forbids
monopolies," says Political Scientist Reo Christenson. "What is a monopoly?
What is an unfair trade practice? When is guilt proved beyond a reasonable
doubt? Those indignant over the lack of specificity in obscenity laws are quite
complacent about vagueness in laws they approve."

QUESTION 5: WHAT CAN BE DONE ABOUT PORNOGRAPHY?

Where should the line be drawn against pornography, or should it be
drawn at all? Given the narrow scope left by the courts to the legal definition
of obscenity, strict laws banning pornographic material from adults will not
stand up in court unless the Supreme Court eventually changes its position. In
its eyes, the dangers of inhibiting freedom of expression are far greater than

those presented by pornography. Beset as we are so suddenly with mountains of pornographic trash and with well-meaning arguments for doing away with it all, it is easy to forget the crimes against political freedom, science and the arts that have been committed in the name of morality. Books by Aristophanes, Defoe, Rousseau and Voltaire have been seized by U.S. customs, and Hemingway, Dreiser and Sinclair Lewis were once banned in Boston. Such past errors certainly do not constitute a conclusive argument against censorship, but they do underline one fact: no apparatus of censorship has ever been devised, or probably can be devised, subtle enough to assure the freedom of the arts or of ideas. Nor does the new freedom necessarily mean that the wave of smut will further engulf the nation. Denmark's experiment in legalizing pornography, for instance, by all accounts has resulted in a decline of the Danes' own interest in it, as well as in the number of reported minor crimes like exhibitionism.

It seems wrong to keep pornography from adults who want it; certainly the attempt is also impractical and wasteful of time, money and effort. But this does not mean that nothing at all should be done. If some have a right to pornography, others have an equal right not to have it foisted on them. The New York State legislature last week passed a law that, if signed by the Governor, ought soon to clamp down on Times Square. This kind of regulation would not put pornography back under the counter but it would at least remove it from the shop windows and posters. As for obscene mail, another unpleasant invasion of privacy, 500,000 orders have already been received by the Post Office to block specific advertising material, and 15,000 requests a week are now coming in to stop all sexually oriented ads, under a new law that went into effect Feb. 1.

Equally important, there are legal, enforceable ways of keeping pornography away from minors—those under 18, 17, or possibly 16, whatever age each community decides—and in fact the pornography commission drafted sample legislation for the states. Logically, of course, if pornography cannot be proved to be bad for anyone, there is no more reason to protect minors from it than to protect adults. But there are strong emotional and cultural arguments for doing so. In order to be effective, however, new laws just be specific.

Any regulation at all is anathema to some civil libertarians, who have a respectable and logical position. It was easier to agree with them when pornography was young and reasonably clean—for instance, back in 1949, when Judge Curtis Bok inveighed against censorship. "I should prefer that my own three daughters meet the facts of life in my own library than behind a neighbor's barn," he wrote. But with pornography what it is today, parents may wonder whether their daughters are not actually better off behind the barn than in the library or at the movies. Even liberal Americans may want to set firmer limits on what their daughters—and sons—will be able to see and read. This should be possible without otherwise blocking the free traffic of ideas.

12
OTHER FORMS OF COMMUNICATION

While linguistic systems of communication (both written and oral) have received the most attention in this book, other forms of communication are of great importance in human association and interrelationships. These forms are becoming even more significant in the 1970s. In the first article of this chapter, Mario Pei discusses some of the many other forms by which people communicate.

The next two articles comment on various types of "body language," such as actions, gestures, postures, and facial expressions. From these, one concludes that at times actions do indeed speak louder than words.

Nonlinguistic Systems
Of Communication

Mario Pei

There was speech in their dumbness, language in their very gesture.
Shakespeare, The Winter's Tale

You are traveling along a motor highway. At the side of the road there appears an octagonal signpost, with no lettering on it. If you do not know the code, you will go right on past it, into the arms of a traffic policeman or, more tragically, into a crash. If you know the code, you will come to a full stop. In like manner, a round disk with a cross tells you you are approaching a railroad crossing, a diamond-shaped sign tells you to slow down, a square sign indicates that you are entering a school zone. Most states have now replaced these symbolic signposts with lettered signs, because illiteracy is rapidly diminishing. They depended upon a visual symbolism of shape and served their purpose well when a segment of the driving population was still semiliterate. But the nations of Europe make use of a system of visual road signs that is designed to surmount the language barriers of a continent where over twenty languages are official. The European round sign with a horizontal bar across it means "no entry" or "one way." The transversal bar through a bent arrow that points left means "no left turn." A triangle standing on its apex means "main road ahead." Similar in nature is the international "snow language," used in Canada and other countries where heavy snows present a problem; here there are visual symbols for snow that is smooth, sun eroded, rain eroded, wind eroded, that has a film crust, a wind crust, a feltlike structure, rounded grains or crystal facets.

The red, green, and yellow lights and "blinkers" which are now so common are equally effective, save in cases of color blindness. They depend upon a visual symbolism of color, in which red arbitrarily stands for "stop" or "danger," green for "safety" or "go," yellow for "slow" or a transitional signal, a blinking light for "caution."

You are trying to pass a truck on a narrow highway at night. In response to the tooting of your horn, the truckman flashed his rear outline lights off and on. If you know the code, you know that you can pass him safely. But if instead of signaling with his lights he waves his arm up and down, you know there is a car coming in the opposite direction and drop behind till he gives the welcome flash. Here we have a symbolism of light and one of gesture.

In none of the cases outlined above has there been an interchange of language, spoken or written. There has, however, been an interchange of meaning, a transfer of significant concepts. If we accept only the narrower etymological definition of language as that which is produced by the human vocal organs and received by the hearing apparatus, we shall have to deny the name of "language" to these transfers. If we accept the broader definition of language as any transfer of meaning, they are forms of language differing in degree but not in kind from a spoken or written message.

In their anxiety to restrict language to a pattern of sounds, too many linguists have forgotten that the sound symbols of the spoken tongue are neither more nor less symbolical of human thought and human meaning than the various forms of activity (gestural, pictorial, ideographic, even artistic) by which men have conveyed significant messages to one another since the dawn of history. It is a commonplace among linguists that the spoken language antedates the written language by thousands, perhaps millions, of years. Insofar as the written language is a symbolical replica of the spoken tongue, this is undoubtedly true. But there is little or no assurance that organized sound language, as distinguished from mere animal cries, antedates pictographs painted on the walls of caves or petroglyphs carved on rocks, whose purpose undoubtedly was to convey a significant message or establish a permanent record.

Some scientists claim that certain animal species communicate by nonlinguistic devices; that bees, for example, convey significant messages to one another by odor and by dancing in their hives, or that ants use their antennae in a significant way. Some of the stories in this connection are impressive. The American nighthawk is said to emit varieties of sounds which convey significant messages to its fellows. Dolphins are claimed to possess a mysterious form of communication (extrasensory, perhaps) which permits quasi-human collaboration between two or more of the species. Attempts to get animals and birds to "talk," or at least to understand human speech, range all the way from experiments with the anthropoid apes (a chimpanzee is said to be able to pronounce "papa," "mamma," and "cup" in a hoarse whisper) to the speaking crow, parrot, and mynah bird, whose vocabulary can be quite extensive. Professor Eckstein, of the University of Cincinnati, claims that higher forms of animal life, such as the bird, dog, or chimpanzee, are capable of changing man's words into symbols and thus understanding them. But even in the best attested cases, there is no evidence that any of the animals in question are able to project their "language" into nonimmediate situations, which is a characteristic of all human speech. The dog or bird can give warning of a present, immediate danger or notice of a present, immediate desire; it cannot warn you, as the most primitive human being can, that there is a danger lurking in wait many miles away, or inform you that it desires to do or have something, not now but tomorrow. This nonimmediate feature seems reserved to the systems of communication of human beings, be they oral, gestural, symbolic, pictorial, or written.

Meaning may be transferred by devices that have nothing to do either with the spoken language or with its written counterpart, and this basic proposition few will be so hardy as to deny. A logical corollary is that language as we know it did not necessarily have to become the great thought conveyor that it is. Granted a different historical development, it is conceivable that the human race might have reserved its oral passages for purposes of eating and breathing only and developed an entirely different machinery for the transfer of meaning. That this might have been so is proved by the truly vast number of auxiliary meaning conveyors that the human race has actually devised and employs side by side with the spoken and written language. Our justification for discussing them here lies partly in the fact that they *are* auxiliaries to language, partly in our partiality for the broader definition of language as that which serves to convey meaning, partly in the fact that a historical discussion of language would be incomplete without them.

In the written language, as will be seen in a subsequent chapter, there are two possibilities: the written language may follow the spoken language, symbolizing its sounds, or at least its words; or it may avoid any connection whatsoever with the spoken language and symbolize thoughts, ideas, and objects. In the former eventuality, the written language is, of course, a handmaiden to the spoken tongue; in the latter, it is altogether free of spoken-language restrictions. In either case, it resembles the spoken tongue in that it depends upon symbols which require common acceptance. The same is true of any nonlinguistic system of communication. There must be common agreement upon a symbol before the latter can become meaningful, serve the purposes of transfer, and be dignified, even figuratively, with the name of "language." We may assume that common acceptance of the symbol takes place through a process of individual innovation and piecemeal acceptance rather than through mass creation. The innovator is one who enjoys prestige and is therefore imitated. If the leader of a group decides upon the use of a certain symbol, oral or otherwise, with a given value, a few of his followers will imitate his usage, which later spreads from individual to individual until it becomes universal within the group.

The systems of communication that have been devised by man's fertile brain since the inception of civilization are numerous, not to say innumerable. An interesting question that arises in connection with them is that of historical priority: namely whether and to what extent the mutual acceptance that characterizes them is based on a previous understanding depending upon spoken language. The story of the fall of Troy, for instance, tells us that the news of the final victory was relayed from Asia Minor to Greece by a series of signal fires. Signal fires have been in use ever since and are believed to have led to the use of the heliograph, whereby the sun's rays are reflected from a mirror at significant intervals. But was not the meaning of the signal fires of Troy previously agreed upon through the agency of the spoken tongue?

The same question arises in connection with the tom-tom used by African natives as a long-distance telephone. Its significantly spaced beats antedate the Morse code by several centuries, and their rate of transmission by a skilled operator is as speedy as that of the telegraph. It was once thought that there was no connection between the tom-tom and the spoken language, but more recent research indicates that the two-toned tom-tom imitates the tones of the native words, to which additional "qualifying" words are added to avoid confusion between two or more words having identical tones. This gives us practical assurance that the tone signals were originally arranged at a series of spoken-language conferences. The same may be said of the smoke signals of the American Indians. If it could be proved that all non-linguistic systems of communication were originally systematized through the spoken-language medium, the historical priority of the spoken language would be established. While this proof is readily forthcoming in the case of many systems, it is lacking in others, notably in the field of gestural language.

Certain nonlinguistic forms of communication come close to the spoken, others to the written language. The "uh-huh" uttered in three distinct tones, and without accompanying gestures or nods, to signify "yes," "no," and "maybe" in some sections of the South is so close to spoken language that one is left in doubt whether it should be mentioned in this chapter. Very close to the spoken language is also the whistling language used by the natives of Gomera, in the Canary Islands, who communicate by means of it over very long distances (some say six miles); it seems established, however, that this whistling language is based on Spanish rhythms and pitch. A similar type of whistling language is employed by the natives of Kusnoy, a village in Turkey. The sounds are described as formed with tongue curled around the teeth and lips not puckered but tensely drawn, with the palm of the left hand cupped around the mouth, and high pressure applied from the lungs. The villagers are said to speak, argue, and even woo in whistles.

Volumes have been written on the imitation of animal and bird calls to convey signals, particularly in warfare. In the production of the film *Home of the Brave*, a birdcall specialist was employed to identify and reproduce the twelve Pacific island bird calls used by the Japanese in their surprise attacks, to keep liaison among the advancing units.

Other auditory forms of communication not based on human speech or the vocal organs include U.S. Army bugle calls, over forty in number, each invested with its own peculiar significance; the applause which may take the form not only of hand clapping but also of stamping the feet, banging canes or umbrellas on the floor, or even rushing up to the front and beating the palms of the hands on the stage. There are the long and short blasts of the locomotive whistle, which engineers often use in various combinations for special messages (one short toot for "I'm coming to a stop"; three shorts for I'm about to back up"; four shorts as a request for instructions; two longs to indicate a start).

Symbols of this sort, however, serve to express only one basic emotion or information and are therefore to some extent disqualified for the status of language, which must express a variety of things. On the other hand, they share one important characteristic of language; they are based on mutual agreement and become quite meaningless if the requisite general acceptance is not there. In World War Two, American WACS were quite bewildered by Italian clucks, and Italian girls by American wolf whistles, until the meaning was explained. In like manner, the American hiss in token of disapproval and loud whistling in sign of enthusiastic applause are quite misunderstood in many European countries, where violent disapproval is expressed by whistling and the hiss is never heard. In Japan a variant of the hiss, a loud sucking-in of the breath, betokens polite recognition. Among quasi-vocal sounds that hold different meanings in different lands may be mentioned the "tsk-tsk" which we use to deplore something but which means "no" in the Mediterranean countries and the Near East; our shushing sound to demand quiet, which means "hurry up" in Germany; the "pst-pst" which some countries use to call a cat, others to draw the attention of people. There is even an account of a joint American-Yugoslav attack that failed during the war because the American did not use the right noises to the Yugoslav mules that carried their supplies and so could not get them started.

Laughter can be a language of limited powers. By it we can express friendliness, agreement, flattery, derision, unbelief, surprise, and many other emotions. A giggle may indicate embarrassment or humility and is so used by the Japanese. There are other noises produced through the instrumentality of the vocal organs that do not qualify as standard speech yet carry a burden of meaning. The uncouth "Bronx cheer" is elevated by the Neapolitans, under the euphonic name of *pernacchio*, to a full-fledged semantic post.

One of the most elaborate meaning codes, involving both visual and auditory devices, appears in a pamphlet issued by the Civil Air Patrol for the guidance of owner pilots of private planes. A series of colored lights, red, white, and green, indicates to the pilot while still on the ground a clear take-off, a clear runway, return to ramp, stop; while similar light signals tell the pilot in flight to return and land, to give way and circle, to use caution. In radio communication, pilots use distinctive words as an audible language code to spell out letters (Bravo for B, Juliet for J, X ray for X, Zulu for Z). Then there are visible ground to air signals, eight feet long, where a single L means "require fuel and oil," a double L means "all's well," two L's back to back mean "not understood." Lastly, there are panel signals, given with two- or three-colored cloths, which can also be used at sea, where they have different meanings (yellow-blue-yellow in parallel bars indicates on land the direction of the nearest civilization, at sea the direction of rescue craft). All this is in addition to radio, mirrors, fires built from piles of kindling wood, flares, and smoke grenades.

Other varieties of nonlinguistic forms of communication come close to the written language and are supposed by some to have given rise to it. Under this heading fall firstly the pictographic drawings of prehistoric groups concerning whose ability to speak there is some doubt; secondly the knotted ropes and notched sticks of the ancient Chinese, and South American Indians, and West African and Australian natives. For the first, the question of priority in time appears insoluble. Did the Cro-Magnons and other still more primitive men who developed a very effective rudimentary form of pictorial art, whereby they left significant messages and records, possess speech? Or are their efforts indicative of an abortive tendency to communicate by means of pictures before connected language began? For the second, the problem that poses itself is to what extent the mutual understanding of the symbols in question rested upon a previous linguistic understanding. All we can say with definite assurance is that the meanings conveyed by the ropes and sticks are independent of the spoken languages of their users and of such a nature as to afford the possibility of international use among speakers of different languages. The *quipu*, or "knots," used by the Peruvian Incas, for instance, included red ropes to symbolize soldiers, yellow ropes for gold, white ropes for silver, green ropes for grain, with a single knot signifying 10, two knots 20, a double knot 100, and so forth. The messages conveyed by means of the *quipu* were so complicated that special officials called *quipucamayocuna*, or "keepers of the knots," were ordained to interpret them.

Another curious form of visual symbolism is the Zulus' "language of the beads," where brightly colored beadwork in various patterns can be used to transmit even love letters. Receipt of a beadwork necklace bearing many white beads assures the young Zulu that his bride-to-be thinks highly of him and that all is well. The addition of a few red beads indicates that her heart is full and she is in good health. Purple, symbolical of the sunrise, and yellow, symbolical of the sunset, mean that the young lady misses him particularly at dawn and dusk. But deep yellow means "I'm jealous," and beige-gray means "You are too poor in livestock for me to marry you." "Wish I were with you" is betokened by nut-brown beads.

Before we smile at this symbolic "language" of largely illiterate groups, let us recall that in our own highly developed civilization in a day, not too remote, when only one out of five could read the written sign, figures of Indians were used to indicate tobacco shops, while carved Chinese stood for tea shops, Beau Brummels for tailors. Our brightly colored barbershop poles and the three-ball insignia of pawnshops are in the same class (the latter was in origin a group of three pills, from the coat of arms of the Medici family, which started its existence with medicine as its profession but later shifted to banking and moneylending). The visual symbolism of advertising is not as widespread as it used to be; but who does not recall the old-fashioned phonograph and the listening dog, with or without the caption "His master's voice," or lovely Phoebe Snow traveling in immaculate white along a "Road of Anthracite" which is today run by electricity and Diesel engines?

Hoboes and gypsies have a way of carving symbolic messages on the bark of trees, or scratching them on rocks, for the benefit of their fellows who may follow. A pair of spectacles, in gypsy symbolism, means "Beware! Danger and trouble here!"; but a small circle inside a larger one spells out "Very kind people. Don't impose on them." As early as the seventh century A.D., the Chinese used fingerprints as distinctive signatures on documents, while the illiterate's cross or mark runs through the Middle Ages and down to the end of the nineteenth century.

Perhaps the most elaborate visual code of all is that of medieval heraldry, now widely adopted by our automobile manufacturers. The designs and colors used in the various coats of arms of noble families not only served the purpose of positive identification (in fact, the medieval terminology was "to read someone's arms"), on the battlefield and elsewhere; they also told a complete story. The arms of France's heir to the throne, called Dauphin or Dolphin, for obscure reasons, show a field of black with red diamonds on which are three dolphins diving over a crown. Could anything be plainer than the coat of arms of the city of Oxford, an ox above two wavy lines, to record the fording of the Thames by an ox at the city's present site? In the static "language" of Persian rugs, singing birds portray happiness, brooks symbolize the life force, and trees are indicative of contemplation.

With so many partial systems of visual symbolism in use, it is not to be wondered at that the idea of a system of elaborate picto-ideography for international communications should repeatedly have arisen in the course of the last few centuries. The first serious attempt was made by Leibnitz. More recently, Charles Bliss, an Australian, devised what he called "semantography," a system of one hundred basic visual symbols which could be combined to produce all sorts of complicated meanings. Margaret Mead favors a code of glyphs, or visual symbols, for use at the UN and other international gatherings, and this idea is being actively sponsored by internationally minded groups in Washington and New York.

Another great division of nonlinguistic communication is gestures, which have no connection, save in a few specific instances, with either the spoken or the written language. Here the problem is more complicated. Granted that many conventional modern gestural signals, like those of a baseball umpire, football coach, boxing referee, or traffic policeman, are based upon previous linguistic understanding, the fact nevertheless remains that gestural language is commonly conceded to have preceded oral speech, some say by at least one million years. It is further estimated that some seven hundred thousand distinct elementary gestures can be produced by facial expressions, postures, movements of the arms, wrists, fingers, etc., and their combinations. This imposing array of gestural symbols would be quite sufficient to provide the equivalent of a full-blown modern language. It is quite conceivable: first, that a gestural system of communication could have arisen prior to and independently of spoken language; second, that such a system, had historical conditions been favorable, might have altogether supplanted the spoken tongue; third, that it could today supply the world's needs for an international common system.

The third part of this proposition requires no proof. Many North American Indian tribes are known to have developed a system of sign language whereby members of different groups, speaking dissimilar languages, could carry on lengthy conversations about any topic (the northern tribes generally used two hands, the southern tribes one). The Indian system of sign language has been repeatedly described in books from as far back as the early nineteenth century. It is unaccompanied by facial expressions and characterized by rich imagery. To indicate that one is sad, for instance, one points to oneself, makes the sign for "heart," then draws the hand down and away in the direction of the ground. A question is indicated by rotating the raised hand in a circle by wrist action; a lie by two spread fingers, showing "double talk," or a man with a forked tongue; "friend" by the two forefingers raised together, symbolizing brothers growing up in each other's company.

The International Boy Scout movement, with a courage based on ideological conviction, resolutely adopted the Indian sign language and proceeded to develop a science of pasimology, or gestures, which serves the Jamborees in perfect fashion. Representatives of as many as thirty-seven different nations have met at various times and carried on both general business and private conversations in pasimology. The use of Indian sign language for international purposes has repeatedly been advocated. Sir Richard Paget and the American Tourist Association, in recent times, have both advanced the possibility of "handage" to replace language.

The gesture-language idea was carried on by teachers interested in the training of deaf-mutes. Here, however, we have a secondary ramification. Some deaf-mute language systems express gesturally and by means of facial expressions only ideas and states of mind, in which case they can be internationally used. Others spell out words, which means that a particular language is called into play, whereupon the gestural system becomes a mere auxiliary of the spoken tongue. Still other systems combine both approaches. A fourth approach is that of lip reading and the consequent reproduction of audible speech by the "deaf oralists," but this, of course, is merely a phase of the spoken language.

It is interesting that the American Indians should have contributed to the world's civilization their own particular form of pasimology, used for the avowed purpose of avoiding international language difficulties. Their systematic reduction of meaning to gestures, however, has less developed counterparts in other portions of the world. It has been noted by students of pasimology that many gestural forms are universal. For example, the gestures describing a beard, a headdress, and a cupped hand raised to the mouth denote respectively a man, a woman, and water in Armenia, Russia, among the Australian Bushmen, and among the deaf, while American Indian signs for "child," "man," "no," "tear," and "night" have been traced in Egyptian, Chinese, and Mayan symbols on monuments, representing the same ideas. Both ancient Egyptian and ancient Chinese monuments represent "no" by a pair of outstretched arms or hands.

Gesticulation used as an aid to the spoken language is universal, but to different degrees and with different symbolisms. Southern Europeans use many more gestures than the inhabitants of northern Europe. There is a story that King Ferdinand of Naples, coming back to the city after the 1821 revolt, tried to address the crowd from the balcony of the royal palace but found it impossible to make himself heard above the shouting of the multitude, whereupon he lapsed into a gestural harangue, in which he gave a silent but eloquent series of reproaches, threats, admonishments, and pardons, thus winning over a mob to which those gestures were a part of daily life.

Differences in gestural symbolism are often striking. To the ancient Greeks, a downward nod of the head meant "yes," an upward nod "no." The modern Neapolitans express "no" by an upward jerk of the head, coupled with the sticking out of the lower lip. Americans usually wave goodby with the palm of the hand down, but many Europeans give the same wave with the palm of the hand up and the fingers moving back and forth, which gives their signal a come-hither look. An Italian downward motion of the forearm, with the extended fingers sweeping down past the chin, which they barely touch, means "nothing doing!," while a wave of the forearm, with the fingers and thumb cupped close together and coming to a point, means "What is it all about?" Wolf whistles and clucks to express admiration of feminine charms give way, in many parts of the world, to visual gestures, such as pressing the forefinger into the cheek, or even both forefingers into both cheeks, while at the same time rolling the eyes. South Americans will often open one eye wide with thumb and forefinger; a word translation of this gesture would probably run: "My, but you're an eyeful!"

Among ancient gestures that have given rise to language clichés is the *pollice verso* ("thumbs down," in our parlance, but the thumb was actually turned up) of the ancient Romans, which meant death to the gladiator who had been overcome. The Romans' expression for "to applaud" was *pollicem premere* ("to press the thumb"), but actually they displayed their approval by clapping, snapping their fingers, and waving the flaps of their togas.

A few special gestures have interesting historical origins. Our military salute goes back to medieval times, when knights raised the visors of their helmets on meeting so they could recognize one another. The Fascist salute, with extended arm and outstretched hand, goes back to the days of ancient Rome; its significance was in origin a peaceful one, indicating that there was no concealed weapon, and the American Indians used a very similar greeting. The clenched fist of the Communists arose in opposition to the Fascist salute.

Gesticulation used for a specific, even professional, purpose is an ancient phenomenon. In the traditional dancing language of Japan, China, Korea, Indo-China, and Indonesia there is a series of conventionalized gestures which serve to convey both the narrative and the emotional states that are to be symbolized. Among the latter, there are said to be some two hundred symbols to express various phases of love. The flirt language of the fan, widely used by lovers in past centuries, conveyed very complicated messages.

The casino croupiers of Monte Carlo also have developed a complete system of sign language. Finger tips touching the table mean, "There's a chiseler here"; a finger behind the ear is a distress call for the head man; the finger of one hand touching the thumb of the other means, "O.K.; let him play"; crossed index and third finger is "please take over"; palm and fingers extended downward means "They are cleaned out."

In all these phases of gesturing, however, previous understanding achieved by linguistic means is implicit. The same may be said of scientific and semiscientific systems of communication such as semaphores, flags, cable codes, and the universal weather-reporting code, intelligible in all parts of the world, devised by the meteorological division of International Civilian Aviation and based upon the use of groups of five figures.

To the question why did gestural language not become generalized in the place of spoken language, a fairly satisfactory, though somewhat mechanistic, answer was given by Darwin. Gestural language requires use of the hands, while the spoken language can operate in the dark and around obstacles. On the other hand, the international advantages of gestural language are more apparent than real, since spoken language could, if desired, be made equally international, while gestural language, as has been seen, is not necessarily international in scope. Even the greater expressiveness and emotional release of gestural language is largely hypothetical, in view of what can be and is achieved along these lines by the spoken tongues.

In sum, systems of communication not based on speech, while extremely useful on specific occasions, are generally inferior to the spoken tongue as meaning conveyors. The one great exception to this general statement is writing, which by sublimating and multiplying symbolical values has succeeded in implanting itself by the side of the spoken tongue, of which it is a substitute and an auxiliary, to the point where some prefer it and consider it an instrument of transfer superior to its oral counterpart.

Can You Influence
People Through
"Body Language"?

Julius Fast

THE BUS WAS crowded when Peter boarded it and he found himself close to a very pretty girl. Peter enjoyed the bus ride and admired the girl; in fact, he couldn't keep his eyes off her. Staring at her, he noticed that she had light blue eyes and dark brown hair, a pleasant combination.

His innocent enjoyment was shattered when the girl turned to him angrily before she left the bus and said loudly, "You should be ashamed of yourself!"

"What did I do?" Peter asked the driver in honest bewilderment. "I only looked at her."

"It takes all kinds. . . " the driver shrugged, but did he mean Peter or the girl? Peter spent a miserable evening wondering just what he had done that was wrong. He would have known what was wrong if he understood some of the rules of body language. Peter violated a very basic law. He looked at the girl beyond the proper looking time.

For every situation there is a proper looking time, a definite period during which you are allowed to meet and hold someone's eyes. In an elevator the time is so brief that it can hardly be considered looking at all. Your eye catches that of a stranger and you look away at once. In a crowded bus, a subway or train, you can look a little longer. But go beyond the proper time—some 10 seconds—and you violate the unwritten but rigid code of body

306

language and take the chance of getting into the same situation that embarrassed Peter.

The girl Peter admired interpreted his stare as insolent or arrogant or insulting in the same way that a cripple interprets the stares of the curious. If we have any consideration, we look only briefly at a cripple or a deformed person, pretending not to look at all.

We look at celebrities in the same way, taking care not to catch their eyes, not to stare at them with too curious a look.

The unwritten laws of body language allow a longer time for staring when we talk to someone, but it is still a limited time. In all conversations we look away frequently and break eye contact. Only a lecturer or a politician addressing an audience can hold eye contact as long as he wishes.

Just what are these unwritten laws of body language? For that matter, just what is body language? Are the rules learned or are they acquired instinctively? Do we all know them, or are they something we must learn? If so, how do we learn them?

These questions have intrigued psychologists ever since they discovered that we communicate with more than the words we speak. Words are only one part of communication. How we use those words is another part. Are our voices loud, angry, overbearing, confident, soft, shy? The quality of a voice can communicate as much as the words. The same words can be tender, mocking, sarcastic or angry, depending on how they are said. We can signal our own authority by talking in a loud, overbearing way. We can use the same words to signal our humility by talking softly and hesitantly. But even beyond voice communication, there are the messages our bodies send out constantly. Sometimes the body message reinforces the words. Sometimes the messages are sent with no accompanying words and we speak in body language alone.

But what gestures make up body language? Most of us are familiar with the common hand gestures. Some people cannot talk without using their hands. They reach out as they explain, almost shaping the words, emphasizing and exaggerating and punctuating with their hands. Other people hardly use their hands at all when they talk. How people use their hands and whether they use them depends on their cultural background. Italians are great hand movers. So are Russians and Latin Americans. Englishmen are stingy about their hand movements; they appear as more controlled and rigid in their behavior.

In the United States, almost any type of hand movement can be found because we have a mixture of cultures. American etiquette books tell us that waving the hands and gesticulating is ill-mannered and distasteful. It is "unrefined." Refined behavior is always tight and formal. True etiquette can be equated with control and discipline. It can also be equated with an Anglo-Saxon, overcontrolled culture. But our cultural mix in the last century has been too much for books of etiquette.

It is just this cultural mix in America that makes some men more eloquent than others. When body language is used to emphasize the spoken language, to reinforce it, the man who cannot use it is crippled. Too many politicians, awkward with their hands, have learned this to their sorrow. Many have had their images revamped by a reeducation in body language.

A man who uses hand movements when he talks appears freer, more open and more honest to an audience than a controlled nonmover. At certain times, however, a limited amount of hand movement indicates things like solidity, reliability and confidence.

A good politician knows this instinctively and matches his hand movements to the image he wishes to project. Former President Johnson was apparently taught the proper hand movements because his image was too distant and withdrawn. There was a period, before he learned the gestures, when he appeared awkward and uncomfortable.

It seems obvious that President Nixon has had his body language changed and tailored to match his new image. He does not come across now as the same man who lost the election to John Kennedy in 1960, and the change is largely due to a more controlled, but not nearly so stiff, body movement.

Fiorello H. La Guardia, New York City's mayor in the '30's and early '40's, used to campaign in English, Italian, and Yiddish. When he spoke Italian he had one set of hand gestures, another set for Yiddish and still a third for English. Each language demanded its own set of body-language gestures.

But body language is more than hand movements. The eyes play a large part, too. Try holding a fellow pedestrian's eyes a bit longer than the proper time. You create an awkward situation and often the only solution is to smile and offer a casual remark, "How are you?" or "Nice day." You may find yourself in conversation with a complete stranger.

The eyes give hidden signals as well as obvious ones. Scientists have found that the pupils dilate unconsciously under pleasant circumstances. Show a man a naked lady, or show a woman a pretty baby, and their pupils dilate. Do the pupils also dilate when a man has a good hand at poker? If so, then perhaps the "natural" poker player is one who unconsciously reads this body-language sign.

What of the rest of the body? Does it also send out unconscious signals? It does, and the fact that these signals are unconscious means that they are beyond our control. We are not aware that we are sending them out and, therefore, they are more honest than words. It is easy to lie with our voices. but harder to lie with our bodies.

Actors are the exception to this rule. They are trained to lie with their bodies. Recently I talked to Lily Tomlin, who plays a number of characters on "Laugh-In." One of them, a telephone operator, is a masterpiece of body language. The operator torments a customer as she plucks at her breast and twists her face and body. Discussing her movements I told Miss Tomlin that the breast-touching indicated loneliness and introversion; the foot-twisting, self-satisfaction.

"That's what she is," Miss Tomlin agreed. "Lonely and yet self-satisfied with what she is doing. The gestures? They just came naturally once I knew the character."

This is an unconscious adoption of body-language gestures by an actress who first created the character, then lived it and, in living it, naturally used the right body-language gestures.

In addition to the messages we send with our bodies, we also use the space around us to communicate. All of us have our own territories—comfortable distances that we like to keep between us and our friends. We stay closer to people we love, farther away from strangers. When a stranger intrudes on our territory—comes too close to us—we may find it uncomfortable. If the intruder is a wife or husband or lover, we may like the intrusion. It tells us, "I care for you. I love you."

Parents often use space to dominate a child. By looming over him, a parent proves her superiority. The child feels the parent as overpowering and himself as helpless. On the other hand, a parent can draw a child into the circle of her arms and by forcibly invading his space, communicate love and warmth. To do this more easily, the parent may kneel down to the child's level and do away with the looming quality of an adult-child encounter.

Teachers, too, can take a tip from body language in relating to their pupils. The teacher who sits behind a desk is placing an obstacle, the desk, between herself and her pupils. In body language she's saying, "I am your superior. I am here to teach you. You must obey me."

Many educators feel that this is an important and necessary attitude to establish if any "real" teaching is to be done. Other teachers, however, try to do away with the barrier of a desk. They perch on the edge of it and have nothing between them and their students. Still others feel that this is an elevated position, putting the teacher above the student and creating resistance to the teacher. They prefer a position in the center of the room, surrounded by the students, some of whom must turn in their seats to face the teacher.

"This," a teacher once explained to me, "puts me in the center of things. I never sit in a student's seat because I'd be too low. I'd be no better than a student, and a teacher has to be better or why be a teacher? I sit on a student's desk in the center of the room. I'm one of them and yet still a teacher. You'd be amazed at how well they respond."

She is using space to communicate a body-language message. "I'm one of you. I'm on your side even though I'm your teacher."

Which method is most efficient? It's hard to say, except that each teacher must adopt the method that works best for her. If her body language is restricted and tight, sitting on a student's desk may seem simply an affectation—false and unnatural.

The use of desk as a protective device is familiar to everyone who has watched the Johnny Carson show. Carson uses a desk to separate himself from his guests and to achieve a certain formality. David Frost, when he interviews a guest, does away with a desk and sometimes even does away with chairs, sitting on the stage steps with his guest and using territorial invasion and touch to communicate closeness and warmth. Frost's interviews have a different quality from Carson's because of this different use of space. Perhaps not better, but surely more personal.

The quality of an interview depends not only on the body language of the interviewer, but on his personality as well, and every personality has its own characteristic body-language gestures, even as each culture has its own gestures. We shake our heads up and down for "yes." In India they use the same gesture for "no." To really understand a person's body language we must understand something of their personality, as well as something of their cultural background.

But there are some gestures, such as smiles, that seem to cut across cultural lines. In America there are many common gestures in spite of our cultural mix. Arm-crossing and leg-crossing are two of them. If someone is trying to persuade us and we cross our arms tightly, it is often a sign of resistance. Crossed legs can also be a sign of resistance. When a woman crosses them tightly at the knees and at the ankles, sort of intertwining them, it may indicate resistance to sexuality or a tight, closed personality. (However, it may also be a necessary pose because she's wearing a miniskirt.)

Women in pants tend to give better clues to their emotions by the positioning of their legs. They can sprawl out comfortably. If they sit with open laps they may indicate acceptance, not only sexually, but also intellectually. The well-organized woman may tend to run her legs parallel–as orderly as her life. But I say "tend" because these are still just tendencies. With a skirt, parallel legs are simply a model's pose. Girls are taught in charm schools that this is more graceful. They are also taught the proper arm-crossing.

If all this is true, can we ever really tell anything from a person's body language? Can we use it to control other people or to interpret the true meaning of the messages they send?

We can. We can learn certain tricks of domination to control a situation. We can arrange to be higher than our subordinates, or we can allow our boss to be higher than we are. We can be aware that we dominate our children when we hover over them, that certain facial gestures should be matched to certain body gestures for a smoother appearance–but these are tricks and rather superficial. The real value of body language lies in the insight it can give to our behavior.

Are we tight and rigid about life in general? Our body language can give us a clue to how we are acting and allow us to change our behavior for the better. How a woman sits next to a man on a couch contains a dozen clues to her personality. Does she use her arms as a barrier? Does she cross her legs away from him? Does she turn her body toward him?

How we react to other people's zones of privacy, and how strong our territorial needs are, give other clues. Do we feel uncomfortable when people are close to us? Are we afraid of touching, of being touched? If we are, it might be a sign of our own insecurity, our own fear of revealing ourselves. Understanding this can allow us to take the first step toward dropping the barriers that stand between us and the world.

Only when these barriers begin to fall is it possible to realize not only our own potential as human beings, but the potential of the entire world around us.

Body Language

SATURDAY REVIEW OF EDUCATION

SEVERAL YEARS AGO a psychology professor at Stanford was teaching a graduate course in Skinnerian theory. His students secretly decided to try behavior modification on the professor himself. They wanted him to lecture as if he were Napoleon Bonaparte.

Whenever his right hand came near his torso, the students would lean forward, open their eyes wide, and start taking notes. Whenever he slumped or slurred or gestured with his right hand, they would look away, feign boredom, and talk to each other.

By the end of the semester, the professor was unknowingly lecturing in short, crisp sentences, standing stern and rigid, with his right hand inserted into his shirt over his stomach.

Body language is always present in the classroom, although not usually as an intentional device of the students. Yet most teachers are insensitive to facial or body cues inside their own classrooms. A study conducted by Nathan Maccoby at Stanford found that experienced teachers were little better than novices in judging whether children had understood their lessons.

Using hidden cameras, Maccoby filmed student behavior as the teachers conducted regular classes. Teachers were then shown the film and asked to predict how their students would fare in an objective test on the lesson's contents. Teachers were no better than other observers at perceiving nonverbal cues (amount of blinking, raising of eyebrows, hands on the face, etc.).

"Educators," says Dr. Charles Galloway, a leading authority on body language in the classroom, "are multi-sensory organisms who only *occasionally* talk." Yet he points out, little attention is paid to their nonverbal behavior. In a normal, nonprofessional conversation, the total message communicated is estimated at 55 per cent facial, 38 per cent vocal, but only 7 per cent verbal. Here are some typical nonverbal cues found in most classrooms.

EYE CONTACT

Sometimes a student will avoid eye contact when the teacher asks him a question. He may act very busy taking notes, rearranging his books and papers, dropping a pencil. Non-verbally he is saying to the teacher, "I don't know the answer; I don't want to be called on." Eye contact signals that the communication channel is open.

ARMS EXTENDING

Have you ever seen a professor lecture all period without moving his hands at all? Galloway has shown that teachers who extend their arms toward the class have students who test better than teachers who keep their hands in their pockets. Arm movement can also communicate specific feelings. People more often stand with their hands on their hips when they are talking with people they dislike than with those they like. Arm folding is known to show disapproval and defensiveness.

NODDING

Teachers who nod affirmatively to their students encourage them to respond more and to respond better. Depending upon individual teacher, grade level, and class size, the optimum number of nods is usually one every 30 seconds. However, if the teacher consciously adopts the 30-second pattern, the kids pick it up, and it becomes ineffective.

HAND RAISING

In volunteering classroom information, a clever student knows how to make his raised arm look tired, as if he's been waiting interminably to be called on. He also knows how to raise his hand tentatively, as if he does *not* want to be called on. It seems that the hand-raising technique is not innate; students learn all these subtleties by around the fourth grade.

TERRITORY

Teachers stand; students sit. The teacher puts himself at the front of the class, placing a buffer zone between himself at the first line of students. Standing higher and removing himself from the masses, the teacher nonverbally insists on his superiority in the classroom. "In the past," Galloway points out, "teachers moved around their desks as if they were isles of security. They rarely ventured into the territories of student residence unless they wished to check or monitor seat-work. To move forward or away from students signifies relationships. Distance establishes the status of interaction."

A professional educator, then, needs to move about the classroom, make repeated eye contact with his students, extend his arms, nod, smile, and encourage nonverbal responses from his students. A recent study made use of time-lapse photographs of a high school social studies class, the photographs candidly revealed changes in the students' posture as the class progressed. As the teacher droned on and boredom set in, students slumped lower and lower in their seats. At the final bell, some students could hardly be seen above their desk top, but the teacher was oblivious to what was happening before him. It is essential not only that an educator be understood but also that he understand how he is being understood.

13

MODERN LIVING AND BEHAVIOR

This chapter on modern living and behavior opens with an article on a lighter subject: poker and the many expressions it has contributed to the English language.

The next article criticizes the excessive and debased language of violent protest so common during recent years. In a closely related essay, Melvin Maddocks argues that the contemporary American is so overwhelmed with a deluge of words that words have a tendency to lose both their meaning and their effect. Thus, echoing the views of other observers, Maddocks finds that there is the danger that much of value will be lost from the American language.

You'd Be *Tongue-Tied*
Without Poker

WEBB GARRISON

STRIP OUR LANGUAGE of words or phrases that got their present meaning from the game of poker and your everyday conversation might lose a lot of its fizz (not a poker term).

The word *bluff* is old in the English language, and has many meanings. One obsolete meaning is "blindness"; in fact *bluff* is a term for a horse's blinkers.

Now poker is a game where you go it blind. You bet that your cards are better than cards hidden from your view in others' hands. You can do just about anything to mislead your opponents about your own holding, to which *they* are blind. You can put on acts. Tell outrageous lies. In poker, Hoyle says, anything can go, short of cheating. Poker is such a blind game that it was called *bluff* (meaning blind) as frequently as it was called *poker* in its early days. The "blind" meaning of *bluff* died out of our general language entirely. In poker, bluff came to mean an act one puts on to deceive his "blind" opponents, especially the act of a player who bets strongly with a poor hand to scare out all the players with better hands, and thus steal the pot.

Today, when we say somebody is *bluffing*, meaning "faking," we owe the usage to poker. And the fellow who is not scared off by someone else's bluster *calls his bluff*, whether in poker, politics, business or whatever.

Ante, of course, is a Latin word meaning "before." In poker it was used in exactly that sense, to describe chips that players were required to put in the pot *before* the cards were even dealt. Of course, all poker players didn't speak Latin, and in no time *ante* didn't mean "before" to them, it only meant the ante in poker. Which is why, when we tell somebody to *ante up*, we mean for him to pay what he owes. It's plain English. In Latin it is most confusing.

People wear three kinds of faces in poker: happy, sad and straight.

The real tough players never change expression. Their faces are set and immobile, neither happy nor sad, whether they hold nothing better than a 9-high hand or a royal flush. They are unreadable. And so, of course, anyone whose facial expression never changes has a *poker face*. Straight-faced Helen Wills Moody, the great tennis star, was affectionately known to a whole generation as "Little Miss Poker Face."

Almost every way in which we use *ace* in our common language is a poker usage. In some situations, in five-card stud poker, the man whose single hidden, or "hole," card is an ace *knows* that his hand is better than all the others. The others can only guess, and may be inclined to bet against a man who needn't see their hidden cards to know he is best. Hence, in any situation in which you secretly know you have the best of others you have an *ace in the hole*. That's legal. But if you have an *ace up your sleeve* you are cheating to win.

If, among your equals, you are your boss' favorite, you stand *aces high* with him. That's because in poker, where two or more hands are tied—in that each has a straight, or a flush, or a pair, or two pairs, or a full house—the holding topped by an ace or by aces beats all others. *Aces high* are tops among equals.

And then there's the fellow who drew one card to improve his hand, and if he'd gotten an ace he would have held the winning combination. He was *within an ace* of victory.

Of course, not all of this is surprising, especially to poker players. But our language debt to poker simply goes on and on and on. It was poker that decreed that when all the talking, bluffing and betting ends, the remaining players must reveal their cards to determine the winner, in a *showdown*. Now we have showdowns in war, politics, business or to bring any argument to an end. It's the hard moment of truth after all the jockeying.

Pray what is a *clip joint*? Originally, it was a gambling establishment in which the houseman had special *clips* up his sleeves to hold cards that he could sneak into his hand to win a big pot for the house in poker. A *clip joint* soon became any low dive (or even a fancy night club) where you could expect to be cheated if you were sucker enough to venture in.

Poker went up the Mississippi on river boats and spread east and west.

Equipment was often crude. A token was frequently used to indicate the position of the deal, being passed along from dealer to the next player on his left. One of the commonest pocket objects available was a big-bladed knife with a buckhorn handle, known as a "buck."

Sometimes a cautious gambler wanted to avoid the responsibility of the deal. Certain advantages go with the deal, but in the old West an accusation of stacking the deck could be followed by bullets before you could say, "I did not, either." When the knife came to a man who wanted no part of such doings, he slyly shoved it along to the next man. Today, if you try to avoid responsibility in anything, someone may accuse you of *passing the buck*.

And, of course, we use *to deal from a stacked deck* to mean that one has fixed just anything his way, in a shady manner, from the start. Or, if you haven't a chance of succeeding in just anything, *the cards are stacked against you*.

Poker has a very clumsy term, known as the "age." The person who has the last turn to bet in a round of betting is the age, or has the age. The word may possibly have meant "senior," the "most aged" turn in the round of betting. There is advantage in having the age, for you needn't commit yourself until you have heard what everyone else has had to say about betting his hand.

Perhaps because it is a clumsy term, it never made much literal sense to poker players and they easily changed it to *edge*, based purely on its sound, without reference to its meaning. Anyway, today it isn't only in poker that you *have the edge* on someone if you have the advantage of him. The *age* or *edge* is a dead term in poker in many parts of the country today, where variations of the game which give a special role to the age, such as "blind and straddle," have gone into disfavor.

For a game whose vocabulary was to color the language of a continent, poker had a strangely inconspicuous start. Nobody knows who actually invented it.

French sailors are thought to have blended their own *Poque*, or *Poche* (meaning "pocket"), with an Oriental game such as the *As Nas* of old Persia. Their queer hybrid proved to have a strange fascination for everyone who became acquainted with it. "Pocket" has the same sense as "blind"—the hidden cards might as well be in your opponents' pockets and it is quite clear that *poker* itself came from *Poque* or *Poche*. There were already plenty of pastimes designed to help redistribute wealth. None of them had the precise flair that makes poker unique—a game compounded upon approximately equal portions of luck, skill with cards and proficiency in psychology.

Almost from the beginning, poker experts preferred to use special counters, called chips, instead of cash. This means that on every deal, those who wanted to stay in the game had to *chip in*. Today your neighbor may ask you to chip in for the Red Cross.

Blue chips were commonly valued at $25 and up—always more than red or white chips—which is why the very best stocks, bonds and other negotiables on Wall Street are called *blue chip* securities.

No matter what their color, chips were swapped for cash when the game ended for the night. Win, lose or draw, it was all over. So the gambling phrase became linked with the game of life. When one dies he is said to *cash in his chips*.

It is absolutely illegal in poker to withdraw a bet once you have placed it in the pot. You can't change your mind. Thus when *the chips are down* you must face the music. The time for backing out is over, and not only in poker. In battle, the soldier likes a man by his side who's still there when the chips are down.

Experts say that in ordinary play, using 52 cards and no joker, there are 2,598,960 possible poker hands. Precisely 1,302,540 of them have less value than one pair.

This adds tremendously to the tension of a popular version of draw poker. Said to have originated in Toledo about 1870, its distinctive rules stipulate that play can be opened only by a man who has a pair of jacks or better.

The game is called jackpot. Every man must ante before the deal. If nobody has jacks or better, the hand is thrown in, the pot stays on the table and there is a new ante all around and a new deal. In one variation called "progressive jackpots" it then takes a pair of queens or better to open—if that fails, a pair of kings, then a pair of aces. With a new ante each time from each player, and with a higher and higher holding needed to open, the pot can grow without any winner. Finally someone can open, and two rounds of betting follow—once on the opening round and again when those who stay in have drawn new cards. The pot is now so big that temptation for all players to chip in for one more round, in hopes of improving even a poor hand on the draw, tends to swell the pot even more. The final winner now takes the whole pot—guaranteed to be a big one. And thus, into our language, came the phrase for receiving any windfall of a large size—*hitting the jackpot*.

Whether poker or pinochle players were the first to allude coyly to a special fund "to buy milk for the cat" is uncertain. Poker seems to have started it. In poker, money to pay for the cards, buy drinks for the players, tip a bellhop for setting up the table in a hotel room, etc., may be set aside a little at a time from each pot, and held in a separate container. "What's that for?" challenges a greenhorn, seeing part of his first winnings withdrawn. "Why, it's to feed the kitty," the other players sneer, thus obtusely suggesting he abide by the rules of the group and not ask questions. Let's hope the greenhorn doesn't look around the room for the cat.

The special fund or container has become the *kitty*, and putting money in it from the pot is *feeding the kitty*.

Long since, the term ran through our language. "Let's throw a party for the kids," suggests a member of a social club. "There isn't enough in the kitty," snaps the treasurer. Later the members vote a special assessment to have the party anyway. Now the treasurer rattles a cup in front of the member who first proposed it. "Come on, feed the kitty," he says.

Cheaters in poker added more than *clip joint, stacked deck* and *something up one's sleeve* to our language. A player might risk *holding out* a good card when tossing his hand in, to put it slyly to use, if possible, after the next deal. That's why you may be said to *hold out* for your own terms on a business deal, hoping to get a better break; though it isn't necessarily dishonest.

According to Webster, the word "deal" comes from an old English word "dele" meaning to separate. But it is odd that *dealing* cards and *dealing* in goods carry meanings allied to the act of putting things on a table. A "deal" once meant a fir plank, and from that a table top. Dealing cards is not only separating them, but spreading them on the table. And one of the oldest forms of dealing in business was the act of a merchant in spreading his wares out on a table or counter for people to select them. "Table" itself has become a verb in parliamentary law—the act of "tabling" a proposition that a group doesn't want to discuss by "laying it on the table."

In any event, many of our uses of the word *deal* come from poker and other card games, especially those in the sense of setting forth terms or conditions, i.e.: "what cards we will hold." *New deal, fair deal, raw deal, dirty deal, square deal* all refer to wanting a "new hand" or having been dealt cards honestly or dishonestly. A union whose power to strike could cripple an industry may "hold all the cards" or at least the *best of the deal*.

Many shades of this use of *deal* spring not precisely from the mere act of dealing cards, but from the custom in many poker games of permitting each player to name the variation of poker that will be played when he is the dealer. "What's the deal?" means "What kind of a game are we playing this time?"

Or, in any situation in life, "What plan are we agreed on?" It also means, "What is your proposition?"

A dealer who is trying to preserve his last few chips may elect to play a game in which the total betting is not apt to go high, to the exasperation of the big money men. Their reaction may be a cynical, "Big deal!" . . . Meaning, of course, "What a pathetic proposition!"

No matter how much they have been bluffing, if the last bet in a poker game has been called, all the active players must put their hidden cards on the table, face up, for all to see. Hence, of course, *lay your cards on the table* is in the language as an imperative to tell the truth about what's on your mind. And when you reveal what you've secretly been up to all along, you *show your hand.*

Pat is a good old English word, one of whose meanings is that something is exactly right or exactly suited to a purpose or occasion. An argument in support of something which offers all the favorable elements and omits anything contradictory may be said to be "just too pat."

Poker picked up the word "pat" and put "stand" in front of it. In draw poker, a player who is perfectly happy with the first five cards dealt him refuses to discard any of his holding and draw new cards when he has the right to do so. What he already holds is exactly suited to his purpose, so he *stands pat.* (And did you see that word *discard* back there, meaning to get rid of cards? Without it, you could sometimes find yourself tongue-tied in ordinary conversation. You might use "sluff off" of course—but that's a card-game word, too.)

A player who stands pat has a dangerous holding, in the eyes of his opponents. At the very least he has a natural straight, unless he's bluffing. It could even be an unbeatable royal flush. His pals don't waste any love on a fellow who holds such a strong hand that he won't budge from his position. Mark Hanna, the noted political leader, blasted Republicans as *standpatters* when they refused to lower the record-high tariff of 1897. He didn't mean that their position was exactly right. Far from it. Just that they were unpleasantly inflexible. The emotional overtones of standing pat in poker, rather than its precise meaning, have ever since applied to a *standpatter* in human affairs. He's just stubborn.

During an evening of play, the cards absorb body heat from players' hands, and their temperature rises slightly. If some cheater had a perfectly matching deck, already stacked in his favor, and slyly intruded it into the game, some of the experts might suspect just from the chill of their cards that they'd been *slipped a cold deck*. That's what someone does whenever he secretly changes the conditions of what you think are the agreed terms of a transaction.

Before much had been written about poker it had already become the favorite game of innumerable people in all walks of life. Its language spread first by word of mouth. Tradition has it that Henry Clay and Daniel Webster once boosted a pot to $4,000, long before any literary people admitted in writing that the game existed. No significant work was written purely about the game until 1871. That year, a treatise appeared by one Robert S. Schenck. No western gambler, he was our Envoy Extraordinary to Britain, and his work started when he jotted down the rules of the game for the edification of Queen Victoria. A storm of criticism broke over his head for explaining so vulgar a game to the Queen. But the record indicates that he was unperturbed, stood pat and refused to draw new cards. He called his critics' bluff and published his work.

Without writing specifically about poker, Brett Harte and Mark Twain spiced many of their finest tales with its language. Harte's "Outcasts of Poker Flat," is an American classic.

Crusaders in California only a few years ago tried to close local card rooms and found that they couldn't shut down poker-playing establishments. Under a state law, poker is considered a game of skill and is exempt from anti-gambling statutes.

Most players would agree that the law is just and proper. Skill and nerve govern the play of the game. For example, given suitable circumstances, a shrewd operator can convince opponents in five-card stud that, if his four face-up cards are spades, his hold card is also a spade, and he has a flush (five cards all in one suit). His hole card may be a club, heart or diamond, making his hand worthless. But nobody will know he is a *four-flusher* unless they pay to find out. Luck has nothing to do with making them back down. His skill in dissembling is everything.

There's nothing wrong with this kind of *four-flushing*, it's part of the game. But then there's the crook who, at the showdown, claims to win with a flush. He shows four hearts, and just the red corner of a diamond, pretending that it too is a heart. This fellow is an out-and-out crook, a low-down, ornery four-flusher. When it's his deal he may have the deck stacked and riffle the cards without really mixing them. Then he gives you a *fast shuffle*.

In nearly all other card games it is absolutely illegal to tell lies. But until the showdown, there's nothing in the least dishonorable in lying about your hand in poker. Hence the other players don't eject a player from the game and stop speaking to him forever if he makes a lot of big noises about the great strength of a weak hand while pondering whether to bet or not. They simply tell him to bet or drop out, to *put his money where his mouth is, to put up or shut up*. That's mild to what they'd do to him in bridge. He could be ruled out of tournament play for any intended verbal deceit. It's far more serious than *talking a good game* in poker.

Violent Protest:
A Debased Language

Time

Words, LIKE TREES, bend with the prevailing wind. In the climate of opinion of the past few years, the word dissent has undergone a decided transformation. For most of U.S. history, it clearly meant speech—the unorthodox opinion, the challenging idea. Then, during the 1960s, civil rights protesters took to the streets to fight segregation, and the word became associated with demonstrations as much as with speech. As protests have continued to broaden and increase, dissent has come to be used to describe and defend a wide variety of physical acts, including violence toward property and even toward people.

The explanation many protesters offer for their switch from verbal to physical dissent is that no one pays attention to words alone any longer. However eloquent it has been, however imaginative its uses, language has not succeeded in eliminating racial discrimination or ending the war in Indochina. So the protesters have resorted to what Social Psychologist Franklyn Haiman of Northwestern University calls "body rhetoric"—sit-ins, lie-ins, marches —and more and more bodies have started colliding. Such public confrontations are an expression of gathering frustration over a society that no longer seems to respond to more traditional forms of dissent.

COMMUNICATION OF FEELING

This argument contains a measure of truth. It is also true that in many cases the massed forces of dissent—as at most of last week's rallies mourning the Kent State four—have demonstrated a commendable restraint in not letting verbal protest build into violence. The fact remains, however, that all too often these days dissent is a matter of arson and rock throwing. The reason may be that protesters have despaired of the efficiency of words before they have really mastered them. It is significant that this generation of dissenters has failed to produce a literature, or even a polemic that is likely to endure. On the contrary, it has been persistently, even proudly, nonverbal. It has emphasized a communication of feeling rather than of words. The vocabulary of protest, often weighted down with an outmoded Marxism, is relentlessly conventional and conformist. The same phrases—"up against the wall," "get the pigs," "tell it like it is"—are endlessly repeated, less for their intrinsic eloquence than for their emotive and symbolic value. And that sort of thing gets tiresome; to borrow the jargon, it "turns people off." Even the most outrageous obscenities lose their impact when they are used ad nauseam.

There is often a disconcerting inexactness about today's rhetoric of dissent. To denounce the Establishment in blanket terms makes little sense in a society composed of several establishments, each with its own ideology and set of mores—many of them surprisingly competitive. "Power to the people" is an admirable democratic slogan—except that, as used presently, what it really seems to mean is power to the leftist radicals who seek to control any revolution in America. It is verbal overkill to describe every mild demurral by whites against the most bluntly radical of black-militant demands as nothing but "racism." And the case for political dissent is weakened when almost any attempts, however peaceful, by college authorities to restore law and order on campus are automatically condemned by militant radicals as proof that the U.S. is a "fascist Amerika." Taken at face value, many protest slogans suggest that the dissenters have seriously misestimated U.S. society and its possibility for evolutionary change.

The ultimate debasement of language, of course, is violence. Except for protesters who simply want to destroy—and there are more than a few—most dissenters turn to violence in a desperate effort to communicate their profound feelings of grievance. Yet surely this is too crude a way to get their message across. A bomb, for example, lacks specificity; its meaning is as scattered as its debris. Some people may interpret such an act as a signal to pay more attention to the protester and his cause; many more are likely to read into it a need to make life a lot tougher for the protester. Violence is, essentially, a confession of ultimate inarticulateness.

Throughout history, dissent has been more effectively expressed by the word than by the weapon. The French Revolution was betrayed by the ruthless masters of the Terror who silenced all opposition with the guillotine. The enduring importance of the revolution lies, rather, in the principles enunciated on its behalf by the philosopers of the Enlightenment, who bequeathed the notion of human equality to the modern world. During its bleakest hours, the American Revolution was resuscitated not so much by brilliant military strategy as by brilliant words—those of Tom Paine in the "times that try men's souls." Even less persuasive and more recondite words can have an impact that dramatic acts do not. Wrote Lord Keynes: "Madmen in authority, who hear voices in the air, are distilling their frenzy from some academic scribbler of a few years back. I am sure that the power of vested interests is vastly exaggerated compared with the gradual encroachment of ideas."

Debasement of the language cannot be blamed on protesters alone. The news media, the advertising agencies, the Government—even President Nixon himself—have all helped flatten and attenuate the English tongue. When radicals misuse language, they are only applying the lesson they have been so well taught by their society. That lesson has been reinforced by philosophers now in fashion—Marshall McLuhan, for instance, who says that pictures are more important than words and contemplates a society of inarticulate tribal emotions based on instant sight and sound. Or Herbert Marcuse, who teaches that protesting words are as empty as air in a technological society where power is concentrated in a few hands. Such a contempt for language makes people impatient with the orderly processes of thought. No sooner is something glimpsed or considered than it is demanded. Not only is dialogue destroyed, but so is rationality, when protesters insist upon immediate capitulation to their "nonnegotiable demands." This is what infants demand—and totalitarians.

EXAMPLE OF AGNEW

Reactionary as the thought may seem, words are still as powerful a force as ever, when they are cogently used. It was, after all, language alone that catapulted Spiro Agnew from a political nonentity to a national figure with an enthusiastic personal following. Agnew, to be sure, can be accused of appealing to the raw emotions of the body politic in his now-famous attacks on "effete snobs" and "tomentose exhibitionists." On the other hand, a protester would have a hard time telling the Vice President that mere speech is not capable of stirring people. Unwittingly, he has shown his antagonists on the left that it can still be done.

During a period of national turmoil and self-doubt, it is all the more imperative for protesters to put down their rocks and find their voices again. As a commentary on the Kent State tragedy, President Nixon's remark that "when dissent turns to violence it invites tragedy" is callously inadequate. His warning, however, carries the weight of history: in a general unleashing of violence, dissent is the first casualty. Today the nation is in considerable need of healing, as well as elevating, language; often in the past that need has been filled by protesters whose perspective on society matched their passionate commitment to its improvement. Now is the time for dissenters to assert their own dignity and maintain their tradition by upholding the ultimate value of the word.

The Limitations
Of Language

MELVIN MADDOCKS

IN J. M. G. LE CLÉZIO'S novel *The Flood*, the anti-hero is a young man
suffering from a unique malady. Words–the deluge of daily words–have
overloaded his circuits. Even when he is strolling down the street, minding his
own business, his poor brain jerks under the impact of instructions (WALK–
DON'T WALK), threats (TRESPASSERS WILL BE PROSECUTED), and newsstand
alarms (PLANE CRASH AT TEL AVIV). Finally, Le Clézio's Everyman goes
numb–nature's last defense. Spoken words become mere sounds, a
meaningless buzz in the ears. The most urgent printed words–a poem by
Baudelaire, a proclamation of war–have no more profound effect than the
advice he reads (without really reading) on a book of matches: PLEASE CLOSE
COVER BEFORE STRIKING.

If one must give a name to Le Clézio's disease, perhaps semantic aphasia
will do. Semantic aphasia is that numbness of ear, mind and heart–that tone
deafness to the very meaning of language–which results from the habitual and
prolonged abuse of words. As an isolated phenomenon, it can be amusing if
not downright irritating. But when it becomes epidemic, it signals a disastrous
decline in the skills of communication, to that mumbling low point where
language does almost the opposite of what it was created for. With frightening perversity–the evidence mounts daily–words now seem to cut off and
isolate, to cause more misunderstandings than they prevent.

Semantic aphasia is the monstrous insensitivity that allows generals to call war "pacification," union leaders to describe strikes or slowdowns as "job actions," and politicians to applaud even moderately progressive programs as "revolutions." Semantic aphasia is also the near-pathological blitheness that permits three different advertisers in the same women's magazine to call a wig and two dress lines "liberated."

So far, so familiar. Whenever the ravishing of the English language comes up for perfunctory headshaking, politicians, journalists, and ad writers almost invariably get cast as Three Horsemen of the Apocalypse. The perennially identified culprits are guilty as charged, God knows. At their worst–and how often they are!–they seem to address the world through a bad PA system. Does it matter what they actually say? They capture your attention, right? They are word manipulators–the carnival barkers of life who misuse language to pitch and con and make the quick kill.

So let's hear all the old boos, all the dirty sneers. Paste a sticker proclaiming STAMP OUT AGNEWSPEAK on every bumper. Take the ribbons out of the typewriters of all reporters and rewrite-men. Force six packs a day on the guy who wrote "Winston tastes good *like* . . . " Would that cure for semantic aphasia were that simple.

What about, for example, the aphasics of the counterculture? The ad writers may dingdong catch phrases like Pavlov's bells in order to produce saliva. The Movement propagandist rings his chimes ("Fascist!" "Pig!" "Honky!" "Male chauvinist!") to produce spit. More stammer than grammar, as Dwight Macdonald put it, the counter-culture makes inarticulateness an ideal, debasing words into clenched fists ("Right on!") and exclamation points ("Oh, wow!"). Semantic aphasia on the right, semantic aphasia on the left. Between the excesses of square and hip rhetoric the language is in the way of being torn apart.

The semantic aphasia examined so far might be diagnosed as a hysterical compulsion to simplify. Whether pushing fluoride toothpaste or Women's Lib, the rhetoric tends to begin, rather than end, at an extreme. But there is a second, quite different variety of the disease: overcomplication. It damages the language less spectacularly but no less fatally than oversimplification. Its practitioners are commonly known as specialists. Instead of unjustified clarity they offer unjustified obscurity. Whether his discipline is biophysics or medieval Latin, the specialist jealously guards trade secrets by writing and speaking a private jargon that bears only marginal resemblances to English. Cult words encrust his sentences like barnacles, slowing progress, affecting the steering. And the awful truth is that everybody is a specialist at something.

If the oversimplifier fakes being a poet, the overcomplicator fakes being a scientist. Perhaps it is unfair to pick on economists rather than anybody else—except that they are, after all, talking about money. And as often as not it turns out to be our money. Here is a master clarifier-by-smokescreen discussing the recruiting possibilities of a volunteer army if wages, military (W_m) are nudged seductively in the direction of wages, civilian (W_c): "However, when one considers that a military aversion factor must be added to W_c or subtracted from W_m, assuming average aversion is positive, and that only a portion of military wages are perceived, the wage ratio is certainly less than unity and our observations could easily lie on the increasing elasticity segment of the supply curve." All clear, everyone?

The ultimate criticism of the overcomplicator is not that he fuzzes but that he fudges. If the cardinal sin of the oversimplifier is to inflate the trivial, the cardinal sin of the overcomplicator is to flatten the magnificent—or just pretend that it is not there. In the vocabulary of the '70s, there is an adequate language for fanaticism, but none for ordinary, quiet conviction. And there are almost no words left to express the concerns of honor, duty or piety.

For the noble idea leveled with a thud, see your nearest modern Bible. "Vanity of vanities, saith the Preacher . . . " In one new version his words become, "A vapor of vapors! Thinnest of vapors! All is vapor!"—turning the most passionate cry in the literature of nihilism into a spiritual weather report. The new rendition may be a more literal expression of the Hebrew original, but at what a cost in grace and power.

Who will protect the language from all those oversimplifiers and overcomplicators who kill meaning with shouts or smother it with cautious mumbles? In theory, certain professions should serve as a sort of palace guard sworn to defend the mother tongue with their lives. Alas, the enemy is within the gates. Educators talk gobbledygook about "non-abrasive systems intervention" and "low structure–low consideration teaching style." Another profession guilty of non-defense is lexicography. With proud humility today's dictionary editor abdicates even as arbiter, refusing to recognize any standards but usage. If enough people misuse disinterested as a synonym for uninterested, Webster's will honor it as a synonym. If enough people say infer when they mean imply, then that becomes its meaning in the eyes of a dictionary editor.

Con Edison can be fined for contaminating the Hudson. Legislation can force Detroit to clean up automobile exhausts. What can one do to punish the semantic aphasics for polluting their native language? None of man's specialties of self-destruction—despoilation of the environment, overpopulation, even war—appear more ingrained than his gift for fouling his mother tongue. Yet nobody dies of semantic aphasia, and by and large it gets complained about with a low-priority tut-tut.

The reason we rate semantic aphasia so low—somewhere between athlete's foot and the common cold on the scale of national perils—is that we don't understand the deeper implications of the disease. In his classic essay, *Politics and the English Language*, George Orwell pointed out what should be obvious—that sloppy language makes for sloppy thought. Emerson went so far as to suggest that bad rhetoric meant bad men. Semantic aphasia, both men recognized, kills after all. "And the Lord said: 'Go to, let us go down, and there confound their language, that they may not understand one another's speech.' " Is there a more ominous curse in the Bible? It breathes hard upon us at this time of frantic change, when old purposes slip out from under the words that used to cover them, leaving the words like tombstones over empty graves.

How, then, does one rescue language? How are words repaired, put back in shape, restored to accuracy and eloquence, made faithful again to the commands of the mind and the heart? There is, sadly enough, no easy answer. Sincerity is of little help to clichés, even in a suicide note, as Aldous Huxley once remarked. Read, if you can, the Latinized techno-pieties of most ecologists. Good intentions are not likely to produce another Shakespeare or a Bible translation equivalent to that produced by King James' bench of learned men. They wrote when English was young, vital and untutored. English in 1971 is an old, overworked language, freshened sporadically only by foreign borrowings or the flickering, vulgar piquancy of slang. All of us—from the admen with their jingles to the tin-eared scholars with their jargon—are victims as well as victimizers of the language we have inherited.

Concerning aphasia, the sole source of optimism is the logic of necessity. No matter how carelessly or how viciously man abuses the language he has inherited, he simply cannot live without it. Even Woodstock Nation cannot survive on an oral diet of grunts and expletives. Mankind craves definition as he craves lost innocence. He simply does not know what his life means until he says it. Until the day he dies he will grapple with mystery by trying to find the word for it. "The limits of my language," Ludwig Wittgenstein observed, "are the limits of my world." Man's purifying motive is that he cannot let go of the Adam urge to name things—and finally, out of his unbearable solitude, to pronounce to others his own identity.

14
THE FUTURE OF ENGLISH

The final chapter of this book is devoted to the future of English. In the opening essay Mario Pei discusses the possible revolt against the wide use of English around the world as countries increasingly assert their cultural independence and stress their own national heritage.

The chapter closes with a forecast by the same writer on the state of the English language a century from now.

The Revolt
Against English

MARIO PEI

ANY COMPETENT SOCIOLOGIST will readily admit that the way in which a language is viewed internationally depends in large measure upon the prestige of its speakers. But "prestige" is a very elastic term and lends itself to a variety of interpretations. What constitutes prestige? Is it a nation's military might; its financial and economic power; its scientific and cultural achievements; a combination of all these, plus that very elusive psychological factor often summarized under the term "good will"? Granted that the status of certain languages is grounded in history, do the current forms of behavior of its speakers, or the vicissitudes those speakers may be undergoing, have a reflection in the way the language is regarded and sought after?

Historically, languages have risen and fallen with the people who spoke them, even though centuries may have intervened between the rise and fall of the speakers and the rise and fall of the language. The Latin of the Roman Empire, once established as a world language, continued in that role, though in modified form, through the Middle Ages and early Renaissance. The international prestige of French, initiated at the time of the Crusades, underwent numerous ups and downs before it blossomed forth into the position of prominence it held from the sixteenth to the late nineteenth century. English, beginning its career of overseas conquests in the seventeenth century, finally burst forth in the twentieth, particularly during and after the Second World War.

Americans, who were isolationists in matters of language as well as politics down to the 1940s, became acutely language-conscious when some 12,000,000 of our young men and women were scattered over the earth. But at the same time that we were giving up our insular mentality and accepting far-flung commitments, we began to develop a form of linguistic neoisolationism. This was based on premises altogether different from the old, which was rooted in indifference to the rest of the world. Now the argument ran: "Everybody is learning English. The world wants to use English. English is the world language of the future." The unspoken corollary was: "So we don't really need to learn other languages."

This attitude is fully reflected in high school and college foreign language enrollments. After an impressive spurt in the days of the war and the launching of Sputnik, they again became fairly stationary. Now, only about 35 per cent of all high school and college students are studying one or more foreign languages. This is a higher percentage than we had thirty years ago, but it doesn't measure up to that in other countries. Also, the percentage rate of increase is nearing a halt.

Is the premise "Everybody wants to learn and speak English" really valid, or are there omens of change? Let us remind ourselves that there are other old, established languages which had to take a back seat while we enjoyed a status of absolute preponderance in all fields during and after World War II. It is unrealistic to expect the speakers of these languages to continue to worship at the English shrine now that their economies are back in working order. Let us also remember that there has been unleashed upon the world, for better or for worse, a series of exasperated neonationalisms (they are often masked under the guise of anticolonialism), affecting primarily the newly formed nations. These necessarily have linguistic as well as other manifestations. Lastly, it is a psychological quirk in human nature that when we don't like the speakers, we also don't like their language.

This is superlatively an American reaction, attested by the fact that the bottom dropped out of the study of German during World War I, and that in World War II the study of German, Italian, and even French (looked upon as the tongue of Vichy–Pétain and Laval) suffered extensively. Other countries are seldom as childish as we in this respect; they continue to study the languages of actual and potential enemies on grounds of self-defense, if nothing else. But even they are to some extent influenced by factors of like and dislike. The British segment of the English-speaking world has grown progressively weaker and less influential in recent times, the American segment more unpopular. All this adds up to a revolt against English, a phenomenon which is still in its infancy, but of which there are clear indications.

Only a few months ago a distinguished scientist wrote me a long letter of which the following is the gist:

> I feel quite strongly that the people who worry what the international language shall be may already have had that decision made for them. Not that a truly international language is now in existence, but I feel that a trend in that direction has already taken place to such an extent that it could be reversed only by a very major upheaval in the world's power structure.

The writer goes on to tell to what extent he feels that English has already become an international language. He cites the Scandinavian countries, where, it seemed, everybody he met spoke English; the fact that the signs at the Moscow airport are in Russian and English; that the proceedings of the scientific society to which he belongs were conducted largely in English, though on Soviet soil. He then describes the preponderant use of English in international scientific journals. He concludes: "Although the process is far from complete, English has an enormous head start toward becoming the international language in tourism and science. I believe this is matched in trade, aviation, military affairs, and communications."

This picture is probably accurate as far as it goes. What it fails to take into account is the underground rumble of revolt, of which we have a number of distressing symptoms. The growing predominance of English has always been viewed with a jaundiced eye by the speakers of French, the great European language of diplomacy and culture. Under the leadership of President Charles de Gaulle, who poses a serious threat to the Anglo-Saxon world, French speakers' resentment finally burst its bounds late last year in a U.N. resolution designed to offer a sizable salary bonus to those U.N. employees who could use French as well as English in their work. France wasn't alone in sponsoring this motion. She was backed by no fewer than thirty-six other states, including French-speaking African countries and (this is perhaps the most painful blow) a number of Latin American states, which also avowed their intention to press for greater use of Spanish at the next General Assembly session.

In demanding their "legitimate rights," the advocates of French also complained about a report that had unnecessarily praised "the excellence and influence of the English language." At the same time, it was brought out that UNESCO carries on most of its work in French, not English, and that the French Foreign Ministry spends nearly half its budget to maintain 32,000 French teachers abroad and to export French books. Of course, the English-speaking nations have been doing the same thing with their British Council and Ford Foundation schools and their USIA and other libraries, so they should not mind the competition.

In one of his speeches dealing with Quebec, President de Gaulle said: "Whether the French language loses or wins, the battle of Canada will weigh heavily in the struggle that is being waged for it from one end of the world to the other." The "battle of Canada" is going rather well for French. By recent accounts, 5,000 English-speaking federal employees are being taught French at a cost of more than $5,000,000, and there are plans to teach 12,000 more. French-speaking Canadians will no longer put up with a situation such as that in Ottawa where they "must speak English almost all the time to succeed." Not content with taking the Union Jack out of the Canadian flag, French Canadians now want to revise the national anthem so that every line will be bilingual:

> O Canada! Our home—*nôtre pays*.
> *La feuille d'érable*: one flag from sea to sea.

For other U.N. languages, it is known that Soviet representatives have almost invariably used Russian in their addresses, letting the translation chips fall where they might. The Chinese Nationalist delegation has almost as invariably used English, but on their one and only appearance at a U.N. session the Chinese Communists insisted on using Mandarin. In the recent Near Eastern crisis, we were regaled with speeches made in Arabic, which is not an official U.N. tongue. Whatever the causes of the special dispensation on this occasion, the principle was established that other tongues besides the official five could on occasion be used.

This goes hand in hand, perhaps, with other manifestations of rampant linguistic nationalism, such as the giant study demonstration against the use of English that forced Delhi University in India to close down last December. These demonstrations, it is true, were both preceded and followed by similar outbreaks in Madras against the use of Hindi as the sole national language and, if only by implication, in favor of the retention of English as a co-official language for all of India.

Until recently Africa had been singularly quiescent on the linguistic front, with most of the nations seemingly content to retain the old colonizing languages—notably English and French—as the common communications medium in countries where there are dozens of mutually incomprehensible native tongues. But a survey was recently initiated, with the collaboration of the national universities of Ethiopia and Kenya and UCLA, to determine which, if any, of the local languages could serve, with a little encouragement, as official national tongues, to be used widely on radio and TV, in school classrooms, in the selection of standard forms, and the creation of scientific and literary terminologies. It was pointed out that Swahili, which is fairly common in East African countries, might easily qualify. It is equally significant that there has been a modest interest in learning Swahili both in Britain and in the United States. We expect English to become the international language, but it doesn't hurt to be on the safe side.

At the same time, countries and cities in all the former colonial areas have been renamed in accordance with local tongues. In the Congo, such names as Leopoldville, Stanleyville, and Elisabethville have disappeared. Northern Rhodesia has turned into Zambia; Tanganyika and Bechuanaland have now changed their names to the localized Tanzania and Botswana. In the Far East—where Batavia turned into Jakarta many years ago—the capital of the Malaysian state of Sabah changed its name very recently from Jesselton to Kinabalu, because Jesselton, named for a British empire-builder, represented the old colonialism.

Some derisive comments appeared recently in the American press over the fact that the Italian State Railways, which already uses English, French, and German in its official timetables, had decided to add Esperanto. But Esperanto is a symbol of linguistic independence to many citizens of smaller nations, which cannot hope to compete for the post of international language. Their argument runs: "Why must speakers of languages like English and French always have the advantage of being able to use their own tongues, while we, whose tongue no one bothers to learn, must forever defer to them? Let's have some equality by using a language which is native to nobody and which everyone must make an effort to learn!"

It may be admitted at this point that other big languages have their troubles, too, in the face of old or rising nationalisms. French, which wants to spread its influence throughout the world, encounters occasional resistance on its own soil by speakers of Breton, Catalan, German, and Italian. Spain has long had trouble with its users of Catalan and Basque. The speakers of Ukrainian, unable to resist Russification on their own soil, sometimes link language and statehood in their protests abroad. On the main island of Britain, Welsh and Scottish nationalists extol the merits of their Cymric and Gaelic tongues over English.

Nationalism is still abroad in the world, and language is one of nationalism's chief standard-bearers. Rightly or wrongly, English-speakers are accused of not only military and economic but also cultural and linguistic imperialism. As these accusations mount, the rosy path of international English may acquire a few brambles and briars as yet unsuspected by those who claim that the trend to English is irreversible.

English in 2061:
A Forecast

Mario Pei

If a modern-day Rip Van Winkle went to sleep and didn't wake up for 100 years, how well would he be able to understand an American of 2061?

It does not take a linguist to know that language changes. Educated laymen know that the language they speak was once Elizabethan English (a little difficult to follow today, especially in the pronunciation of Shakesperian actors), and before that the half-incomprehensible language of Chaucer, and before that the Anglo-Saxon that no one today can read, let alone speak, unless he has had a graduate course in it.

Yet many people fail to realize that language is also going to change in the future. The English of 1,000 years from now (granted that English is still a living tongue by the year 2961 A.D.) will probably be as different from the language of *Saturday Review* as the latter is from the spoken tongue of the Venerable Bede.

The big difference between the past and the future is that we know, or can reconstruct with some degree of accuracy, what has happened in the past, while we have no way of knowing—or so it sometimes seems—what course the future will take.

But is the last proposition altogether true? We know that governments, business organizations, even private individuals make projections into the future, based on present tendencies and trends. These forecasts do not, of course, have the same value as recorded history, since they may be thrown completely out of kilter by the unexpected or accidental. Nevertheless, barring the unexpected, it is quite possible for our government experts to say: "We anticipate that the population of the United States, growing at an average yearly rate of about 2,000,000, will reach the 200 million mark, more or less, by 1970." In like manner, a business firm may say: "Our profits have grown about $1,000,000 a year over the past ten years. Barring a major depression, we estimate that by 1965 they will be about $5,000,000 higher than they are today." When you estimate your income tax for a year that is just beginning, as the Treasury Department somewhat unreasonably asks you to do, you go through this process of reasoning: "My income over the past five years has been about $10,000. As of this moment, I cannot anticipate any sizable change. Therefore, I am putting down the same figures for 1961 that appear in my 1960 declaration."

It is quite possible to do the same thing with language, always with the understanding that some outside factor may come along to knock the calculation into a cocked hat. One such factor in the development of the English language, for instance, was the Danish invasions of England that antedated the Norman Conquest. One effect of them is that today we say, "Take the knife and cut the steak" instead of "Nim the metter and sned the oxflesh," which is the logical development of the Anglo-Saxon of King Alfred without Scandinavian interference. Another factor was 1066 itself, by reason of which we say, "The army pays out large sums of money" instead of "The here tells out great tales of gild."

A projection of the English language into the future on the basis of present-day indications is something like the predictions of an IBM machine on election night when only the first 2,000,000 votes are in. It can be fascinating, though many things may come along to upset our predictions. Nevertheless, despite the hazards, the questions can legitimately be asked: What can we prophesy at this moment about the English of 100 years hence? How will our descendants of 2061 A.D. speak and write?

By looking at the changes that have taken place in the past, and at the way the language is changing now, I think we can make some reasonable predictions.

Let us first of all recall that language consists of sounds (or phonemes, which are sounds that are distinctively significant to the speakers); of grammatical forms (like *love, loves, loved,* or *see, sees, saw, seen,* or *child, children*); of word arrangements, like the characteristic "John loves Mary," which indicates that John, coming before the verb, is the doer of the action, and Mary, coming after the verb, the recipient; and of individual words, laden with their distinctive meanings. Language change may and does occur in any of these four divisions: phonology, morphology, syntax, and vocabulary.

But the changes do not occur at the same rate or to the same extent in all four. In times of trouble and stress, when communities become isolated, or when an alien tongue comes in direct contact with the native language of an area, changes in sound and grammatical structure seem favored; when conditions are stable, sounds and grammar change moderately, but vocabulary grows quickly.

For this reason, the big sound-and-grammar changes in the English tongue took place primarily in the days of the Anglo-Saxons, the Danes, and the Normans, then again through the troublous times that preceded the stabilization of English society down to the days of Queen Elizabeth I. There were numerous vocabulary changes in those days, too, but the most dramatic vocabulary accretions have come since the dawn of the scientific era.

Our projection for the next hundred years, assuming there will be no major cataclysm (such as an atomic war that plunges us back into medieval conditions), therefore involves a very limited amount of sound changes, a very moderate amount of grammatical transformation, and extensive vocabulary changes, mainly along the lines of accretion.

In the sounds of our language, the omens point to a process of stabilization and standardization, with local dialectal variants tending to be replaced by a uniform style of pronunciation. Indeed, it is likely that even the cleavage between British and American English will tend to be effaced. There are many reasons for this. Large, centralized government units, easy communication between speakers of different areas, widespread trade and travel, and widespread education all favor unification and standardization. This was proved in the days of the Roman Empire, when a strong central government, good roads, unrestricted trade among the provinces and a fairly good educational system (at least for that period) led to the use of a standardized Latin throughout the western part of the Empire and a standardized Greek in the eastern regions. Today we have not only the American Union and the British Commonwealth, with their highly centralized features; we also have highways, railroads, swift ships, and jet planes, bringing the speakers of the various English-speaking areas into fast and easy contact with one another; we have public schooling for all social classes, with illiteracy practically eliminated;

above all, we have the ubiquitous printing presses, radio, TV, and spoken films, bringing a standard King's English and a standard General American to all readers, viewers, and listeners. The local dialects will probably never quite disappear; but they will be driven more and more underground, particularly with the new generations of speakers. Only those mispronunciations that have spread throughout the country, like *marjerine* for *margarine* and *Febuary* for *February*, will come out on top. As for the cleavage between British and American English, the tendency has been toward reunification since the First World War. Spoken British films were almost incomprehensible to American audiences when they first appeared, while American plays presented in England often were accompanied by printed glossaries in the programs (or should we spell it programmes?). Today, a British accent barely causes us to strain our ears, while the British have grown quite accustomed to the Midwestern voice. Actually, we are slowly and insensibly modifying some of our forms of pronunciation to conform with the British, and they are doing the same with regard to ours.

The pronunciation of the year 2061 will probably not differ very widely from the General American of our best radio and TV announcers today. There will be an elimination of marked vulgarisms and localisms, which will be looked upon as old-fashioned (Cicero, writing in the first century B.C., used such expressions as *rustici dicebant*, "the rustics used to say," and *rustico sermone significabat*, "in rustic speech used to mean"; his use of the imperfect past in this connection is a dead giveaway that these local forms of speech had gone out of fashion by his day).

In the matter of grammatical forms and arrangements, our language today is far too standardized to permit of much change. It is possible that a few stray levelings may take place (*oxes* and *deers* for *oxen* and *deer*, for instance; or *I heared him* in the place of *I heard him*). But despite the widespread rantings of the apostles of "usage" (however that much-belabored word may be defined), it is not likely that substandard forms will make much headway. The primary reason for this is that such substandard forms are normally in the nature of localisms. Such rank atrocities as "Them dogs are us'ns," "I seen the both'n of 'em," and "I'll call you up, without I can't" are too localized to survive the impact of schools and TV. The only grammatical changes that have a real chance of becoming part of the standard language are those that have nation-wide currency, such as "It's me," "Who did you see?" and "ain't." Judgment may be suspended for some ignorant uses in sentences like "I should of done it" and "I seen him."

One historical factor that may blast our calculations to smithereens, however, is the possible growth of a pidginized form of English for international use, and its influence upon the native speakers. If this happens, it is possible that we may get such analogical standardizations as *childs, mouses, gooses, foots* (so that all nouns may form their plurals the same way without exception), and *I did see, I did go* for *I saw, I went* (so that the basically simple English verb may be further simplified by having a universally regular past).

The really big changes will come in vocabulary. It will be the multiplicity of new words that will really make the English of 2061 a startingly different language from that of today.

Here there are several factors at work. As man's activities become increasingly complex and multiform, new words have to be coined, combined, borrowed, or otherwise created to take care of such activities. All we have to do is to go over the list of vocabulary accretions since 1900 to realize what is in store for the language in the next hundred years. Think of *futurama, micromatic, jitterbug, genocide, corny, snafu, gremlin, smog, zoot-suit*—all words that would have been meaningless to Dickens or Edgar Allan Poe. Add to these the words of specialized fields of activity (*megavolt* and *psychosomatic, electronic* and *morphophonemic, isotope* and *positron, kodak* and *latex*), and consider also the words that pre-existed the turn of the century, but which are now used in a variety of new acceptances (*atomic fission, integration, featherbed, release,* etc.). It is easy to see that the language of the future will be only partly comprehensible to the speaker of present-day English, even if the basic sounds, forms, sentence structures, and connecting words remain largely unchanged.

The future tongue will sound, from the point of view of present-day speakers, somewhat like double-talk or, better yet, those nonsense sentences that linguists often construct when they want to get away from meaning and concentrate on form-sentences in which the sounds, the grammatical forms, the word order, and the connecting words are all standard English, but in which the vocabulary is imaginary: something like "Foring mests larry no granning sunners in the rones." Yet this vocabulary will of course be easily understood by speakers who have grown up with it.

How many of our present, current, everyday words will be altogether obsolete, or even archaic, by 2061? A good many, no doubt. All we have to do is to look closely at the vocabulary of 100 years ago and notice how many words were in current use that we can still recognize, but would not think of using ourselves, words like *drawing-room* and *trencher, conscript* and *sparking light, eximious* and *mansuetude,* or, to go a little further, *vocular* and *viduous, gossipaceous* and *dandiacal*. If we care to go a few centuries further back, we can find *deruncinate* and *suppeditate, whirlicote* and *begeck, yuke* and *pringle, toom* and *mizzle, jarkmen* and *priggers, assation* and *clancular, dignotion* and *exolution*.

Since the language of radio and TV, in the English-speaking countries, is largely a matter of commercial promotion, a special word may be in order for the future ramifications of the Madison Avenue tongue.

In the field of sounds, the promotional language tends to avoid, save for occasional picturesque effect, localisms and special accents. It is a powerful, perhaps the most powerful, factor in the standardization we anticipate. It is only occasionally that we get a deliberate distortion of pronunciation, like *halo* for *hello*. This laudable conservatism does not, by the way, extend to spelling. Forms like *nite, kool, Duz*, and *chaise lounge* are there to plague us, and to confuse the foreigner and even the native learner of English.

In grammar and syntax, the language of promotion tends toward those vulgarisms that are nation-wide ("like a cigarette should" is a good example), but not toward local or extreme forms.

In the advertising vocabulary, two distinct and contradictory trends are noticeable. One is the tendency to stress the short, pithy, monosyllabic elements of vocabulary, as when an earlier "If headaches persist or recur frequently" was replaced by "if headaches hang on too long or keep coming back." But side by side with this, we have droves of commercialized scientific and pseudoscientific long words, like *hydramatic* and *irradiated, homogenized* and *naugahyde, chlorophyll* and *duridium* even *oldsmobility* and *beaverette*.

One grammatical peculiarity of the language of commercialism is the avoidance of the personal pronouns *it* and *they*, replaced with endless and annoying repetitions of the name of the sponsor or product. This may eventually lead an as yet unborn chronicler of the English language to say in the year 2061: "Personal pronouns, still quite alive in British English, are obsolescent in American. This is particularly true of the third person neuter pronoun *it*, which only the older generation of American English speakers occasionally use today. Instead, Americans prefer to repeat the noun over and over again, often with ludicrous effects."

But all in all, despite the multiplying of human activity, the advances of science and its nomenclature, the ravages of commercialism, it seems to this writer that we are not justified in expecting too radical a change in the language, particularly in its sound-and-grammar structure, provided the present trends continue.

Remember, though, that this picture may be violently changed by the unexpected and unforeseeable. A historical upset, a political upheaval, a military disaster may place the English language in swift motion once more, so that a century or two could bring on the same differences that appear between the Anglo-Saxon of Aelfric and the Middle English of Chaucer.

BIBLIOGRAPHY

GENERAL WORKS

Abrahams, Roger D. and Rudolph C. Troike, Editors. *Language and Cultural Diversity in American Education.* Englewood Cliffs, New Jersey: Prentice-Hall, Inc., 1972.

Abrams, Charles. *The Language of Cities.* New York: Equinox, 1971.

Adler, Bill. *Graffiti.* New York: Pyramid Books, 1967.

Adler, Mortimer J. and Charles Van Doren. *How to Read a Book.* New York: Simon and Schuster, 1972.

Asimov, Isaac. *More Words of Science.* Boston: Houghton Mifflin Company, 1972.

Asimov, Isaac. *Words of Science and the History Behind Them.* New York: New American Library, 1969.

Bailey, Richard W. and Jay L. Robinson. *Varieties of Present-Day English.* New York: Macmillan Company, 1973.

Baugh, Albert C. *History of the English Language.* 2nd Edition. New York: Appleton-Century-Crofts, 1957.

Barnett, Lincoln. *The Treasure of Our Tongue.* New York: Alfred A. Knopf, 1964.

Berry, Thomas E. *The Study of Language.* Encino, Calif.: Dickenson Publishing Company, 1971.

Bloomfield, Morton W. and Leonard Newmark. *A Linguistic Introduction to the History of English.* New York: Alfred A. Knopf, 1963.

Borgmann, Dmitri A. *Language on Vacation: An Olio of Orthographical Oddities.* New York: Charles Scribner's Sons, 1965.

Caldwell, Nancy. *Word People.* New York: Random House, 1971.

Chomsky, Noam. *Aspects of the Theory of Snytax.* Cambridge, Mass.: M. I. T. Press, 1965.

Chomsky, Noam. *Language and Mind.* New York: Harcourt Brace Jovanovich, 1972.

Clark, Virginia et al. *Language: Introductory Readings.* New York: St. Martin's Press, 1972.

Dean, Leonard F. et al. *The Play of Language.* New York: Oxford University Press, 1971.

Dillard, James. *Black English.* New York: Random House, 1973.

Estrin, Herman A. and Esther Lloyd-Jones. *How Many Roads? . . . The '70s.* Beverly Hills, Calif.: Glencoe Press, 1970.

Fast, Julius. *Body Language.* New York: Pocket Books, 1971.

Finne, W. Bruce and Thomas Erskine, Editors. *Words on Words: A Language Reader.* New York: Random House, 1971.

Funk, Wilfred. *Word Origins and Their Romantic Stories.* New York: Funk and Wagnalls, 1968.

Gleason, Henry Allan. *Linguistics and English Grammar.* New York: Holt, Rinehart and Winston, 1965.

Gleeson, Patrick and Nancy Wakefield. *Language and Culture: A Reader.* Columbus, Ohio: Charles E. Merrill Company, 1968.

Greenough, James Bradstreet and George L. Kittredge. *Words and Their Ways in English Speech.* Boston: Beacon Press, 1962.

Guth, Hans P. *English for a New Generation.* New York: McGraw-Hill Book Company, 1973.

Guth, Hans P. *English Today and Tomorrow.* Englewood Cliffs, New Jersey: Prentice Hall, 1964.

Hall, Edward T. *The Silent Language.* Greenwich, Conn.: Fawcett Publications, 1959.

Hayakawa, S. I. *Language in Thought and Action.* 3rd Edition. New York: Harcourt Brace Jovanovich, 1972.

Hayakawa, S. I., Editor. *The Use and Misuse of Language.* Greenwich, Conn.: Fawcett Publications, Inc., 1962.

Katz, Jerrol J. *The Philosophy of Language.* New York: Harper & Row, 1966.

Keils, R. M. "Pentagon English Is a Sort of Newspeak." *College Composition and Communication* (a publication of National Council of Teachers of English), Vol. XXIV, No. 5, December, 1973, pp. 386-391. This is an interesting and thought-provoking article, although the author mistakenly relates the expression "the GI's"—referring to diarrhea—to the army term "General Issue." The medical term derives from "gastro-intestinal," and has no military significance, even though many soldiers are subject to such disorders through accidents of their calling. Dr. Estrin asked that we include Mr. Keils's article in this volume, but we were unable, on short notice, to find the author to obtain his permission to reprint. We do recommend close attention to the media indexes and to the list of publications of NCTE; a number of articles on the general subject of language distortion have been written very recently and will appear in print in the immediate future. – Ed.

Kerr, Elizabeth M. and Ralph M. Aderman, Editors. *Aspects of American English.* 2nd Edition. New York: Harcourt Brace Jovanovich, 1972.

Kronhausen, Eberhard and Phyliss. *Pornography and the Law.* New York: Ballantine Books, 1970.

Laird, Charlton. *Language in America.* Englewood Cliffs, New Jersey: Prentice-Hall, Inc., 1972.

Laird, Charlton and Robert M. Gorrell. *Reading About Language.* New York: Harcourt Brace, 1971.

Leary, Bill. *Graffiti: Those Private Scrawls on Public Walls.* Greenwich, Conn.: Fawcett Publications, 1969.

Marckwardt, Albert Henry. *American English.* New York: Oxford Book Company, 1960.

Marckwardt, Albert Henry. *Linguistics and the Teaching of English.* Bloomington, Indiana: Indiana University Press, 1966.

Maurer, David W. *Whiz Mob.* New Haven, Conn.: College and University Press, 1964.

McDonald, Daniel. *The Language of Argument.* Scranton, Penn.: Chandler Publishing Company, 1971.

Mencken, Henry Louis. *The American Language.* 4th Edition with Two Supplements. Edited and Annotated by Raven I. McDavid. New York: Alfred A. Knopf, 1963.

Morris, William. *Your Heritage of Words.* New York: Dell Publishing Company, 1970.

Muller, Herbert J. *The Uses of English.* New York: Holt, Rinehart and Winston, 1967.

Nierenberg, Gerard I. and Henry H. Calero. *How to Read a Person Like a Book.* New York: Pocket Books, 1973.

Pei, Mario. *The Many Hues of English.* New York: Hawthorne Books, 1969.

Pei, Mario. *The Story of English.* New York: Mentor Books, 1966.

Pei, Mario. *The Story of Language.* New York: Mentor Books, 1972.

Pei, Mario. *What's in a Word?* New York: Hawthorne Books, 1968.

Pei, Mario. *Words in Sheep's Clothing; How People Manipulate Opinion by Distorting Word Meanings.* New York: Hawthorne Books, 1969.

Postman, Neil, Charles Weingartner, and Terence P. Moran. *Language in America: A Report on Our Deteriorating Semantic Environment.* New York: Pegasus, 1969.

Postman, Neil and Charles Weingartner. *Linguistics: A Revolution in Teaching.* New York: Delacorte Press, 1966.

Pyles, Thomas. *The Origin and Development of the English Language.* New York: Harcourt Brace, 1964.

Pyles, Thomas. *Words and Ways of American English.* New York: Random House, 1952.

Reed, Carroll E. *Dialects of American English.* Cleveland: The World Publishing Company, 1967.

Rembar, Charles. *The End of Obscenity.* New York: Bantam Books, 1968.

Roeburt, John. *The Wicked and the Banned.* New York: Macfadden Books, 1963.

Rosten, Leo. *The Joys of Yiddish.* New York: Pocket Books, 1970.

Salomon, Louis B. *Semantics and Common Sense.* New York: Holt, Rinehart and Winston, 1966.

Schwartz, Alvin. *A Twister of Twists, A Tangler of Tongues.* New York: J. B. Lippincott Company, 1972.

Shores, David L. *Contemporary English: Change and Variation.* Philadelphia: J. B. Lippincott Company, 1972.

Skidmore, Max J., Editor. *Word Politics: Essays on Language and Politics.* Palo Alto, Calif.: James Freel & Associates, 1972.

Sledd, James and Wilma R. Ebbitt. *Dictionaries and THAT Dictionary: A Casebook on the Aims of Lexicographers and the Targets of Reviewers.* Chicago: Scott, Foresman & Co., 1962.

Stewart, James. *Names on the Land.* New York: Houghton Mifflin, 1967.

Strunk, William and E. B. White. *The Elements of Style.* 2nd Edition. New York: The Macmillan Company, 1972.

Vann Laan, Thomas F. and Robert B. Lyons, Editors. *Language and the Newsstand.* New York: Charles Scribner's Sons, 1968.

Wallwork, J. F. *Language and Linguistics.* London: Heinemann Educational Books, 1970.

Williamson, Juanita V. and Virginia M. Burke, Editors. *A Various Language: Perspectives on American Dialects.* New York: Holt, Rhinehart and Winston, 1971.

Wilson, Kenneth, R. H. Hendrickson and Peter Alan Taylor, Editors *Harbrace Guide to Dictionaries.* New York: Harcourt, Brace, and World 1963.

Wise, David. *The Politics of Lying: Government Deception, Secrecy, and Power* New York: Random House, 1973.

REFERENCE WORKS

Barnhart, Clarence L., Sol Steinmetz, and Robert K. Barnhart, Editors. *The Barnhart Dictionary of New English Since 1963.* New York: Barnhart / Harper & Row, Publishers, 1973.

Bernstein, Theodore M. *The Careful Writer: A Modern Guide to English Usage.* New York: Atheneum, 1972.

Compact Edition of the Oxford English Dictionary, The. Oxford: Clarendon Press, 1971. Two Volumes.

Follett, Wilson. Edited by Jacques Barzun and Others. *Modern American Usage: A Guide.* New York: Grosset & Dunlap, Inc., 1970.

Hodges, John C. and Mary E. Whitten. *Harbrace College Handbook.* 7th Edition. New York: Harcourt Brace Jovanovich, Inc., 1972.

Perrin, Porter G. et al. *Writer's Guide and Index to English.* 5th Edition. Chicago: Scott, Foresman, 1972.